Salthouse

George and Taffy, Salthouse 2002

Some of the oldest Contributors, at the Manor House 'get-together', 4 October 2001

Left to right: Phyllis Jackson, Roland High, Muriel Brown, Ken Brown, Ivy Nightingale, Janette Dams, Jim Radley, Elsie Radley, Gerald Cubitt, Bridget Cubitt, Kathleen Thomas, Vivian High, Stan Barker, Madge Barker and Jasper Woodhouse.

Salthouse

The story of a Norfolk village
by
FRANK NOEL STAGG

and a continuation of the story up to the present day
by people from old Salthouse families:

Ken Brown	Ray High	Mary Lemmon (Dawson)
Joyce Childs (Dawson)	Vivian High	Jim Manson
George Cooke	Alice Holman (Woodhouse)	Primrose McGlinchey (Dawson)
Leslie Cooke	Betty Holman	Suzanne McKnespiey (Cooke)
Richard Cooke	Brian Holman	Freda Morse (High)
Gerald Cubitt	Doris Holman (Holman)	Ivy Nightingale (Holman)
Janette Dams (Cooper)	Freda Holman (Duffield)	Florence Radley (High)
Harry Dawson	Phyllis Jackson (Brown)	Jim Radley
Lorna Fox (Hancock)	Carrie Large	Doreen Sayer (High)
Marybeth Gibbons	Ivan Large	Jasper Woodhouse
Kath Gray (High)	Macala Large	Anne Wright (Large)
Jimmy High	Tracey Large (Wright)	Zoë Wright

and by friends and residents, past and present, of Salthouse:

Harry Apling, Madge and Stan Barker, Steve Benson, C.D. Borrer (Sea Pie), Peter Brooks, Jill Coleman, Sarah Dawson, Jim Deterding, Hermia and Sebastian Eden, Ted Ellis, Wendy Elsden, Chris Evans, Tom Fox, Louise Grattan, Jane Hales, Daphne Hanlon, Steve Harris, Birkin Haward, Jonathan Hooton, Giles Hunt, Cyril Jolly, R.W. Ketton-Cremer, Ian Keymer, C.L.S. Linnell, Tony Palmer, H.N. Pashley, Russell Reeve, Betty Ringer, Elizabeth Robertson, Andrew Rogerson, Edwin Rose, Derek Schofield, Stephen Shipley, Betty Smith, Jim Sutton, Gwen Szabó, Kathleen Thomas, Dorothy Thomson, Charlotte Upcher, Alex Vines, Winnie Walton, Olga Ward, Sylvia Townsend Warner.

Edited by Val Fiddian

First published in Great Britain by
The Salthouse History Group
July 2003
© Val Fiddian
ISBN 0-9543547-0-2

ABOUT THIS BOOK

This book is grant aided, and is aimed at a wide section of the community and, though it contains much that is scholarly, it should not be regarded as a historian's text book but rather as a local history project. Commander Stagg's research in the 1930s was—(as he states in his own introduction which can be seen on page 9)—a rich mixture of the scholarly and the naïve. His work is reproduced here as it stands. Only where some of his more obscurely involved passages were left unresolved, has some of his work had to be cut. The type-written manuscript is in the Special Collection of the UEA library in Norwich, but a photocopy is in the keeping of the Blakeney History Society, where it may be available to any interested member of the general public.

GRATITUDE

A big thank you from the editor to all the Salthouse people who have given of their best memories to make this book a success, and sincere regrets to those who might have done so but didn't do it in time! Grateful thanks to the generous people who helped to finance it (whose names are listed at the end of the book) and also to those who gave time and care to their independent researches. Finally thanks to two members of my own family: my brother Jem, who introduced me to desktop publishing and was always there at the end of the phone; and my daughter Sue, the copy editor, who also made the index and had the idea of the fold-out map. It is thanks to her maddeningly eagle eye that there are less mistakes than there would have been, and it is her tireless polishing and trimming that has made this book the excellent thing it is.

All Rights Reserved
No part of this publication may be reproduced, stored in a retrieval system, or transmitted in any form or by any means, electronic, mechanical, photocopying, recording or otherwise, without the prior permission of the publishers or copyright owner.

Sponsored by the Local Heritage Initiative which is a partnership between the Heritage Lottery Fund, the Nationwide Building Society and the Countryside Agency.

Designed and produced by Val Fiddian, Salthouse.

Front cover : From a watercolour by Adrian Taunton, Kelling, Norfolk.

Back cover : The Coast Road and the Dun Cow, with Kayleigh Holman, Marybeth Gibbons and Zoë Wright, the future of the villlage, descended from the oldest families.

Photograph on first page: George Wright is descended from sea-faring Salthouse ancestors, while Taffy Sinclair represents one of the newest families in the village.

Printed and bound in the U. K. by Antony Rowe Ltd, Chippenham, Wiltshire.

Editor's note

When electricians needed to move the safe in the vestry of Salthouse church in the winter of the year 2000, it was found to have been standing upon a small mysterious iron chest which was later identified as 'the Parliament Box', which had once been in the vestry but had gone missing.

A locksmith was fetched to open it, and the box was found to be full of calf-bound account books dating back to 1742 and exciting brown paper envelopes—one of which contained a petition made in 1815 by two Salthouse men in Norwich gaol who needed money to alleviate their suffering.

The Bishop's Committee had listed and labelled the contents of the box in 1959. Studying the list, I became obsessed with one item which wasn't there.

A *History of the Parish of Salthouse in the County of Norfolk,* by Frank Noel Stagg R.N., was clearly listed among the contents of the box but was definitely not present, though one or two older Salthouse people had heard of its existence and remembered it having been lent to different people who had since died.

R.W. Ketton-Cremer was a friend of Stagg, and his hand-written note (see page 10) explains how Lady Champion de Crespigny gave him a copy of her brother's typescript. He later bequeathed the manuscript to the University of East Anglia and it was this copy that I discovered in the Special Collection on the lowest archive floor of the University library. I was lucky enough to meet Deirdre Sharp, the Chief Archivist, who photocopied the whole thing for me and wished me luck with my idea of trying to get the manuscript published.

My brother Jeremy in Ireland, who has worked in publishing for many years, pointed out that Commander Stagg's history ended in 1840 and then dropped a bombshell in my lap by saying that it ought to be continued up to the present day and that I should be the one to do it.

This challenge, together with the fact that Commander Stagg had in his foreword hoped that some Salthouse person would carry on his work one day (see page 9), weighed rather heavily on me until I had a wonderful idea—I was already collecting material from Salthouse people for an exhibition of village history (on the strength of the recently-found contents of the parish box) and I suddenly saw that it was *the people of Salthouse themselves* who should carry on the history.

Salthouse material has filled this book to bursting and the result is a very rich mixture of memories, photographs and forgotten news items, beginning with excerpts from the treasures in the Parliament Box, and going on to embrace the living history of the present day.

Commander Stagg researched and wrote his history, surely out of a love for Salthouse. Without knowing it he started something which, seventy years on, was to be the inspiration for a great gathering together of Salthouse people who belong to the same history. The people of Salthouse today have written the second part of his book and, as editor, I have had the wonderful, exhilarating job of collecting and arranging the contents, which I wouldn't have missed for the world.

Val Fiddian 2003

Contents

Part 1   Frank Stagg's History of Salthouse

Editor's note 5
F.N. Stagg's foreword 9
A note from R.W. Ketton-Cremer 10
Early and Middle Ages 12
Sixteenth century and the Heydons 19
Seventeenth century... 32
Eighteenth century.. 41
Nineteenth century.. 48
Fields of Salthouse, 1838... 50
Marshes... 54

Part 2   Continuing Frank Stagg's research

The Marshes:
   The Trading Port and the channels, *Jonathan Hooton* 60
   Landscape, history and bird life, *Steve Harris*............................ 66
The Church: Clergy, Church Goods, the Jewel, the Ruin, Graffiti 75
   The Bells, the War Memorial and the Graveyard........................ 87
   The Buried 16th-century Records and the Record Office 91
   Churchwardens' Accounts, 1742-1843, *Derek Schofield*.............. 94
   The Poor Prisoners' Petition (document from the Parliament Box) 101
   The Relief of the Poor, *Derek Schofield* 104
   The Property Valuation of 1854 110
   Church and Chapel memories, *Giles Hunt* 112
   Lady Charlotte Upcher's diary, *Olga Ward* 115
The Chapel: 1851 Religious Census, Preachers and personal memories:
   Jimmy High, Cyril Jolly, Florence Radley, Mary Lemmon............ 116
Main landowners, lords of the manor and notable characters:............. 127
   Onesiphorus Randall, *Peter Brooks* 128
   Present lord of the manor, *Jim Deterding* 131
   James Olley, *Steve Benson* 133
The Heath: History and wildlife, *Steve Harris*................................ 136
   Heath Award, *Tracey Large*, and documents from the Parliament Box....... 140
   Flag-cutting, *Colin Wells*.. 144

Part 3 Memories of fishing, farming and family life

Florence Radley (née High) (early memories)... 149
Jimmy High (farmer's boy in 1890)............... 156
'Sea Pie' and H. N. Pashley (Gabriel Piggot)..... 164
Jim Radley (childhood and Common Rights)... 167
Betty Holman (family photographs) 172
Lorna and Tom Fox (the Hancocks)............... 175
Lorna Fox (James Dix, Master Mariner)......... 181
Jasper Woodhouse (baker's boy, 1930s)............ 185
Stephen Shipley (his grandfather Charles High) 190
Ian Keymer (tracing ancestors)...................... 194
Freda Morse (née High) (early shopkeeping).... 198
Ray High (early milking co-operation, ducks).. 203
Tracey Large (née Wright) (Cattle Association) 207
Vivian High (farming and fishing) 211
George Cooke (fisherman, marshman).......... 222
Leslie Cooke (wildfowler)............................ 226
C.D. Borrer (Sea Pie) (wildfowler, taxidermist) 229
Suzanne McKnespiey (née Cooke) (crab shop) 230
Kath Gray, Doreen Sayer (Cliff High in WWI)... 231
Mary Lemmon (née Dawson) (Manor House).... 234
Gerald Cubitt (Cross Street and the marl pit)... 239
Janette Dams (née Cooper) (family life)........... 243
Phyllis Jackson (née Brown) (family life).......... 248
Ken Brown (boyhood memories)................... 254
Dorothy Thomson (church memories)............ 259
Freda Holman (née Duffield) (memories)........260
Brian Holman (village memories)................. 262
Ivy Nightingale (née Holman) (memories)..... 264
Betty Ringer (Friday Forsdick and fishing)....... 265
Primrose McGlinchey (née Dawson) (memories) 268
Joyce Childs (née Dawson) (Hall guest house).... 270

Kelling School: *Jill Coleman* (the log book, 1877)... 272
  Daphne Hanlon (Head Mistress 1947-1977)......... 274
  Alice Holman (walking to school 1912)............... 278
  Anne Wright (walking to school 1992)............... 279
Rocket House (Randall's Folly):................... 280
  Florence Radley, Jimmy High (shipwreck)........ 282
  Louise Grattan (née Jopling) (the Joplings)....... 285
  Sylvia Townsend Warner (from her diary)......... 287
Radar Pylon and Lancaster bomber................ 292
  Russell Reeve (German pilots on the heath)........ 295
Two Windmills: *Harry Apling, Tony Palmer*...... 297
Post Office and Village Stores: *Gerald Cubitt*....... 304
  Kathleen & Madge Haylock, Elizabeth Robertson 306
Dun Cow: *Ian Keymer* (memories, 1950)............ 313
  Jim Manson (landlord 1967-1996) 314
  Ken Brown (Salthouse football team).............. 317
Local Archaeological finds: *Alex Vines*............ 318
  Paul & Vivian High, Carrie & Macala Large....... 320
Myngs Terrace, Catriona Court and Bloomstiles:
  Wendy Elsden, Winnie Walton, Chris Evans.......... 324
Flood: *Jane Hales* (from 'The East Wind')............. 328
  Mary Lemmon and Harry Dawson..................... 331
  Kathleen Thomas, Madge and Stan Barker........ 334
  Jim Manson, Hermia Eden (rebuilding)............ 341
  Doris Holman (the three cottages) 346
  Jim Sutton (flood and sea-defence)................... 348
Shingle bank: *Birkin Haward, Jack Cooke,*
  Harry Dawson, Jim Manson, Ivan Large............. 352
At Little Eye: *Ted Ellis*................................. 360
Poem: *Sebastian Eden*................................. 361
Acknowledgements 362
Map Index 363
Index.. 363

Frank Noel Stagg

It was a hard job to hunt down a living relation of Commander Stagg but after a long search his niece, Gwen Szabó, was discovered living with her Hungarian husband in a remote and wild part of Hungary, and her response to my request for her approval was full of encouragement. Here she describes her uncle:

Commander Frank Noel Stagg R N,
Knight of St Olave, Order of Dannebrog.

My uncle was 'special' and the photo he gave me is there for all time. It was taken, he told me, during one of his broadcasts to one of the Scandinavian countries at the end of the war.

Let me introduce you to him as he was soon after the photo was taken. He was a tall, well-built man whose hands moved in expansive gestures as he talked with enthusiasm on his favourite subjects—literature, history, and people who he had known. His sense of humour was gentle but infectious and he was incredibly compassionate regarding mankind generally. I understand that in his later years he worked in some capacity for the Church but, since he never spoke of this himself, I have no idea in what capacity. It was quite evident that he was a 'practising Christian'. Sadly I have no childhood memories of him.

His family over generations had built up a business in fell-mongering and wool-stapling and, in this, his grandfather had done well enough by the 1880s to send his daughters to finishing schools and his sons to major public schools. However, my uncle, the younger of two sons, wished for a career in the Navy and he was sent to Osborne Naval College (now at Dartmouth).

As a young officer in the first world war, his ship was involved in the Battle of Jutland and afterwards when he visited Denmark he had a sense of homecoming or déja-vu. He became intensely interested in all things Scandinavian, learning the Norwegian and Danish languages in addition to the three or four European languages he spoke fluently. As a Naval Officer he held diplomatic posts in both countries. Both Norway and Denmark decorated him with their highest honours in respect of undercover work and services to their countries carried out by him.

In the early 1950s Allen & Unwin published his History of Norway in three volumes—I

F. N. Stagg's Foreword

imagine this has been out of print for many years. He would never talk about himself so it is difficult to ascertain exactly what his wartime activities were. His passion was the study of History, something I could well appreciate, being in a very small way of the same mind. I didn't know him until I was grown up, but when I was living in London we frequently met. He would ring me and say 'Put your coat on, we're dining at the Danish Club tonight'—or maybe it would be the Norwegian Club; even his own Club, the Junior Carlton, which was stuffy by comparison.

He died quite suddenly after a very short illness in 1956 and I missed him so much. There was a Service of Thanksgiving for his life, at St Olaves, Mark Lane, a church he had campaigned to rebuild after the bombing.

That's all I can tell you about F.N. Stagg, except that I am so glad to have known him even for such a short space of time.

Gwen Szabó

Was it not Rudyard Kipling who wrote:—
God gave All Men All Earth to love,
But, since our Hearts are small,
Ordain'd for Each – ONE SPOT should prove
Beloved over All.

For those whose ONE SPOT happens to be Salthouse I have collected these notes concerning its history in the hope that they may be able to re-people its cottages, fields, lovers-walks and churchyard with the ghosts of some few of their predecessors.

I have stopped at the year 1840 and have not dwelt on the history of the Heath and its Trusteeship at all. Perhaps some enthusiastic resident will fill in the many blanks on the spare pages provided, and also correct what I fear will be found to be numerous mistakes.

When I started on this History of Salthouse I had not realised how intimately allied it was to that of Kelling, whilst it appears to have had little in common with its other neighbour Cley.. A combined history of Salthouse-Kelling should be the work of greatest interest, and I hope some lover of both villages will undertake it.

I am no Antiquarian or Archaeologist and I fear this is but the tale of an ignorant amateur – full of errors and stupidities.

F.N.S.

19th January 1934.

The history of the parish of Kelling, so closely knit with Salthouse in the past, now waits for an enthusiast to pick up Kelling's story and carry it through to the present—as we have done for Salthouse in the following pages.

A note from the historian, R.W. Ketton-Cremer

This hand-written explanatory note was attached to Commander Stagg's manuscript:
These notes on Salthouse were compiled by the late Commander Frank Noel Stagg, R.N. They were left to me by his sister, Mabel Lady Champion de Crespigny, who lived with her husband Commander Sir Frederick Champion de Crespigny, R.N., at Salthouse Hall from about 1925 until 1940. She died in 1955.

During the 1939-45 War the parish registers of Salthouse were buried by the Rector in a misguided effort to preserve them from enemy action. They emerged in a totally illegible condition, little more than a mass of fungus. So far as I know, this volume contains the only existing extracts and transcripts of any portion of these registers.

R.W. Ketton-Cremer, 1956.

PART ONE

Early History
up to the Nineteenth Century

by

FRANK NOEL STAGG

Early and Middle Ages

We know that prehistoric man roamed the fields of Salthouse before the dawn of legend, for he has left behind those tumuli, called the 'three-farthing' and 'three-halfpenny' hills, on Salthouse Heath. These were both opened in 1850, and urns of brown clay containing burnt bones found therein were declared to be Bronze Age relics.

During the greater part of the 400-year-long occupation of England by the Romans, it is almost certain that they would have used Salthouse Harbour, secure as it then was from desultory attacks by roving pirates thanks to its tortuous and narrow approach, which made it easy for Roman foot soldiers to defend. The Roman bricks and pottery found on Gramborough Hill in 1855 may have been in use by a Roman military detachment from Brancaster, where that important Roman Official, the 'Count of the Saxon Shore' had his headquarters for a couple of centuries—to which fortified post the Peddars Way led from Colchester. Gramborough Hill would have made an ideal site for a small Roman military station, since its precipitous sides would then have dropped down to marshy slush all round, whilst it would have commanded the Salthouse Main Channel, which still in our time flows—or rather stagnates—around its southern side. The Romano-British craft could then have lain in safety at Kelling and Weybourne hards.

The Angles swept over Norfolk from the fifth to the ninth centuries, and must have effectively mixed their blood with the Romano-British found there. The only actual finds from this period were made in 1851, when some Anglo-Saxon coins were dug up in the extreme north-east of the parish, where a field named Spanish Pits* falls into the marshes. But it may be that the foundations of the church would be found to be of Saxon workmanship. [see p 75]

At the end of the ninth century the Danes commenced their Viking-raids on Norfolk, to be followed shortly after by their occupation and settlement of East Anglia. For a while they were bought off by ransom, and under this tax (called Danegeld) the towns of Sheringham and Salthouse had to find the sum of eleven pence halfpenny per annum.

But eventually the Danish occupation of Norfolk became complete. Their forts, called 'Danish Camps', are to be found in many parts of the county, whilst the frequent ending 'Thorpe' or 'Torp' in village names indicates their villages, since that word is purely Danish in origin. The Danes are known to have been cruel and oppressive rulers, and during the reigns of the four Danish kings of England there is said to have been a Dane quartered in every Anglo-Saxon household. He had full powers over the fates and actions of all its inmates.

On 8 June 1042, Hardicanute (the last of the Danish kings) died from a stroke at Lambeth, and Edward the Confessor ascended the throne. The day of the Danes' rule and power was irrevocably past, and the Angles of Norfolk (who had inevitably absorbed much Danish blood) enjoyed once more a short-lived freedom of 24 years under their own kings: Edward the Confessor and Harold.

---

* *For field names mentioned, see map p 51.*
NB *In places, Stagg's marginal notes have been inserted into the text, and material added from an alternative, shortened version made by him.*

By 1042 the lands of Salthouse, Kelling and Weybourne were in the possession of two Danes named Seiar Bar (meaning 'victorious' in Danish) and Osgot. Seiar Bar's holding appears to have been entirely in Salthouse and to have consisted of about 600 acres. Osgot, who probably lived in Kelling, had a holding in both parishes of about 375 acres of arable, 844 acres of meadowland and 7 windmills.

Both of these Danes were ejected during Edward the Confessor's reign, and it is known that a portion of Osgot's lands was divided amongst twelve freemen who were under the protection of King Harold at the Norman Conquest. There appears however to be no record as to who acquired Seiar Bar's lands between the time of his ejection and William the Conqueror's partition.

At the Norman Conquest the landowners were for the most part required to surrender their estates, and the French feudal system was gradually enforced. King William I was determined to extort as much tribute as possible from his conquered subjects, and the Norman barons and minor landowners placed in charge demanded a toll in kind and service from those under their control.

We know that Seiar Bar's lands in Salthouse were given by William the Conqueror to William de Scohies (or de Escois), and consisted of 360 acres cultivated by 4 free peasants, which constituted his own demesne, whilst 240 acres were farmed by his tenants, and that there were 10 tied peasants (or 'bordars') on his lands.

SOKEMEN, VILLEINS AND SERFS

Below the lord and his family there were several classes of peasants: Sokemen were free men and were holders of land. They formed the upper stratum of peasant society, and corresponded roughly to the 'yeomen' of later days. Demesne was the land kept in the lord's possession: not leased out, but worked by villeins to supply the lord's household. Villeins were free peasants of relatively high status and, at the time of the Domesday book, they were the most numerous element in the English population, providing the labour force for the manors. Serfs were at the bottom of the system. They worked on their lord's lands in return for being allowed to cultivate some for themselves. They could not be sold as if they were slaves, but they could not leave the estate to live or work elsewhere without permission.

We learn this from the entry for Salthouse in the Domesday Book, compiled 1086 (which is where the written history of Salthouse begins):

The Land of William de Scohies. Hundret (of) North Erpingham. Salthus was held by Seiar Bar (as) 3 plough lands. Then as now (there were) 4 villeins (and) 10 bordars. Then (there were) 3 (ploughs) on the demesnes and afterwards a half, now one, then as now 2 ploughs belonging to the men. Wood(land) for 100 swine then as now (semper) it was worth 40 shillings. And William (ille) has the soke and sac. And it is included in the measurement of Siling(eham) [Sheringham].

Osgot's lands, including that part which Harold's twelve freemen had occupied, were granted by William I to Hugh d'Avranches, Earl of Chester. This Earl Hugh, who was the son of the Conqueror's sister, governed his earldom of Chester virtually as an independent ruler, and fought the Welsh and the Norsemen on Anglesea in many a hard battle. Besides his earldom he held lands in twenty other English counties and was a faithful supporter of William Rufus. He died without heirs as his only son was drowned in the 'White Ship'. It is probable that Hugh never even saw Salthouse or Kelling, for we know that he let his holdings here to Ralph de Toesny (who died 1102) as a reward for his services in the conquest of England. This Ralph, sometimes called Ralph de Conches, married Isabel de Montfort and was afterwards a friend of William Rufus. Under the overlordship of Hugh Earl of Chester, he held in Kelling, Weybourne and Salthouse 375 acres of arable and 844 of meadowland,

THE MANOR

*T*o appreciate the position of the lord of the manor in feudal times one must understand the nature of the tenure of the land. The manor was the unit of land and could not be subdivided. Neither could it be devised by will: if heirs failed, it lapsed to the Crown. At the Norman Conquest all land was assumed to have reverted to the King, but his ownership consisted mainly in the right of bestowal. Some of the land he gave back to its former owners, some to Norman followers as his tenants, and some to the clergy as tenants for life. The laity held their lands on condition of military service, the clergy on condition of performing religious offices. Thus the King granted lordships and manors, and those on whom they were bestowed were tenants of the King, with the right to make what they could out of the land provided they paid him the service and rent he demanded and did not encroach on the rights of the people.

The manor was a sort of petty kingdom with a constitution. The people had rights as well as the lords. The demesne was the lord's home farm; in the rest of the village he had restricted dominion. The arable land was cultivated by the people for their own use, with fixity of tenure so long as they paid their dues in rent and service. If they died without heirs, their holding reverted to the lord to be re-apportioned by him. Both lord and people had their respective rights in the pasture, waste and woodland.

Thus the land belonged to the people and the people to the land, and the lord was the owner of both, but with distinctly restricted ownership.

which were cultivated by one free peasant and twenty-five tied peasants. There were also seven windmills on his property. Ralph held many other lands in England and Normandy, and it is quite likely that he, like Hugh, saw little or nothing of North Norfolk. No doubt Salthouse and Kelling lands were controlled by an agent.

At the start of the twelfth century, we read of four manors in Salthouse and Kelling, (though it is sadly impossible to define their boundaries now):

1) The capital lordship of William de Scohies in Salthouse, was sold at some unknown date to Walter Giffard, Earl of Buckingham. By an heiress of that family it came to the ancestor of the Earls of Clare, who owned it up to about 1350.

2) The principal lordship of Kelling, which extended into Salthouse, was held after Ralph de Toesny by the family of de Kelling. As Ralph died in 1102 that is probably the year in which the family of de Kelling began its knightly occupation. They brought no noble name with them from Normandy, so it may be assumed that they 'rose from the ranks'; it is also likely that they lived in Kelling and built that moated house near Kelling Hall whose slender ruins are still standing.

3) The lordship of the lands formerly held by King Harold's twelve freemen, then by Ralph, was acquired by the family of Ilketeshale. The first of this name would seem to have been Sir Gilbert de Ilketeshale, who in the twelfth century was also lord of Hedenham in Norfolk and Ilketeshale in Suffolk, whence they took their name.

4) At the Conquest a portion of Salthouse and Kelling was owned by Wester, a freeman of Guert, who was a brother of King Harold. On Wester's eviction it was given to a Norman named Roger, who held twelve other manors in Norfolk. Roger leased it to one Ralph,

Oak trees at Kelling Hall which were young acorns in the time of the de Kelling family.

the son of Hagan, and the extent of the manor was 240 acres, six free peasants, and twenty tied peasants. It then came into the hands of the ancient family of Braunche of North Barsham

The de Kellings would seem to have early acquired the sub-lordship of Manor 1 from the Earl of Buckingham, and thus extended their control over most of Salthouse parish as well as that of Kelling; they became patrons of both village churches. The first of the de Kellings seems to have been a Sir Hubert, and we know of his signature to a deed (unfortunately undated) of an agreement between himself and Sir Thomas de Weybourne, whereby Hubert's men of Salthouse should work at the Weybourne mill and Sir Thomas' men of Weybourne at the Salthouse mill, when either of them could not grind.

Side by side with this feudal lordship of Salthouse we must remember that the Church had its fingers in the ownership of land. We know that in 1240 Sir Peter Braunche, son of Richard Braunche of Gresham, conveyed all his estate in Kelling and Salthouse to the Prior of Binham for twenty-five marks (except a parcel of land which he gave to Salthouse Church). This grant was confirmed by Sir Nicholas Braunche in a deed of 1321, and the manor then became known as Binham Priory Manor, and was held by the Priory until John Heydon acquired it, either by purchase or exchange, in about 1470.

The family of Braunche of North Barsham drifted away to Somerset in 1314 leaving a junior branch in Norfolk, one of whom, Richard Braunche, was Mayor of Lynn in 1349 and has been immortalised by the 'peacock brass' in the church there. The name does not occur again in Salthouse, unless a manor called Brache's (which bobs up in the late fifteenth century) perpetuates the name of him who gave a parcel of land to Salthouse church in 1240—which parcel is perhaps the very land on which the present church stands, since the date of the old tower's construction is believed to coincide.

On the other hand, the piece of land may have been the portion of glebe adjoining the north-east side of the churchyard where it seems almost certain the rectory used to stand. [see page 76]

Other small portions of Salthouse lands were added to this Manor 4 (Binham Priory Manor) to provide masses for the souls of the donors. During the reign of Henry III (1216-1272) one William, son of Sir Thomas de Weybourne, gave lands

The 'slender ruins' of the moated Old Hall at Kelling as they are today.

16

in Kelling and Salthouse, with Grenberew (Gramborough) Windmill, for the souls of Alice his wife and Aldreda his mother.

And in 1247 Robert, son of Sir Hubert de Kelling, gave to Binham Priory half a mark rent per annum out of Grenbergh (Gramborough) Mill, and sixteen acres of land in Kelling and Salthouse. Peter Stoun of Kelling and Salthouse also gave rent and lands, as did Roger de Langham.

In 1251 Thomas Weybourne, son of William mentioned above, conveyed by fine* to Richard, Prior of Binham, the fourth part of a fee* in Kelling and Salthouse, the Prior engaging to find Thomas for life several pittances of meat, drink, oats etc (a medieval form of life annuity).

In 1286 Binham Priory claimed 'view of frankpledge'—the right of inspecting twice a year the frankpledge* men in the small district, presumably the manor in this case—and 'assize of bread and ale' (the regulation of the price of bread and ale by the price of grain).

After the Reformation this holding of the religious orders was confirmed to the Heydon family, on 20 June 1546. As this family controlled the destiny of our parish for so long, and in such exciting times, their family history is told in the next chapter.

When John Heydon died in 1479, he had amassed several manors into his estate including Brache's in Salthouse. He had purchased half of the Kelling manors in 1466, and acquired the Salthouse advowson about 1473—at all events he presented in 1476.

With the advent of the year 1500, great changes came over the face of England. The Wars of the Roses had given the nobility such hard blows that they never recovered their pre-eminent position in the life of the country. Shortly after the birth of the sixteenth century Henry VIII clipped the wings of the clergy in the Reformation. The feudal age became a thing of the past, and the King and his people entered their own. The embryonic chicks of our modern democracy began to wriggle in their shells.

The history of Salthouse also took a complete change at this date, for the by no means insignificant remains of the feudal age were gathered into the hands of the Heydon family. The actions of the Heydons during the sixteenth century are preserved in numberless documents, showing them to have taken a leading part in the life of North Norfolk during those stirring times. They lived hard by at Baconsthorpe Hall and must have influenced the lives of their people at Salthouse advantageously, for they were a most enlightened series of masters.

Before shutting up the pages of Salthouse in the feudal age we must list the rectors who cured the souls of the nameless parishioners. Only the names of these old priests and their patrons are known; anecdotes and details concerning them are completely absent.

1266 Robert de Salthouse (son of Robert de Kelling compounded first-fruits)
12— Simon de Bodham
1322 John de Oxenden, presented by Sir Walter de Holewell

---

* Fine: a lump sum of money payable as a premium at the beginning of a tenancy.
* Fee: an estate in land held in feudal law from a lord on condition of homage and service.
* Frankpledge: a system of mutual responsibility where householders formed a group to bring criminals to justice.

1327 Robert Inge, presented by
    Sir Walter de Holewell
1337 William de Rythere, presented by
    Sir Walter de Holewell
13— John de Rose, presented by *unknown*
1360 John Blaunchard, presented by Sir Warine
    de Bassingborn and Mary his wife
1361 Henry Attewell, presented by John, son of
    Sir John de Avenel (deceased)
13— Henry Knoff, presented by John, son of
    Sir John de Avenel (deceased)
1370 Robert Archer, presented by
    Nicholas de Stivekele
1397 John Clerk, presented by the King
1398 John Playford, presented by the King
1409 John Wychingham, presented by Nicholas
    Kymbell
1416 Nicholas Kent, presented by John
    Cornwalleys Esq & John Torell Esq
1417 Henry Bamme, presented by
    Thomas Walsingham
1420 William Kyrre, presented by
    Thomas Walsingham
1421 Edmund le Ker, presented by
    Thomas Walsingham
1443 Robert Colyn, presented by
    Thomas Walsingham
1458 William Brewster, presented by
    Thomas Walsingham
1476 William Rougham, presented by
    John Heydon
1495 William Herwer, presented by Sir Henry
    Heydon
[William Herwer was the last priest of the old Church]

The entrance of the ruined chapel today, taken from the interior.

The architectural remains of the feudal age in Salthouse are limited to the ruins of a chapel in the north-west corner of the churchyard (perhaps built as a chantry chapel where masses might be sung in perpetuity for the soul of some devout donor to the Church or Priory). Above all, stands that fine old weather-beaten church tower which must surely be an object of veneration to all present and future parishioners, for it has looked down on the lives and deaths of more than thirty generations of their grandfathers and grandmothers.

The Sixteenth Century and the Heydons

The life of Salthouse through this century centred round the fortunes of the Heydons, an old Norfolk family which originated in the village of Heydon with one Thomas de Heydon, who was a 'Justice Itinerant' in 1221. William Heydon settled at Baconsthorpe about 1418, and John Heydon (his son) was appointed to arbitrate as to the right of ownership of Kelling Manor in 1460.

This John Heydon of Baconsthorpe was an eminent lawyer during the reigns of Henry VI and Edward IV. He was Recorder of Norwich in 1431 and was greatly attached to the house of Lancaster. He it was who built the massive tower of Baconsthorpe Hall which is still such a thing of beauty. By his wife Jane, daughter of his neighbour Edward Winter of Barningham Winter, he had a son Henry who succeeded to his Salthouse properties.

John died in 1479, having acquired an interest in two of the manors in Kelling and Salthouse and both advowsons.* He was buried in the Heydon chapel of Norwich Cathedral which he himself had built.

Sir Henry Heydon, his son, was steward to Cecilia, Duchess and widow of Richard Duke of York (and mother of Edward IV). He married Elizabeth (some references call her Ann) daughter of Sir Jeffery Boleyn, a Lord Mayor of London, whose arms are impaled with Heydon on the shields in the nave of Salthouse Church. This Lady Elizabeth, or Ann, was aunt of Ann Boleyn. Sir Henry Heydon was knighted in 1485, and built a noble house and the fine church at West Wickham, Kent, some ten miles from London. But his interest in Norfolk must have been keen for he exchanged his lands in Scarning and Didlington in order to obtain control of the Wychingham manor (sometimes also called Berdwell's) in Salthouse, in addition to agreeing to pay 30 shillings per annum rent to William Berdwell junior. He was now in possession of the whole of Salthouse parish, though it cannot now be determined where were the boundaries of Brache's and Wychingham (or Berdwell's, as it was afterwards called).

All that remains today of the magnificent quadrangular Hall at Baconsthorpe: the gatehouse with John Heydon's tower beyond.

Sir Henry exchanged his lands at Walsingham for the Priory holdings at Melton Magna and Thursford, and built a causeway from Thursford to Walsingham. In the course of six years he erected the magnificent quadrangular Hall at Baconsthorpe, whose walls are still standing behind John Heydon's solid tower: all damaged, presumably by Cromwellian soldiers. He acquired the last remains in Salthouse of the de Kelling family's holdings, by exchange, and rebuilt its church. He died in 1503, the same year in which Salthouse Church was completed, and was buried in the Heydon chapel of Norwich Cathedral, which has com-

---

*ADVOWSON: the right of nomination or presentation to an ecclesiastical benefice. An Advowson is held by a patron who may be an individual or an institution, clerical or secular. The patron presents the candidate to the appropriate bishop for institution and induction though the nomination may be refused. An advowson is a form of property which may be bought sold or given away and is subject to civil law.

pletely disappeared (together with his tomb).

Henry was followed in 1503 by his eldest son John, aged thirty-three, who was owner of all the Salthouse manors for the forty-seven years until he died in 1550. During his father's lifetime he was a great courtier and lived on a lavish scale, but after succeeding to the Norfolk estates, appears to have spent most of his time upon them and was created KCB at the coronation of King Henry VIII in 1509. His youngest brother William was killed by the rebels in Kett's rebellion in 1549, and is buried in St Peter Mancroft, Norwich.

Sir John married Catherine, daughter of Lord Willoughby of Parham, and had several sons and five daughters. He built the Hall at Saxlingham whose ruins are still standing. Sir John and Catherine are both buried in the north aisle of Baconsthorpe Church: he died in 1550 at the age of eighty-one, and she in 1542 at the age of seventy-one. They were pre-deceased by their eldest son Sir Christopher who died in 1540. He had married Ann, daughter of Sir John Heveningham of Keteringham, and had four children, one of which, Sir Christopher, succeeded his grandfather in 1550.

During the twenty-nine years Sir Christopher owned his Norfolk estates he was held in great esteem and veneration and was noted for his justice, charity, and remarkable hospitality which was equal to his ample means. One memory which has survived through the ages is him entertaining thirty 'master-shepherds' of his own flocks, at a Christmas dinner at Baconsthorpe Hall. We do not even know the name of his Salthouse shepherd (or should we call him 'bailiff'?) nor for certain what breed of sheep grazed the fields of Salthouse.

Blomefield's visitor to Salthouse Church in 1748 refers to the remnants of a stained glass image of this Sir Christopher in the east chancel window, and also to a portrait in the church porch. He must certainly have sometimes come over from Baconsthorpe to worship here.

Sir Christopher died 10 December 1579 and is buried in the south aisle in Baconsthorpe Church with his two wives, Lady Anne and Lady Temperance. The following is a translation of the original Latin:

> Here under this tomb lyeth ingraved the bodies of the Ladie Anne Heydon, daughter of Sir William Drury, Knighte, sometime wife of Sir Christopher Heydon of Baconsthorpe in the county of Norfolk, Knt., which Ladie Anne deceased the 7th day of September Ao 1561, and the said Sir Christopher the 10th day of December 1579. And also the Ladie Temperance, second wife of the said Sir Christopher, daughter of Sir Wymunde Carewe, Knt., which Ladie Temperance deceased the 9th day of October in Ao Di 1577.

Sir William Heydon, eldest son of Sir Christopher, succeeded in 1579 at the age of thirty-nine. He married Ann Woodhouse of Hickling and had three sons—Christopher, William and John. The eldest, Sir Christopher, was living at Saxlingham Hall (whose ruins still stand close to Saxlingham Church) with his first wife, Mirabel,

Norfolk Longhorn sheep

in the year of the Spanish Armada, 1588.

The following entry appears in the Registers of Holt Church for that year:

> In this year was the town of Waborne fortified both with a continuall garrison bothe of horse and foote with skonces [earthworks], ordinaunce and all manner of warlike appoyntment to defende the Spannyardes landinge theare. Sir Willm Heydon being leiftenant appoynted Sir Xper Heydon his prime captaine, with meny other gent wch in order cam in wth their companies.

That field in the extreme north-east of Salthouse parish called Spanish Pits was no doubt the site of some of these 'skonces' dug by Heydon's men.

Some five years after the Armada the fortunes of the Heydons crashed, Sir William having become heavily involved in some unsuccessful speculation in London. He was obliged to mortgage many of his manors, including those of Berdwell in Salthouse and Ilketeshale in Kelling and Salthouse, to Thomas Croft Esq of Sheringham who in 1593 transferred the mortgage to Thomas Thetford Esq 'with all rents, services, foldcourses (sheep walks), & clear of all encumbrances done by him, Sir William Heydon, or Sir Christopher, his father'. In that same year Thomas Croft delivered to Henry Sidney of Walsingham Esq the manors of Saxlingham, Nowers and Linacres, which had also been Heydon properties.

Possibly through worry over his financial embarrassments, Sir William died 19 March 1593 at the age of fifty-three and he lies buried in the south aisle of Baconsthorpe Church. The following is a translation of the Latin inscription on his monument:

> To Sir William Heydon a most noble Knight of Norfolk, once Admiral and High Sherif, Justice of the Peace—Lady Anne Heydon, his wife, daughter of Sir G. Woodhouse, Knight, longing and hoping, has during her life-time placed this monument in token of her faithful and undying love. He lived fifty and three years and four months. Died on the 19th day of the month of March 1593. Amongst his fathers and forefathers, Heydons, William is here, one of the nobles, a lover of religion, faithful to his county of Norfolk, by land & by sea he was renowned in the offices of war and state. Enriching by arms, arming by laws far off lands, he gave the gifts of peace, he has the reward of peace.

If the last paragraph of this epitaph is not empty praise from a devoted widow, it points the way to a pretty tale of adventure and patriotic endeavour which should repay some student of imperial history.

Although with Sir William's mortgage of the manors of Salthouse and Kelling in 1593 the connection with the Heydon family ends, our interest in that splendid family prompts us to follow the fortunes of the Heydons for two or three more generations. We recall Sir Christopher in 1588—then about twenty-five years of age—as living in Saxlingham Hall with his first wife Mirabel, daughter of Sir Thomas Rivet Knt, a London merchant. This Lady Mirabel Heydon was buried in Saxlingham Church beneath a tomb which almost filled the chancel and nearly reached the roof. It was in the form of an Egyptian pyramid, and there was a figure of a lady kneeling before a bible open at 'I am sure that my Redeemer liveth'. This bible page and a small female figure are all that remains from the hands of the restorer. Sir Christopher (a lead-

Pedigree of the Heydon family

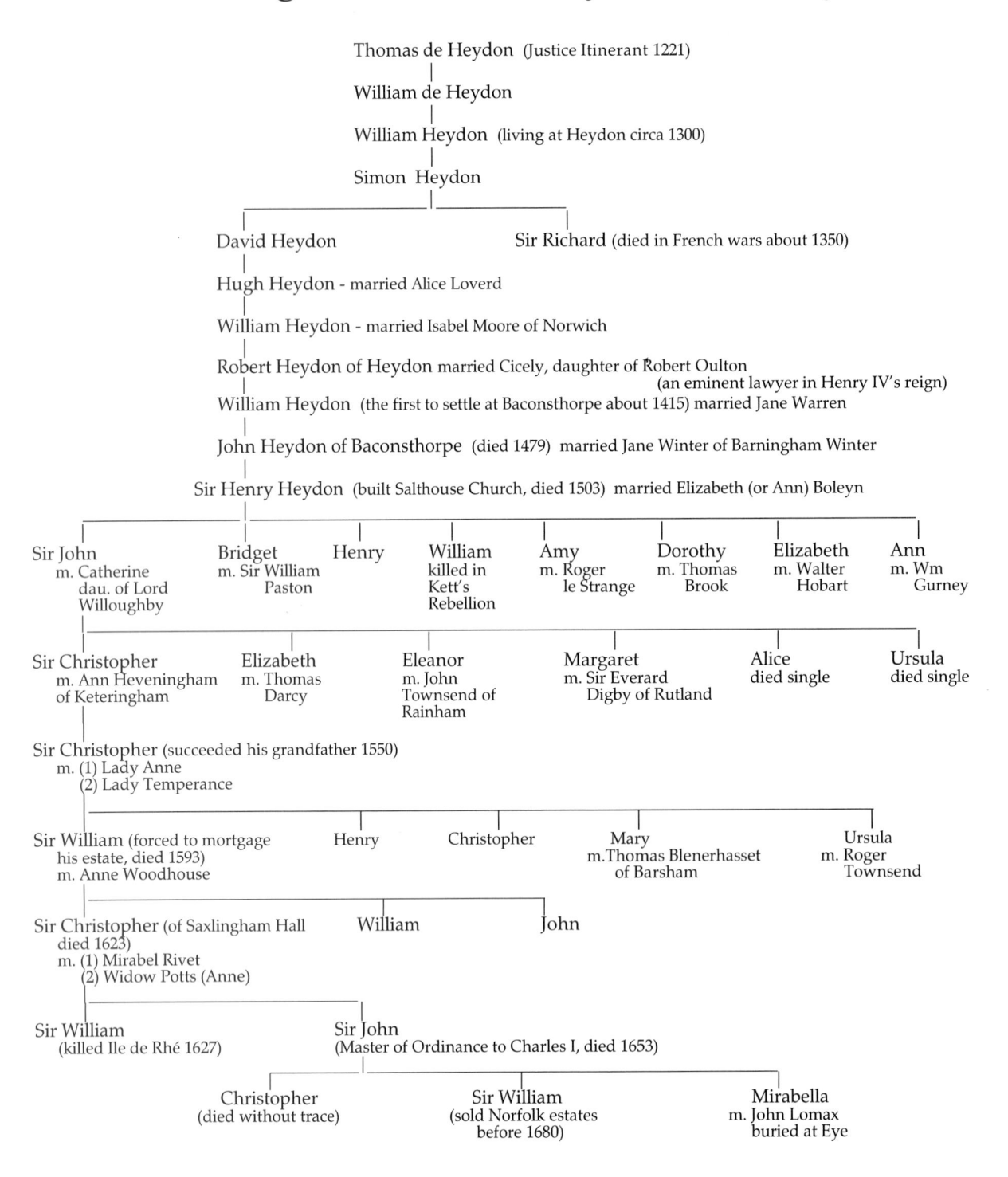

Thomas de Heydon (Justice Itinerant 1221)
|
William de Heydon
|
William Heydon (living at Heydon circa 1300)
|
Simon Heydon
├── David Heydon
| |
| Hugh Heydon - married Alice Loverd
| |
| William Heydon - married Isabel Moore of Norwich
| |
| Robert Heydon of Heydon married Cicely, daughter of Robert Oulton (an eminent lawyer in Henry IV's reign)
| |
| William Heydon (the first to settle at Baconsthorpe about 1415) married Jane Warren
| |
| John Heydon of Baconsthorpe (died 1479) married Jane Winter of Barningham Winter
| |
| Sir Henry Heydon (built Salthouse Church, died 1503) married Elizabeth (or Ann) Boleyn
└── Sir Richard (died in French wars about 1350)

Children of Sir Henry Heydon:
- Sir John m. Catherine dau. of Lord Willoughby
- Bridget m. Sir William Paston
- Henry
- William killed in Kett's Rebellion
- Amy m. Roger le Strange
- Dorothy m. Thomas Brook
- Elizabeth m. Walter Hobart
- Ann m. Wm Gurney

Children of Sir John:
- Sir Christopher m. Ann Heveningham of Keteringham
- Elizabeth m. Thomas Darcy
- Eleanor m. John Townsend of Rainham
- Margaret m. Sir Everard Digby of Rutland
- Alice died single
- Ursula died single

Sir Christopher (succeeded his grandfather 1550)
m. (1) Lady Anne
   (2) Lady Temperance

Children:
- Sir William (forced to mortgage his estate, died 1593) m. Anne Woodhouse
- Henry
- Christopher
- Mary m. Thomas Blenerhasset of Barsham
- Ursula m. Roger Townsend

Children of Sir William:
- Sir Christopher (of Saxlingham Hall died 1623) m. (1) Mirabel Rivet (2) Widow Potts (Anne)
- William
- John

Children of Sir Christopher:
- Sir William (killed Ile de Rhé 1627)
- Sir John (Master of Ordinance to Charles I, died 1653)

Children of Sir John:
- Christopher (died without trace)
- Sir William (sold Norfolk estates before 1680)
- Mirabella m. John Lomax buried at Eye

ing astrologer of the day) had the tomb covered with hieroglyphics, and is said to have published a book specially to explain their meaning.

> *Another account of this extraordinary tomb comes from Noël Spencer in his book on monuments in Norfolk churches:*
>
> I cannot leave this century without mentioning a monument, now gone, that stood in the chancel of Saxlingham church, near Holt. This had been erected by Sir Christopher Heydon, to the memory of his first wife, Mirabel Rivett, who died in 1593. About 1740, a Thetford antiquary, named Tom Martin, gave a description of it, accompanied by sketches. "Tis lofty," he wrote, "and encompassed with iron rails and almost fills the chancell, there being hardly room to walk about it." His sketches reveal it to have been one of the strangest structures imaginable. The base is a hollow cube in which kneels the figure of Lady Mirabel and, towering above it, is a tall pyramid covered in hieroglyphics (for Sir Christopher was a mystic) and topped with a flaming urn, which is the symbol of eternal life. All that remains today is a kneeling figure, possibly of Lady Mirabel, and an open stone bible. Walter Rye and Ketton Cremer have written about the monument; the former blamed Sir Alfred Jodrell for destroying it when he restored the church in 1898. However, it had gone a century earlier, for a faculty was obtained to remove it in 1789, when it was described as "dilapidated and dangerous".
>
> *Sculptured Monuments*, Noël Spencer
> Norfolk Churches Trust Ltd, 1977

In 1931 there was living an old resident of Saxlingham who remembered that all the children in his boyhood days were scared to go near the avenue leading to the Hall after dark, for fear of meeting Lady Heydon (Mirabel) on her nightly ride to Bayfield Hall. His elder sister who had been in service as a girl in the farm house which was then within the ruins of the Hall, remembered an indelible red spot on the stone stairs which was believed to have been the blood of a serving wench killed by Lady Mirabel. One wonders whether the uneducated among the Saxlingham inhabitants had taken the mysterious signs on her tomb to have denoted a pact with the Powers of Darkness and therefrom attributed to a lady (who may have been as sweet as her name sounds to our ears) all the evil which imagination could conjure up.

This Sir Christopher graduated at Cambridge in the days when the Danish Astronomer Tycho Brahe was propounding theories regarding the universe which caused the intellectuals of all nations to turn their thoughts to the skies and stars. Sir Christopher must have been bitten badly, for not only did he cover the entombed body of his Lady Mirabel with zodiacal emblems, but he wrote voluminously on the 'science' of astrology and was a leading figure in the defence of astrology in the intellectual disputations of his time. In 1602 he published *A Defence of Judiciall Astrologie* and, in 1605, *An Astrological Discourse . . . in Justification of the validity of Astrology*. He also wrote a pamphlet called *A Recitall of the Coelestiall Apparitions of the present Trygon now in being*—which, however, was never published.

In political life, Sir Christopher was induced by the 'immoderate brag' of one Thomas Farmor to oppose his candidature for the representation of Norfolk in Parliament in 1586. The election, on account of the contested return, attracted some attention, but finally the House of Commons adjudged the seats to Farmor and Gresham. But Sir Christopher represented Norfolk in 1588 though he soon after travelled abroad, perhaps hoping to forward his father's interests ('enriching by arms, arming by laws far-off lands,' as Sir William's epitaph has it).

In 1596 Sir Christopher was knighted by the Earl of Essex, at the sacking of Cadiz; he and his brother, John, got involved in Essex's mad rebellion, for which crime, however, they were both pardoned in 1601. This brother John appears to have been somewhat of a fire-eater. He went to Ireland with Essex in 1599, and in that year had a duel with Sir Robert Mansfield which resulted in the loss of Sir John's hand. This hand is still preserved in Canterbury Museum.

In 1620, in the early days of the Thirty Years War when King James I was trying to assist his son-in-law the Protestant King of Bohemia, the Privy Council issued letters to all the nobility and gentry in England, requesting a loan for the recovery of the Palatinate. This was earnestly desired by Sir Christopher, who sent a letter to the Privy Council stating that the Papists were as ready to support the Emperor of Germany as the King was the King of Bohemia, and that they met at the house of Mr Henry Kervile at St Mary's Marshland (Terrington St Mary's). Kervile was sent for and imprisoned, but the charge was dropped and he was soon released.

Sir Christopher had several sons by Lady Mirabel, of whom the eldest—Sir William—was killed in the expedition against the Île de Rhé in 1627. By his second wife, Anne, widow of Sir John Potts of Mannington, he had four daughters and a son.

Sir Christopher died in 1623 at the age of sixty, and lies buried at Baconsthorpe together with his wife Anne who died in 1642. His second son by Lady Mirabel, John, succeeded him.

Sir John Heydon was a great mathematician and soldier, and succeeded his brother William as Lieutenant-General of Ordnance on the latter's death in 1627. Between 1627 and 1643 he was actively engaged in furnishing men, provisions, arms, guns and ammunition for the service of the King. When Charles I raised his standard at Nottingham, on 26 August 1642, Sir John was in charge of cannon and ammunition at York. He soon joined the King, was made a member of his Privy Council, and accompanied the Royalist Army from Shrewsbury towards London in October 1642. He suffered much for the King's cause. His goods were sequestrated, and there is an inventory of them in the British Museum entitled 'Inventarye of part of the Goods and Chattells of Sir John Haydon, knight, taken the 28 Julye 1643', and also of 'the goodes of Edward Stevens, seruant of Sir John Haydon, Knight'.

Sir John died on the 16 October 1653 (one reference says 1657), leaving two sons and three daughters, of whom Mirabella married John Lomax and lies buried at Eye, Suffolk. Sir John's eldest son, Sir Christopher, died without trace (presumably done to death in the Commonwealth disturbances) while his second son, Sir William (to whom some parts of the estate were returned after the Restoration), sold the Norfolk estates some time before 1680 to Mr Bridges, a woollen draper of St Paul's Churchyard, London.

The Church that Henry Heydon built
and the beginning of Parish Records

Drawn by Charles High (see p 190)

There was great life and bustle in Salthouse when the year 1500 dawned, for masons and builders were hard at work on a new church which Sir Henry Heydon was erecting. It is probable that these masons and carpenters came over from Baconsthorpe as soon as they had completed the Hall there—after six years' continuous work.

Recent work on the restoration of the chancel has brought to light the possibility that it may be far older than the nave, since the work on the walls has a far different and older appearance than the rest of the structure. It is possible that the extreme shortness of the chancel could be explained by the same plans being used for the nave as were drawn up for the reconstructed nave of the Heydon church in West Wickham in Kent; part of Salthouse church's old chancel may have been sacrificed in order to make full use of these plans for the nave, leaving the chancel the length that it is now which has caused surprise in all ages—as witness an entry in the Parish Register in 1630:

It is also to be noted that the Chancell of Salthouse Church extendeth towards the Church no further than the first principall spanne which is not above one foot four inches beneath the first and lowest step which goeth up towards the East end of the said Chancell.

—Thos Dawney rectorem de Salthouse.

The tower of Salthouse church was not built by Henry Heydon. It belongs to an earlier church on the site, see p75.

The rectors must have been anxious to establish how small a portion of the fabric they were liable to repair out of their own stipend. It is possible that the width of the chancel was the width of the church which was pulled down in 1500: that is about the same width as that of Kelling Church.

The rectors of Salthouse through the sixteenth century were:

1500 Robert Fevyr, presented by
  Sir Henry Heydon
15— Stephen Prowet, presented by
  Sir John Heydon
1559 Gregory Madys, presented by
  Sir Christopher Heydon
1560 Christopher Nuttall, presented by
  Sir Christopher Heydon
1589 Stephen Gervys, presented by
  Sir William Heydon
1592 Robert Hetherington, presented by
  Sir William Heydon

In 1531 the clergy were required to designate the King as 'Protector and only Supreme Head of the Church and Clergy of England'. This many of them did, with the reservation 'so far as is allowed by the law of Christ'. Stephen Prowet was rector here when this 'Submission of the Clergy' was required, and it is likely that he willingly submitted, for he was the nominee of John Heydon who was a vigorous supporter of Henry VIII.

In the Public Records Office there is a paper which gives one last peep at pre-Reformation conditions in Salthouse. It is called 'Augmentations Office: Miscellaneous Book No 466—for Muster Roll and Clergy List in Hundred of Holt', circa 1523, in which Sir Robert Fever, rector of Salthouse is mentioned. His benefice is valued at £20 0s 0d and his goods at £23 13s 4d, and Sir John Rede's 'stypend' is £5 6s 8d. 'Sir' was a courtesy title given to all priests. Sir John Rede was probably a chantry priest saying masses for the dead either in the old building in the churchyard, now in ruins, or else in one of the two chapels in the east ends of the side aisles.

In pre-Reformation days the office of churchwarden was solely ecclesiastical. The 'custodes ecclesiae' were wardens of the goods of the church. In the reign of Henry VIII civil functions were added to their duties: they were made relieving officers to deal with the widespread poverty caused by the suppression of the monasteries and chantries, and they also had to provide arms for the soldiers. By the year 1600 much of the burden of local government rested on their shoulders: for instance, they had to see to the upkeep of roads, appoint local officials, and keep the parish free from vermin. (The early accounts of Salthouse are lost, but from 1742 they are full of interesting details of parish life.) [eg. p 95]

There were important ecclesiastical changes in the reign of Edward VI and in 1546, when he ascended the throne, the Book of Common Prayer came into use. The second Prayer Book was sanctioned in 1552, and ten years later the English Bible, which for two years past had been set up in the churches, was ordered to be read to the people in the public services. In 1547 injunctions were issued that the clergy were to preach at least once a quarter, that images were to be removed from the churches, stained glass windows to be broken up, and the inside walls of the churches to be whitewashed. When Queen Mary came to the throne in 1553, all the statutes of her brother Edward VI were repealed and the Book of Common Prayer declared heretical. In 1554 five thousand clergy and many of the bishops were ejected—but possibly Salthouse was too far removed from the lynx eye of Cardinal Pole, even if Parson Prowet did not conform to his order. When Elizabeth I became Queen in 1558, the legislation respecting the Reformation again came into force.

But what gives this century such a hold on our imagination after the blankness of the previous ones was the beginning of the keeping of parish registers under an order from Vicar-General Thomas Cromwell. Salthouse registers must all have begun in 1538, and that of marriages still does, but one folio of christenings has been torn off, apparently since they were rebound in 1748, and two pages of burials likewise, so that baptisms now begin in 1546, and burials in 1558.

We have not the handwritings of the rectors prior to Robert Hetherington, since up till 1593 they are in the hand of a scribe who was sent round the country to transcribe the presumably bad writing of the earlier priests.

Thanks to these registers we know at least the names of the parishioners and what christian names were then in fashion. The great families were the Tucks, Parrs and Stanforths. Of course the Heydons must have controlled the bulk of the economic life of the parish since the grazing rights would have been entirely theirs—but who their bailiff was, that went to Sir Christopher's Christmas banquet at Baconsthorpe, we do not know. The only name that has been immortalised is that of Tuck, who gave his name to the field of Tuck's Close. Should we be correct in assuming that the Tucks were agriculturalists? The Parrs we know were later on owners of ships or small craft, while the Stanforths call themselves merchants in the 1700s and were also millers.

Mill Drift taken from land just east of Grout's Lane and above the coast road. Little Eye is in centre distance.

27

Extracts from the Salthouse Registers in the Sixteenth Century

CHRISTENINGS

38th year of Henry VIII (1546)

Henry Cowp, the son of John Cowp, 6 June
Margaret Tucke, the daughter of William Tucke, 20 July
Agnes Tucke, the daughter of William Tucke, 27 July
Alice Burne, the daughter of William, 9 August
Emme Niccollys, the daughter of Godfrey, 20 October
Robert Peersonne, the son of Robert, 20 October
John, the sonne of William Burne, 26 October
Andrew Howesgoe, the son of Rbt, 1 December
Margaret, the daughter of John Jamys, 28 March

1st year of Edward VI (1547)

Katerine, the daughter of Richard Tucke, 8 May
Robert Carman, the son of Robt Carman, the last of May
Katerine, the daughter of Robert Stanforth, 1 July
Margaret, the daughter of George Parr, 18 July
Eele Cotton, the daughter of George Cotton, 28 August
Frederica, the daughter of Richard Cotts, 7 September
John, the son of Jeffery Ipworth, 22 September
John, the son of James Wysse, 28 October
Agnes, the daughter of Thomas Tompson, 6 December
John, the son of Thomas Gart, 6 January

2nd year of Edward VI (1548)

Margaret, the daughter of James Magnus, 26 August
George, the son of Robert Stanforth, 2 October
Andrew, the son of Godfrey Niccollys, 6 October
George, the son of John Jamys, 16 February
Alice Peerson, the daughter of Robt Peerson, 16 February

3rd year of Edward VI (1549)

James, the son of Reynolde Andeley, 21 April
Richard and George Parr, sons of Robt Parr, 13 May
William, the son of Robt Howsgoe the younger, 26 May
Johanna, the daughter of John Cowp, 30 May
Alice, the daughter of Wm Tucke, 21 June
Robert, the son of Andrew Niccollys, 7 July
John, the son of Thomas Camplin, 7 August
Cecelie, the daughter of Richard Tucke, 21 September
Alice, the daughter of Jeffrey Ipworth, 17 October
George, the son of William Burne, 16 November
Avis, the daughter of James Mangles, 20 January

The above is a copy of the earliest complete page of christenings (there is only a fragment of an earlier page).

In the Middle Ages documents were dated not by calendar years but by regnal years, starting from the time that the monarch ascended the throne. Thus, a document of the third year of Henry VI, would be shown as such. In later records the Anno Domini year either replaced the regnal year or was given in addition to it. The calendar years have been added here in brackets. Before the introduction of the Gregorian calendar (which we did not accept until 1752), the inaccurate Julian calendar—dating from the time of Julius Caesar—was in force in England. The year began on Lady Day, 25 March, yet Margaret Jamyss, born on 28 March, was listed at the end of the year 1546 (above). The then rector of Salthouse, Stephen Prowet, may have been observing Old Lady Day (6 April) as the beginning of his calendar year.

Even today old customs die hard; one of our present-day dates, the starting of the official financial year on 6th April, is a survival of the Old System.

MARRIAGES

30th year of Henry VIII (1538)

Thomas Thorneton and Anne his wife, 29 January
William Stanforth and Emme his wife, 12 November
William Unthanke and Rose his wife, 25 November

31st year of Henry VIII (1539)

Robert Parr and Margery his wife, 4 January
Richard Marr and Alice his wife, last of April
George Parr and Alice his wife, 10 November
Richard Hunte and Alice his wife, 11 November

32nd year of Henry VIII (1540)

Henry Stubb and Katerine his weif, 25 November
William Parsonne and Agnes his weif, 24 January
Robt Jamys and Johanne his weif, 20 August

33rd year of Henry VIII (1541)

Cutbert (?) and Isabel his weif, 20 January
Thomas Allen and Alice his weif, 24 January
Edwarde Saunders and Christian Stabell, 25 October
Reynolde Andeley and Margaret his weif, 12 November
Richard Tucke and Elizabeth Parre, 27 November

34th year of Henry VIII (1542)

William Burne and Alice his weif, 20 January
Robert Standforth and Margaret 6 August
Robt Starburgh and Katerine, 3 September
Robt Howsgoe and Johanne his wife, 9 September

35th year of Henry VIII (1543)

Robt Trumpe and Johanne his wife, 9 June
Wm Bredcocke and Margaret, 27 September

36th year of Henry VIII (1544)

Null

37th year of Henry VIII (1545)

Robt Goene and Johanne his wife, 15 November
Godfrey Nicholls and Johanne, 21 November

38th year of Henry VIII (1546)

Andrew Nicholls and Johanne, 8 November

1st year of Edward VI (1547)

Robert Boge and Johanne his wief, 6 November
James Magnus and Margaret his wife, 13 Nov
George Cotton and Johanne, 21 January

2nd year of Edward VI (1548)

Thomas Cumplyn and Johanne his wife, 18 Nov

This ends the first sheet of the Marriage Register

Ketton-Cremer of Felbrigg, in a note he inserted into Stagg's MS (see page 10), said that, as far as he knew, this work contained the only existing extracts and transcriptions of any portion of those early Salthouse parish registers (which were ruined after being buried during the war). On pages 91-93 there are photographs of these ruined records in their present state. Some of the pages are still readable and the Norfolk Record Office with newly developed techniques might, if funds were to be found, be able to restore them (read what Antoinette Curtis, the Conservator at the NRO, says on page 91).

BURIALLS

1558

Wm Trowby, 12 January
Robt Harde, 5 February
Cecilie Garth, 8 March
Katerine Howsgoe, 7 June
Richard Mangles, 23 June
Johanne Marroll, 1 July
Johanne Niccolls, 6 July
Avis Boge, 23 July
Johanne Niccolls, 27 July
Margery Cotton, 1 August
John Wagstaffe, 3 August
Thomas Vevian, 10 August
Robt Howsgoe, 17 August
Isabel Vevian, 25 August
Thomas Marroll, 28 August
Ann Pedder, 28 August
Thomas Tucke, 3 September
Margery Tucke, 6 September
John Niccolls, 10 September
Wm Tucke, 14 September
Robt Howse, 7 November
Andrew Niccolls, 9 November
Elizabeth Tucke, 12 November
Margaret Parre, 21 December

1559

Barthelemew Heywarde, 21 May
Henry Niccolls, 26 May
John and James Carman, 2 June
Emme Garth, 3 July
Cecelie Harde, 7 July
Darse (?) the son of the parson of Kellinge, 10 December

1560

Thomas Garth, 5 April
Margery Niccolls, 6 May
Edmonde, the son of Wm Tucke, 7 July
Margaret, the daughter of Anne Niccolls, 17 August
Cecilie, the daughter of Roger Ellis, 18 November

The above are on the first sheet of the Burial Register. In 1579 there were thirty deaths and in 1580 there were 26 deaths.

CHRISTENINGS

1593

Elizabeth the dau of Peter Tucke 29 April
John the son of Nicholas Tucke, 20 May
John the son of John Gyrleton (Girdlestone), 20 May
Cecelie the daughter of John Baker, 10 June
Henry the son of Thomas Parr the younger, 24 June
Elizabeth the daughter of Robt Harrysonne, 29 July
Peter the son of Richard Ipworth, 29 July
Margaret the daughter of Thomas Lambard, 26 August
John the son of George Smarte, 31 August
Suzan the daughter of John Hamonde, 23 September
John the son of Robt Cotton, 30 September
Rose the daughter of Richard Skoss, 30 September
John the son of James Mason, 21 November
Dorothee the daughter of Peter Abraham, 25 February

1594

Agnes Fakener daughter of Richard, 25 August
Johanne the dau of Wm Howse, 25 August
Joseph the son of Wm Holmes, 20 September
Margerey the daughter of John Gyrleston (Girdlestone), 28 October
Dorothee the daughter of Ralphe Bloome, 25 December
Margery the daughter of Robt Cotton, 25 December
Marie the dau of Ambrose Watherson, 27 December
Marie the daughter of John Lyon, 6 January
Rebecca the daughter of Robt Tucke, 1 March
Elizabeth the daughter of [?] Sallowes 22 March

1595

Robt the son of Thomas Parr junior, 22 April
George the son of John Whitaker, 1 June
Robt the son of John Grey, 13 July
Marten the son of Peter Tucke, 3 August
Ann the daughter of Christopher Pattersonne, 17 August
Thomas the son of Peter Abraham, 7 September
Sarah the daughter of Wm Saunder, 7 September
Margery the daughter of Wm Holmes, 26 October
Robt the son of James Parre, 23 December
Richarde the son of Peter Tompson the younger, 20 March

The following entries in the Burial Register of the sixteenth century are of the Girdlestone family:

Christopher Gyrleton, last of October 1576
Ellen Gyrlestone, 13 April 1592
Humfrie son of John Gyrleston, 2 June 1593
Henry Gyrlestonne, last of August 1595
Helen Girlton, 23 April 1600
Whilst 3 Girdlestones buried at Salthouse 1604

One result of Blomefield's visit, 2 centuries later (see p 46), seems to have been that the Registers of both Salthouse and Kelling were sent away for rebinding. That of Kelling still keeps its 1748 binding and is in a good state of repair, but that of Salthouse has disappeared, and with the cover has gone the first folio of Christenings and apparently the 2 earliest folios of Burials.

The Seventeenth Century

We left off our description of the manors of Salthouse at the moment when Sir William Heydon, owing to financial embarrassments, had mortgaged his holdings to Thomas Croft of Sheringham, who in the same year had transferred the mortgage to Thomas Thetford Esq.

It does not seem that Thetford was an absentee landlord, for a son of 'Thomas Thetford Esq and Margaret his wife' was baptised at Kelling in 1634, and a daughter in 1637. 'Esquire' meant something in those days, and surely the Thetfords lived at Kelling Old Hall. Michael Foster was presented to the living of Kelling in 1608 by the assignees of Thomas Thetford.

It would seem that Thetford alienated* his Salthouse holding to Sir Henry Sidney* soon after acquiring it but continued to hold Kelling until somewhere about 1640, soon after which date there is reason to believe a Thomas Fermor Esq became the squire of Kelling, holding it until about 1680. If these assumptions are correct, it would appear that the first eighty years of the seventeenth century were the only period in which the two parishes of Kelling and Salthouse were not united (by ownership being in one pair of hands).

But to return to the family of Sidney: the Sir Henry of this family busied himself collecting all he could of the wreck of the Heydon properties. He amassed a considerable fortune and acquired vast properties in North Norfolk, including the manors of Salthouse, though in which year he obtained them from Thetford is not quite certain. We do know, however, that he acquired those of Saxlingham direct from Thomas Croft in 1593. Sir Henry married Jane Jermy, the daughter of Francis Jermy of Brightwell, Suffolk, presumably a relation of the Jermys who lived at Bayfield Hall in those times. He died 2 November 1612 leaving all his lands to his widow, who lived till 1638. They are both buried under perfectly preserved ornate tombs in the Sidney Chapel of Little Walsingham Church. On Dame Jane's death in 1638, her properties passed to Robert Sidney, Earl of Leicester, but no record has been found as to who owned Salthouse in the troubled years of Civil War that followed, nor any record as to whether the manors reverted to the Heydon or Sidney families after the Restoration of Charles I in 1660. *[Here there is a handwritten 'No' in the margin, and again 'Palgrave'.]*

The Leicester branch of the Sidney family was divided between allegiance to the Crown and adherence to the Commonwealth, whilst North Norfolk was peopled by many wealthy landowners of Puritanical persuasion, such as the Jermys of Bayfield Hall and the Reymes of Edgefield, who would have seen to the dispossession of any Royalist neighbours. A letter dated 4 December 1650, written by Robert Jermy of Bayfield Hall to the authorities in London, provides a good example of this:

> In the first outbreaking of this insurrection the whole country seemed in a flame, and had been, had not the Lord even in the moment appointed for your and our sure overthrow showed that He was God, our God, who hath saved and would not now forsake us ... They had so many parties appointed, and in so many places, that we could apprehend no place safe ... There were many of

---

*ALIENATE: *a law to convey or transfer (eg. property or a right) to another, usually by a specific act (eg. a deed or will).*
Commander Stagg was not entirely sure if it was the Sidney family or the Palgraves who bought the Salthouse holding from Thomas Thetford. A handwritten note has been inserted here in his typewritten MS saying, 'No? Palgrave?'

power and eminency named as engagers with them . . . But this is too plain that many, yea we justly fear so many of the middle ranks of men are engaged in it that it will be no end to try them by jury, but either to make some exemplary by a martial trial or by the High Court of Justice.

feelings of churchmen. This Robert Jermy of Bayfield was serving as Colonel of Horse and Dragoons of the Norfolk Militia in the Parliamentary Army, and was one of the four Norfolk members in that much ridiculed 'Little Parliament' which Cromwell summoned in 1653 (and was despised by no one more than himself).

Royalists

The Government raised 4,000 foot in November, and sent down to North Norfolk a special court of three judges which sentenced twenty-four of the Royalists to death. Some of the executions, including that of the Rector of Little Barningham, took place at Norwich on Christmas Day 1650, as an insult to the

Jermy may possibly have consented to the destruction of the Royalist Heydon's home, Baconsthorpe Hall, about the year 1650; and at the same time, perhaps, defaced the Rood Screen of Salthouse Church and damaged its stained glass windows.

Admiral Sir Christopher Myngs

The events occurring at Salthouse in the early seventeenth century are overshadowed by the birth of its only hero whose name has been immortalised: that of Christopher Myngs in 1625. His mother, Katherine Parr of Salthouse, was baptised at Kelling on 16 June 1605. Her marriage is recorded at Salthouse in 1623 to John Myngs 'of ye parish of Snt Katherines in ye Cittye of London'. She was the daughter of a well-to-do landowner, whose father had been the owner of some ships which sailed out of Salthouse Port. Samuel Pepys is inaccurate in his diary of 13 June 1666 where he describes Sir Christopher's father being 'always, and at this day, a shoe-maker, and his mother, a hoyman's daughter, of which he was used frequently to boast'. His parents were of well-to-do families.

It is probable that from his early youth Sir Christopher was brought up to the sea in the local coasting trade, for while still a mere lad he entered on board one of the state's ships and served as a shipmate of Thomas Brooks (a fleet-chaplain during the Commonwealth) for several years before 1648. He followed an illustrious career in the war against the Dutch; he was knighted in 1665 for his services at the Battle of Lowestoft and he died from his wounds in the great battle off North Foreland in June 1666.

On the fourth day Myngs, in the Victory, lead the van and engaged the Dutch vice-admiral, De Liefde, broadside to broadside, the yardarms of the two ships almost touching. De Liefde's ship was dismasted, whereupon Myngs made an unsuccessful attempt to burn her with a fireship. The Dutch pressed in to support De Liefde; the two admirals, Van Nes and Ruyter, brought up other ships, and the battle raged fiercely.

Admiral Sir Christopher Myngs from a portrait owned by his descendant Geoffrey Minns.

Myngs was shot through the throat but refused to leave the deck, even to have the wound dressed. He remained standing, compressing it with his fingers till he fell, mortally wounded by another bullet which, passing through his neck, lodged in his shoulder.

Pepys, who was at his funeral in London, described how 'about a dozen able, lusty, proper men came to the coach side with tears in their eyes, and one of them that spoke for the rest said to Sir William Coventry:

We are here a dozen of us that have long known and loved and served our dead commander, Sir Christopher Myngs, and have now done the last office of laying him in the ground. We would be glad we had any other to offer after him and in revenge of him. All we have is our lives; if you will please to get his Royal Highness to give us a fire-ship among us all, choose you one to be commander, and the rest of us, whoever he is, will serve him and if possible do that that shall show our memory of our dead commander and our revenge.

The Victory (80 guns). Myngs' Flagship from April 1666 until he was fatally wounded on her quarterdeck on the last day of the Four Days Battle, 1-4 June, 1666.

Courtesy of Scheepvaart museum, Amsterdam

There must have been some epidemic in 1604-1605, since forty-one burials occur in less than two years, but whether it was smallpox or typhoid we shall never know; and the same applies to 1657-8 when there were 56 deaths in less than two years. There were 140 communicants in 1603, and it would be a fair allowance to add 60 to this figure for unconfirmed children, which gives a population of about 200 souls. So that even allowing for the high rate of infant mortality then prevalent, there must have been a thorough decimation of Salthouse dwellers during those two epidemics.

On the back of this page of Stagg's typescript, R. W. Ketton-Cremer has written about four Salthouse men impressed to serve in the Navy in 1602, and their descriptions. It is headed 'Stiffkey Papers (Camden Soc., 1915)' and, as well as I can make out the difficult handwriting, it reads:

> *The four men from Salthouse impressed to serve in the Navy in 1602 included Thomas Parre of the age of xl years of a middle stature with a black heade and bearde. John Stanforth of the age of xxiij years of a middle stature with a small thinne bearde – discharged at Norwich imposte repaid for W. Kinge. The other two were James Howsegoe and George Clarke.*

The Tucks, Parrs and Stanforths appear very frequently in the registers throughout the seventeenth century. The Parrs, I think we can safely say, lived in the Manor House—in which case Sir Christopher Myngs was born there. When the latter acquired some small degree of wealth, he bought a property in Salthouse and everything points to its having been what is now called the Hall [*here there is a large asterisk in the margin and a 'no', and Stagg's words 'what is now called the Hall' are crossed out. Handwriting that is not Ketton-Cremer's and may be that of Stagg himself supplants it with: 'The building in Long Chats Lane opposite the Hall'. (Long Chats Lane, according to Richard Cooke, is probably a misheard representation of 'Long Church Lane' heard pronounced by a Norfolk speaker!)*].

If so, it must have been in that house that his daughter Mary died in 1697-8, but Myngs' second wife Rebecca must have disposed of it probably soon afterwards to one of her husband's maternal relations, the Parrs.

The century opened with Robert Hetherington as rector, he being succeeded in 1613 by Thomas Dawney (presented by Dame Jane Sidney) who 'compounded for first fruits'* as did his son Edward who succeeded him in the living in 1643, though I cannot find who presented him to it.

The fact of their being in a position to compound for first fruits indicated that they were men of some substance, and it seems that one of them found the Rectory either too small or too dilapidated to occupy (though it was undoubtedly in existence at that time on the piece of glebe just north of the Manor House). They evidently built a house of their own: a house which was still being referred to as 'Dawneys' in the churchwardens' accounts for 1742 and must have been erected by them before 1663, for Edward Dawney was made rector of Kelling as well as Salthouse in that year, and must surely have chosen to live in that pleasing rectory in Kelling, if he had not already been dwelling in a house of his own. There are definite indications that this was the Manor farmhouse [*'Manor farmhouse' is crossed out and 'what is now called Salthouse Hall' substituted*] and that its erection was prior to 1663.

---

* First fruits: *the profits of a benefice during the first year after the death or resignation of an incumbent, originally made to the see of Rome.*

In 1662 the Act of Uniformity ordered exclusive use of the new Book of Common Prayer and required that all ministers should assent publicly to its use. Because of this hundreds of priests abandoned their livings, and parsons must have been hard to come by. Michael Foster had been presented to the Kelling living in 1608 and, after his death in 1658, there was only a curate in Kelling for the next three or four years—one August Underwoode. One might guess that the patron of Kelling who was then Thomas Fermor Esq, unable to find a rector because of the exacting demands of the Act of Uniformity, decided to join the two parishes into one living for the first time. As a result Edward Dawney was called upon to cure the souls in the two parishes till his death in 1677, when the livings were once again in separate hands. Kelling was given almost directly to Thomas Wilson the parson of Thornage, but Salthouse seems to have been without a rector until 1680 when Charles Worsley was presented (by whom we do not know, but it is likely that it could have been by Zurishaddai Lang of Baconsthorpe Hall).

The Manor Farmhouse

This Zurishaddai Lang, whose name in Hebrew means 'God is my rock', had bought the Heydon estates from the Commissioners in Bankruptcy when Mr Bridges, the woollen-draper of St Paul's Churchyard London, went bankrupt. It is impossible to say whether the Salthouse manors ever came back to the Heydons, but it seems highly improbable, for Charles II was anxious not to penalise any section of the community by dispossessing those who had acquired Royalist property during the Commonwealth regime. However vague

The west end of the village seen from Long Church Lane. Salthouse Hall is on the left, and the houses grouped around the Dun Cow centre and right, the marshes beyond them. The white line is the shingle bank and beyond it is the sea.

we may be as to the ownership of the manors and advowsons of Salthouse between the death of Dame Jane Sidney in 1638 and the year 1680, we do know for certain that they were acquired then by Dr Lang.

Charles Worsley only held the living for two years, from 1680 to 1682; his burial in the chancel of Letheringsett church is recorded in the Salthouse register. Blomefield states that there was a mural tablet in Letheringsett Chancel with this inscription:

> Charles Worsley late rector of Salthouse, descended from an antient family of the Worsleys of Plat in Lancashire, and son of Edw. late rector of this Church, and Mary Playford, of North Repps, his mother, which said Charles, with Mary Claxton of Booton, his wife, lye interred under these marbles, in hope of a blessed resurrection.

A visit to Letheringsett church shows that this marble slab has been removed, probably during the comparatively recent restoration, and its whereabouts are unknown. I think there is every possibility that Worsley lived at Letheringsett and did not occupy the Salthouse rectory, which by this time was probably in a dilapidated condition.

Worsley was suceeded at Salthouse by Thomas Bainbrigg, who was also headmaster of Gresham's School at Holt, and his handwriting in Latin begins to cover the church registers, and also those of Kelling, from about 1695 which must have been the date that Lang had presented him to that living also. He held the two livings till his death in 1713 and lived at Kelling during the last years after he left Holt School. It seems certain that he never lived at Salthouse, so we can assume that Edward Dawney was the only rector to run both parishes from Salthouse; that Worsley was the last independent rector of Salthouse; and that Thomas Bainbrigg around 1695 began his reign over both parishes from Kelling—a situation which has continued until the present day.

Reading between the lines of the registers, we can see a little tragedy connected remotely with Mary Myngs. Her father's great friend Sir John Narborough had many relations in the neighbouring villages and perhaps Philip Narborough of Wiveton was one of these. He married Elizabeth Roose (or was it Loose?) at Salthouse in 1687 and they had three children—Elizabeth, Mary and John in 1688, 1690 and 1692 respectively—and then Philip died (was he perhaps killed, or drowned at sea?). In 1695 the registers record a baptism, 'Rose, the Base daughter of Elizabeth Narbr'o widow, baptised 20 October'. Was this poor widow being befriended by Mary Myngs and possibly even living in her house? One wonders what happened to the widow Elizabeth and 'Base' Rose. Let us hope that the tolerance of Charles II's court towards such offences against social custom reached as far as Salthouse and that their lives were not too unhappy.

The registers of Kelling, throughout the seventeenth century, contain many entries of the name of Heydon but what relation these Heydons bore to the great family of the previous century has not been traced. Their fortunes cannot have been flourishing though, since there is no trace of an 'Esquire' affixed to any of their names.

A study of the Kelling registers presents a curiosity concerning the status of the Salthouse Parr family; in the title page of these registers, among many other names of parsons and esquires, written apparently haphazardly, there is finally a carefully scrawled: 'Henry Parre de Salthouse'. Also, the birth of Frauncisca Parre at Kelling in 1599 seems to have been an event of great importance judging by the detail given in the entry, but Parr was essentially a Salthouse family, and the name appears in the Kelling register but two or three times. Dix, on the other hand, was a purely Kelling family and provided churchwardens for Kelling Parish through the seventeenth and eighteenth centuries. The Dixes did not enter Salthouse till 1777.

Extracts from the Salthouse Registers in the Seventeenth Century

BAPTISMS

1625

Ciceley the daughter of John Smart, 24 June
Dorothee the daughter of Thomas Learner, 15 July
Thomas the son of James Flawes, 7 August
Margerie the daughter of William Tucke, 7 August
James the son of Edmond Cooke, 9 September
Ciceley the daughter of Thos Flawes, 23 September
Anne the daughter of Edmond Momford, 28 October
Christopher the son of John Mings, 22 November
    (Thos Dawney, rector; Peter Abraham
    William Stanforth, churchwardens)

In 1643 the following entry occurs:

Memoranda that Thomas Bredcocke son of Thomas Bredcocke of Salthouse beinge slaine in Winterton roade in the Parliament service in a shippe called the Hopefull Luke upon the 30th of August 1643 being Wednesday, was buried in Great Yarmouth Churchyard the 31st of the same, being Thursday.
    Ita testatur Edw Dawney rector ecclesiae de Salthouse.

BURIALLS

1657

In 1604 there were 23 burials. In 1605 there were 18. In 1645 there were 22 burials, but in 1657 there were as many as 34 in a few months:

    Thomas Larners, 1 April
    Sarah Leverington, 2 June
    Edmund Mountford, 12 June
    Anne Cricke, 16 June
    Cicelye the wife of Tho Beverlye, 18 June
    Elizabeth the wife of Henrye Stanforth, 10 July
    Margerye Furlock, 2 August
    Christopher Dobson, 30 August
    Cicelye Cooke, 2 September
    Agnes Tucke, 4 September
    Elizabeth Fuller, 5 September
    Francis Gurnott, 7 September
    Cicelye Stanforth, 10 September
    Willm Fuller son of Willm Fuller, 22 September
    Elizabeth the wife of Mark Tucke, 2 October
    Ann Jervie, 5 October
    Temperance Bask, 6 October
    John Jervie, 9 October

William Stanforth's son, 13 October
William Kinge, 13 October
Dorothy Pestale, 19 October
Margerye Watson, 19 October
Mary the wife of Mark Niccolson, 2 November
Benjamin Danks, 4 November
Anne Bourne, 7 November
Frances Cricke, 17 November
Johanne the wife of Peter Tuck, 22 December
Robt Bredcocke, 23 December
Sarah the wife of Christopher Kinge, 30 December
Martyn Harde, 16 January
Peter Tucke, 19 January
Cicely Larner, 28 January
Sarah the wife of Thomas Waterson perishing in the extremity of reathes [reeds?] the 20th of February betwixt Holt and Salthouse, was found and buried the 23rd February
Elizabeth the wife of John Gurnott, 24 February

1671

Henrie Stanforth the son of Henrie, and Robert the son of Robert Stanforth, being drowned at the seashore while trying to save the men of a ship wrecked and aground off Wims [?] Sept 12th, were taken up at Cromer and Runton Sept 15th, and buried at Salthouse Churchyard Sept 18th.

1680

Mary Bretland widdow was buried the 4th Sept in woolen according to the late Act of Parliament provided for that purpose*

*see the 'Burial in Wool' Act, page 92.

1682

John Man the son of Mary Man widow was buryed the 16th July (found drowned in the channel)

1683

John Brown a Scothsman of Preston-pans was buried on the 8th day of December in woollen

1688

Robt Teasdal a Stranger was buried 1st Oct

BAPTISMS

1656

Filia populi. Margerye, the daughter of Martha Mode, was borne the 1st Oct and baptised the 25th of the same month

1673

Filius populi. James, the son base-borne of Margerie Priest, was born about the 28th May 1667 and baptised the 20th April 1673

1688

Elizabeth, the daughter of Philip Narborow and Elizabeth his wife, was baptised the 14th Nov

1690

Mary, the daughter of Philip Narborow and Elizabeth his wife, was baptised the 4th May

1692

John, son of Philip Narborough and Elizabeth his wife, baptised 21st Aug

1695

Rose, the Base daughter of Elizabeth Narbr'o widow, baptised 20th Oct

MARRIAGES

1686

Anthony Dunn and Ann Narborough were married 5th Sept

1687

Philip Narborough of Wiveton and Eliz. Roose of Salthouse, 28th Feb

BURIALS

1620

Margerye wife of Edmond Girdlestonne, 17th Nov

1623

Edmond Girdlestonne, 23rd Sept

1638

Cicelye Girdlestonne widow, 1st May

Richard Burrage clerke and minister of the Church at Happisburgh, 5 Jan [buried in Nave of Salthouse]

1639

Augustine Anderson an Holland man, 25 Aprill [probably employed damming the marshes]

Peter Abraham, 3 May [cited in lawsuit concerning marsh damming of 1638]

1642

Thomas Dawney, clerke and minister of the Church of Salthouse was buried 7 Jan

1682

Carolus Worsley, hujus Ecclesiae Rectr sepult in Letheringsett Chancel, 28 Dec

1697

Mary Myngs, 29 Jan

Extracts from the Kelling Registers that have some bearing on Salthouse history*

1599

Frauncisca Parre filia Xtoferi Parre et Elizabeth uxis ejus baptizat fuit secundo dio Martii: et nata primus Februari ante horam nona ejusdem diae: in Edibe Edmundi Gyrlestonn (Girdlestone) mo° Willm Daul (Dale) in Kellinge

1605

Katherine Parre filia Christopheri Parre et Elizabetha uxoris ejus baptisata fuit decimo sextio Dio Juni
(Mother of Admiral Myngs)

1608

Elizabeth Parre the daughter of Christopher Parre and Elizabeth his wife was baptised 16 Oct

1624

Willm Parr of Salthouse and Mary Lile were married 13 Sept

1631

Christopher Heydon was buried 2 April
William Heidon and Margaret Allen were married 16 Jan

These Kelling entries are a selection only, from Stagg's MS.

The Eighteenth Century and the changing Property Owners

Although the Langs of Baconsthorpe were the lords of the manor until 1754, this century might really be called the 'Girdlestone Century'. The last of the Langs was John, and it seems he must have been lacking in finer feelings or else to have been possessed of a keen sense of humour. A contemporary letter tells the tale that as the funeral party left the graveside of his first wife, Lang called out in a loud voice: 'Does anybody here want a husband?—I want a wife!' On his death in 1754 he left most of his estates, and certainly all his Salthouse ones, to the Rev Girdlestone, rector of Baconsthorpe, in whose family they remained until 1870. This Zurishaddai Girdlestone was baptised at Kelling in 1719, being the youngest child of John and Sarah who begat a large family in that village. There must have been some friendship between Squire Lang and John Girdlestone, for surely no father would have christened his son with such a name unless he had expectations from Zurishaddai Lang's family. The fortune of the Girdlestone family would seem to have had its beginning in this legacy of 1754, since they were an ancient Kelling family who do not seem previously to have had great worldly possessions. The Rev Zurishaddai Girdlestone lies buried in the chancel of Baconsthorpe Church, whilst his son William became rector of Kelling-Salthouse in 1782.

It was at the beginning of this century that the custom of placing gravestones in churchyards commenced. Previously crosses or other emblems of wood were used to mark the place of burial. There was a time when the churchyard cross was seen in every parish. It was the common memorial of all those who slept in nameless graves. Shakespeare's 'Alas poor Yorick' was a cry that gravediggers must have frequently uttered when they struck some skull of a recent burial which then found its way to the charnel house. The corpses were left undisturbed only so long as to allow complete decomposition—had this not been the custom, our churchyards would be so large as to cover half the parish.

The rectors during this century were: Thomas Bainbrigg the old schoolmaster, Thomas Turner (1714), John Beale (1745), William Brooke (1778), and William Girdlestone (1782). They all lived in Kelling Rectory and the last three at any rate are buried in that church.

The old Salthouse families died out in this century: the Tucks (whose name exists in Salthouse now only as the name of a field) died out in 1739, the Parrs in 1742 and the Stanforths in 1786. Captain John Parr, who is buried in the nave of Salthouse Church, died as a man of considerable property in 1742.

We come to some definite information in the first Churchwardens' accounts book of 1742. From this we know that Mrs Pirdy (sic) was paying the Churchwarden's rates due from the lord of the manor (Lang), and for the 'foldcourse' (sheepwalks—probably the grazing rights on the heath). She was presumably farming the Lang property at Kelling, and living at Kelling Old Hall. In 1758 Mrs Purdey (sic) took over the above payments, and continued to make them for twenty years when Mr Hagon paid them in 1778. There is a stone in Letheringsett nave to a Mrs Henry Hagon, the wife of a 'common brewer', who died in 1773; presumably Hagon owned Letheringsett

Brewery previously to the first William Hardy. In 1782 Charles Starling paid rates for the lord of the manor, whilst Mr Marsham Purdy an outsetter (a land owner living outside the village), becomes a ratepayer for the foldcourse.

To return to 1742, at which date virtually the whole of the parish rates were paid by the two main landowners, Captain John Parr and Henry Stanforth, in the proportion of 8:5 respectively. The holdings of Captain Parr consisted of two properties of nearly equal rateable value. These two holdings are both referred to as 'late Captain Parr's' until 1756, in which year the smaller one became known as 'Mrs Marberley's' and the larger as Hardy's, Hardie's or Hardey's. There seems little doubt that Captain Parr was the big farmer, while the Stanforths called themselves 'merchants' on their gravestones.

> *R.W. Ketton-Cremer has written a note here, in the margin of Stagg's manuscript:*
>
> 'In *The East Anglian*, iv. 296-8, is a most interesting account of a suit in 1734 between John Parr and his wife Eleanor (née Bally). She had left him, embarked on 'a certain ship lying at anchor in the bay of Salthouse' and sailed to Flanders where she hoped to join her lover Christopher Alcock. He had been recalled home by his father, and Mrs Parr returned in the greatest agony and confusion to find that her husband not unnaturally refused to restore her conjugal rights. Four children are mentioned: Muriel (aged 14), John (11), Eleanor (7) and Ann (3). John must have died, and Muriel (later Marbellow) became the Parr heiress.
>
> R.W.K.C.

The Manor House (known as Parr's in the first half of the eighteenth century) where John Parr lived with his wife Eleanor, until she deserted him to follow her lover to Flanders. After 1756 it was known as Marbeley's. In 1796 this Parre property was acquired by the Johnsons who held it for over a century. This pencil drawing (c 1850) is by William Johnson Jennis Bolding (1815-1899), the grandson of William and Hannah Johnson who are commemorated on a slab in the centre aisle of the church (in the picture), and nephew of John Francis Johnson who died on 20 October 1844, and is buried in the churchyard.

[The above drawing appears here by courtesy of Richard Jefferson of Cley]

EIGHTEENTH CENTURY

The Stanforths were collecting property all through the eighteenth century. They became owners of Poulter's, Dawney's, Hembling's, Bainbrigg's, and other parcels of land. In 1742 Henry Stanforth's estate was divided into ten assessments for payment. The largest was Mr Dawney's, slightly smaller was Poulter's, and Hembling's was less than half the size of Dawney's. The smallest rate was for their Malthouse; the Stanforths were sometimes referred to as maltsters and sometimes as merchants.

Then, in 1781, Henry (the last of the male Stanforths) sold his properties to Thomas Purdy, and went to Ingoldisthorpe to live with his only child Margaret, who had married Dixon Hoste Esq, the squire of that place. Henry Stanforth was buried in the centre aisle of Salthouse nave in 1786. The Stanforths' property which Thomas Purdy acquired is described in this deed of conveyance:

> One Mansion House with the Millhouse, Barns etc. in Westgate Street in Salthouse [*this is now called Salthouse Hall*]. One Malthouse with the kilnyards in Westgate Street, One Malthouse with the kiln Millhouse etc. next the Saltmarsh towards the north. One House with Barns, Stables etc. in Westgate Street, then in the use of Edmund Hunt Harvey, Gentleman. One House with barns etc next a little lane or footway leading to Cley-next-the-Sea towards the north [*in 1938, occupied by Mr F. Woodhouse*] and a piece of land called the Old Orchard adjoining. Two 'double' cottages in Westgate Street, 213 acres scattered all over Salthouse Parish, 50 acres scattered all over Kelling Parish. The whole for the sum of £6,000.

And so the name of Purdy entered Salthouse in 1780 and the last of that name was buried in the family tomb in Salthouse Churchyard during the Great War (1914-18). This particular Thomas was buried in Kelling Church in 1802 and is described as 'late of Salthouse'.

The name of Poulter appears frequently in the registers and on the early tomb stones. One epitaph reads: Anne dr of Robert Stanforth, wife of Luke Poulter, Oct 20, 1717. 39.

Here Anne doth sleep, betimes she's gone to bed
But will not rise till trumpets rouse the dead
In her own sphere as truly did she move
As a bright star in its own sphere above.
By pious means eternal joy she sought
And up to them her soul the angels caught.

Marberley's became Hipkins in 1778. From the registers we know that William Hipkins was born in 1744 and died in 1788, and that he married Ann Bussee and had four children by her between the years 1780 and 1787. And so we can understand the first tithe valuation which is given for 1781 as follows:

Mr Bussy [Bussee] paying for Hipkins, £44
  [*The Manor House Farm*]
Mr Passon [Parsons] for Hardy's, £49
  [*Myngs' Farm*]
Thos Purdy for Stanforths, £70
  [*Salthouse Hall*]
Mr Dichal for the lord [*of the manor*] £10

In 1782 a new valuation shows:

Mr George Bussee, £105 (divided between
Mr Ditchell for Bussey £70 and Mrs Hipkins for other parts £35)
Mr John Parsons for James Hardy, £99
Thos Purdy Farm, £147
Thos Purdy Marsh Malthouse, £10
Thos Purdy Upper Malthouse, £10

In 1791 Mr Dew acquired Mrs Hipkins.

In 1795 Mr Proudfoot acquired Mr Parsons.

In 1796 John Johnson acquired Ditchell's & Dew's.

As the Johnson property has remained more or less constant till our own days we can definitely trace the Manor House and the eastern farmlands from Captain John Parr, Mrs Marberley, Bussee and Hipkins, Ditchell and Dew, to Johnson.

'Poulters' may have been the top house on the left going towards Bard Hill, whilst 'Hemblings' one must just guess at. The Churchwardens Accounts for 1796 and 1811 are missing so we shall never know.

In 1744 died that great optimist Robert Colls, Gent. He is the only 'Gent' that I have found in the Salthouse registers, and not one single 'Esquire'. The gravestones are rapidly disintegrating—the inscriptions on them read:

> Here lyeth the Body of Elizabeth, the second wife of Robert Colls, who departed this Life, the fifth day of February, Ann. Dom. 1738, Aged 80 years ye 28 of Jan last. Rob and Elizabeth Colls do agree to give ye minister ten shillings apece yearly to preach A funeral Sermon on each of our Burial days each serm' to hold A full houre or the money not to be paid ham (*sic*) wee do give to ye poore five shillin worth of Bred after my serm' and 5s wor' after my wife's serm' and 5s wor' at Christmas and 5s wor' at easter ye Clerk to have one of the loaves every time to keep ye letters cleare of Moss all these three stones it is our will yt all should be fulfiled as long as ye world endure ye Bre' to be given at Church. Annales Die pace hic. Here lyeth the Body of Robert Colls who departed this Life the 19th of Sept 1744, aged 71 years. Writ by my own hand Rob Colls 1733.

> Here lyeth ye Body of Martha, ye first wife of Robert Colls. Who departed this life ye 13 day of March, in ye 37 year of her age, Anne Dom 1699. Here also lyeth ye Body of Sarah, ye third wife of Rob Colls, who died April ye 24th, 1742, aged 36 years.

The three grave stones of Robt Colls

Left: The north side of the church yard, looking west towards the ruined chapel amongst the trees. Robert Colls' three flat grave slabs can be see in foreground. *Right*: Robert's instructions to the rectors of the future are still just discernable. Ten shillings to be given the minister to preach a funeral sermon on each anniversary of his and his wife's burial days, with five shillings' worth of bread to be given to the poor after the sermon. The poor would no doubt help to pray for Robert's soul, and for that his second wife, while they waited an hour for their bread. (His first and third wives evidently missed out on this protection.)

Extracts from the Registers in the 18th century

A new Register was started in 1713, and on the back of its cover is the following:

'October the 29th 1713: Boute by William Goate and Robt Abraham Church Wardings. This booke cost fortenn shillings.'

BAPTISMS

Henry Par, 23 December 1719
Ann Standforth dau of Henry and Mary, 7 February 1721
John the son of Captain John Par and Elinor his wife, 9 Nov 1721
Robt Standforth son of Henry and Mary, 17 July 1722
Henry Stanforth son of Henry and Mary, 15 January 1723/4
Henry Par son of John Par and Elinor, 24 September 1723
Mary Standforth dau of Henry and Mary, 6 November 1724
Robert Standforth son of Henry and Mary, 25 February 1726
Catherine Standforth dau of Henry and Mary, 16 December 1730
Sarah High dau of William High and Hester his wife, 24 January 1735 *
Ann Codlin baseborne child of Thomasine Loose, was borne January 18 1742
Maria dau of Muriel Marbellow, 14 November 1756
Margaret dau of Henry and Ann Stanforth, 3 May 1757
Thomas Ewen Parr son of Muriel Marbellow born 8 January and baptised 21 January 1759
Ann Chilcot dau of John and Ann Chilcot Vagrants, 19 May 1776
Elizabeth Purdy dau of James and Eliz Purdy, 8 April 1778
John son of Thos and Mary Ann Girdlestone, 12 April 1778
Jane dau of Thos and Mary Ann Girdlestone, 18 June 1780
Elisha son of John and Sarah Girdlestone, 27 August 1780
Robert son of William and Ann Hipkins, 31 December 1780
Mary dau of Thos and Mary Ann Girdlestone, 3 June 1781
Thomas son of Thos and Mary Ann Girdlestone, 24 May 1782
Wm son of Susanna Blogg, bastard, 14 January 1783
Pleasant Ann dau of William and Ann Hipkins 21 September 1783
Ann dau of Eliz Learner and Thos Olley illegitimate, 21 August 1784
Maria dau of William Hipkins and Ann (late Bussee), 9 November 1784
John son of William Hipkins and Ann (late Bussee), 26 May 1787
Henry son of Anne Platten, widow (late Cook, spinster) Illegitimate, 20 April 1787

BURIALS

Elizabeth Tuck [*last of the Tucks*], 4 September 1739
Captain John Par [*last of the Parrs*], 28 May 1742
Robert Colls Gent, 21 September 1744
Thomas Matthews, 29 December 1745
John Stanforth, 29 October 1749
Henry Stanforth, 15 July 1751
The Revd Mr Robt Stanforth, 25 November 1751
Maria Marbellow, 18 May 1757
Robert Ram, 24 April 1759
Mary Stanforth, 19 September 1761
Amy Woodhouse, January 1769
Thomas Girdlestone, 26 February 1772
Muriel Marbellie, 9 December 1772
Sarah Kendal Dix, 19 October 1777

---

* *Stagg refers to this entry in a later note: The name of High appears to be the oldest still existing in Salthouse and begins with Sarah High's baptism in 1735.*

Mary Ann Stanforth, 21 June 1780
Jane Girdlestone, 14 August 1780
Mary Girdlestone, 30 July 1781
   daughters of Thos and Mary Ann
Robt Woodhouse, drowned in the marsh, 12 March 1782
Henry Stanforth, Widower, son of Henry and Mary (late Heydon), 17 February 1786
William Hipkins, married man, son of William and Pleasance, aged 44, 25 May 1788
A body taken out of a wreck, 21 December 1788
Robt son of Robt Keymer and Hannah Rose, shot by accident, 11 February 1793
Sarah Anne dau of William Cubitt and Elizabeth (late Strutt), 18 May 1793
Anne dau of John Lynn and Elizabeth, 21 June 1799
Henry son of Henry Monument and Mary (late Buscall) aged one month, 4 May 1803
Hannah wife of Thos Dew, (late Driver), 22 August 1803

Blomefield's Report on Salthouse Church

In the year 1748 Salthouse was visited by a reporter for the History of Norfolk which is now known as 'Blomefield'. He has given us a description of the church and its churchyard which it would perhaps be most satisfactory to quote verbatim where references occur to matters that have not already been mentioned.

[NB: What follows seems to be a collection of extracts made by Stagg from two early versions of Blomefield. Edwin Rose, of Norfolk Landscape Archaeology, says that nothing like the reference to a strong-room known as 'Hell' (see next page) occurs in Parkin's 1808 edition of Blomefield, and he wonders if it comes from the original edition which Parkin largely re-wrote when he edited it.]

The Church here is a most lightsome uniform building built on the site of the old Church but much less; for the Charnel House that was under part of the old building is now in the Churchyard on the N. side of the present Church. The Cemetery is very large... [as all adjoining the sea coast generally are, I suppose laid out so at first on the supposition that the many bodies washed up by the sea might find sufficient room for sepulchre without incommoding the parishioners.] In the N.W. corner of the yard are the ruins of an old chapel which was 7 yds long and 6 broad. The Rectory joins to the East side of the Churchyard, but the Glebe is inconsiderable.

The Tower is that which belonged to the old Church; it hath 3 bells. The Nave, 2 aisles, Chancel, N. vestry, and N. & S. Porches are all built of stone and leaded, and its situation on a high hill by the seaside is very pleasant in summertime.

It was rebuilt chiefly at the care and expense of Sir Henry Heydon Knt, then patron, and Mr Robert Sawyer (Fevyr) then rector, and at the entrance the patron's arms remain still carved in the stone and several times in the Aisles quartered with H??? and his effigies with his arms in his surcoat and a collar of S.S. still remains in the East Chancel Window, and in the East Window of the S. Aisle was Fevyr's effigies, now lost, and only this broken superscription remains...'Rectoris Ecclesiae. Anno MCCCCCiii'.

There are many capital 'N's crowned on the screen denoting the Church to be dedicated to St Nicholas, and the Chapel at the E. end of the N. Aisle is dedicated to St Mary Virgin.

In the Churchyard and the N. side are the remains of a small house at some distance from the Church, now called the Vestry, but supposed by some to have been a school formerly. On the same side at some distance is an arched vault now made use of as a charnel house.

Over the Church door on the inside of the Porch are two coats of arms. One of Sir Chris Heydon with his coat of arms upon his garment—

Left: One of the rooms in the tower under the belfry with a double trapdoor in the floor.

Commander Stagg thought the room—described by Blomefield as 'Hell'—to have been below ground-level, for on the next page he suggests that 'Hell' could have been filled in when the tombs in the centre aisle of the church were dug out.

a collar of S. S. about his neck reading a book which lay open before him. There is an inscription on a label over his head which is so much broken that there are only very few letters remaining. Upon the South Window in the Chancell this: '... ecclesiae A°M° VIX '. On the East Window in the South Aisle are some words which I am not able to read and after them this date: MCCCCCIII.

In the second pew from this window on wooden panels are X apostles with labels on their heads; over the third is: *Animae propitieture Deus*, and over the fourth: *Anno Xiii-Xv°-Xiii°*. At the East end of the N. Aisle is a strong private room down two steps, of no use now. In the 2nd pew from this room on wooden panels are X apostles very much erased. Upon a stone in the middle alley is a brass, with a cup and ball in it, and under it on a brass plate this inscription: 'I Sir Robte Fevyr ...etc.' A woman in brass praying, and under her on a brass: 'peilwyse (?) Charlys'.

Within the steeple under the belfry is a very strong room with two doors called 'Hell', which probably was made use of as a dungeon, Hereticks prison or a Purgatory, it is now only a lumber room. Within it is a strong press in which is kept the Communion Plate—'Ye TOWNE. OF. SAVLTHOVS. 1567.'

There are several old records of 15 and 16 hundred date in that Press and 2 printed books viz: one a Defence of ye Apologie of the Church of England Anno 1571. The other is a book of sermons 1595. In the Steeple are 3 bells upon one is: Anno Elizabeth 41. Anno Domini 1599.
Upon ye 2nd: W. Anno Domini 1599.
The 3rd is broken, upon it is: 1637.

There is a small spire upon the steeple. The points in the Escutcheons stand for as many Bulls Heads couped and ye coats are ye same as in Kelling Church. I have not blazoned these because they are plaister work. <u>N.B.:</u> Part of ye foundation of ye old Church is to be seen between ye Church and Charnel House.

The Nineteenth Century

There are those living who remember the sale of the effects of the last of the male Johnsons, and saw at least one of the books mentioned by the 1748 visitor (as well as a piece of Church plate) included in the Sale. Personal effects had been mixed up with Churchwardens' wards.

In 1811 the Easter accounts of the churchwardens show that a high rate was levied and a large sum raised for a thorough repair of the church. There were no bazaars or appeals in those far-off days, but the parishioners set to work to mulct themselves to repair their own church in a delightfully independent spirit. A rate of 18/- in the £1 yielded the sum of £461.1.6, of which sum William Purdy paid £285.15.0 and Elizabeth Johnson paid £114.15.0 (together £400) and all the other ratepayers paid between them £60.11.6.

The iron (which included two old bells) and planks sold, realised £70.13.4, so that the sum available was £531.14.10. The total cost of repairs was £537.16.7, leaving the churchwardens to find £6.1.9.

The nature of the repairs effected is not given in detail but from the amount of wood used it would seem that the roof must have had serious attention. The iron and planks that were disposed of would have probably been invaluable today. Presumably it was in this major restoration that 'Hell' was filled in.

This century might well be called 'the Purdy and Johnson century', for those two families controlled Salthouse's economic life throughout almost the whole period.* Their railed-in tombs in the churchyard are memorials of their leadership of village life for a hundred years. The Purdys as we have shown came from Kelling, where they had been living through most of the eighteenth century, but the Johnsons entered Salthouse in 1796 from an unknown district.

The Baptismal Registers of the early 1800s show the beginnings of some of the families still residing in the village [in the 1930s]:

Charlotte, the dau of Peter <u>Grout</u> and Christiana his wife (late Ottey), born 30 March 1811.

Susannah, dau of Wm Hardingham and Sarah his wife (late <u>Duffield</u>), born 14 July 1812. (The Duffields were at Kelling before this date)

Thomas, son of John <u>Hearne</u> and Sarah his wife (late Adams), born 7 November 1812.

Marianne, the dau of Francis <u>Ives</u> and Sarah his wife (late Jackson), born 7 October 1816.

In 1837 there was a wreck on Salthouse beach, and this account was published in the *Norfolk Chronicle* of 24 February that year:

During a severe gale from the NNW, accompanied by heavy snow squalls, the *Raby Castle* of 60 tons burden went ashore at Salthouse, and became a total wreck. She was bound from London to Stockton with a valuable cargo. The crew and passengers were saved. When she broke up the beach was strewed with spirits, wine, oranges, nuts, teas, toys, hampers, boxes &c. The scene beggared description. The most outrageous and beastly conduct was exhibited. Here might be observed a group broaching a spirit cask, and letting it run into their oilskin hats, shoes, &c. There another stood filling their pockets and handkerchiefs. Plunder, wholesale plunder, appeared to be the order of the day, in spite of contingents of coastguard men. Many who were charged to watch the property became themselves intoxicated. Many were conveyed from the beach literally dead drunk, and it is with disgust we add that many women were in the same state. The cargo of the *Raby Castle* was worth £5,000: about £800 was recovered. The vessel was sold by auction for £41.

For list of main 19th-century landowners, see p 127

We know the names of some of the villagers who may have indulged in the above-mentioned 'glorious drunk', for we have a complete list of the inhabitants for that year, and a valuation of their dwellings. These particulars have been taken from a 'Valuation of the Messuages, Lands, and other Hereditaments liable to Poor-rates in the Parish of Salthouse', which is a document in the church safe referring to a survey made by Edward Houghton in 1838 [see following pages 50-53]. In the survey, the village is classified under four roads which were then called Holt Road, Church Lane,* Kelling Road and Cley Road.

In Holt Road (now Purdy Street) lived the big farmer Robert Purdy at the Hall. He occupied a farmhouse and a dwelling-house and farmed 440 acres. Also: John Moy the glazier, Thomas High, Thomas Ives and William Pigott.

In Church Road* (now Grout's Lane) lived George Larner Neave, the miller (working the mill belonging to Parlett Starling), Thomas Proudfoot, Peter Grout (junior), James Tinker, Robert Woodhouse, Charles Moore, Thomas Andrews and James Hancock. There were also two unoccupied cottages in this lane.

In Kelling Road (now Cross Street) lived John Francis Johnson in the Manor House (farming 360 acres, partly with his partner John Bolding), William Dew, the grocer (in James Massingham's house), James Hardingham, the grocer (in Mary Waller's), James Hancock (junior) (who kept a beer shop and bakery in Samuel Hancock's house), Lewis Fenn, Thomas Dix, James Pooley, Robert Farthing, James Massingham, Ann Bastard, Mary Mack, James Lynn, Elizabeth Pratt, John Gibbs, Eliz. and Mary Meck, Jonathan Vial, John Jary, Robert Bone, William Dix, and Ann Spence. One house unoccupied (probably the Manor farmhouse).

In Cley Road (now the Coast Road) was a chapel leased by the Ranters Society,* and close to it were evidently three tenements belonging to Francis Pegg (who lived in one and leased the others to Philip Keymer and John Matthews). Also living in Cley Road were: Thomas Dew (senior), Robert Spence the wheelwright (on his own property), William Keymer (junior), Peter Williams publican of the 'Dun Cow' (which belonged to William Hardy of Letheringsett), Edward Spence, James Moy, William Cubitt, John Parfrement, John Moy (junior), William Keymer, John Proudfoot, Edward Payne the blacksmith (on Thomas Purdy's property), Robert Nurse, Robert Spence, Thomas Dew (junior), George Bridges, Robert Matthews the blacksmith (on Edward Painter's property), Widow Blogg, Benjamin Overton, William Lowne, David Jary, Thomas Parlett, Jennis Lowne and John Dix.

Stagg has 'Church Lane' and then 'Church Road' in his MS —referring to what is now Grout's Lane.

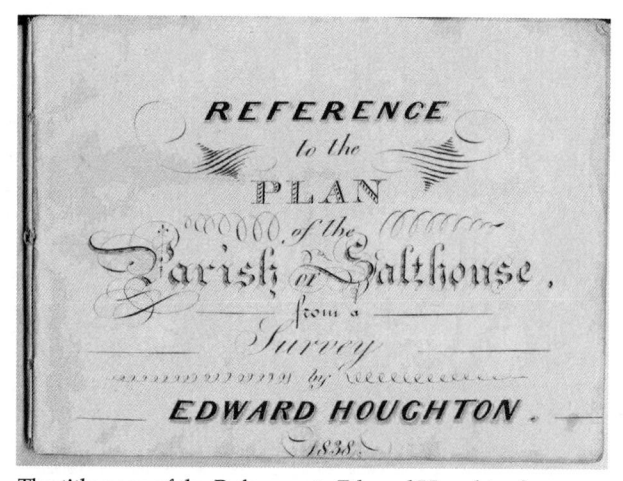

The title page of the Reference to Edward Houghton's survey.

*This definite evidence of 'the Ranters Society' meeting in a building on the coast road is interesting. The chapel on the coast road was not built until 1891, and even the Wesleyan chapel at the top of Cross Street was not erected until 1842. The Primitive Methodists had a chapel in Grout's lane, built two years before, but evidently it was not for Ranters!

Edward Houghton's 1838 Plan of Salthouse

This is the village section of the plan, the original copy of which shows only numbers of fields and properties corresponding to the fields listed by Stagg on page 52. Where the numbers are discernable, the field names have been superimposed and, in addition, the road names of 1838 have been marked in capitals (with their modern names in brackets). NB Nowadays 'Church Lane' refers to the approach from Cross Street.

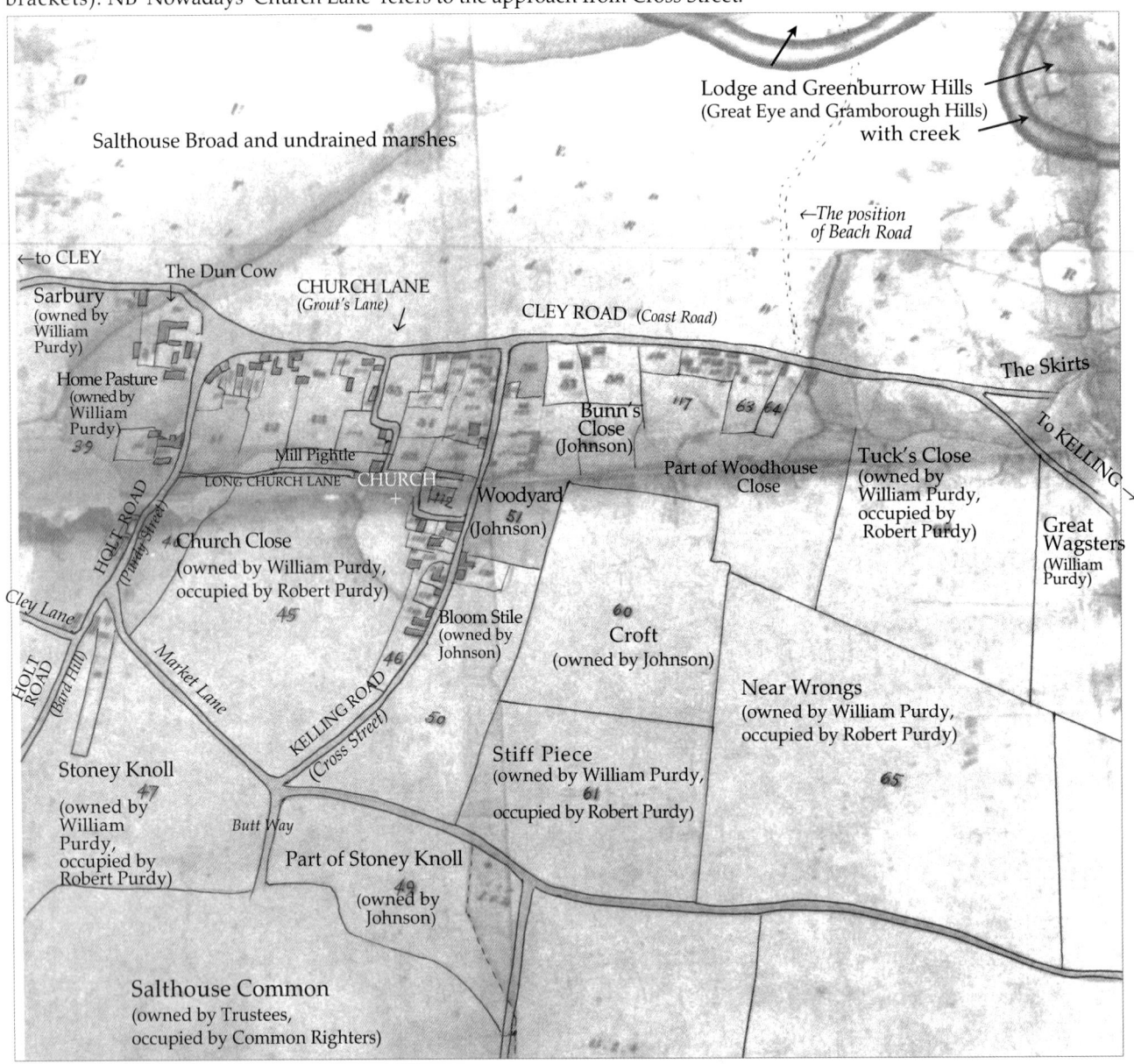

Lodge and Greenburrow Hills (Great Eye and Gramborough Hills) with creek

Salthouse Broad and undrained marshes

←The position of Beach Road

←to CLEY

The Dun Cow

CHURCH LANE (Grout's Lane)

CLEY ROAD (Coast Road)

Sarbury (owned by William Purdy)

The Skirts

Home Pasture (owned by William Purdy)

Bunn's Close (Johnson)

Mill Pightle

Part of Woodhouse Close

Tuck's Close (owned by William Purdy, occupied by Robert Purdy)

To KELLING→

LONG CHURCH LANE

CHURCH

Woodyard (Johnson)

Great Wagsters (William Purdy)

HOLT ROAD (Purdy Street)

Church Close (owned by William Purdy, occupied by Robert Purdy)

Cley Lane

Bloom Stile (owned by Johnson)

Croft (owned by Johnson)

HOLT ROAD (Bard Hill)

Market Lane

Near Wrongs (owned by William Purdy, occupied by Robert Purdy)

KELLING ROAD (Cross Street)

Stiff Piece (owned by William Purdy, occupied by Robert Purdy)

Stoney Knoll (owned by William Purdy, occupied by Robert Purdy)

Butt Way

Part of Stoney Knoll (owned by Johnson)

Salthouse Common (owned by Trustees, occupied by Common Righters)

This portion of the map [reference number: DN/TA 100], photographed by Gerald Cubitt, is reproduced with the permission of the Norfolk Record Office. These plans have been inserted into Stagg's text, to illustrate his material.

THE SITUATION OF SOME OF THE FIELDS NAMED IN THE REFERENCE TO THE PLAN OF 1838

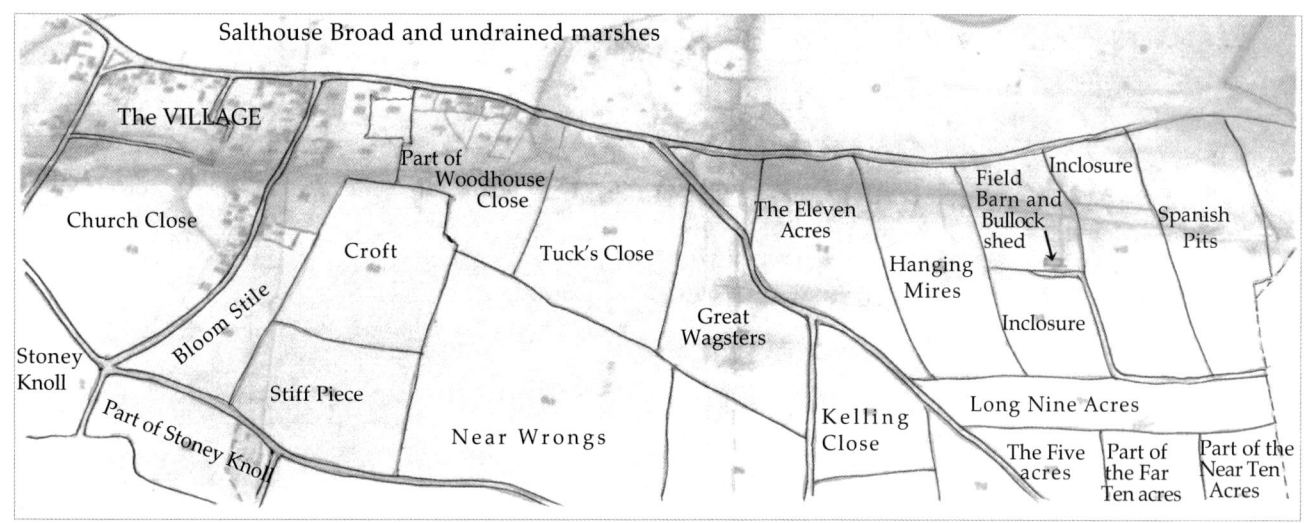

Above: Some of the fields east of the village, largely farmed by Johnson.

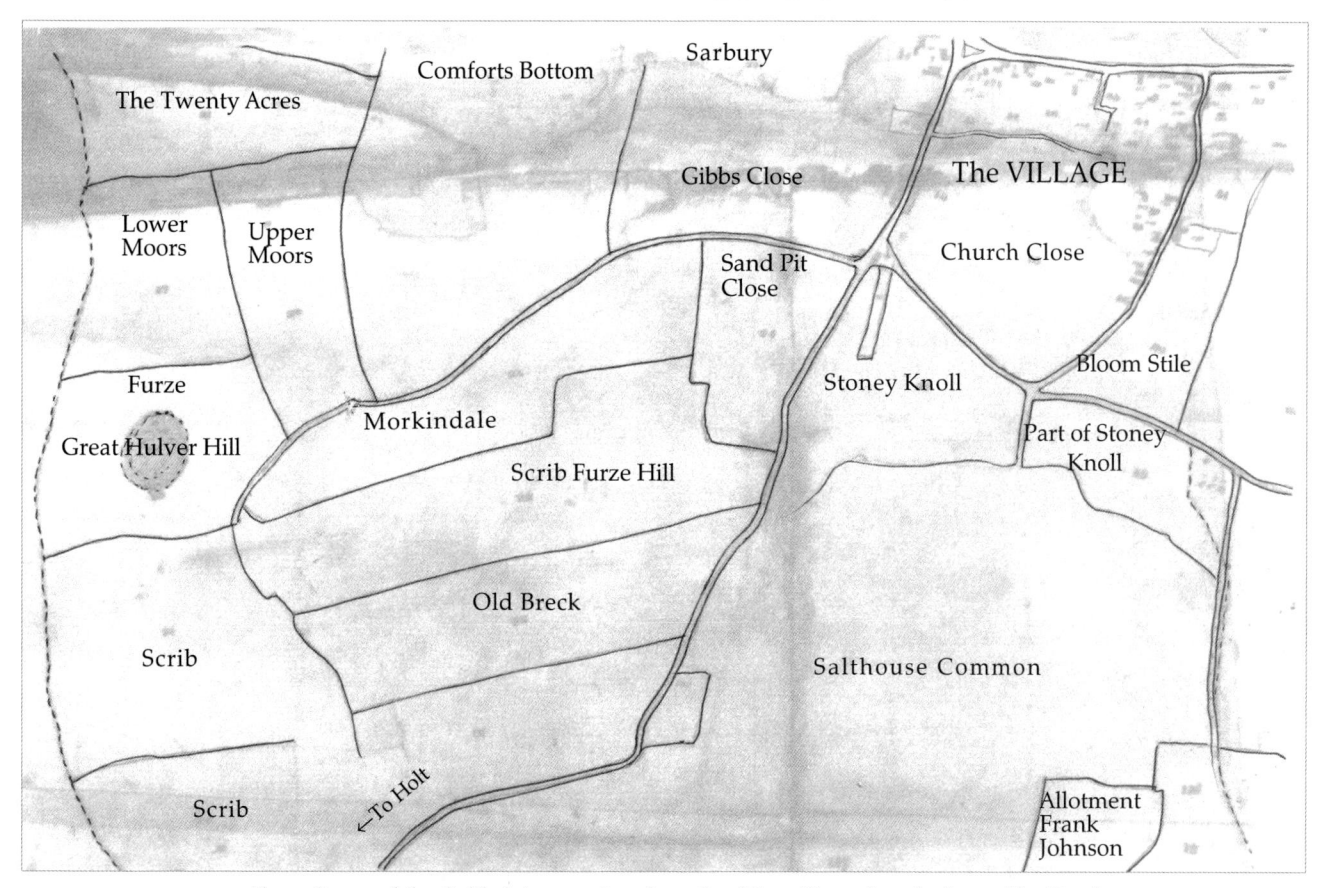

Above: Some of the fields lying west and south of the village, largely farmed by Purdy.

The Fields of Salthouse in 1838

The land lying south of Salthouse Heath would seem to have all belonged to Phoebe Maria Girdlestone, and in this year was being farmed by John Francis Johnson and John Bolding as partners. This consisted of seven fields as follows:

No.		Arable a r p	Pasture a r p
1	Part of Lows Meadow		9 1 24
2	Lawn Breck	34 0 9	
3	Part of Little Warren	27 3 23	
4	Part north of last		48 1 18
5	Inclosure	23 3 1	
6	"		7 0 2
7	Lows Home Piece	10 2 36	

Salthouse Common vested in Trustees is shown:

8	Salthouse Common	153 3 11

The western part of the parish, south of the Heath, was mainly being farmed by Robert Purdy from the Hall, and the ownership of the following fields was vested in William Purdy (presumably of Kelling Old Hall) except where otherwise stated:

9	Inclosure	2 1 11	
10	Glebe in No. 9	1 0	
	(in name of Rev W. E. Girdlestone)		
12	Allottment	1 2 05	
14	Part of Westmoor Pit	6 3 21	
15	ditto	17 1 04	
16	Glebe in No. 15	0 0 20	
	(in name of Rev W. E. Girdlestone)		
19	Maiden Hill	15 2 10	
20	Glebe in No. 19	0 0 20	
	(in name of Rev W. E. Girdlestone)		
21	Scrib	21 2 05	
22	Old Breck		12 2 33
23	Scrib of Furze Hills		27 3 0

No.		Arable a r p	Pasture a r p
24	Sand Pit Close	9 3 23	
25	Morkindale	16 2 15	
26	Great Hulver Hill	13 0 36	
27	Lower Moors	11 2 03	
28	Cley glebe in Lower Moors	0 3 00	
	(in name of Rev Ch. Codd)		
29	Cley glebe in Upper Moors	0 1 00	
	(in name of Rev Ch. Codd)		
30	Upper Moors	10 2 36	
31	The Twenty Acres	25 0 28	
32	Upper Walcey	14 1 25	
33	Lower Walcey	19 0 02	
34	Little Hulver Hill	17 3 29	
35	Comfort's Bottom	19 3 12	
37	Sarbury		
38	Gibbs Close	11 2 36	
39	Home Pasture		8 0 26
40	Orchard & Stack Yard		2 1 0
41	Paddock		1 0 20
42	Lown's Pightle	1 2 11	
45	Church Close	14 0 25	
47	Stoney Knoll	13 2 04	
61	Stiff Piece	9 2 31	
62	Part of Woodhouse Close	8 1 27	
65	Near Wrongs	23 3 19	
66	Tuck's Close	14 0 30	
67	Great Wagsters	10 3 04	
68	Far (Farther) Wrongs	9 2 37	
69 & 72	Kelling Close	10 1 12	
70	Part of Long Mire	5 1 12	
73	Little Wagsters	3 0 27	
84	Part of Spanish Pits	7 0 32	
146	Part of Woodhouse Close	1 11	
147	Part of Woodhouse Close	1 3 28	
	(owner of this portion was Thos. Purdy)		
153	Furze Ground (Walcey Hill)		4 3 23
154	Furze (Hulver Hill)		1 2 29
158	Cley glebe next Walcey	1 0 00	
	(in name of Rev Ch. Codd)		

The 'a' of 'a. r. p.' stands for acre, the 'r' stands for rood (which is roughly a quarter of an acre), the 'p' is perch (which is a 160th of an acre or 30¼ square yards).

So that in 1838 Robert Purdy was farming 440 acres and the rateable value of his holding was £440. That he farmed a part of Spanish Pits and other fields in the east of the Salthouse parish is presumably due to their being part of William Purdy's Kelling property.

Living in the Manor House in Kelling Road was John Francis <u>Johnson</u>. He owned and farmed on his own account the following fields:

No.		Arable			Pasture		
		a	r	p	a	r	p
11	Inclosure	8	0	28			
13	Allottment				10	1	24
17	Scrib Allottment	7	3	26			
18	Johnson's Scrib	9	2	04			
49	Part of Stoney Knoll	6	0	00			
50	Bloom Stile	7	0	28			
51	Wood Yard				1	3	21
56	Pightle				0	2	15
59	Bunn's Close	2	3	00			
60	Croft	10	3	34			
74	The Eleven Acres	11	2	24			
75	Hanging Mires	12	1	12			
76	Inclosure (north of Field Barn)	7	0	00			
77	Inclosure (south of Field Barn)	5	1	29			
82	Inclosure	12	1	13			
83	Spanish Pits	12	2	32			
112 & 141	Garden (being garden of Manor House)	0	2	32			

So that John Francis Johnson was farming 139 acres of his own property of a rateable value of £159-5-0.

<u>Johnson and Bolding</u> in partnership farmed (in addition to the Girdlestone land south of the Heath) the following which they also leased from Phoebe Maria Girdlestone:

No.		Arable			Pasture		
		a	r	p	a	r	p
85	Green Burrow and Lodge Hills with Creek				59	1	26
88	Part of Gallow Hill Field	0	2	12			

<u>Unoccupied</u> in 1838 was:

86 Salthouse Broad & undrained Marshes 467 0 9 of waste

<u>James Massingham</u> who lived in one of the better houses in Kelling Road was the only other occupier of land and farmed the two small pieces of glebe:

| 48 | In Kelling Road | 0 | 2 | 00 |
| 52 | In Kelling Road | 0 | 2 | 09 |

He later became a farmer in a somewhat larger way, for the Directory of 1861 mentions Purdy, Johnson and Massingham as farming the land of Salthouse parish.

The churchyard—consisting of 2 roods and 20 perches—was let to Robert Farthing as pasture.

In 1838 the land of the parish was described as follows:

	a	r	p
Arable	631	2	15
Pasture (including the marshes and Heath)	905	1	37
Roads	22	2	36
Total	1,559	3	8

Salthouse's Ancient Marshes

If there be one physical feature which is unique in the parish of Salthouse it is its marshes. Their history shows a continuous encroachment of the sea, and one can but hazard a guess that in the course of a couple of centuries they will be no more.

It is definitely known that in the past 275 years the sea has encroached quite 275 yards, and has all but completely wiped out of existence the Salthouse Main Channel up which the sea-going craft of British, Roman, Angle, Norman, Plantagenet and Tudor days used to sail or pole to Salthouse, Kelling and Weybourne Hards, to load and unload the produce and imports of the countryside.

The stream at Weybourne turned due west on the beach where now there is a pond filled with reeds, the water from which is now compelled to percolate through the piled-up shingle to find an outflow.* This Weybourne stream in its westward course then met (in about half a mile) the little Kelling Beck, and as one stream it then flowed—and still flows, or rather stagnates—as the 'Salthouse Main Channel' to the southward of Gramborough Hill, round which it curves till it can take a straight course for the Rocket House on Great Eye. To the eastward of Great Eye there was in Elizabethan days—and long since—an islet called Flat Eye which has almost if not entirely been engulfed by the sea and by the shingle. The Salthouse Main Channel then curved south-westwards between the Great Eye and Tubb's Hill, and can still be traced in its almost due north course between Great and Little Eyes. The remainder of the Salthouse Main Channel has been virtually swallowed by the sea until we come to abreast Walcey Hills in the extreme north-west of the parish, where it used to take a southerly bend just to the east of what is called Cley East Bank.

The Salthouse Main Channel in its flow westwards then joined up with the Cley Main Channel, and so into Blakeney Harbour and the open sea at the spit there.

With modern ideas of seagoing craft it is difficult to imagine how at any time such ships could have sailed up channels which have now become obliterated, and which must have been very tortuous, narrow and tidal. In those far-off days the more difficult a harbour was to approach, the safer it became from Vikings, pirates and such other marauders. Also the vessels were flat-bottomed tubs requiring little water to float them, for it was not till the time of the Tudors that 'beating to windward' was discovered, necessitating finer lines for the hulls and a consequent deeper draught. The fact remains that till the death of Elizabeth I seagoing vessels used to sail to Salthouse, Kelling and even Weybourne via the Salthouse Main Channel, whose course has been described. All through the Middle Ages a considerable export of wool and corn to the Low Countries, and import of manufactured goods from the

Map of channel overleaf pp 56-57

Continent, was carried on by Salthouse ships and sailors trading with the Hansa towns. [*But see page 60 for the article by Jonathan Hooton whose research on Salthouse's port and its possible trade with the Continent disagrees with this.*]

It has often been said that the fine churches of Norfolk were built from the profits of the wool trade; and it was from the small ports of the north coast that most of it was done.

In a Muster Roll of 1570 there is the following table:

	ships	mariners
Blakeney	11	52
Wiveton	8	43
Cley	13	65
Salthouse	-	38
Kelling	-	5
Weybourne	4	17

From this it must be reasoned that in 1570 the encroachment of the sea was already making the Salthouse Main Channel almost unnavigable for anything but the smallest of craft, called in those days 'doggers' (the name has survived in the Dogger Bank), and it is known that the Salthouse mariners beached their small boats on the south bank of the Main Channel at a point in the extreme north-west of the parish, opposite Walsey Hills, called 'Dogger Layer Point' in an early seventeenth-century chart of the marshes [*see p 56*]. This point would appear to have been about 100 yards east of Cley East Bank and 70 yards south of the 1855 sea wall.

In 1621 there began a perfect orgy of reclamation of marshland throughout the east of England. This was probably caused by the Thirty Years War which occasioned a cessation of practically all husbandry on the Continent, where there was burning and ravaging from one end to the other. The demand for English produce in the devastated areas must have been great, and consequently there was a great call for good corn land, with the result that the Fens were drained between 1621 and 1640.

Finding that the Salthouse Main Channel no longer served its purpose as a waterway, and that the marshland was brackish through its being open to the ebb and flow of the tides, the authorities set a Dutchman named Van Hasedunck to work in 1637. He threw up a bank in that year from a point close to where the Dun Cow Inn now stands, for about 150 yards due north, and then bent his line north-east, straight for Little Eye. He then built a dam between Little Eye and Great Eye, exactly where the present owner has just built a causeway for a road. [This causeway, built in the 1930s, lies under the sea in 2003.] One result of this banking work was a series of lawsuits. It seems that Van Hasedunck had not sufficiently sluiced his enclosed marshland, with the result that instead of it being only submerged at spring tides (with tidal brackish water) it was perpetually covered with the flow of fresh water from Weybourne Stream and Kelling Beck. Lady Sidney, as owner of Gramborough Hill (where there was undoubtedly a windmill), went to law with the complaint that:

> the said new embankment made over the mayne channel between the great and little eyes stopped and penned up the fresh water flowing from Waborne Mill and Kelling becke that the said Ladie cannot feed her grounds lying on the North side of the mayne channel which always have been known to be the right of the town of Salthouse... The inhabitants are excluded from 'their fishing in the said channel

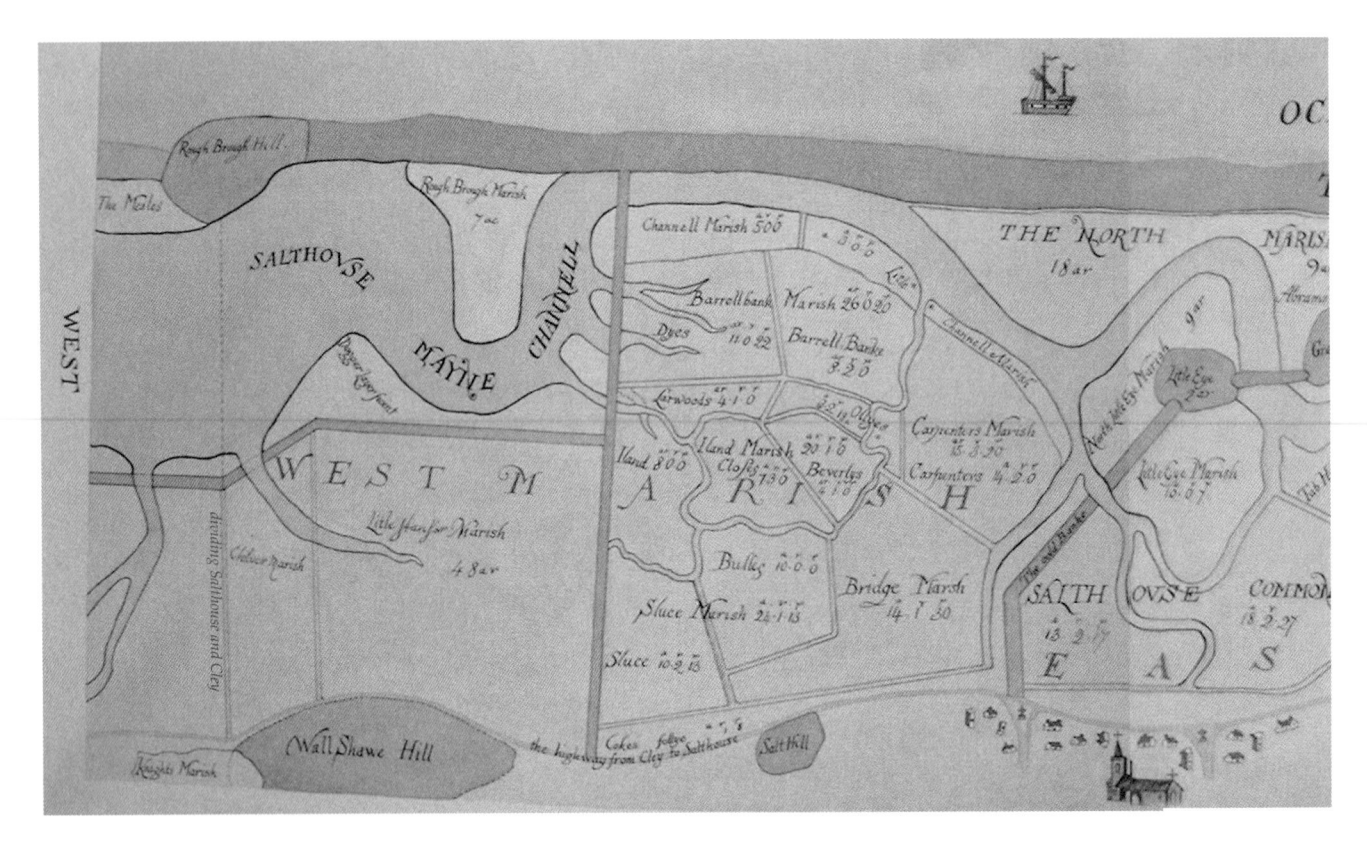

and crick' . . . and from the sea 'Their chief means of livelihood' and . . . are forced to beg and seek new habitations.

Unfortunately there is no record of the results of the lawsuits, and perhaps with the death of Lady Sidney they were not pressed to a decision.

In any event reclamation was so much the fashion of the day that it was probably heresy to object, for in 1649 a new bank was built from the east end of Walsey Hills due north to the seabeach, and one was also constructed east and west from the middle of this north and south bank (its point of junction would now be close to the southward of the 1855 sea-wall) to join up with the Cley embankment. So that after 1649 the only part of the Salthouse Main Channel left with communication to the open sea was in the extreme north-west of the parish at Dogger Layer Point.

As late as 1850 a resident of Blakeney, now [1931] recently dead, stated that he had sailed his boat round the north end of Cley East Bank as far as Dogger Layer Point. Just north of Walsey Hills was an enclosed portion known as Little Harnser Marsh in 1649, then (as recently) the home of herons.

Thus matters remained with Salthouse Marshes until 1855, when (and no doubt long before) they had once again become tidal and brackish like the marshes off Morston and Stiffkey. In that year a sea-wall was built from

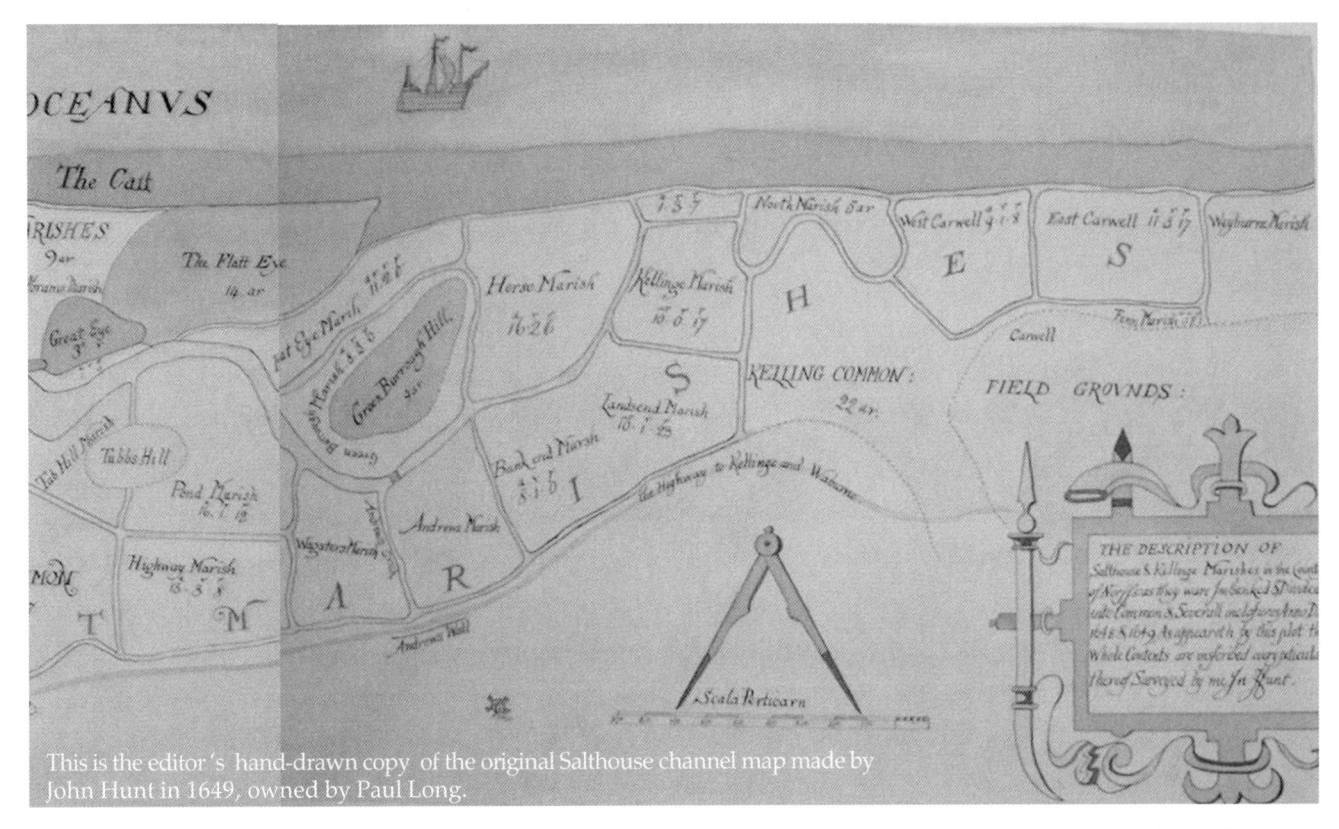

This is the editor's hand-drawn copy of the original Salthouse channel map made by John Hunt in 1649, owned by Paul Long.

the northern end of Cley East Bank to Kelling Hard. But six years later, in 1861, a storm breached it once more and Salthouse Broads (as the western portion of the marshes is known) again became brackish. Kelling Beck was then diverted through a new channel which runs alongside the Coast Road and out of Salthouse parish just before reaching a sluice in Cley East Bank. But new cuts are necessary from time to time, and there will surely come a day when a repetition of the storm of 1897 will have let the sea into this picturesque tract of marsh to such an extent that either drainage or reclamation will be rendered impossible.

There is in the possession of a neighbouring squire a free-drawn sketch of Salthouse Marshes in the year 1733. It shows the Salthouse Main Channel as a considerable waterway with a large tract of land to seaward along all its course *[whereabouts now, sadly, unknown]*.

On the north side of this Channel there is drawn not merely Lodge Hill (Great Eye) with a red and white striped structure on it (presumably a beacon) but four other hillocks or 'eyes' rising from the marshes. Gramborough Hill appears well inland, whilst to the westward of Great Eye and to the north of the Channel (which is then called Ruburgh Channel) is a marsh called 'Eighteen Acres' and to the westwards of that again is 'Mr Lang's Marsh',

For a simplified version of this map, see page 62. Compare it to the aerial photograph of marshes and channel, page 63.

in the extreme north-west of Salthouse parish. It is interesting to note that Blakeney parish boundary is marked along the west side of 'Mr Lang's Marsh', and thus Blakeney abutted Salthouse until all the land to the north of Ruburgh Channel was swallowed up by the sea—probably since the middle of the nineteenth century.

On the south side of Salthouse Main and Ruburgh Channels a 'New Bank' had been constructed in 1733, along its whole course, and this bank continued along the parish boundary between Ruburgh Channel and Walsey Hills. Between Cley East Bank and Salthouse Boundary Bank there is marked 'Mr Thos. Royall's Marsh' in Cley parish.

| Population in 1813 - 199 souls |
| " 1821 281 " |
| " 1831 262 " |
| " 1841 266 " |
| " 1871 215 " |
| " 1881 - 207 " |
| " 1891 - 215 " |

Ketton-Cremer has added in the margin of Stagg's MS:

Census 1961 - 233
and we can add: 2000 - 190

Although Commander Stagg's manuscript officially ends here, he did write a later note:

The XIXth Century seems to have passed Salthouse by without causing any events of interest, except perhaps the story of the wreck of the 'Raby Castle' on its beach,

So we leave our story of Salthouse in the year 1900, and we leave it thinking what tale there will be to tell of the place and its people by the time the year 2000 comes??

THE EXTRAORDINARY THING—

—is that it was in the very last months of 2000 (which for Commander Stagg was a date so distant that it was unlikely ever to arrive) that the Parliament Box was discovered in Salthouse Church vestry (see page 5) and the adventure of publishing his work and building upon it, to create this book, was born! Frank Stagg's enormous research began it and we, the people and friends of Salthouse, now continue this story . . .

PART TWO

FRANK STAGG'S RESEARCH
is continued by many people

St. Nicholas' Church, Salthouse.

Tim Groves Collection

Jonathan Hooton looks at the marshes and Salthouse the trading port

Jonathan Hooton, pictured right, is well known as the leading authority on the Glaven Ports (which is the title of his book). Now he has been inspired by Stagg's chapter on the marshes to do more research on the port of Salthouse.

It is undeniable that the medieval economy of Salthouse was linked with the sea. It is most likely that the major use of the salt it once produced was for salting the fish caught by the ships that sailed from the Glaven estuary. However, by the Middle Ages they were visiting France and Spain where the salt was more plentiful and of a much better quality. Blakeney was a major centre for fish, specialising in cod and ling and regularly visited by purveyors for the royal household. The trade was of such national importance that in 1357 a statute was passed attempting to regulate trade and stamp out the abuses that had arisen (Statute cap 1 31 Edw III 1357). It included a clause that forced all 'doggers and Lodeships' belonging to Blakeney and the adjacent coast (which mentioned Salthouse) to discharge their catch only at the quays of Blakeney and Cley, presumably so that the statute could be enforced. This is likely to have restricted the use of Salthouse channel to inshore fishing boats only, from this date onward.

The popular belief, voiced by Commander Stagg, that medieval Salthouse carried on a direct trade with the continent, can not be supported by historical documents, unless it was the trading of Salthouse mariners sailing in the ships of Blakeney and Cley.

It is true that Salthouse was frequently coupled with the other Glaven towns in official documents, such as the Statute already mentioned, and in the Close Rolls for 25th June 1322 when Edward II ordered the towns of 'Snyterle, Wyveton, Cleye, and Salthous' to provide two ships, in addition to the one previously granted for the Scottish campaign. However, references to ships owned by Salthouse are very rare. In 1317, William de Bald was arrested for Piracy having 'robbed at sea a ship of Salthouse belonging to John Atte Hill and killed 20 men therein, viz. Robert le Mowe and his companions.'(C.I.M. No. 357, 1317) The Patent Roll for February 28th 1437 gives a long list of fishing vessels released from the king's service which included a 'lodeship' belonging to Roger Wryght of 'Salthous', although it is by no means certain that it operated from Salthouse rather than sailing from Cley. The importance of Salthouse as a fishing centre at this date is further put into context when the number of ships belonging to other places mentioned in the same document are considered:

Cromer	14 ships
Sheringham	3 ships
Cley	18 ships
Wiveton	6 ships
Blakeney	7 ships

By the time that references to ships become more frequent, in the 16th century, there is, as yet, only one document to show that Salthouse participated in mercantile trade. This is the port book for Blakeney from Easter to Michaelmas 1587 (PRO E122 Customs 4/2 reprinted in Norfolk Record Society Vol 8 1936). This records that the *'Mary Robert of Salthouse'* 20 tons arrived on 6th June from Newcastle when Robert Howsego, the master of the vessel, imported 15 chaldrons of coal. The same vessel and master also left Blakeney on 7th August for Newcastle, with 60 quarters of malt shipped on behalf of Richard Jerveis. Robert Howsego presumably returned with more coal, but not to Blakeney before Michaelmas as the vessel does not appear again in the port book. The *'Mary Robert'* was quite a small vessel, but it was still likely that it used the quays at Cley rather than the winding channels to Salthouse. It is also interesting to note that a Thomas Howsego, presumably a relation, entered the port on 27th December as master of the *'Margaret of Cley'* (60 tons) bringing cloth, hemp and '2 turney tikes for beads' from Rotterdam. The Muster Roll of 1570, as Stagg points out [*page 55*], does not show Salthouse as owning a ship and only records the numbers of mariners or fishermen dwelling there.

The winding channels, broad though they were, were too tortuous for anything but inshore craft. However, the Salthouse marshes, and their gradual disappearance, played a big part in the prosperity of the Glaven ports. This was because at high spring tides they were covered with a large quantity of water, which scoured the channels as it ebbed, keeping them deep and navigable. The gradual loss of the marshes through embanking and erosion was a major factor in the silting of the channels of the Glaven estuary and a contributory factor in the cessation of trade at Blakeney and Cley.

The first embanking took place in 1522 and is found in the manuscripts of the Duke of Rutland (vol iv. 1905). Here there is an item for expenses for John Carleton, who rode to Norfolk for the purpose of 'seeing and viewing the decay of the haven there through the winning of a marsh at Salthouse by Sir John Heydon, Knight'. This is a very early date for embanking and already there is the connection between embanking and its effect on navigation.

Little seems to have happened until the next century. It was then that Hasedunck carried out the embanking mentioned by Stagg and referred to as 'the ould bank' on John Hunt's map. This brought about the litigation on behalf of Lady Sidney and although the result of the law suit is not known, it was presumably successful as the 'ould bank' is shown as broken through on Hunt's map, thus allowing free drainage for the channel that ran between Little Eye marsh and Salthouse Common.

Litigation seemed to dog Hasedunck. In 1642 he petitioned the House of Lords: 'That he having in Order of this House, to quiet his Profession in some Fens in Holme, in Northfolke, the said Order is disobeyed, his Corn spoiled, his Ditches thrown down in a riotous and tumultuous Manner, and spoke divers contemptuous Words, and tore the Orders, as appears by an Affidavit' (Journal of the House of Lords 1642 p 101). It is also very likely that he was responsible for the bank thrown across the Glaven in 1637, which also had to be taken down after the angry mariners of Cley had

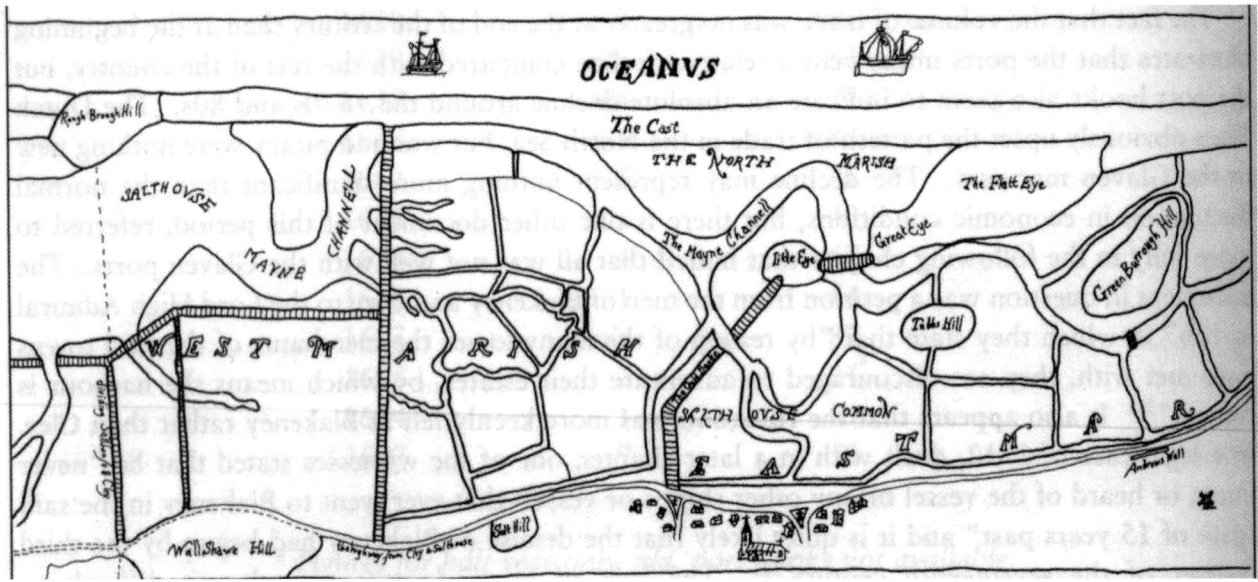

A simplified version of John Hunt's map of Salthouse Marshes, 1649.

petitioned the Privy Council.

However this only delayed the inevitable as further banks were constructed in 1649 which reclaimed most of the marshland in Salthouse. This is shown on John Hunt's map above, which was entitled 'The Description of Salthouse & Kelling Marshes in the County of Norffs: as they were Imbanked & divided into Common & Severall inclosures Anno Dom 1648 & 1649'.

Since Hunt's map is such an invaluable document it is worth assessing its accuracy. The horizontal line of the spit at the top of the map appears at odds with today's spit which diverges from the land diagonally in a north westerly direction. However, Hunt did not orientate his map to the north. If instead, Hunt's coast road (which rises to the east of the map) is placed near to the horizontal, then the spit does indeed veer off diagonally to the north west.

The linear scale on the map is labelled 'Scala Perticarn' which is Latin for perches (i.e. 5 ½ yards). The scale, although not entirely accurately drawn, is approximately 4 inches to 80 perches, or 1 inch to 20 perches (110 yards). This would give a scale of 1:3960 (110 x 36 inches). With suitable adjustments this can then be compared with measurements taken from the 1:10,000 Ordnance Survey map. The problem with this is in identifying points common to both maps that have not shifted their positions in the intervening years. There are no definite points, but an idea of the general accuracy can be obtained by comparing the junction of the coast road with Purdy Street and Cross Street and the central southern side of Little Eye and Gramborough Hill (assuming that the 5 metre contour line on the O.S. map correlates with the boundaries of the Eyes on Hunt's map). There is one other feature common to both maps and that is the parish boundary with Cley.

If measurements are compared between the two maps it appears that Hunt under-recorded distances by an average of 0.94%. Indeed, one measurement—between the junctions of Purdy Street and Cross Street with the coast road (the points that could be most accurately located on both maps)—was exactly the same on both maps. It can be concluded then that John Hunt's map was both carefully and consistently surveyed and surprisingly accurate, assuming a scale of 1:3960.

If measurements are taken on Hunt's map from the parish boundary and the road junctions perpendicular to the coast and compared with the O. S. map, then an estimate of the amount of land lost can be made. The O. S. map gives both high and low water marks and it is not known which of these Hunt used. If compared with the high water mark there appears to have been an average loss of 0.88 yards per year, and 0.76 yards per year if compared with

An aerial photograph taken after flooding 25th February 1993, by Derek A. Edwards. ©Norfolk Museums and Archaeology Service, Gressenhall. The dark lines indicate the probable position of the main channels shown on John Hunt's map of 1649. (See page 56-57)

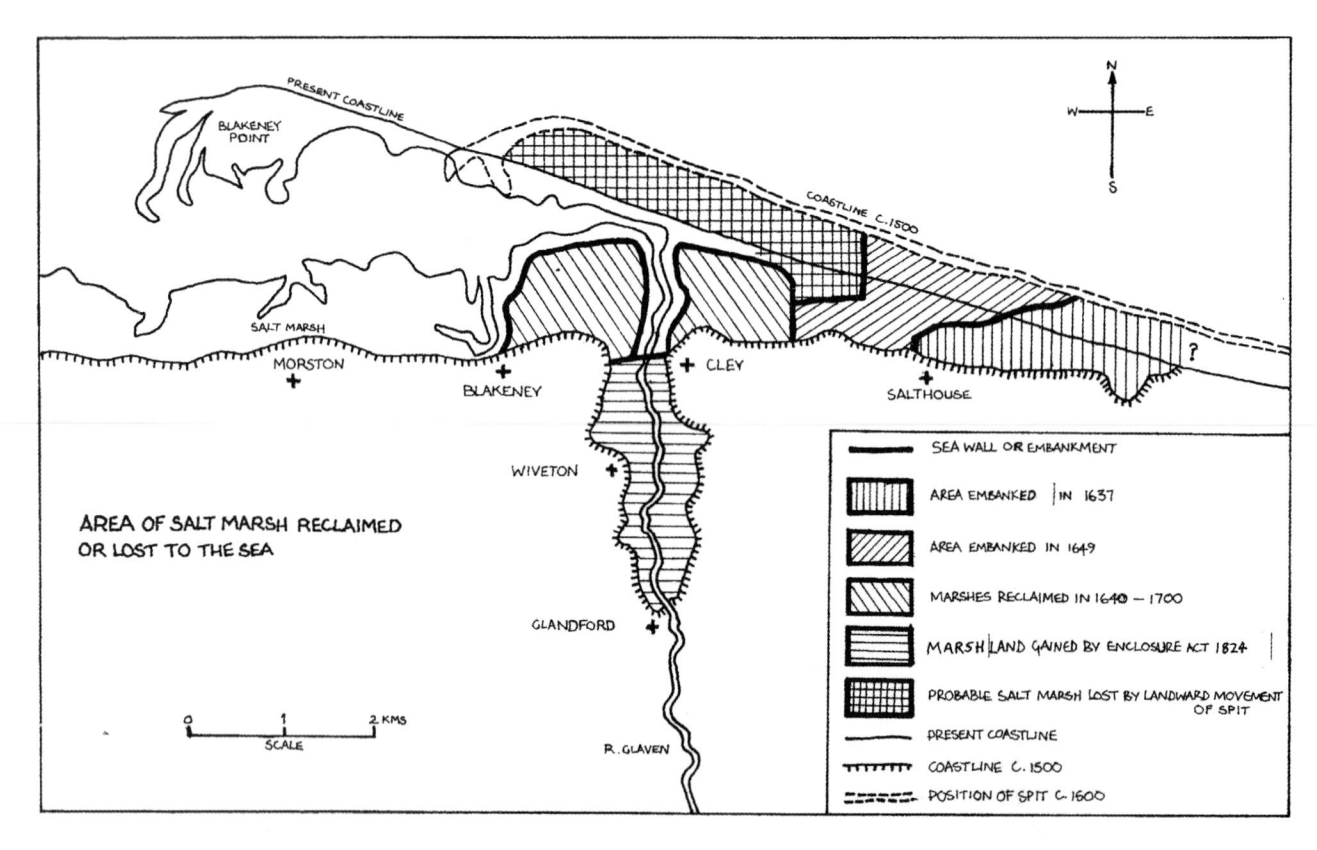

[Map: Area of salt marsh reclaimed or lost to the sea, showing Blakeney Point, Morston, Blakeney, Wiveton, Glandford, Cley, Salthouse and the R. Glaven. Legend: Sea wall or embankment; Area embanked in 1637; Area embanked in 1649; Marshes reclaimed in 1640–1700; Marshland gained by Enclosure Act 1824; Probable salt marsh lost by landward movement of spit; Present coastline; Coastline c. 1500; Position of spit c. 1600.]

low water. Stagg gives the figure of one yard per year, a figure proposed by Basil Cozens-Hardy in the Transactions of the Norfolk and Norwich Naturalists' Society Vol XII part 3, p360. Although one must not put too much emphasis on the above calculations it does seem reasonable to suggest that the average yearly rate of retreat over the past 300 years is probably nearer to 0.8 of a yard, rather than Stagg's assertion.

Can anything be seen of the details shown on Hunt's map today? Surprisingly, the answer is yes, especially when the area has been flooded. The aerial photograph on page 63, taken on 25 February 1993, shows Salthouse marshes as the flood water was receding so that minor depressions (too small to be recorded on an O.S. map) reveal the former positions of the channels that Hunt surveyed in 1649.

The channel to the south of Gramborough Hill (mentioned by Stagg to be still in his time flowing—or rather stagnating—around the hill's southern side) shows up well, as does the meander that winds between Great and Little Eyes. The most prominent feature, still distinguishable without flooding, is the loop of the channel running south of Little Eye Marish and parts of the channel that led off this through Salthouse Common to the coast road at its junction with Cross Street. Most of the channels to the west have been lost to the sea, or lie buried beneath the shingle. However, Dogger Layer Point and part of the old embankment can be identified to the east of Arnold's Marsh, which is the remnant of what is called the Salthouse Mayne Channel on Hunt's map.

The map opposite, illustrating the reclamation of marshland, indicates the importance of the Salthouse marshes to the ports of Blakeney and Cley. In addition to the embankments of Hasedunck and others, much land was also lost as the shingle bank was pushed inland during tidal surges. The remnant of the Salthouse main channel, known as Salthouse Broad, was finally prevented from draining out to sea around 1850 when the channel was blocked by shingle being heaped upon Cley Eye. In 1846 Joseph Hume, in his report for the Tidal Harbours Commission, blamed the embankments for the decline of trade at Blakeney and Cley. It is worth quoting some of his conclusions at length (H.L.R.O. 2nd Report of the Tidal Harbours Commission—in Sessional Papers (1846) [692] [756] xviii parts 1 & 2 and Appendix A). He visited the area on 28th October 1845 and states:

I examined the Salt-House Broad extending several miles from Weybourne west to Cley marshes. The present area of the broad is considered to be between 500 and 600 acres and the rise of the tide through the shingle bank on each side is now several feet, but the communication which, by that map, appears to have formerly existed is now closed, although within the memory of some of the witnesses there was a passage to admit boats from Cley harbour to the Broad . . . The channel which ran to Salthouse broad, between the embankment on the south and the Shingle bank on the north, was closed by shingle being forced inwards by the sea so as to join the north side of the embankment. It is evident that if that embankment had not been formed, the tidal water would have resisted the encroachment of the beach and thus have preserved to the harbour not only the scour of 431 acres, or 1 million tons of water, but it would have preserved the scour of another million for the Salthouse Broad.

The result of the loss of these marshes, and those of the Glaven valley (which was embanked in 1824), led to witnesses reporting that within living memory the channel to Cley had silted up four feet and was up to one third narrower in places. The water in the Pit (an area of deepwater behind the Point) which used to have 11 feet at low water and had accommodated up to 140 vessels taking refuge in a gale, now only had 3 or 4 feet and could only shelter two vessels. The depth of water at the harbour entrance had also reduced by 5 feet at high tide. This led Joseph Hume to conclude that 'a public harbour (has) been almost destroyed by the encroachment on its tidal lands' and that 'measures should be taken to remedy the existing evils of this nature and to prevent their recurrence in future'. However, it is worth concluding that had none of these embankments taken place, the coming of the railways to north Norfolk would have just as quickly brought an end to shipping in the Glaven Valley.

Jonathan Hooton, July 2002

The Landscape, History and Birdlife of the Marshes

by Steve Harris

Salthouse's defining landscape-features, the marshes and the shingle bank, have for thousands of years been shaped by entirely natural processes. The shingle, now thought to be largely glacial in origin has, in fits and starts and averaging about 0.75 metres a year, rolled in towards the rising land. At the same time Blakeney Point has extended, as sand from the west has built up at its tip.

At the start of the 1500s the view from the village green would have appeared little changed from that when the settlement was first established, and reminiscent of the scene from Blakeney Quay now. The shingle ridge would have been nearly a quarter of a mile further away and the intervening land, where cattle now graze on grass pastures, would have been dissected by creeks and channels and covered by saltmarsh plants. At least three more 'eyes' would have been visible: Great Eye, with Flat Eye beyond, and Rough Brough Hill (Ruburgh Hill) more or less opposite Walsey Hill. On spring tides, Gramborough Hill would have been an island, as all the marshes would have been flooded. Towards the landward edge of the saltmarsh, vigorous spring activity would probably have added sufficient fresh water to the estuary for there to have been a reed fringe to the rising land, extending for a distance out onto the marsh.

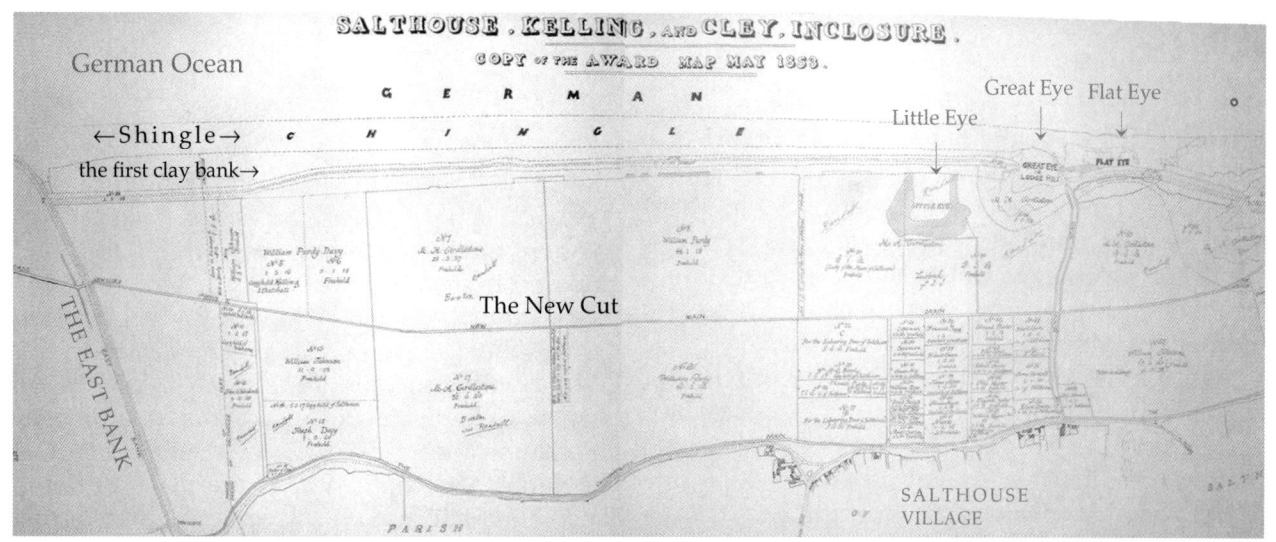

This section of the Salthouse Kelling and Cley Inclosure Award 1853 (made from the copy in the possession of Ivan Large), shows how small a gap there was between the first clay bank and the shingle. (For an enlargement of the land allotments just north of the village, see page 71)

And so it would be today, if Dutch embankers had not set about claiming land from the estuary. Jonathan Hooton's article details the sequence of the bank creation, but perhaps the one with most significance to Salthouse was the bank built in about 1650 which encloses the Cley Marshes, the area that is now the Norfolk Wildlife Trust's reserve. Through the first half of the nineteenth century, a major channel around the north side of the Cley enclosure connected Salthouse to Blakeney harbour and beyond. Salthouse people still had access to the sea, and the sea continued to have tidal access to the marshes.

All this changed dramatically on a stormy night in 1845. That night, crashing waves spread the shingle southward and filled in the channel, cutting off the village's access to the sea. With any argument about whether or not to enclose the marshes effectively redundant, it is easy to see that the reclaimers saw the chance to take the marshes from the sea once and for all. To prevent saltwater that could come through and over the shingle, from spoiling the intended grazing, a clay bank was proposed running the length of the marshes just inland of the shingle. This bank was built between 1851 and 1855, and the reclamation it permitted was formalised by the Inclosure Award of 1853. The map of the Award (above) is curiously silent about the nature of the ground being enclosed. It divides the marsh into neat rectangular blocks without reference to the creeks, sand flats and pools which persist even today. At that time water on the marshes had no easy means of escape, and the area must have been, for most part, a large brackish lagoon.

The remains of this ill-fated attempt at keeping out the sea, can be seen today running east from the Cley East Bank just behind the shingle. Sometimes, after a scouring tide has removed shingle from the beach, the remains of the bank can be seen on the seaward side of the shingle ridge, with the grass that used to grow on its sides still visible, browned and preserved.

The mistake that the Victorian embankers made was to fail to realise that, in an overtopping event, the space between the shingle and the new bank of 1853 (see map), would soon be filled and seawater would spill over and down the back of the clay bank and erode a breach. So, by 1861 or 62, the bank was destroyed in many places, and the money raised for its construction completely wasted. As a result, the village's common land on the marshes, which had been mortgaged for the purpose of raising funds for the project, was lost to Salthouse residents. [*Salthouse Common* on map p 56]

Once more the marshes became a brackish lagoon, and a noted bird haunt: a source of food for local people, and of specimens for Victorian collectors. As any flood or seepage water had to drain out through the Cley marshes—from the 1860s until the 1920s when the New Cut middle drain was improved—it is likely that the marshes would have been more or less totally flooded in winter and partially so in summer, with islands and a few more extensive dry areas. The slow drainage of Salthouse was made worse in 1921 when shingle infilled the Glaven's course round the north of Blakeney Freshes. At this stage Cley marshes too became permanently flooded. An account at the time eloquently describes Salthouse 'Broads', as they had become known after the disastrous 1921 flood: 'Such a sight as was witnessed here during the last summer could surely not have been equalled elsewhere in the British Isles. With numerous small islands dotted about on a shallow inland sea or broad . . . here indeed was a spot such as many birds must have been on the lookout for . . .'

The rising interest in natural history at this time means that from the end of the nineteenth century we have regular recording of the bird life, and it is possible to detect changes in the landscape of the marshes from the naturalists' diaries of the time.

NOTABLE BIRDS ON THE MARSHES

There are two main sources of information about the bird life of the marshes: firstly *Notes on the Birds of Cley,* by H. N. Pashley, the taxidermist whose diary spans 1887 to 1924, and secondly the reports on the birds of Cley and Salthouse in the 'Wild Bird Protection' section of the *Transactions of the Norfolk and Norwich Naturalists' Society*, from 1920 onwards.

One of Salthouse's early claims to fame was its colonies of terns, particularly those of the Sandwich tern, named after the place in Kent. The Sandwich tern was a very rare bird in the nineteenth century, but in 1922 a colony was established on islands somewhere south-east of Arnold's Marsh. The colony increased yearly until, in 1940, over a thousand nests were counted; soon after, a decline set in and breeding last took place in 1944.

A common wader which put itself in the record books at Salthouse is the dunlin. This bird visits the Norfolk coast in thousands in winter but always retreats to upland moors to breed, except in 1938 when a pair raised a brood on the marshes here. This was the first time the species had bred in Norfolk and possibly the first time for anywhere in the south east of England.

Another wader for which Salthouse is noteworthy, is the avocet. The avocet became extinct as a breeding bird in Britain in 1820, and Pashley suggested that Salthouse Marshes were the last place that they bred: 'When a youngster of 17 or 18, I talked many a time with two old gunners who had taken their eggs. They used to call them clinkers from their note'. Interestingly, the first eggs to be laid in Britain after the avocet's extinction in the 1820s, were at Salthouse in 1941, six years before the species re-established in Suffolk.

Salthouse continues to attract scarce and rare birds, and undoubtedly the biggest crowd-puller was the little whimbrel that was on the marshes close to the duck pond over the 1985 August bank holiday weekend. It had only occurred in Europe twice before, and the mingled crowd of enthusiastic 'twitchers' and ice-cream-buying visitors was one of the biggest for any rare bird.

Little Whimbrel

For many, however, it is the numbers of birds that are impressive here, and none more so than the brent geese which visit in winter. When you look out over one of the flocks of several thousand that occurs now, it is hard to appreciate how rare brent once were. Pashley, writing in 1924, stated: 'Not one seen in some recent winters'! The almost growling sounds of a feeding flock of brent on the grazed pastures, are now an integral part of a Salthouse winter. One particular goose was ringed as a youngster on the marshes in front of the Dun Cow in 1974, and returned annually to Salthouse for over twenty years.

One bird that is being seen more frequently these days is the black-tailed godwit. It could, possibly, one day breed, and fortunately is not now under the sorts of pressure it was in Pashley's day. His diary for August 1923 says, '9 black-tailed godwits for some time at Salthouse, but nearly all gone by 17th—shot and eaten no doubt by the Salthouse people...'!

The wading birds are a special feature of these marshes. The tumbling 'nuptial' displays of the lapwing are easy to take for granted here, but in many areas of Britain lapwings are now totally absent as breeding birds. Through the summer, the omnipresent alarm calls of the redshank, the raucous courtship clamour of the oystercatcher, the 'kleeping' of avocets and soft piping of ringed plovers, combine to be a constant reminder of the huge importance of these marshes to wetland birds.

Steve Harris, February 2003

1922 - the wildfowler's view

From a newspaper cutting dated 19 August, 1922

SALTHOUSE BROADS.

A BIRD PARADISE IN NORTH NORFOLK.

"THE story of Salthouse Broads" is the title of an article by Mr. J. Wentworth Day in the current issue of "The Field." Mr. Day tells how 140 acres of poor quality grazing marsh have been turned into "the most wonderful duck marsh in England."

During last winter, 852 head of birds were bagged—and that was done in the worst wildfowl season for many years. A very great variety of birds frequent the marsh, Mr. Day points out, including spoonbill and avocet. These results have been obtained by the "expenditure of a good deal of hard work, no extravagant amount of money, and plenty of commonsense."

The owner, Mr. Day says, realised that wild duck do not require a great deal of water—"What they want is a place where they can feed in peace, and stand on their heads with their bills on the bottom." He set out to give them it. Tufts of reeds have been put down from boats, and fresh water conveyed in wooden troughs to the fifteen and twenty-acre sections into which the marsh has been divided.

The measure of the owner's success is the increase in the yearly bag, which has risen in the last three years from 121 head to the 852 head mentioned above. Yet the owner does not shoot his marsh more often than once a fortnight, sometimes less frequently.

The record individual bag was one of 130 duck made on September 26th last year, when, says Mr. Day, "it was blowing a westerly gale and raining in torrents. The duck kept coming in from the sea, and the gale kept them low."

Salthouse Broads were formed thirty years ago, when an irruption of the sea left behind a chain of brackish pools. During the war, the marshes were again flooded, this time deliberately—to prevent a German landing.

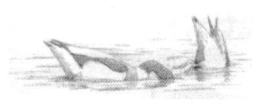

The birdwatcher's view in the early 1900s

IN SALTHOUSE MARSHES.

Among the haunts of rare or vanishing birds of Norfolk few names occur more frequently than that of Salthouse Marshes and the bank of shingle which runs thence westward to Blakeney Point. The former attracts mainly the birds which have now deserted England and have found a refuge in Holland. The latter is the chosen alighting-place of rare migrants which are seldom, and in some cases never, seen elsewhere in our islands, but after snatching a brief repose of a few hours from the weary journey across the Northern sea, instantly take flight again for some distant and congenial region of the South. To the marshes of Salthouse, and the more ancient reclamations adjacent, the City Levels, the spoonbill flies almost yearly to see if the times are mending, and the marshes becoming wet enough for the "return of the *Plateleidæ*," and the avocets drop in to look again at their old haunts, where 60 years ago they fed in black and white flocks like sea-magpies on the muds. There, too, the cranes wing their ordered way, and after dancing a solemn dance on the flats, fly off before the fowlers can fetch their guns to shoot them. There the black tern and the phalarope, and sometimes the sand-grouse (on the Weybourne Beach adjoining) and Temminck's stint, and many more whose names are chronicled in the lists of Norfolk naturalists, touch like passing ships, and then disappear by night over land and sea, on their invisible voyages.

It is not difficult to account for the attraction of this strange fringe of shore for the ancient tribes of the birds. It is intensely solitary, protected for mile after mile against the sea by an immense pebble ridge, which runs as straight as a railway embankment for miles along the shore, and forms a natural barrier against the onset of the sea. Indeed this, and below the level of the flood tide, are marshes for ever and ever, a grey-green region, level and featureless, a land without foreground, and devoid of trees, bridges, or even gates and rails, to break the flat. Looking inland the whole of the marsh fringe is backed by hills, on which, from point to point, stand the great empty churches, tall and embattled, big enough to hold twice the population of the stark and stony little fishing villages which lie along the shore below with their feet in the marshes. Through this interminable shingle wall the North Sea breaks from time to time, and pours down over the levels, engulphing all in one roaring flood, rushing up into the villages, and drowning out the people, who at Salthouse had to fly, like sheep and cattle on the flats, and take refuge by night from the storm in their church upon the hill.

Two years ago the sea made a breach upon Salthouse Marsh, and now for miles the northern levels lie sea-soaked and waterlogged, with plovers and stints feeding in what were the furrows of cornfields. This gives some food for the waders, but otherwise the transformation of what was an immense "meal-marsh" of crabgrass, sea-lavender, and samphire into thin, sour pasture has made Salthouse a mere desert resting-place, and not a nine-mile table of food, for the birds of the fen and foreshore. Towards Blakeney, beyond the west bank, are the more ancient reclamations of Cley, and beyond that again the natural river, bedded in rounded banks, set with masses of grey and green orach, like sea-heather. Here the tide flows up the channel, and here alone is the survival of the natural vegetation of the shore. The colouring, seen from the sea inland, or looking over the immense reclamations on either side, is like nothing else in England. On the ancient fresh marshes it is green like emerald, changing into amethyst under the distant sky, with hoary grey orach beds, red-green samphire, and gleaming waters up the creek, and northwards the golden ridge of the shingle bank, tipped by the flinty sea.

It is possible to make the circuit of the whole marsh on the banks which bound it. Not a living soul will be seen in the levels, not a sail on the sea, not a sign of human life on the eastern line of shingle, narrowing till it is lost in the mist of foam flying from the breakers on the shore. But there is no limit to the chances of seeing rare birds at such times as fancy sends

THE ALLOTMENTS ON THE MARSH 1853

Salthouse Kelling and Cley Inclosure

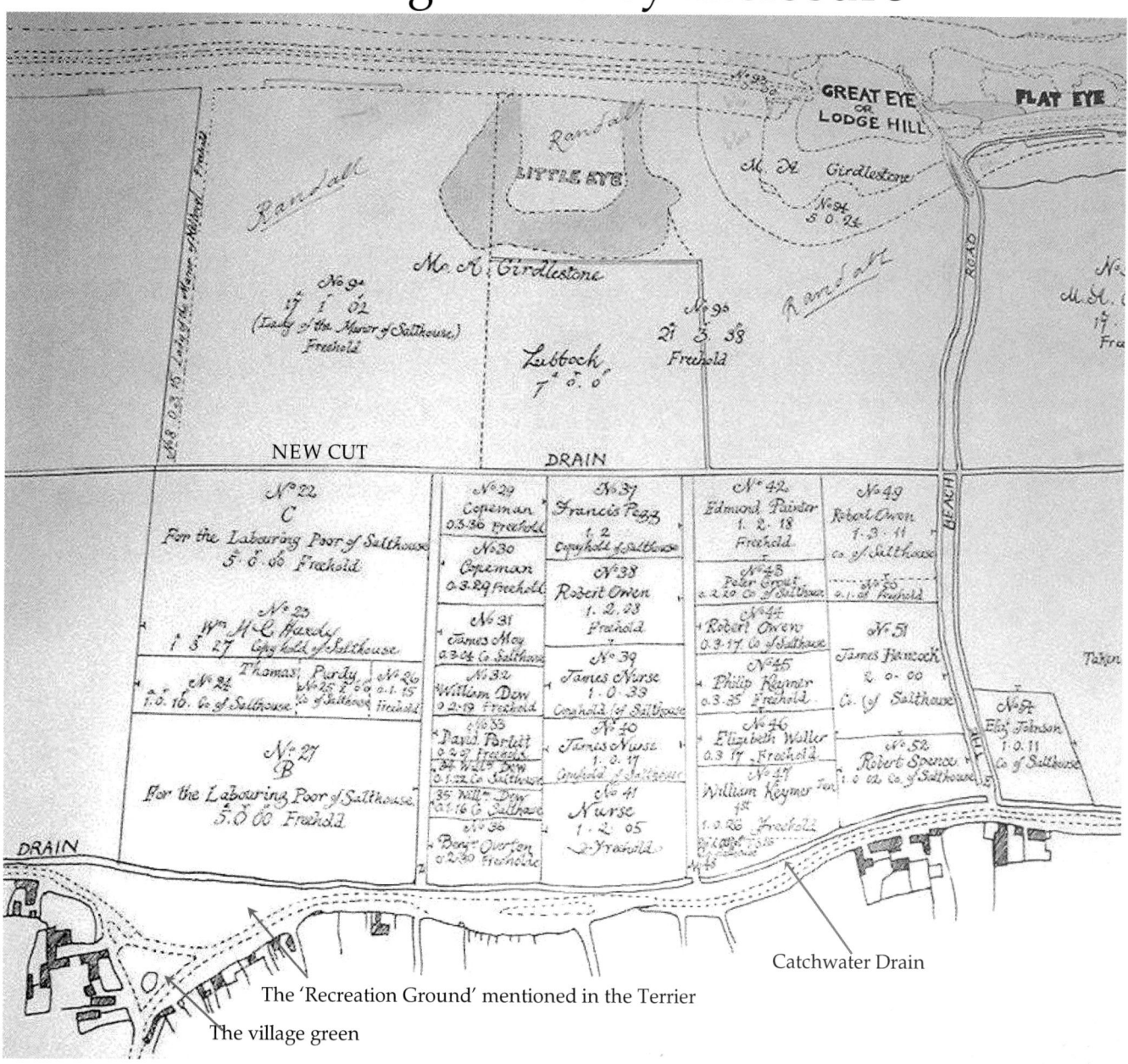

Detail from the Award Map of 1853, showing the allotment holders (from the copy in the possession of Ivan Large).
(*for a larger section of this map see p 67*)

Henry Lewis, Overseer of the Poor, seeks counsel's opinion concerning the allotments on the marsh:

Salthouse July 21st 1880 Frank Page. Ch Warden

Salthouse 29th July 1880

Gentlemen

The Churchwarden has put off answering the questions, sent to him, until after seeing the Auditor, who had requested a Terrier of the Poor lands, Also to know if he would excuse the Poor Rates now Charged on the Allotments (as he would not) we this day held a Meeting in Vestry when it was unanimously agreed that the Overseers should take Counsels opinion thereon, Should you be able to give any advice and would kindly do so you will greatly oblige

Your obedient Servant

Henry Lewis Asst Overseer

P.S. This letter also a copy of the Terrier are sent to you by the request of the Churchwarden

A Terrier of poor lands in the Parish of Salthouse

The Terrier (right, undated) has been copied out to be included with the letter on previous page (which, though dated, is not addressed):

'Two' acres of 'Recreation ground' (situated in the centre of the parish) 'Ten acres' called allotments, now used as marsh, bounded on the North by land belonging to 'O Randall's Executors'—and now occupied by Frank Page, on the East by Mill Drift, on the West by a Marsh belonging to W. Purdy Esq. and on the South by the recreation ground.

'The above allotments are now occupied by about 27 Tenants and are part of Land reclaimed from the sea by raising a Bank' in the year 1851. The rents of the afore said allotments were then collected by the Allotment Wardens and after paying the Interest to <u>W. D. Spurrell</u>, the Mortgagee, the remainder was added to the 'Poor Rate Fund' (see balance of poor Rate December 1854)

In the year 1862 the Bank gave way, since which time the sea (at times) flows over all the Marshes, and does them a considerable amount of harm, and for years the Mortgagee has taken what Rents he can get, <u>The Tenants now refusing to pay the Poor Rates.</u>

A letter from marsh owner Roy Pope to the E D P, 18 April 1940

SALTHOUSE AND CLEY MARSHES

Sir—Being the owner of Salthouse marshes, I was very interested in the report of the Erpingham R.D.C., and the protest made by Mr. A. E. Stangroom about the state in which these marshes had been allowed to get into through the drains and the main drain not having been cleaned out for years. What land I have been able to reclaim since the new cut was made into Cley channel is let to Salthouse smallholders.

I am one of the biggest ratepayers to the Internal Drainage Board. Apart from these rates I have to pay a rate of some £18 a year which the Erpingham R.D.C. claim from one for owning land that is not agricultural, but water. I have appealed against this unjust rate, but the Board have turned the appeal down. A lot of this land could be brought back to grass, like the marshes I have reclaimed, if the main drain banks and drains were mended and kept clean.

I have to take nearly all the water from the Norfolk County Council marshes. Here again the main drain banks are all broken. I cannot get rid of my water until Cley marshes are clear. Here again it is all held up by bad drainage, and the fact that the main sluice into Cley channel is so bad that more water at high tide comes back than goes off. No work has been done to the Kelling and Salthouse fresh water drain for two years, yet the rate goes on.

I am a member of the Salthouse and Kelling Drainage Board, our chairman being Mr. H. E. S. Upcher. We are, however, powerless to do very much as we have very little money to spend and out of this I am given to understand that a certain grant has to go to the Catchment Board, why, I fail to see.

I agree with Mr. A. A. Holmes when he stated that Salthouse and Cley marshes are good grazing land and it certainly is a case to go before the Norfolk War Agricultural Executive Committee when we are told by the Government that all land must be put to the best advantage. Flooding by sea water we shall always get from time to time, but if the sluices and drains are put in good order the land would soon clear itself.— Yours faithfully,

ROY POPE.

Manor Hotel, Blakeney.

from the Collection of Tracey Large.

The Church—three churches on one site?

Edwin J. Rose, of Norfolk Landscape Archaeology, made a detailed report on the church building in November 2000, and after thorough consideration, he favoured the idea that there was not one earlier church on this site, but two. He said that if the ridge along the north wall of the church (covering a buried wall footing) does mark the edge of an earlier church, then either that church was wider than the present one or else there are three periods here: a church to the north, replaced by a church on the present site (of which only the tower remains), reconstructed to form the present building.

He pointed out another factor to be taken into account—the doorway from the north aisle into the sacristy (shown left): 'This door is round-headed and very crude, it very much gives the impression of a fragment of a Norman church incorporated into the present building. But if this is the case then the foundations to the north must presumably be pre-Norman; it is very difficult to work out any plan of an earlier church on the present site that would satisfactorily incorporate this doorway. It is something of a mystery.'

The comparatively large stone-rimmed, blocked-up hole in the south wall of the church's thirteenth-century tower is another mystery; early churchwardens have referred to it as a walled-up Hermit's window (through which, perhaps, very early parishioners wanting prayers might have shown their respects, or offered food, to the holy man inside), but Mr Rose didn't think much of this fanciful idea. 'The opening in the tower base cannot be an anchorite's walled-up cell' he explained. 'Such cells were always positioned with a view of the high altar so that the occupant could watch the Elevation of the Host.'

Could it have been a window through which bread was handed out to the poor by the Overseers? This is one more of the mysteries of this church's construction waiting to be solved.

The door to the vestry.

The South side of the tower showing the blocked-up window.

The blocked-up window in close-up.

[For Blomefield see pages 46-7, and for early church building history, see pages 16 and 25]

The Church and the Clergy since 1836

1836	W. E. GIRDLESTONE	1945	George Hodson FOOTE
1865	John Gay GIRDLESTONE	1949	Felix YOUNG
1883	J. W. FLAVELL	1963	Giles Butler HUNT
1885	Charles Ernest LOWE	1968	Jeremy D. SAVILLE
1904	William Bramley Sayle DALBY	1971	Harry OLDALE
1915	James Richard BOWDEN	1984	Michael H. SELLORS
1930	Charles SWAINSON	1992	Peter BARNES-CLAY
		1998	Angela DUGDALE (Curate)

THE SITE OF A PARSONAGE HOUSE IN SALTHOUSE

A 1954 view from the Churchyard, looking down onto the empty glebe pightle where once stood a parsonage house with bake-house and barn, and where later the British Columbia Hall would be erected. Andrew Gray's barns and cattle houses can be seen beyond on the other side of Cross Street, and a wire fence keeps chickens confined to the churchyard.

In the early seventeenth century, in the time of Parson Thomas Dawney, the rector had a parsonage house in Salthouse. 'Terriers', which were inventories of the possessions, profits and endowments associated with a benefice, had been required by law since 1571 and one of these—a glebe terrier of 1735—reports:

Imprimis a parsonage house with a kitching and other rooms convenient in ye said house with Bakehouse in ye same yard with a Barn belonging to the said house standing in ye eastgate in Salthouse by a malthouse of Mr John Pars Gentleman ye Widows Burtons on ye north and abuteth on ye Church yard on ye west.

This was the piece of land now occupied by the British Columbia Hall. The malthouse of Mr John Pars [Parr?] was the building belonging to the Manor House where the Parrs lived at that time and the Widows Burtons must have lived in the Manor Farm cottage.

A brief list of Clergy and Restoration work

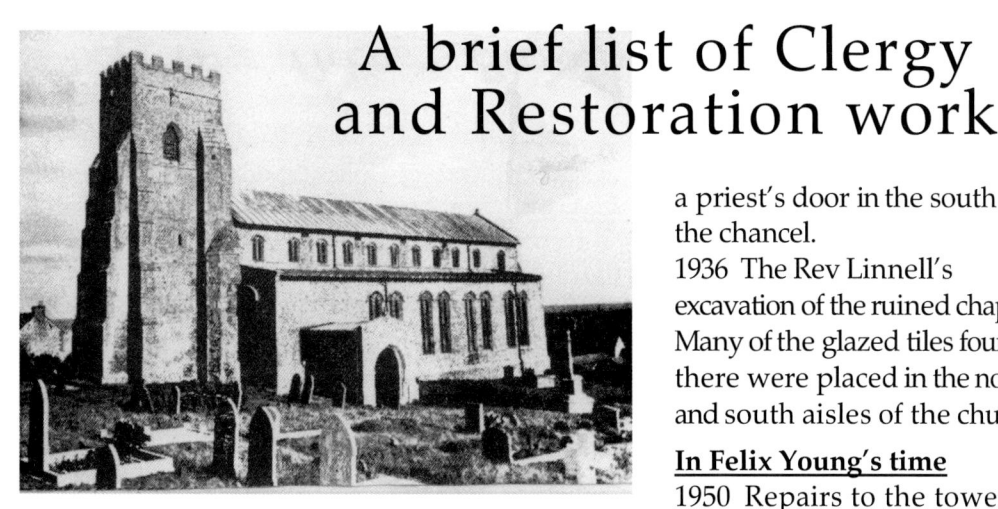

From Tracey Large (née Wright)'s collected notes:

In 1878 a stained glass window in memory of Mrs P.M. Girdlestone was placed in the east end of the south aisle, and in 1887 Salthouse church was entirely restored. Many of the old open benches and carved poppy-heads were retained. The following list of restoration work since that time, will give some idea of the continuing care which is given to this church.

In William Bramley Sayle Dalby's time
1908 Church roof restored.

In J.R. Bowden's time
1917 Bell recast and inscribed in memory of the Cobbold brothers who died in the war.
1918 War memorial erected and dedicated to the memory of thirteen men of the village who lost their lives in the war.
1929 Vestry completely rebuilt.

In Charles Swainson's time
1931 Screen restored.
1932 Portable altar stone removed from the font riser to the centre of the high altar.
1933 Pavement restored. Sanctuary replastered and the inscription of 1639 discovered on the north wall. East window restored to its original size, and remains discovered, and restored, of a priest's door in the south wall of the chancel.
1936 The Rev Linnell's excavation of the ruined chapel. Many of the glazed tiles found there were placed in the north and south aisles of the church.

In Felix Young's time
1950 Repairs to the tower and belfry and to the walls of the nave.
1951 West window of the tower restored.

In Giles Hunt's time
1964 Three-day festival, including visit from John Betjeman, raised £804 towards the £10,000 needed to combat death-watch beetle in the roof timbers.

In J. D. Saville's time
1968 Campaign for £2,500 to save the tower from falling down.

In Michael Sellors' time
1986 £24,000 restoration appeal with a festival—Pat Mattocks co-ordinated an Exhibition in the church to help fund it.

In Peter Barnes-Clay and Angela Dugdale's time
1999 British Heritage Grant to convert the north porch into a lavatory and kitchen. Windows renewed and dedicated.

Giles Hunt

Michael Sellors

Peter Barnes-Clay

Angela Dugdale

NB: Selection of clergy pictured above, is limited only by availability of photographs!

Church Goods

Above: The Remnant of the Host would have been suspended above the altar, enclosed in a pix and placed in an elaborate tabernacle like the example above (which shows the canopy for a pix in the form of a dove). A lamp was always kept burning to advertise its presence.

When Henry Heydon had completed the rebuilding of Salthouse church, in 1503, he equipped it with the furnishings and finery of the time, and although we have no official list of church possessions before 1706 we do have a list of some of the articles sold by the churchwardens in the reign of Henry VIII. The paraphernalia of parish church worship, in those days before the Reformation, must have been spectacular, and this list of items, though certainly only a small part of the original rich apparel of 'Salthows church', helps to give an idea of this:

'In the xxxvij year of the reign of King Henry VIII, [1522] the Churchwardens of Salthows in the deanery of holte, Robert Parre, Edmund Golding and Robert Manys,* sold with the Consent of the hole parysh ther: a sylver crosse, a chrysmatory, paxes and a pixte, a payer of Sensers, copes of redde velvet and purpled velvett, and copis of sylke.'

It was not unusual for goods to be sold to raise money if the need arose to repair the steeple and to mend the church gates, but in this particular year it may well be that they were sold to save them from destruction. Chantry chapels, where prayers were sung for the souls of the dead, had already been dismantled and destroyed.

In the 1930s, when Mrs Matthews was churchwarden, it was obviously common knowledge that the entire north aisle of Salthouse church had once been a chantry chapel. And there is evidence of this in marks where screens were set into the pillars, and grooves in the arches above where memorial plaques would have hung. In Mrs Matthews' time, the private exterior door to the north aisle chapel was still in existence. She writes that it was used by the monk who served there at the private altar, and she supposed that the present vestry may have been erected to house him. The furnishing of the north aisle chapel must have been dismantled earlier in the reign of Henry VIII at the time of the dissolution of the monasteries.

Churchwardens of the sixteenth century must have seen what might be going to happen to the everyday articles of parish church worship (articles such as those sold in 1522), and it is known that items were often disposed of, or hidden away, to save them from ruination.

In the reign of Edward, there was indeed widespread official destruction of church ornamentation. Then, in Queen Mary's reign, 'popish paraphernalia' that had been hidden away might be brought out again, but by the time of Elizabeth, Protestantism was established once more, and it was Queen Elizabeth who ordered that the old chalices be converted into 'decent communion cups'.

According to Mr C. Morgan, in his book *Cupps' Early English Plate*, the old form of chalice (from which only the priest partook of communion) consisted of three parts: 'the Cup or Bowl, the Stem which in the middle swelled into a bulb called the Knop, and the Foot. The

---

* Peter Barnes-Clay points out that the Canons of 1604 (King James I) state that there must be only <u>two</u> churchwardens, and this may indicate that more than two were common before then.

THE CHURCH POSSESSIONS

Above: The brass which is set in the chancel floor on the tomb of the first Priest in Charge of the new church of 1503. The inscription reads: 'I Sir Robte Fevyr was su time As thou arte And thou shal be as I am whatsowere you be Pray for the soule of S. Robte Fevyr for charite qui obit VIII° die Octobr A° d m Md Ve XIX [1519]'

cup was generally quite plain, in order that it might be kept quite clean and pure. The Stem and the Knop were frequently ornamented with enamel or chased work, representing the emblems of the Passion, and on the foot, which was generally made hexagonal to prevent the chalice from rolling when laid on its side to drain, there was always a cross which the priest kept towards himself at the time of Celebration.'

These beautiful works of art were so closely connected with what was thought, at the time of the Reformation, to be superstitious practices, that they were ordered to be removed and replaced by 'decent cups'. The new cups were often newly made, but sometimes, no doubt, the old chalices were sufficiently altered to meet the new conditions. We cannot tell whether the Salthouse chalice, pictured below left, was newly made or adapted from the original but, on a brass of a tomb in the chancel (see left), we do have a picture of the pre-Reformation chalice.

Above: The silver chalice in use today. *Below:* the inscription on the paten reads: Ye TOVNE OF SAVLTHOVSE 1567

Two and a half centuries after that earliest list of items sold, the inventory of Salthouse Church goods for the year 1706 is:
'One Puter Flagon and one Chales of Silver, a carpet for ye communion Table, one Pulpit cloth and Cushion, a cloth for the communion table, one large surplis of Holland, two Common Prayer Books, one large Bible of the last Translation, the Book of Homilies, the Book of Martyrs and the Book of Cannons.'

The pewter flagon.

In 1720 it is notable that the books are listed first, and the few 'ornaments' last:
'One Bible and Common Prayer, book of Paraphrases of Erasmus, the Works of Bishop Juel, Book of Martyrs, one puter Flagon, puter Salver, a silver Cup and plate for Sacraments, one surplis and a Hood, one cushion.'

These lists of goods remain more or less the same (the flagon, the chalice and a surplice) but an inventory of 1879 is specific concerning books, in addition to 'an old Bible dated 1613 and a new one and the Book of Common prayer', the elaborate titles of two books by Bishop Jewell are faithfully recorded:

Dr Jewell's *Defence of the Apologie of the Church of England*, dated 1571, and (the longest title of all) Dr Jewell's *Answer to a certain booke lately set forth by Mr Harding and entitled a confutation of the apology of the Church of England*, dated 1611.

Sea Pie and the Salthouse Jewel

Ornithology and wildfowling are not the only attractions for visitors to Salthouse. There is the glorious parish church perched on its hilltop just inland, still looking out towards the changing, changeless sea. From the church we see to the east the bending coast of Weybourne crag; to the west an almost limitless marsh view as far as the line of Holkham gap and the uplands near the Wash. Below us lies the sea-worn, battered, red-roofed village. The interior of the church was in a sad state when I first beheld it half a century or so ago. Portions of a once lovely coloured rood-screen were propped against the walls of the mouldering aisles. Chickens were running within the sacred precincts. Only once or twice in after years did I scramble up the steep slope, to point out to some interested person certain tombstones of the forefathers of the hamlet, who sleep in the long grass outside the south door of the church.

Now I have been back to Salthouse Church, not to look at half-forgotten graves of "old timers," but accompanied by a noted South Country antiquary, who had come all the way from Sussex to inspect what he described as the "Salthouse Jewel." In my ignorance I was puzzled by his insistence that this would be found inside the church, so it was with some slight trepidation that I opened the porch door.

The interior is in very different trim from that on my last visitation. Pious hands have lovingly restored the priceless screen and replaced it before the chancel. And there my friend speedily discovered the "Jewel" which had escaped my observation, reposing in a glass-topped receptacle on a carefully-dusted ledge of the north aisle.

In case there is somebody in Salthouse who does not know as much about the "Jewel" as I (now) do, I will mention that in the 16th century there lived a deeply religious gentleman named John Jewel, who regarded himself as a kind of official champion of the Anglican Church, as opposed to that of Rome. So he wrote what antiquaries term an "apology," stating his views so forcibly that the delighted Archbishop of the day (Sancroft) ordered a copy of "Jewel" to be placed in every church.

There was formerly a "Jewel" in the neighbouring church of Cley, but a present churchwarden informs me that according to ancient terriers it was lost more than a hundred years ago. It ought to have been chained to the lectern, as is the "Jewel" at Cirencester. The churchwarden complains that although it hardly makes light reading on a sunny afternoon, if he does happen to want a quiet half hour with old John's masterpiece he has to walk a couple of miles, scramble up a steep hill, and find out who has the key which safely guards the "Salthouse Jewel."

6 October 1958   *Sea-Pie.*

From a cutting in the collection of the late Lorna Fox

Sadly the 'Jewel' of Salthouse was considered unsafe in its glass case on the ledge where once there had been an altar, at the east end of the north aisle, and was fetched away to be stored safely several years ago by order of the Bishop's Committee.

The Ruin in the Churchyard

The mass of ivy in the north-west corner of the churchyard completely conceals a rectangle of crumbled stone walls that once belonged to a little building. The absence of any known documentation relating to this structure renders it all the more mysterious. In 1936, when the Rev C.L.S. Linnell of the Norfolk Archaeological Society was carrying out an excavation on the ruin,* he had been unable to find any definite documentary evidence that could help to date it. Even as early as 1735, an account of 'Salthouse in Holt Hundred' could do no more than mention the existence of a ruin, and state that 'it was supposed by many to have been a school formerly.'

It may well have served as a school, but definite evidence of it having been built for a different purpose was provided by Linnell's excavation. The unmistakeable remains of a piscina in the wall of the south-east corner, and a line of brickwork indicating the base of an altar, were enough to convince him that this had been a consecrated building.

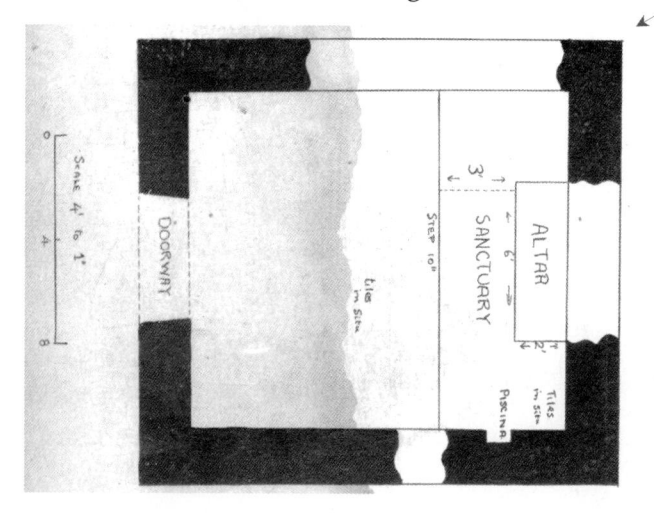

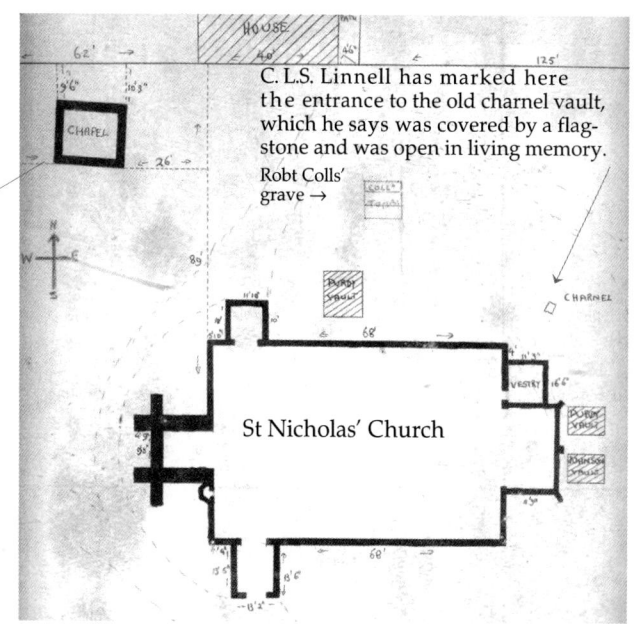

Above: The position and size of the chapel in relation to the church.

In his report, Linnell stated that the place had been used as a rubbish dump for some time. It seemed that it had been deliberately filled up, because the heavier and more chalky soil was on the top while the lighter, surface soil appeared at floor level. He suggested that this may have been done when the Johnson and Purdy vaults were made, to the east and north of the church, and when graves such as the Stanforths' tombs were made within the church itself. But unfortunately Linnell was still not able to say when the chapel had originally been built. In his report 'Some Notes on the Ruin in Salthouse Churchyard' published in *Norfolk Archaeology, Vol. XXVII*, he said:

'The absence of anything in the nature of

---

* His report was published in *Norfolk Archaeology, Vol XXVII, p 345*

dressed stone or mouldings in connection with the site made it impossible to obtain anything like an accurate date for the building.

'As regards finds: in the loose soil, directly above the floor level, a large number of stained glass fragments were found. Most of this is of a brown colour, and there are a few pieces that have a fragment of design—the best find among these being a portion of St Dorothy's basket of loaves. This fragment and one or two other fragments have been dated by the Rev Christopher Woodforde as fifteenth-century work. It seems reasonable to suppose that these may have come from the church, and I suggest that some of it came from the east window when, if it had been smashed outwards (during the iconoclasm of the Reformation), possibly some of the fragments would have been swept up when the vaults were made and carted with the soil to the chapel. Other finds included a number of large pins, a book clasp and some pottery (late mediaeval) out of which it was possible to reconstruct a shallow cooking bowl, heavily charred on the outside.

'A number of coins were found, among them two very worn silver three-penny pieces, a Double Tournois of Francis I of France, a number of Irish farthings of the Jacobean and Caroline periods, and some merchants' tokens with names and mottoes, all bearing the mark: '

Many of the tokens were too worn for the inscriptions to be deciphered, but below are three of the mottoes from tokens issued by Hans Kravwinckel of Nuremburg:

HEVTRODT:MORGEN:TODTT: Heaven's red, tomorrow's dead.

GOTES:REICH:BLIBT:EWICK: God's Kingdom remaineth always.

GLICK:KVMPT:VON:GOT: Luck comes from God.

Archaeological find inside the church porch

A different sort of excavation took place in September 2000, when workmen uncovered a strange object in the floor of the north porch of the church itself. The North Norfolk News interviewed Andrew Rogerson and made this report:

Loos on hold after clay oven unearthed

ARCHAEOLOGISTS are trying to unravel a mystery after builders unearthed a first for Norfolk in a rural church.

Work to construct toilets and a kitchen at Salthouse Church was halted after contractors stumbled across a medieval clay oven under the floor of the North porch.

Experts were called in, and were amazed to discover the oven was used for melting lead to recycle.

Dr Andrew Rogerson, of Norfolk Landscape Archaeology, said: "I haven't seen one of these in Norfolk. They are most often seen when people do archaeological digs at monasteries.

"During the Reformation when monasteries were destroyed, people stripped all the lead off them to melt down and re-use.

"I can't be exactly certain why the hearth is at Salthouse Church. It was probably used during a building programme at the church, perhaps in the 15th or 16th century. It is about 70cm across and would have been a temporary feature cut into a phase of the building."

Dr Rogerson said the find illustrated the importance of Norfolk's unique array of churches.

He said: "They are our most important archaeological relics. They are packed with potentially interesting finds. Every time someone digs at a church they are likely to find something.

"Much of this is because churches have been built on to and altered so many times down the years. Today it it may be a new lavatory or kitchen that is needed, but in the past a change of worship style may have prompted an overhaul."

He said the find also showed the importance of sensitive building work like that carried out by F Woodrow and Son.

"The builders cleaned around it and they have to be commended for leaving it to me to record. Their vigilance and enthusiasm is very encouraging."

Building work will now continue, and the hearth will be covered up again.

Dr Rogerson said "It is very rare that anything is worth preserving in aspic."

Above: Looking inside the porch from the north, showing the exact situation of the kiln. The rim is visible. The outer surface of the clay rim was yellowish but within that the lining was fired to a red colour, becoming vitrified and pink at its inner surface which was lined with a thin 'skin' of lead.

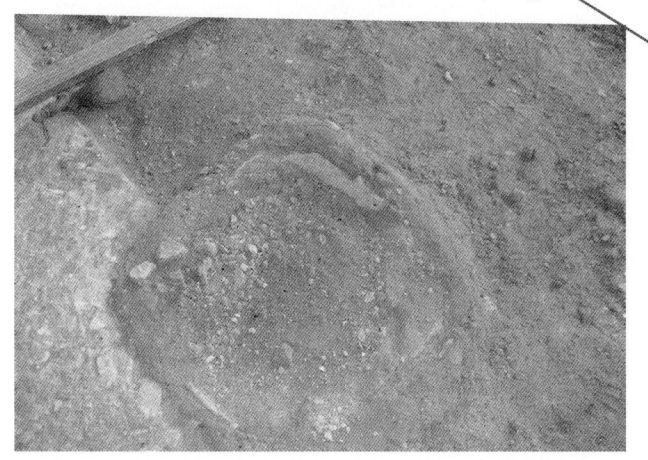

Above: Looking straight down on to the smelter. In his report, Andrew Rogerson wrote: 'The south part of the lead melting hearth was cut through the north edge of a massive level-topped east-to-west flint and mortar wall foundation. The upper surface of this foundation lies no more than 5 mm below the level of the nave floor and is flush with the uppermost surviving elements of the hearth.'

Graffiti in Church

No one can fail to wonder at the carvings on the choir stalls in St. Nicholas' Church, and nor can anyone think up a satisfactory answer to explain them, except to conclude that the benches probably did not begin life inside the church.

There are many seventeenth century dates scattered over the area of the desks and screens, and an article in the Eastern Daily Press in 1938 drew attention to the beaked bows of some of the ships and their even higher curved up sterns, and suggested that these features would seem to establish them as not many years later than the Armada period.

'Most of the ships are three-masted, but in one of them there seems to be a sign of a fourth mast abaft the mizzen, a "bonaventure" as it was called, which dropped out of the old design of ships during the seventeenth century. On another sketch there is apparently an indication of a triangular lateen sail instead of a square sail, and this again would indicate a date not later than the early seventeenth century.

'Boys always like to put the flags in a drawing and these ships are liberally supplied with flags, the diagonal cross on them rules out the possibility that they date from Elizabethan days since the cross of St. George was then the flag of England. We are then left with the probability that the boy intended roughly to represent the first union flag of England which was introduced by James I after his accession to the throne in 1603. Whoever drew these ships needed only to wander down the street to see them. It is an interesting point that most of the ships are in harbour with their sails furled.'

Above: Ships from a map of 1700, showing the same shaped hull.

Above: This square-rigged ship 'John' appears in two places on the choir desks.

The south choir stall bench, covered with 'graffiti'.

Above: The back of the screens that were placed at the west end of the nave in 1936. This particular scratched image has the appearance of being unfinished except for the flags which dominate it.

Above: Saint Simon with a fish, and the prophet Daniel (both faceless) on a panel of the parclose screen in the Lady chapel.

Above: The south choir stall with part of the screen serving as backing. The '**n**' standing for 𝔑𝔦𝔠𝔥𝔬𝔩𝔞𝔰, is topped by a mitre, which can still be clearly seen behind the graffiti.

Most of these ships appear on the backs of the original sixteenth century screens, some of which have been incorporated into the backs of the choir stalls. The faces of the saints and prophets on the screens have been scratched out by those whose job it was to destroy whatever seemed to smack of idolatry in the eyes of the Protestant reformers, but we don't know at what time the screens were dismantled; had it been done in Elizabethan times and the sections stacked in somebody's barn for safety and then more or less forgotten, a boy with a need to draw might have found them a most admirable drawing board.

The scratched ship on the right, each mast surmounted by an enormous flag, is typical of the many that are to be found all over the screens. At first glance these scratchings seem to be the work of a vandal, but on close scrutiny there is an immensity of detail to be seen. The illustration below, of a privateer in dock, is remarkably similar in details of rigging.

Fitting Out an Elizabethan Privateer

The ships carved on the surface of the choir stall desks (right) are quite different from those on the screens and would seem to have been done by another person. They are all smaller craft and most of them are under sail. Perhaps the most extraordinary and delightful thing is the fact that the people in charge over the ages allowed this 'graffiti' to remain.

The Bell in the Tower

From *The Holt, Melton Constable and Wells Post*, 14 Sept, 1917.

Bishop of Norwich at Salthouse

DEDICATION OF A BELL

Last Friday the Bishop of Norwich visited Salthouse and dedicated a bell which had been recast and hung in Salthouse church in memory of Lieutenants R.H.W. Cobbold and E.F.W. Cobbold, two sons of the Rev R. R. Cobbold Rector of Hitcham, Ipswich. There was a good congregation at the service, which consisted of a shortened form of Evensong taken by the Rector of Kelling and Salthouse (Rev J. R. Bowden). The special lesson was taken from St. John's Gospel 1st chapter beginning at the 35th verse. During the service the hymns 'Jesus calls us', 'Jesus Lover of my Soul' and 'Sun of my Soul' were sung, Mrs Matthews being at the organ. The bell was dedicated by the Bishop, who said 'We dedicate this bell to the memory of Robert Henry Wanklyn Cobbold and Edgar Francis Wanklyn Cobbold, in the Name of the Father, and of the Son, and of the Holy Ghost', and then the bell was solemnly rung.

Afterwards the Bishop gave a touching address, alluding to the two dead officers who in days gone by had made Salthouse their holiday home, and of whom many had pleasant recollections, and of whom they would think when the bell gave out its summons to worship.

Above: The inscription on the far side of the bell, according to the Rev Hermitage's notebook.

Left: One of the finds in the Parliament Box was a little notebook of 1930 belonging to Rev E. Hermitage. There is no record of who he was, but he was certainly a lover of Salthouse and a great recorder of detail. Here are his notes about the recasting of the bell, and its dedication to the two Cobbold boys who died in World War I. The bell was originally one of three bells that were hung in the tower in 1599 (as the little drawings on it show). An entry in one of the Churchwardens' account books gives a clue to the fate of the other two bells:

1811 Recd of Mr Baker for
Old Bells: £68 10s. 0d.
Recd for Old Iron: £1 3s. 4d.
Recd for Old plank: £1 0s. 0d.
Signed Willm Girdlestone Rector, Elizabeth Purdy and Robert Mash.

The embossed inscription ELISABETHE can faintly be seen at the top of the bell.

87

World War One

The men who died 1914 - 1918

Edgar F. Cobbold
Robert H. Cobbold
David Cooke
Jasper T. Dawson
Thomas N. Dix
Sydney Dix
Edmund P. High
William Hinnells
Brandon Holman
Ernest J. Leman
Sydney Leman
Frank W. Ramm
Herbert Wall

Those who served 1914 -1918

Isaac Cooke
Marshall Cooke
Robin Cooke
John R. Dack
Matthew Dack
Alph C. Dawson
Harry Dew
Richard Dew
Herbert Dix
James Duffield
Harry Hancock
Isaac Hancock
Leonard Hancock
Clifford High
Harry High
Leonard High
Willy D. High
Frank Holman
Hezekiah Holman
Peter Ives
David Jenkenson
Newton Leman
Matthew Long
George Pigott
John Pigott
Percy E. Ramm
Samuel Talbot
Clifford Woodhouse
Frederick Woodhouse
Thomas Woodhouse

Soldiers marching up Church Lane to attend the funeral of a Private killed by accident in Salthouse, in 1915. (see page 90)

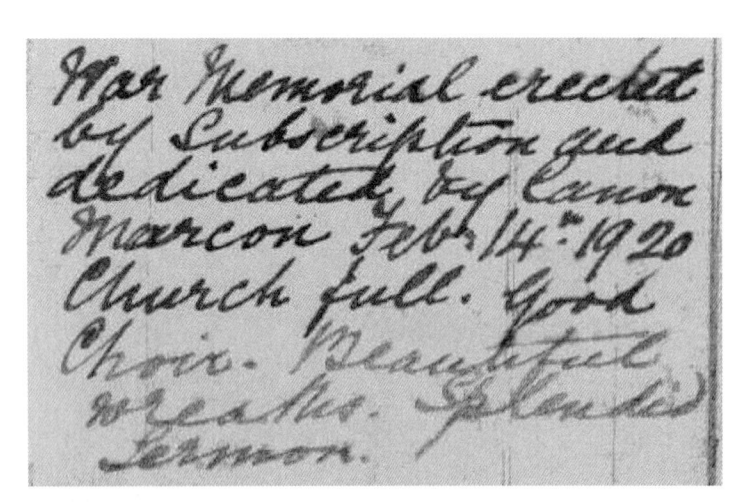

The Reverend Hermitage was present when the War memorial was erected and dedicated in 1920 by Canon Marcon. This description is taken from his notebook found in the 'Parliament box' in the vestry of St Nicholas' church.

The Memorial in 1920.

The War Memorial and W W 2

From the church porch, the Memorial to three wars, with the heath beyond.

Killed in Action 1939-1945

Philip J. Dawson   Stanley Holman

Killed in Korea 1950-1953

Herbert W. Graveling

Those who served 1939-1945

Kenneth Brown
Russel Brown
Ruth Chandler
Ronald Clarke
Basil Cooke
George Cooke
Leslie Cooke
Robert Cooke
Robin Cooke
William Cooke
Walter Cooper
Frederick Ch. de Crespigny
Henry Ch. de Crespigny
Harry Dawson
Jasper Dawson
Mary Dawson
Eric Graveling
Thomas Gray
Vivian High
Harry Holman
John Holman
Peggy Holman
Roy Holman
Dennis Keane
Alfred Lynn
James Radley
James Swainson
Peter Swainson
Jasper Woodhouse

Month In Korea - Killed At 19

Pte. Herbert Graveling, Royal Norfolk Regiment, youngest son of Mr. and Mrs. W. Graveling, of the Dun Cow, Salthouse, who has been reported killed in Korea. He was 19. After being called up for National Service he signed on as a Regular soldier. He had only been in Korea a month.

Herbert Graveling 'Mickie' at work Sheringham August 1949

Pauline Lemon Collection

The north-east corner of the graveyard

Today (eighty-seven years after this picture was taken), this north-east corner has become a tangle of undergrowth. Private Potton's gravestone is on the far right. Could this corner have been the 'Strangers' Corner' mentioned in churchwardens' notebooks as having been reserved for those drowned off Salthouse coast and brought ashore for burial?

Above: The funeral of Walter George Potton, Private 7th Essex Regiment, accidentally killed when his bicycle wheel caught between the planks of the Beach Road raised walkway and he was drowned in the mud and water of the dyke beside the road, 8 August 1915, aged 31.

In November 2002 Zoë Wright and Marybeth Gibbons set about clearing this neglected corner of the churchyard where many graves were lost beneath the growth. Under the ivy roots that they removed on the first day of work, three gravestones that had been completely lost to view were discovered, collapsed on top of each other.

Above: Private Potton's grave before the clearing operation began.

Above: Zoë and Marybeth started on a massive growth of ivy and worked till dark. →

Three buried tombstones—lying one upon another—were discovered.

The Buried Remains of the Earliest Parish Records

When Commander Stagg had access to this book in the 1930s, he described it as being in very good condition.

Now Antoinette Curtis, Conservator at the NRO, has been consulted as to her opinion of the state of it after its ten years' burial in the churchyard.

Antoinette described the cover as a full rough calf leather binding; it was sewn on to five cords and there is still evidence where the cords were. She said the text block was parchment, and apart from suffering dirt, damp and considerable mould damage, several of the folios and sections had become welded together, as a result of the gelatine coming out of the parchment and congealing it together in one lump.

The inks used by the ancient scribes are very stable, made from a mixture of iron sulphate boiled up with oak galls. But though parchment is a beautiful writing surface, it doesn't absorb (as paper does) and the ink tends to sit on the surface, which makes the cleaning process extra difficult for fear of removing any of the writing. Antoinette was unsure if they could get those sections apart; the first five were very bad but the last four were better. She said

IN THE CONSERVATION ROOM AT THE NORFOLK RECORD OFFICE, MARCH 2002. Susan Maddock, Principal Archivist (left), and Jessica Durkota on loan from the USA, view the pulped remains of Salthouse Parish Register, 1538-1812. The cover and the text section lie separate on the table, briefly unwrapped to be photographed.

that if the parish or someone were to come up with several hundred pounds,* there was real hope—with the equipment improving all the time—that quite a lot could be separated, rendered flexible, cleaned, and flattened. She pointed out that the Record Office didn't repair things as a museum does, to put them in a glass case, but to enable them to be used as they were originally intended—to have their pages turned.

Although this document would not stand up to being rebound, after all it has suffered, a very good digital copy could be printed out and bound in the usual way, and made available.

* The arrangement with the Diocese is that the parish meets the cost of putting right any damage caused while a document is in the church's keeping.

Antoinette Curtis says, 'It's interesting: there appear to be many single leaves, as opposed to folios' (folded leaves).

The Burial in Wool Acts of 1667 and 1678

Early legislation, intended to promote the wool trade, required that corpses should be buried in wool. The act decreed that:

> ... no corpse of any person (except those who shall die of the plague) shall be buried in any shirt, shift, sheet or shroud or anything whatsoever, made or mingled with flax, hemp, silk, hair, gold or silver, or in any stuff or thing other than what is made from sheep's wool only ...

Initially the officiating priest was required to certify that a deceased person had been 'buried in wool'; later, relatives of the deceased had to swear an affidavit within eight days of a woollen burial. This was recorded in the registers, as can be seen on the opposite page. Failure to comply resulted in a fine of £5.

Right: This page from the buried parish registers begins with Henry Stanforth's burial 10th January 1682(?). It makes no mention of wool but perhaps, being a well to do family, the relatives were willing to pay the £5 fine. All of the others on this page were buried *'according as the woollon Act in that case directs'*:

James the son of William and Ann Cook, Elizabeth the daughter of John and Elizabeth Moon, Mary the daughter of Robert and Mary Waterson, and Mary the daughter of Edmund and Elizabeth Cook.

Sworn affidavits were given in for the two men, Samuel Swanton and 'John Brown a Scothsman' (who may have been one of the many seamen drowned off the coast of Salthouse).

The hole

Antoinette Curtis said that the hole in the bottom of the parchment (see right) was a natural hole which formed when it was still on the animal's back. It may have been a small wound like an insect bite which, when the skin was cured, opened up.

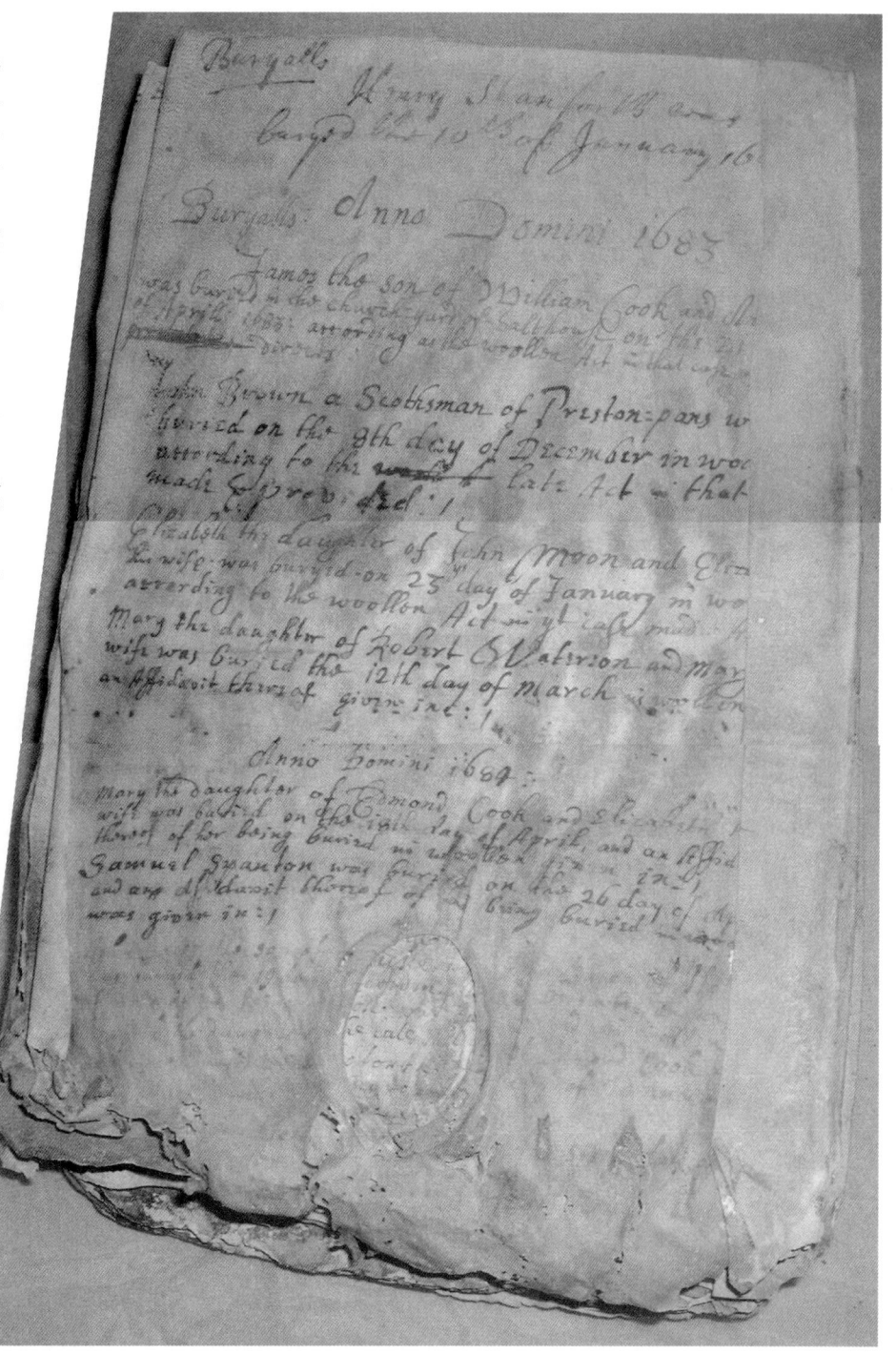

By Hedgehogs and Sundry

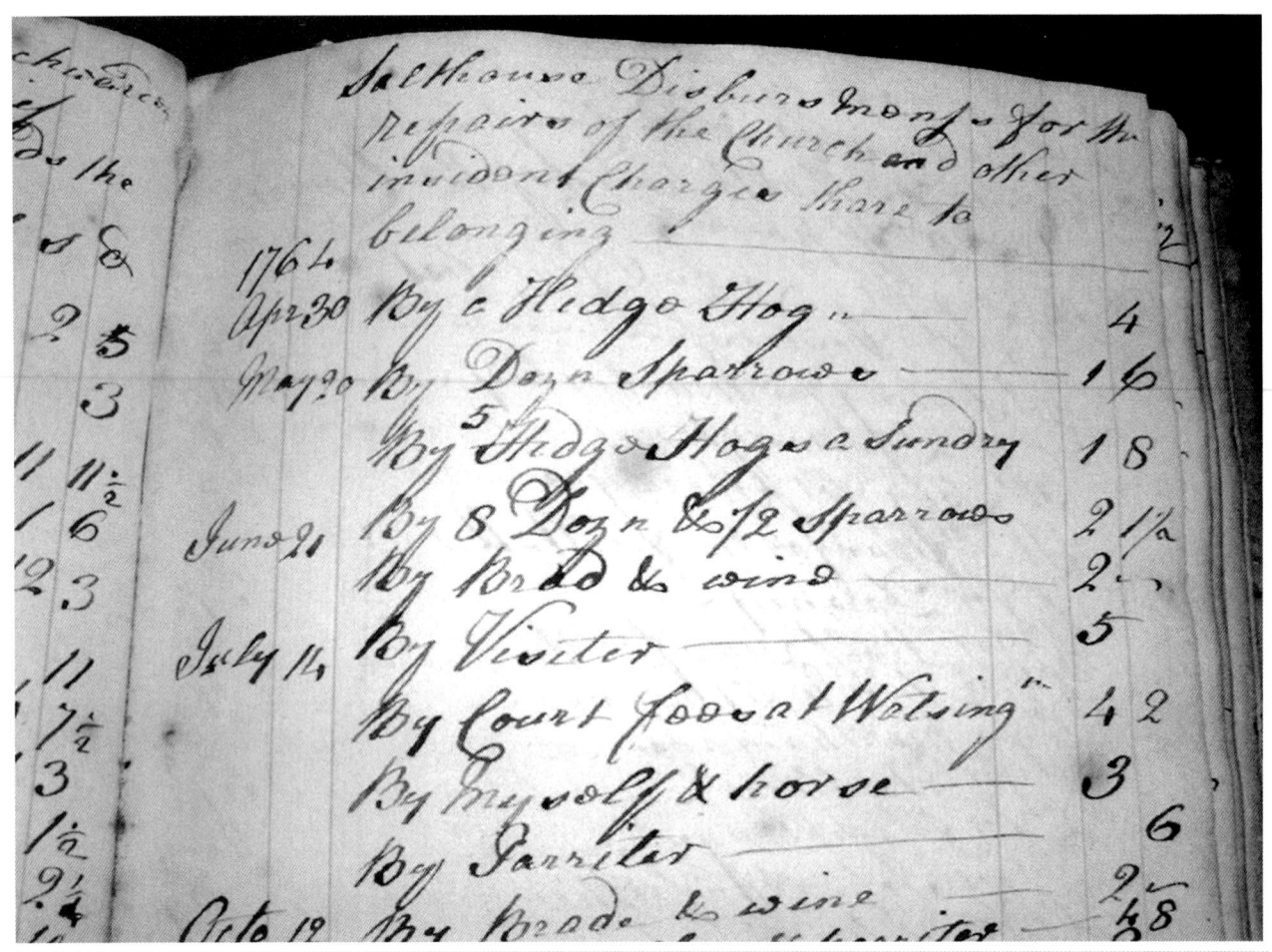

Above: The top half of a page entitled 'Salthouse Disbursments for the Repairs of the Church and other insident charges there to belonging' (1764).

COINAGE APPROXIMATE EQUIVALENTS
Some readers may be unfamiliar with the coinage in use before 1971.

Pre 1971 Coinage	Decimal Coinage
£1 or 20 shillings (s)	£1 or 100p
1 shilling or 12 pennies (d)	5p
1d	0.4p
½d	0.2p
¼d	0.1p

Churchwardens' Accounts 1742-1813

Derek Schofield

The rediscovery of these old accounts (together with a number of other documents) in the Autumn of 2000 caused excitement in the parish and interest in the County Record Office, where the collection is now lodged. The accounts probably reveal nothing to surprise expert historians, but for local people they provide a fascinating insight into the differences—and similarities—in the life of the church two centuries ago, as compared with current practice.

The major difference between the period covered by the accounts and the modern responsibilities of Churchwardens is the source of funding for the life of the church. Whereas now the day-to-day expenditure—and a very great deal of repair costs—can come only from voluntary donations or various fund raising efforts, in the eighteenth and early nineteenth centuries the Churchwardens enjoyed a 'church rate'. The Rector, as parish priest, had the benefit of the tithe—an entitlement to a tenth of the produce of the land—but this was to provide for his own support. The 'church rate' covered expenditure on maintaining services, the upkeep of the building and other necessary expenses—including some which to modern eyes seem strange. The 'church rate' was a tax levied on the owners or tenants of land and on householders within the parish. It was calculated on the national annual value of the land or other property, and then the rate was set at so much in the pound. For example, if the annual value of a property was £50 and the rate was set at 3d, then the owner or tenant would have to pay 50 x 3d (or 12s. 6d in old money). The actual rate fluctuated, but for much of the period covered by these accounts it was only 3d in the pound, and occasionally fell to 2d.

The number of properties rated varied from time to time, as empty property was not charged, but the underlying annual value of each property remained unchanged until a complete revaluation in 1782. The village valuation then rose from approximately £221 to £573 and the number of rated properties from 30 (in 1780) to 66.

The Churchwardens themselves often set the rate but usually after consultation, as can be seen from the first entry in the account book:

> Salthouse April 19th, 1742—a Rate made by the Churchwardens and with the Consent of the Chief Inhabitants for and towards the Repairs of the Church at Six Pence in the Pound

There were then 39 rateable properties in Salthouse plus 3 'Outlayers' also liable. The total proceeds of the 1742 rate were £5 10s. 6d and the two largest individual payments were £1 2s. 3d and £1 4s. 6d, getting on for half the total receipts. The lowest payment was 4½d. The form of words for setting the rate varied from time to time and sometimes the Churchwardens seem to have acted alone. For example, in April 1773 the entry reads merely:

> A Rate made by the Churchwardens of the Parish

of Salthouse for the Repairs of the Church at 3d in the pound

At other times entries, such as the following, refer to a grant:

A rate granted to Thos Purdy Churchwarden from Michaelmas 1797 to Michaelmas 1798

Whatever the formalities, Churchwardens in the 18th century had a more assured income than their modern counterparts, but they also had civil as well as ecclesiastical responsibilities, as will be clear later.

It is in the expenditure entries that the greater interest lies. The maintenance of the church services figured no more predominantly in the accounts than it does today—for the simple reason that the Rector's income was and is covered from other sources. The purchase of bread and wine for communion cost 11s. 5d in 1742-3 and this item of expenditure occurs annually. A new cloth for the communion table cost £1 8s.10½d in October 1789. Other costs connected with services included such matters as:

26 Oct 1795 to a prayer for the King 1s. 0d
29 Sept 1796 to a prayer for Thanksgiving....... 1s. 0d

These special prayers, purchased from parish funds, presumably reflected national concern at King George III's illness and thanks-giving for his recovery. Housekeeping costs figure regularly. Washing the Rector's 'surplis' cost 2s. 6d in 1742—an amount which, with very few exceptions, continued unchanged for 70 years. In March 1743 three brooms were purchased for 6d but one month later another three cost only 4½d—a lower quality or just a harder bargain? In May 1744 a payment was made for 'cutting the Weeds in the Churchyard' but it was not just the churchyard which had to be attended to; Church Lane also had to be kept clear and clean (possibly from horse droppings). For example, an entry in 1786 reads:

Pd Cranfield for Cleaning Church Lane.......1s. 0d

In May 1790 a similar sum was paid for mowing the Lane.

Details of expenditure on the church building, however, are minimal. There are plenty of entries which clearly relate to repairs but omit the details, as in April 1754 for example:

Leond Haddon's Bill...................£10 17s. 10½d

While disappointing, this is by no means surprising since modern accounts are equally unrevealing. Some details in the 18th and 19th centuries are, however, very different. A typical entry (for September 1803) relating to work done in the church is:

Glazier's Bill................................ £1 4s. 0d
Allowance Beer for Glazier.................. 2s.10d

The payment for beer is surprising to modern eyes but it must be remembered that in times past beer was a safer drink than water, and throughout these accounts there are entries for the cost of beer provided for workmen.

The cost of cleaning the church appears for several years. In 1760 an entry records a payment of 1s. 0d, but a more thorough clean, for example after building work, seems to attract a going rate of 10d per day. In June 1783 the entry reads:

Pd two Women 6 Days for
cleaning ye Church........................... 10s. 0d
Pd John Cranfield for helping.................7s. 0d
Pd for a horse fetching the water........ ......1s. 6d

In 1797 there was another cleaning marathon

following a whitewashing of the church, something which was done fairly often in the 18th and early 19th centuries but which has recently been sadly neglected. Several separate but related entries about this work in 1797 read:

> June 12th   To chaldron of lime 10s. 0d
> To carriage & getting into Church................ 2s. 6d
> July 9 Paid J Lynn for whitening Church   £1 11s. 6d
> Paid J Lynn's Bill 15s. 9d
> Paid Woman Spence 10 days at 10d per Day
> for Cleaning Church 8s. 4d
> Oct 5th To a man and Horse
> getting Water to Clean ye Church............. 2s. 0d

By far the greatest expenditure incurred for the whole period covered by these accounts took place in 1810-11 when there was a major repair exercise and the 'church rate' rose to 18s. 0d in the pound. The entry reads:

> A rate made by Willm Johnson and John Cranfield Churchwardens for a therrow [sic] repair of Salthouse Church done under a Faculty at Easter 1811 at 18s. 0d on the pound

This is an astonishing figure as compared with the usual 3d or 6d in the pound—although it was occasionally higher and had, for example, reached 2s. 6d in 1760. For the decade prior to 1810-11 the highest total expenditure by the Churchwardens in any one year was a little over £12 (and the lowest was just under £5). In 1810-11 it rose to £537 16s. 7d—forty or fifty times higher than usual. It was, of course, financed through an inescapable rate, but one can imagine the reaction of the ratepayers. This tremendous expenditure puts into context the repair programme currently (in 2001) under way in the church—costing nearly £100,000 but only eight or nine times greater than the PCC's normal expenditure. How much more could be done if the Churchwardens still had recourse to a 'church rate'!

The nature of the work carried out in 1810-11 is not revealed in the accounts. As on previous occasions, entries merely state that, for example, Mr Jordan's bill was paid. Whatever work was done, however, involved a good deal of timber; entries total £72 8s. 11½d on this material, and there was also a payment of £6 18s. 6d on 'pavement'. A clue also occurs in a note about income for 1810-11. The cost of the repair work (over £537) was offset by:

> Rec'd of Mr Baker for old Bells........... ..£68 10s. 0d
> Rec'd for Old Iron............................. £1 3s. 4d
> Rec'd for Old Planks........................... £1 0s. 0d

Just as in the modern parish, payments to outside authorities were made frequently. There seem to have been regular expeditions to Walsingham close to Easter and Michaelmas each year for the purpose; for example in 1744:

> April 1st Paid the Court fee at Walsingham.. 3s. 4d
> The Parriter... 6d
> Horse and Self.. 2s. 6d

The Parriter (more usually Apparitor) was a minor legal figure who was the official messenger of the Archdeacon. It seems strange, in a modern age used to cheques and a banking system, that in order to make payments totalling 3s.10d the parish clerk had to be paid 2s. 6d to journey to Walsingham and back—unless, of course, he had other business there. Other payments to church authorities appear, for example in October 1801:

> Bishop's fees and general................... £2 0s. 0d

Doubtless such payments were as unpopular within the parish as their latter day equivalents are now.

As well as dealing with church matters, parish authorities had a number of civil responsibilities—for relief of the poor and for maintenance of the highway, amongst others. Expenditure of this kind does not appear in the Churchwardens' accounts but costs of another seemingly non-ecclesiastical kind do. In Tudor times parishes were given the responsibility of controlling 'vermin', and this seems to have been extended over the centuries to include all sorts of animals and birds. The entries in the accounts are illuminating; in 1743 there are:

March 23rd For 2 Jackdaws to Thos Pegg 2d
June 2nd Paid Wm High for 3 Jackdaws 3d
September 21st Paid
Henry Stanforth Junior for a Fox................1s. 0d

From the 1750s this activity increased markedly, with sparrows (at 3d per dozen killed birds) featuring prominently. Jackdaws were at 1d each and foxes 1s. 0d. By 1761 hedgehogs (at 4d each) were included in these bounty payments and in 1764 there is the curious entry for May 20th:

By 5 Hedgehogs and Sundry..................... 1s. 8d

Presumably 'Sundry' attracted no per capita fee! A few years later there was a veritable holocaust, the peak annual payments occurring in 1780 when 40 dozen killed sparrows meant a payment by the Churchwardens of 10s. 0d, and 2 dozen jackdaws were also despatched. Payments for the dead birds seem to have been made mainly between May and October each year but one cannot be sure about the season of the cull since, in the years of the greatest slaughter, there is only one payment entered in each year's accounts. Presumably the killing of the sparrows was to protect the poor yields (by modern standards) of the wheat, barley or rye grown in the old open field system of agriculture—and possibly to protect the Rector's tithe derived from the crops. At all events, these payments recorded in Salthouse accounts were by no means unusual in the 18th century. One authority (W. E. Tate in *The Parish Chest*, p.107) states that extant church records from across England prove the slaughter of several million sparrows.

Although the parish constable had to keep 'watch and ward' and consequently had charge of the 'village gun' (Tate p.187), it was, one hopes, the Churchwardens' somewhat vague duty of dealing with 'vermin' which account also for several other entries—such as that in 1785:

May 4th Paid for powder and shot...................7d

By far the oddest entry in the entire period covered by these accounts occurs in 1800:

December 4 Hair powder Instructions 6½d

One can imagine gentlemen of the time requiring hair powder and, conceivably, instructions in its use, but why the Churchwardens should have charged it against the 'church rate' in the single year of 1800 is puzzling.

How the item could have been accepted by others looking through the accounts is even more puzzling. The accounts were supposed to have been 'signed off' (i.e. checked) annually but, in Salthouse at least, there is no evidence that this was always done. The accounts for 1742 have the following note:

These Accts are examined and alowd by us whose Names are Under Written and we choose Henry Stanforth and Richd Youngs Churchwardens for the Year Insuing

POWDER AND SHOT FOR THE CHURCHWARDENS

			£	s	d
1784	*The Dursments of Tho. Purdy Churchwarden for the parish of Salthouse from Michs 1784 to 1785*				
Octo 17	To Bread & Wine		0	2	4
Decr 26	To Bread & Wine		0	2	4
1785 Feby 6	paid Boothes Bill		0	2	10
	for Morter for the windows		0	0	6
April 3	To the Surples Washing		0	2	6
	To Bread & wine		0	2	4
4	Paid Boothes Bill		0	3	4
	paid for Morter for the windows		0	0	6
	paid to the pareter		0	0	6
21	paid at the General		0	6	6
	pd the pareter		0	0	6
	my Jurne		0	3	6
May 4	paid the Visetors		0	5	6
	paid Robt Spence for 9 Jackdaws		0	0	9
	paid for Powder & Shot		0	0	7
22	To Bread & Wine		0	2	4
June 9	paid Cranfield & Spence for Eight Jackd yd		0	0	8
	pd Cranfield for mowing the Churchyard		1	0	0
	pd the pareter		0	0	6
Octo 4	pd at General		0	7	6
	my Jurney		0	2	6
	The Chars Rate making		0	3	0
			2	11	0

A page from the Churchwardens' accounts Michaelmas 1784-85. Note the 'powder and shot' 4 May, 1785.

signed:
> Thomas Turner Rector of Salthouse,
> Sherwood (?) Bainbrigg,
> Robt Colls,
> Francis Southgate,
> Richard Youngs

In some years there are equivalent notes but in others none. There must, in any case, be doubt about the effectiveness of the examination. The note written on 28th March 1749 reads:

> These Accts are examined and alowed by us whose names are underwritten. We chuse Henry Stanforth and Fenn Lewis Church Wardens for the year ensuing.
> John Jarvis (his mark)
> Edm Rice (his mark)

Although 250 years ago illiteracy was widespread, two people who could neither read nor write could hardly have gone through the accounts with a fine tooth comb. Mr Rice similarly examined the accounts for 1750-51 and made his mark at the relevant entry in April 1751. He became Churchwarden for a year in 1752 but at that time illiteracy would have been, presumably, less of a handicap in that office.

It is interesting to note that there is no evidence, within the accounts, of 'signing off' for thirty-one consecutive years after 1779-80. Not surprisingly, given the colossal expenditure in 1810-11, the procedure was certainly carried out in 1811 when the note reads:

> We the undersigned parishioners have examined and do allow the foregoing Accounts, as Witness our Hands
> Signed: Willm Girdlestone, Rector
>   Elizabeth Purdy
>   Robert Mash

Elizabeth Purdy was the widow of the major landholder in the village and on his death had become the person making the highest contribution to the 'church rate'. No wonder she took an interest in this quite exceptional expenditure. Presumably her position in the village enabled her to do so despite the general absence of women from the records of those participating in church government. How very different from the position in the early years of the 21st century when not only the Churchwardens but also the Priest with particular involvement with Salthouse (among the clergy within the Weybourne Group) are all women.

D. A. Schofield, 2001

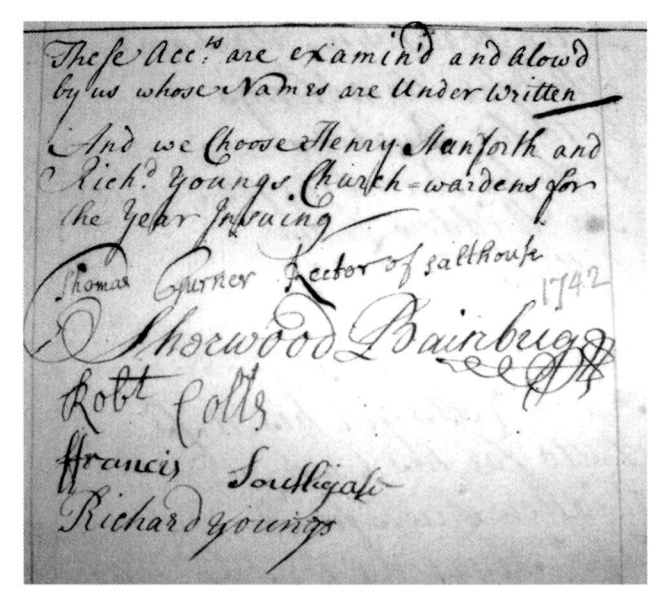

Above: The spectacular signatures at the foot of the page of accounts (April 1741-April 1742) mentioned above, top left.

The Poor Prisoners

In 1815 two men from Salthouse, Robert Spence and John Jeary, were arrested for carting wreckage off the beach. They were taken to Norwich County Gaol to await trial. Their plight is described in a letter which was recently found in the church chest (see right, and transcribed below). The list of names on the reverse of the petition (see following page) shows how many neighbours generously contributed.

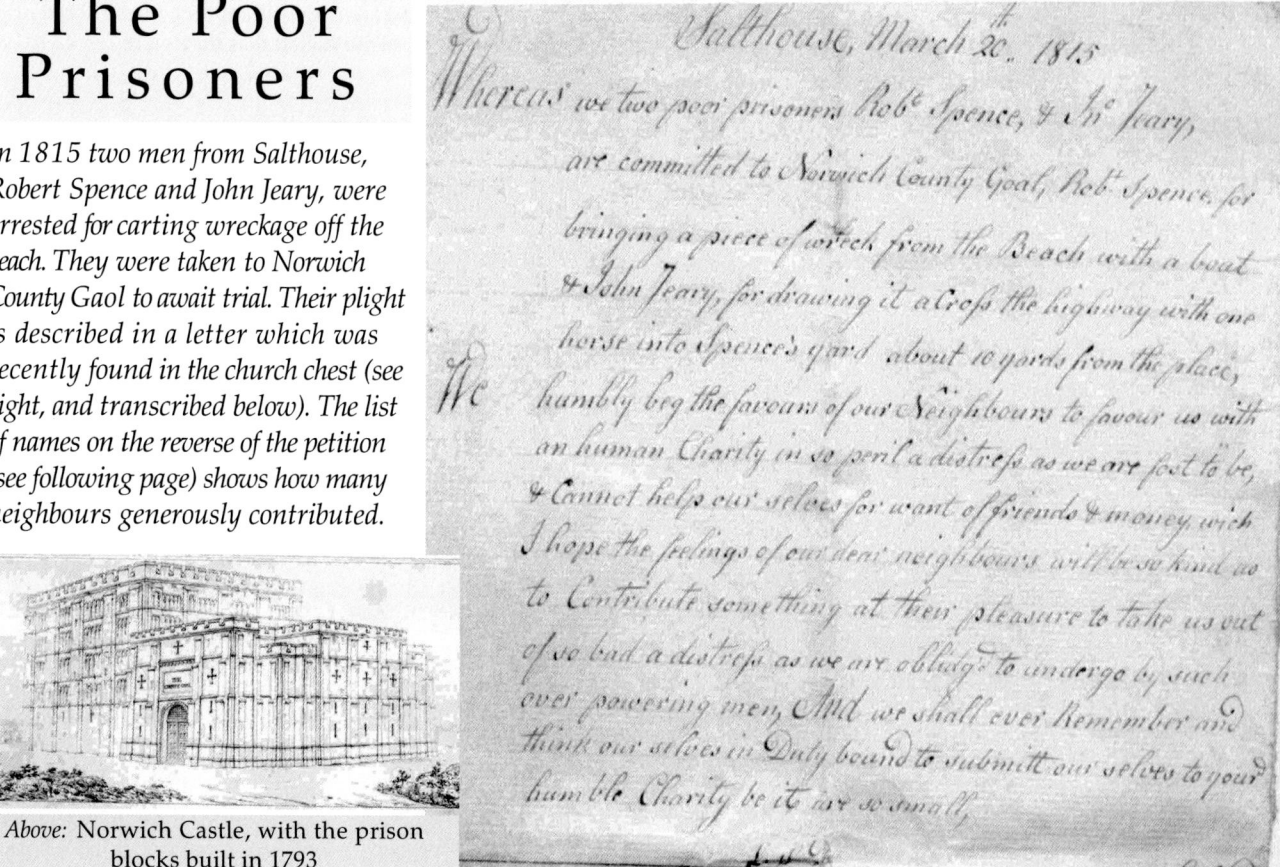

Above: Norwich Castle, with the prison blocks built in 1793

Whereas we two poor prisoners Robt Spence & Jn Jeary, are committed to Norwich County Goal, Robt Spence for bringing a piece of wreck from the Beach with a boat & John Jeary, for drawing it across the highway with one horse into Spence's yard about 10 yards from the place,
We humbly beg the favours of our Neighbours to favour us with an human Charity in so peril a distress as we are fost [*forced*] to be, & Cannot help our selves for want of friends & money, wich I hope the feelings of our dear neighbours will be so kind as to Contribute something at their pleasure to take us out of so bad a distress as we are oblidg'd to undergo by such over powering men, And we shall ever Remember and think our selves in Duty bound to submitt our selves to your humble Charity be it here (?) so small.

THE POOR PRISONERS' PETITION

Below: Part of the list of names which accompanied the petition; supposedly these are the neighbours who subsequently contributed to the collection for the relief of Robert Spence and John Jeary, 'in so peril a distress' as they were forced to be.

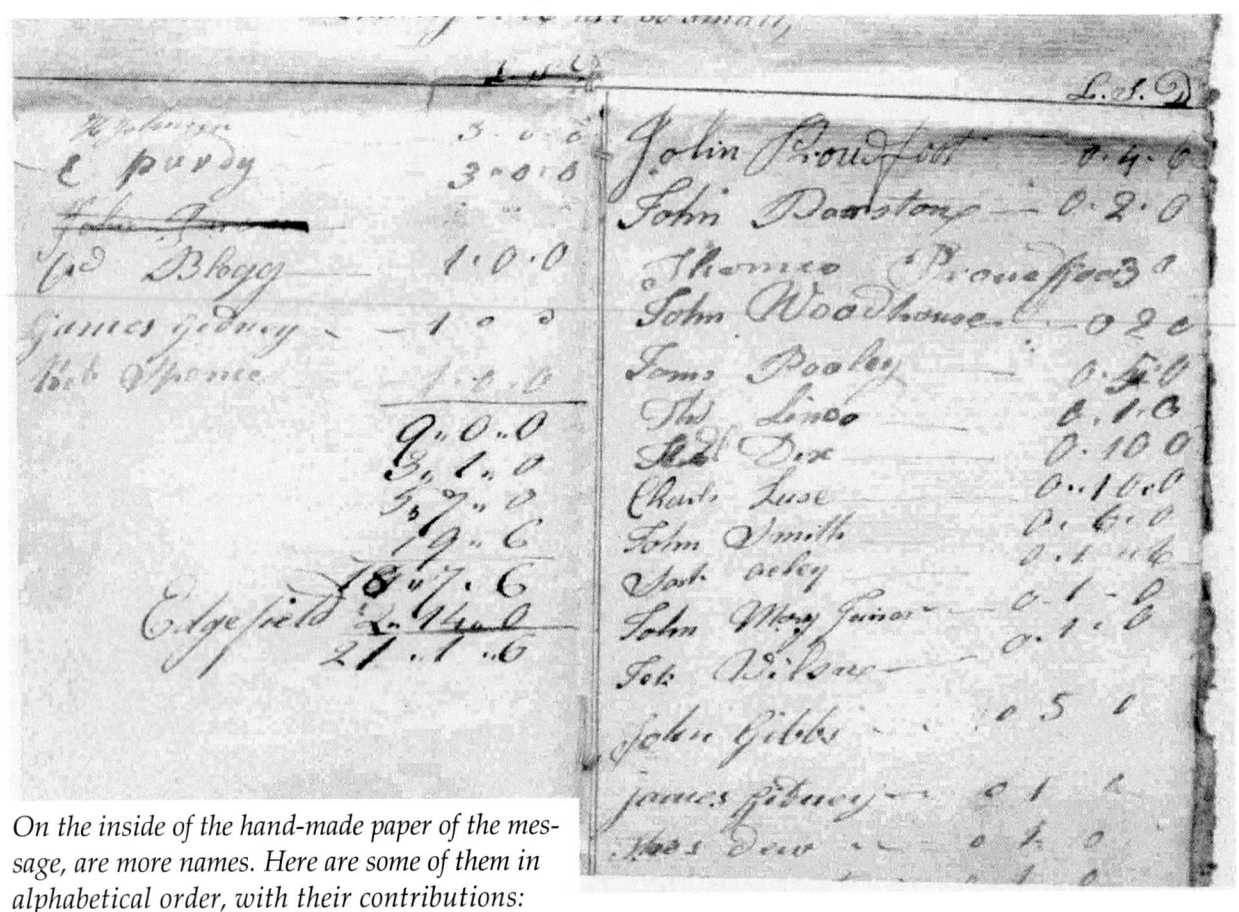

On the inside of the hand-made paper of the message, are more names. Here are some of them in alphabetical order, with their contributions:

? Blogg	£1	Frances Ives	6s	John Moy	10s	Thomas Proudfoot	3s
William Cooke	5s 6d	R? Johnson	2s	John Moy Junior	1s	James Pooley	5s
William Cubitt	2s	? Johnson	£3	John Newell	2s	E. Purdy	£3 0 0d
Thomas Dix	10s	J. Jordan	5s 6d	Samuel Olley	1s 6d	John Ram	5s 6d
John Frost	10s	William Keymer	2s	Rose Otway	1s	William Smith	6d
Thomas Gaffer?	2s	Mrs Larner	1s	Edmund Painter	1s 6d	Rob Spence	£1
John Gibbs	5s	Thomas Lines?	1s	John Parstone	2s	John Smith	6s
James Gidney	£1	Charles Luse	10s	S. Perfrement	2s	William Web	6s
Wil Harding	1s	James Mansbridge	5s	Elizabeth Pratt	3s	John Wilson	1s
John Hardy	1s	Robert Matthews	5s	John Proudfoot	4s	John Woodhouse	2s
B. High	3s						

102

LIFE IN NORWICH COUNTY GAOL IN 1815

Robert Spence and John Jeary must have been taken to Norwich before they had a chance to warn their friends and families.

Life in prison in the early nineteenth century, without any means to procure the few comforts allowed, must have been wretched. According to their letter, John and Robert are not being treated very well by their 'over powering' gaolers. It is clear that money, if they had it, would save them a good deal.

Prison Disciplinary Rule No. 19 states that: 'A criminal prisoner before trial may maintain himself', and permits him to send for 'food and malt liquor' from outside as well as clothing, bedding 'and other necessaries'. This indicates that if anything was provided, it was certainly inadequate. 'Any articles so procured must be paid for out of monies belonging to such prisoners in the hands of the gaoler'—who was instructed to:

Act not to deprive convicts of any allowance made by law - -
Jailers to permit prisoners to send for victuals from what place they please, and to have such bedding, &c. as they think fit - - - -

There is sadly no record to be found of their trial.

The Relief of the Salthouse Poor 1792-1810

Among the documents recently rediscovered in St Nicholas' Church was the 'Account Book of the Overseers of the Poor of the Parish of Salthouse, 1792-1810'.

These eighteen years were a period of great difficulty for the country in general and for the poor in particular. Not only was there virtually continuous war with France but, in the 1790s, there was also a succession of poor harvests. The shortage of food and the resulting increase in prices meant problems for paupers and all poor people, whether existing on subsistence agriculture or on the paltry wage of the agricultural labourer. The number depending on subsistence farming was decreasing as a consequence of the enclosure of the old open fields and of much common land. New systems of farming led to a reduction in the numbers needed to work a given area of land, and at the same time to a decline in wages. This depression in wages became such an acute problem that from the mid 1790s help had to be given not only to the unemployed and unemployable poor, but also to many people who, although they were in employment, were earning less than a subsistence wage.

This supplementation of the workers' earnings, by the parish, resulted not surprisingly in the employers having no need to pay a proper living wage and being content to leave the parish to pick up the shortfall. Wages became further depressed and the incentive to work diminished.

In the years covered by this Account Book, responsibility for 'poor relief' (i.e. helping the poor) rested with each parish. Although 'poor houses' existed, much of the help given was in the form of 'out relief'—the recipients of help continued to live in the cottages or elsewhere in the parish. 'Overseers of the Poor' (usually two) were appointed annually from among the substantial householders in each parish and they had responsibility for the proceeds of a local tax—the 'poor rate'. [For a description of how the rating system worked and an explanation of the coinage in use, see the chapter on 'Churchwardens Accounts' p 95.] From the poor rate, the Overseers had to provide for paupers, and others in need who had a right to live in the parish—the so-called right of settlement. Someone who had no such right would not be provided with relief locally but would have to return (or be removed) to the place where he or she had such a right—whether established by birth, by having worked continuously in that place for a full year or (in the case of a woman) by marriage. Certificates were issued to poor people moving from place to place indicating where the right of settlement (and therefore the cost of poor relief) existed. Frequent arguments and even lawsuits arose between parishes about responsibility for particular individuals, since ratepayers everywhere wished to keep costs down. In the meantime the applicants for assistance suffered even more.

The Salthouse Account Book reveals the payments made to or on behalf of individuals as well as the overall costs falling on the parish. Before turning to the statistics, it is illuminating to outline the history of one regular claimant on poor relief, and to give examples of other calls on the poor rate.

WIDOW PLATTEN

In 1792 Widow Platten was living away, but her place of settlement must have been Salthouse. At all events the Salthouse Overseers paid her £1 6s. 0d for the six months from Easter to Michaelmas—a payment at the rate of 1s. 0d per week. An entry for the same period records:

To Wade for paying the money..................2s. 4d

Later entries in the accounts reveal that the widow was in Norwich and that Wade was the local carrier who, presumably amongst other tasks, took the Salthouse payments to her from time to time. These payments at Norwich continued until the summer of 1795 when she, one assumes with whatever household effects she owned, was moved to Salthouse at the parish's cost. The entry reads:

To Widow Platten's collection.............£3 9s. 6d

She was moved into a house or cottage with John Newell and his wife, and the Overseers paid them directly for her lodgings (at the rate of 1s. 0d per week) while continuing to pay an allowance, at fluctuating rates, directly to Widow Platten. For a few months in the summer of 1800 she was moved to lodge with John Cawston on the same basis but then moved back with the Newells. By the middle of 1801 she had become ill, or had become more ill, and the Overseers paid not only for her lodging (now at 9d per week) but also, in October, made a payment:

To Mrs Newell doing for Wd Platten
26 weeks @ 2s.6d............................ £3 5s. 0d

In the spring of 1803 the accounts reveal:

Sheet making washing and
removing Wd Platten........................... 2s. 0d

but it is unclear where she was taken. Although occasional payments for Widow Platten's 'being' (seemingly synonymous with 'lodging') continued to be made the recipient is not named. In addition, 6 bushels of coal (7s. 0d) were provided for her at this time and sometime after Midsummer 1803 a payment of 6d was made to E. High (presumably Mrs) for washing Widow Platten. In November 1803 a gown and shift (1s. 3d) and a pot (1s. 6d) were purchased for her. Sometime towards the end of 1804 the widow was moved again (at a cost of 1s. 0d), this time apparently in with Widow Brown, also in receipt of regular poor relief. The Overseers recorded:

Pd Wd Brown for Wd Platten's being
12 weeks @ 2s. 0d............................ £1 4s. 0d

In the summer of 1805, probably in August, Widow Platten died. Poor relief was provided for only 7 weeks instead of the usual 13 for each Quarter. A payment of 3s.0d was 'Paid Brown for Platten' (probably for laying out) and 6s.0d was paid for '4 Bearers and Beer'. Such was the life and death of someone on poor relief.

OTHER PAYMENTS

Apart from making regular payments to individuals such as Widow Platten, the Overseers also met costs 'at need' for others. These entries related to both 'one off' cash payments and to purchases made on a pauper's behalf. There are numerous entries but the following selection gives an idea of the range of purchases or services covered:

Easter/Michaelmas 1792
Two shirts for the Boy Mann 6s. 0d
Easter/Michaelmas 1793
Pd Girl Bloom for mending for Boy Mann 6s. 10d
Michaelmas 1794
Two blankets and Rug for Woodhouse....... 12s. 0d
Michaelmas 1795
Shoes mending for the Girl Larner.......... 1s. 2d
Easter/Michaelmas 1798
3 yds Suffolk Cloth for Girl Brown........... 3s. 6d
7 May 1801
Girl Kew Pair of Stays........................ 5s. 0d
22 November 1801
To a pair of half worn shoes for Kew........ 2s. 6d

There were also other more general outgoings, for example:

5 July 1796
To 20 yards Cloth for the Poor at 1s. 0d.. £1 0s. 0d
May 1801
To John Cawston cutting 3,000 flaggs.. 18s. 0d

There are many entries for 'flaggs', presumably turfs to be dried out for firing, as well as similar entries for furze or furze faggots, which would have been used as fuel also.

106

Sometimes payments related not so much to general and continuing poverty but to the relief of an immediate crisis, for example:

Easter/Michaelmas 1793
Dutch Doctor—his Bill £1 16s. 0d
7 February 1802
To Robt Starling for loss of Cloths at Sea.....10s. 0d

There are a good many entries for doctors' bills but only one for a Dutch doctor.

EMPLOYMENT

The Overseers had a responsibility to find employment for the able-bodied poor wherever feasible, and they obviously would wish to do so in order to keep the poor rate as low as possible. One way was to bind pauper youngsters as apprentices, either within the parish or elsewhere, since the employer would then be responsible for board and lodging. Sometimes the apprenticeships were spurious (eg. for 'husbandry' or 'housewifery') but often the indentures were genuine. There are only a very few apprenticeship entries in the Salthouse accounts; in April 1800, for example, the Overseers paid £4 3s. 6d for John Spence's apprenticeship but, unfortunately, neither the name nor trade of the Master is recorded. Other more direct employment took place— cutting flaggs could be undertaken as a means of relieving the poverty of the cutter and the flaggs could be distributed to parishioners on poor relief.

The upkeep of highways, another responsibility of each parish, was also a means of employing local labour. In May 1807 a number of men were paid for 'Hyghway work', including Benjamin Lynn who received £1 6s. 6d. He was someone who had suffered a decline in his fortunes, but whether through the changing pattern of agriculture or his own fault one cannot say. In the mid 1780s he had moved slightly up-market, and until 1796 he held a property with an annual value of £6. By the following year he was in a property with a value of only £4 p. a. and in 1799 only £1 p.a. These values are taken from the Overseers' and Churchwardens' Account Books, (they used a common valuation). There was no revaluation in these years and so Benjamin Lynn either moved to poorer cottages or disposed of some of the earlier holding. He frequently received poor relief in the early years of the new century but must have been able-bodied since in 1807 he undertook highway work. When he died in November 1808, however, he was a charge on the parish. The Overseers paid Mary Mack for sitting up with him and then paid the bearers at his funeral the usual 6 shillings.

TRAVELLERS

As well as helping the poor of the parish, the Overseers had responsibility for removing those paupers who had no right of settlement. Until 1794 people who might become a charge on the poor rate could be removed, but after that date the necessary Justices' warrant could only be obtained when they actually needed help. Poor people travelling the countryside might be helped if they had legitimate reason for doing so—usually established by carrying a pass. Two (out of many) examples give an idea of the far-reaching extent of controls on the movement of poor people around the country:

29 May 1796 To a person with a Pass
to Yarmouth & 3 Children......................1s. 0d
28 August 1796 To 3 Sailors with a Pass.........1s. 0d

Other expenditure no doubt demanded less thought—for example the cash paid (usually 5s. 0d) at the public house for the Town Meeting each year.

DEATH

Inevitably paupers' funeral expenses appear several times in the Overseers' Account Book and not just for Widow Platten and Benjamin Lynn. Sometimes there is a surprise. As in Benjamin's case, it was not unusual for the parish to pay a local woman to sit up with a dying pauper (presumably a pauper without relatives) but, on one occasion at least, refreshment was provided. Sometime between February and Easter 1793, payments (at 6d per night) were made to women for sitting up over a period of 12 nights with Widow Phoker and in addition there is the following entry:

Pd for Bread and Tea when sitting up for the Women 2s. 6d

Not all matters relating to death concerned humans. The Overseers seem to have taken

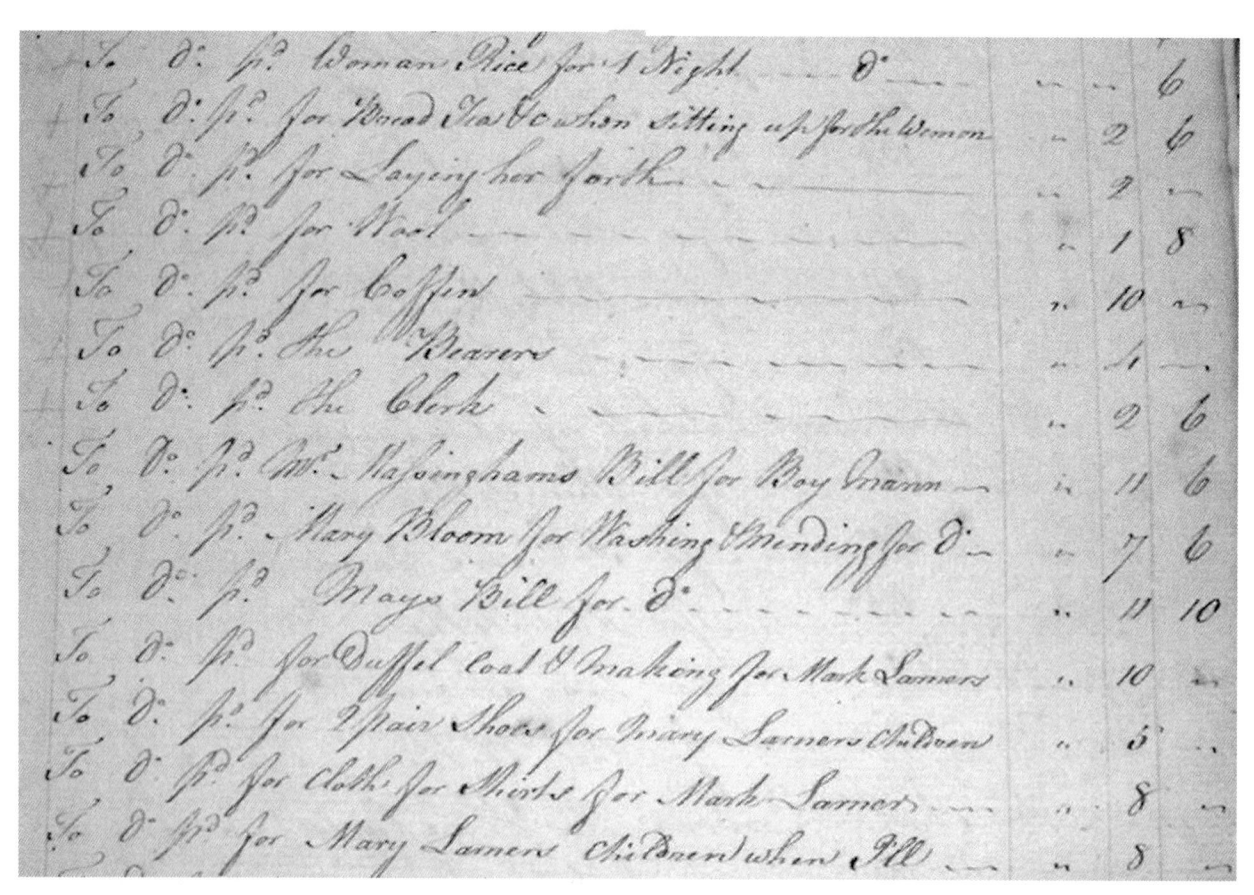

A page from the Overseers' Account Book for 1793 which shows the entries concerning the supply of bread and tea for a woman sitting up with a dying pauper, and remuneration for 'Laying her forth' (see above).

over responsibility from the Churchwardens for culling sparrows. There are a number of entries similar to:

June 1801 To 4 dozen sparrows killing..........1s. 0d

OVERSEERS

In previous decades the Churchwardens' accounts reveal many such payments but the number of entries decline as those in the Overseers' book go up. Perhaps concern about some sort of employment for the increasing number of paupers led to the change—or perhaps it is completely without significance since, in the parish of Salthouse at least, the same individuals frequently held both offices concurrently. For example, Thomas Purdy was both Churchwarden and Overseer (with the exception of a single year) from 1792 to 1800, and John Proudfoot held both offices from 1799 to 1809 (except for 1801-2) and possibly to his death some months later.

Salthouse appears to be unusual in the length of time served by individual Overseers. In the 18 years covered by the accounts only 6 persons held the office of Overseer, and it should be borne in mind that two Overseers were in office at any one time. The usual historical perception is that in many parts of the country the office was regarded as so onerous and unrewarding (it was unpaid) that most individuals would serve for only one or two years.

COSTS

During these 18 years the Overseers in Salthouse witnessed a sharp increase in the number of poor people who had to be helped on a regular basis. In the early years covered by the Account Book, between 6 and 9 persons received regular payments and no more than 2 were men. By 1798/99 the total number had risen to 14, and 4 were men. In early 1805 the number receiving regular relief increased to 17, and no fewer than 8 were men—four times the number of men little more than a decade earlier. This increase in the number of men receiving regular poor relief reflected the changes in agricultural and employment practice referred to earlier. Total costs increased equally sharply. In the twelve months from Easter 1792 the Overseers spent a little over £56, but for the year from Easter 1803 expenditure had risen to £125. By then, setting and collecting the poor rate on a half yearly basis had been replaced by quarterly charges, presumably to ease the payments by ratepayers. Some fluctuations occurred, but for the twelve months from Easter 1807 expenditure had risen to over £195—well over three times the level of 1792 and 1793.

These local figures reflected the national situation. In England as a whole the total proceeds of the poor rate in 1785 were £1.912 million, in 1803 £4.078 million and in 1817 £7.87 million, [W. E. Tate, *The Parish Chest*]. With such a trend it is hardly surprising that complaints about the level of the poor rate led later to the draconian Poor Law Reform of 1834 and the establishment of the dreadful Union Workhouses—a reform which certainly reduced costs but which did little to alleviate the condition of the poor.

Derek Schofield, 2002

1854 RATE BOOK ASSESSMENT FOR RELIEF OF THE POOR *The rate was 8d in the Pound*

The roads named in this list, copied from one of the Rate Books in the Parliament Box, are confusing for those familiar with the road names of Salthouse today. Cross Street—where the Johnsons lived in the Manor House—was known as Kelling Road at the time of this survey (and that of 1838 also), and Purdy Street of today—where the Purdys lived and owned the Hall farm—was known as Holt Road with Bard Hill incorporated. The lane known today as Grout's Lane between the Coast road and the church—where Peter Grout lived—is listed here as Church Lane. On page 50 you can see a map of the village with the alternative road names clearly marked.

	OCCUPIER	OWNER	DESCRIPTION	SITUATION	VALUE £ s p
1	SPENCE Mary	PURDY William	Cottage and garden	Kelling Road	4.10.0
2	SPENCE Robt	Himself	Cottage, Wheelwright's shop and land	"	6.10.0
3	CUBITT Thomas	WILLIAMS Willm	Cottage and land	"	6.5.0
4	DIX William	OWEN Robt	"	"	6.5.0
5	PANE John	PURDY Thomas	Cottage, garden and blacksmith's shop	"	6.15.0
6	CUBITT Robt	"	Cottage and garden	"	3.5.0
7	BRIDGES George	JOHNSON Willm	"	"	3.7.6
8	IVES Francis	"	"	"	3.15.0
9	PIGOTT John	JOHNSON Willm	Cottage and land	"	4.5.0
10	ANDREWS Thos	"	Cottage and garden	"	1.15.0
11	LEWIS Fenn	"	Cottage and land	"	7.5.0
12	SPENCE John	POOLEY Mercy	Cottage and garden	"	2.10.0
13	HIGH Richard	JOHNSON Willm	Cottage and garden	"	4.15.0
14	WOODHOUSE Charles	"	Cottage and land	"	5.0.0
15	DEW Ann	PURDY Willm	Cottage and land	"	6.7.6
16	FARTHING Ann	Herself	Tenement, shop and garden	"	5.10.0
17	HOLMAN Brandon	DEW William	Cottage and garden	"	2.5.0
18	HANCOCK Samuel	HANCOCK James	Dwelling house and baking office	"	7.10.0
19	PARK(E)? John	PURDY William	Cottage and garden	"	3.12.6
20	HARDINGHAM Willm	WALLER Mary	"	"	5.10.0
21	PIGOTT Gabriel	JOHNSON E. M.	"	"	1.17.6
22	MATTHEWS John	PURDY William	Cottage and land	Church Lane	8.0.0
23	LEWIS Fenn	GIRDLESTONE Rev J.G.	Churchyard	"	0.17.6
24	JOHNSON E. M.	JOHNSON William	Farm house and land	Kelling Road	159.5.0
25	PROUDFOOT Thos	"	Cottage and garden	"	4.0.0
26	JARY Sarah	"	Cottage and garden	"	5.0.0
27	POOLE Charles	"	" "	"	8.0.0
28	MASSINGHAM Jas	Himself	Cottage and land	"	5.0.0
29	"	GIRDLESTONE Rev J.G.	Glebes	"	1.10.0
30	DEW William	MASSINGHAM Jas	Cottage, garden and grocer's shop	"	4.17.6
31	POOLEY Mercy	Herself	Cottage and orchard	"	4.0.0
32	DIX John	WILLIAMS Charles	Cottage and garden	Cley Road	4.0.0
33	DIX John	"	Barn and land	"	2.0.0

PROPERTY VALUATION OF 1854

	OCCUPIER	OWNER	DESCRIPTION	SITUATION	VALUE
34	KEYMER William	Himself	Cottage and outhouses	Cley Road	8.10.0
35	PARLETT Thos	OWEN Robert	Cottage and land	"	4.15.0
36	GROUT Peter (jnr)	GROUT Peter (Snr)	Cottage and garden	Church Lane	4.7.6
37	MOY William	NELSON William	Tenement and shed	"	2.2.0
38	WOODHOUSE Rbt	NELSON William	Tenement and land	Church Lane	7.0.0
39	LYNN William	"	Tenement and garden	Church Lane	4.12.6
31	JARVIS John Dewing	PARLETT Starling	Dwelling house, mill and land	Church Lane	17.17.6
41	DIX John	PURDY William	Land	Cley Road	17.6
42	MOY James	Himself	Cottage and garden	Cley Road	5.0.0
43	Unoccupied	PEGG Francis	Cottage and Tenement	"	1.15.0
44	Unoccupied	PEGG Francis	Tenement and shed	"	2.15.0
45	PEGG Francis	Himself	Cottage and land	"	6.0.0
46	JARY Thomas	HANCOCK Jas Snr	Tenement and shed	"	3.2.6
47	HANCOCK Samuel	"	" "	"	2.5.0
48	LOWN William	"	" "	"	3.17.6
49	PARLETT David	Himself	" "	"	3.10.0
50	IVES Robert	PERFREMENT Saml	" "	"	2.17.6
51	PERFREMENT Samuel	Himself	Tenement, shed, and outhouses	"	4.17.6
52	PIGOTT William	MOY John	Cottage and garden	"	2.2.6
53	MOY John	Himself	" "	Holt Road	5.0.0
54	"	PURDY William	Land	"	5.0
55	PURDY William	Himself	Tenement	Church Lane	2.0.0
56	"	"	Tenement and shed	"	3.17.6
57	IVES Francis	PURDY William	Cottage and garden	Holt Road	4.12.6
58	MASH Elizabeth	"	Cottage and shed	"	3.15.0
59	GIBBS John	PURDY William	Cottage	"	2.15.0
60	PURDY William	Himself	Farm house, buildings and land	Holt Road	435.17.6
61	"	"	Land	Kelling Road	7.6
62	"	PURDY Thomas	"	"	2.5.0
63	"	GIRDLESTONE Rev J.G.	Glebes	Holt Road	5.5.0
64	"	CODD Rev	"	Cley Road	1.17.6
65	HIGH Thomas	PURDY William	Cottage and garden	Holt Road	3.5.0
66	MATTHEWS Rbt	PAINTER Edmund	" "	"	6.15.0
67	HIGH Charles	"	Blacksmith's shop	Holt Road	3.12.6
68	WILLIAMS Charles	HARDY W.H.C. Esq	Public House and land	Cley Road	12.7.6
69	DEW Thomas	PURDY William	Cottage and shed	"	2.17.6
70	"	"	"	"	2.10.6
71	CUBITT William	PURDY William	Cottage and shed	"	3.7.6
72	DEW George	"	Cottage and garden	"	5.5.0
73	DIXON Grandison	DAVY W.P.	Land	Kelling Road	19.10.0
74	GIRDLESTONE M.A.	Herself	Land	"	93.2.6
75	" Rev J.G	Himself	Rent change (?)	"	180.0.0

The Church and Chapel: the Rev Giles Hunt

Among the recollections of his years as Rector of Salthouse, Giles Hunt writes about the time when the church was under repair and he was invited to hold church services in the Chapel— a striking example of Christian unity. Today, living in Cley, Giles has just completed his second book 'Launcelot Fleming: a portrait' published by the Cathedral Press, Norwich.

Giles Hunt, 2003.

When I became Rector of Holt in 1962, Kelling and Salthouse had been without a rector ever since the death of the Rev Felix Young. Since the total population of Salthouse was only 227 (of Kelling even less) and Kelling Rectory was in bad repair, I was asked to take on Kelling and Salthouse as well as Holt in 1963. This did not (alas!) entail any extra pay, but did mean that I could have a curate, David Tuck, who was ordained Deacon at Michaelmas 1963, and is still remembered with affection.

My first recollection of Salthouse Church was being shown round by the Bishop of Lynn. It was breathtakingly beautiful, but in all-too-obviously bad repair. I remember saying 'This needs £5,000 for starters'. (£5,000 then equals at least £100,000 today, and building costs have outstripped inflation.) It was not a bad guess.

Salthouse was a breath of fresh air in more senses than one. Holt was much smaller then, so that its rector's every step was watched with sharp and critical eyes. But since Salthouse was basically a 'chapel' village, those who might have formed an awkward squad did not belong to the Church; and relations with the Chapel, whose leading lights were Sidney Craske and Gordon Hancock, were excellent. Gladys High was organist at both church and chapel; and the Hancocks had me to stay for a week each August so that I could get to know the parish better (I was even able to help with the harvest, since Haddon High still used the old labour-intensive reaper-binder).

Haddon High extreme left and his son Don extreme right; could it be a headless rector, helping with the harvest, on top?

The church congregation was small. It was alleged that a previous rector used to take a 20-bore to church, and if he found no congregation he would have a go at the bats in the roof. This was held to be why the clerestory windows were in such a bad state. Sometimes the congregation consisted (I was told) of just the organist and Alice Graveling; her husband was landlord of the Dun Cow and the sermon was invariably against the evils of the drink trade and all engaged in it. Alice Graveling was one of my churchwardens, the other being Bill Holland who had come to Salthouse after being in the Colonial Service in Africa and was Bursar of the new University of East Anglia. They were a wonderful pair.

Certain memories of my four years as rector

The Rector, Giles Hunt, and John Betjeman on their way to the church during the 1964 festival

stand out. In September 1963 a party of undergraduates from Trinity College Cambridge spent a week in Salthouse, staying with families in the village and working as volunteers on church repairs. Bernard Feilden our architect (who charged no fees for his work—how things have changed!) came and explained what they could do: clean out the church tower (we sold the guano for over £10!) and the gutters, down-pipes and drains. The sight of two undergraduates perched precariously over a 30-foot drop as they cleared out the gutters while their transistor radio blared out the latest Beatles music sticks in my memory. Nowadays health and safety rules would make that kind of voluntary work impossible but, as it was, the sight of people doing something for nothing, working as unpaid volunteers, made quite an impression on the village. The Dun Cow did a roaring trade—they found it thirsty work.

The Salthouse Festival in July 1964 was also memorable. It was a triumph of good planning—my input was minimal, and people pulled together in a remarkable way. The Newmans invited us to hold planning meetings in the Manor House and, as a vote of thanks put it, never failed to push the boat out.

The key event of the festival was John Betjeman giving a talk on the Sunday afternoon, which brought in people from a long distance round and gave publicity to the other events as well—in the Village Hall an exhibition by Kelling School, and in the church an art exhibition, a talk from local historian Wyndham Ketton-Cremer of Felbrigg, a concert on Saturday evening, and Evensong on Sunday evening with Gresham's School Choir.

Flower clubs from Fakenham, Aylsham, North Walsham and Holt had done some stupendous arrangements; and when it was all over we realised that the village had managed to raise over £800—not far short of £4 (or in today's values about £75) for each man, woman and child in the parish. It was thanks to all this local effort that we were able to get a grant from the Historic Churches Preservation Trust, and other grant-givers.

By 1967 the most urgent repairs on the church had been carried out. The roof timbers and tower had been treated for death-watch beetle, and the clerestory windows and those in the south of the nave (where deterioration had been worst) had been renewed with clear 'antique' glass. The Victorian stained glass window at the east end of the south aisle was also found to be beyond repair; but Kings the glaziers produced some fragments of fifteenth-century stained church glass that had been found in someone's

David Lincoln Collection

Above: The south aisle of the church and the east window, with (*overleaf*) the medieval glass centre-piece.

The medieval glass in the south aisle east window

summer-house in Suffolk. Skilfully pieced together, they were set into clear glass, being paid for by Mrs Young [the widow of Felix Young] and by Mrs Leach lately of the Manor House, in memory of their respective husbands. Shortly before I left, the Pilgrim Trust agreed to have the medieval screen restored by its experts, a wonderful offer. I was dismayed to find, on a later visit to Salthouse, that for some reason the screen had subsequently been relegated to the back of the church.

All this meant that for three or four months the church was filled with scaffolding and virtually unusable. We were invited to use Salthouse Chapel for our Sunday services—and told we must make ourselves completely at home, bringing our altar furnishings, and must not think of paying for the extra heating they laid on. And the time of the Methodist service was altered for our convenience. Salthouse taught me a lot about what Christian unity could mean.

But the most important Church work was done by David Tuck, not least among the young. Salthouse did not have enough teenagers to form a youth club, but there was one in Holt (despite a total lack of support from the local authority), set up and run entirely on a voluntary basis—its first leader was a local policeman. The church link with Holt made it easier for anyone from Salthouse to join in.

Looking back after nearly forty years, one can be deluded into thinking that the good old days were much better than today. In fact, most people's quality of life has improved since then; but in some ways life in Salthouse probably was more enjoyable then than now. It was not an idyllic community—there were feuds, there were 'bad eggs' as well as 'good eggs'—but in those days there were very few holiday homes empty for most of the year, and there were plenty of people able and willing to play a full part in village life. Certainly I found that there were more lay people in Salthouse willing to play an active part in church life, and much stronger lay leadership, than in most parishes.

I suppose that anyone who can survive those winds coming straight from the North Pole is unlikely to be wimpish!

The bottom of Cross Street c1900. The Methodist Chapel is the building on the right (facing the North Pole).

Olga Ward quotes from the Memoirs of her great-great-grandmother

Salthouse people, it seems, have never been tolerant of what they considered to be 'outside interference', and during the last half of the nineteenth century when men from neighbouring villages were touching their caps to the lord of the manor and jumping to his orders at the double, Salthouse men (having no resident lord) were very independent. The Chapel community which flourished in Salthouse in the late nineteenth and early twentieth centuries was devoutly religious, as the following pages show, but in the field of religion—as in the field of territory and privilege—Salthouse people were mostly unco-operative with 'foreigners'!

The Hon Mrs Upcher by G. Richmond

Olga Ward came upon an interesting reference to Salthouse amongst the pages of her great-great-grandmother's published memoirs, which are entitled: *Memoirs of the Honourable Mrs Upcher (being extracts from her journals and other papers)*, by her daughter Emma Pigott. The Honourable Mrs Upcher of these journals was Charlotte, née Wilson. In 1809 she married Abbot Upcher who bought the Sheringham Estate in 1812. Under the heading 'Bible Society', Emma Pigott writes:

About 1830 my mother visited many villages, far and near, for the Bible Society, and established a district association in nearly all of them. Among the parishes she visited from house to house, were Salthouse, Edgefield, Hanworth, Study (sic), Beeston, Bodham, East and West Beckham, Briston, Kelling, Hempsted (sic), Hindolveston, etc. This extract shows some of her interesting work.

1830, August 7th, District 31:

Mary Moy, a pious young woman, having offered to collect, I visited every house save one in Salthouse. In 50 houses there were eleven families without Bibles or Testament, six were out, or houses empty. The two principal farmers appeared sadly opposed and avaricious. In this parish there is no day charity school, and the Sunday School is held only once a fortnight, reading not taught in it. Promised the loan of a Testament to a Waterloo soldier, PARTLELL (interesting character), till he could purchase one for himself, he has since paid for a 5s. Bible.

In 1830, when Mrs Upcher made this report of her visit to Salthouse and met with such 'sad opposition', the Methodist Church had not yet been established in the village. Although the 1851 religious census states that Primitive Methodism reached Norfolk in 1820, the first Primitive Methodist chapel in Salthouse was not erected until 1836 (see p 117).

The Methodist Chapels of Salthouse

This 1885 map gives the positions of the two earlier chapels described opposite in the Religious Census of 1851: the Primitive Methodists in Grout's Lane, and the Wesleyans in Cross Street.

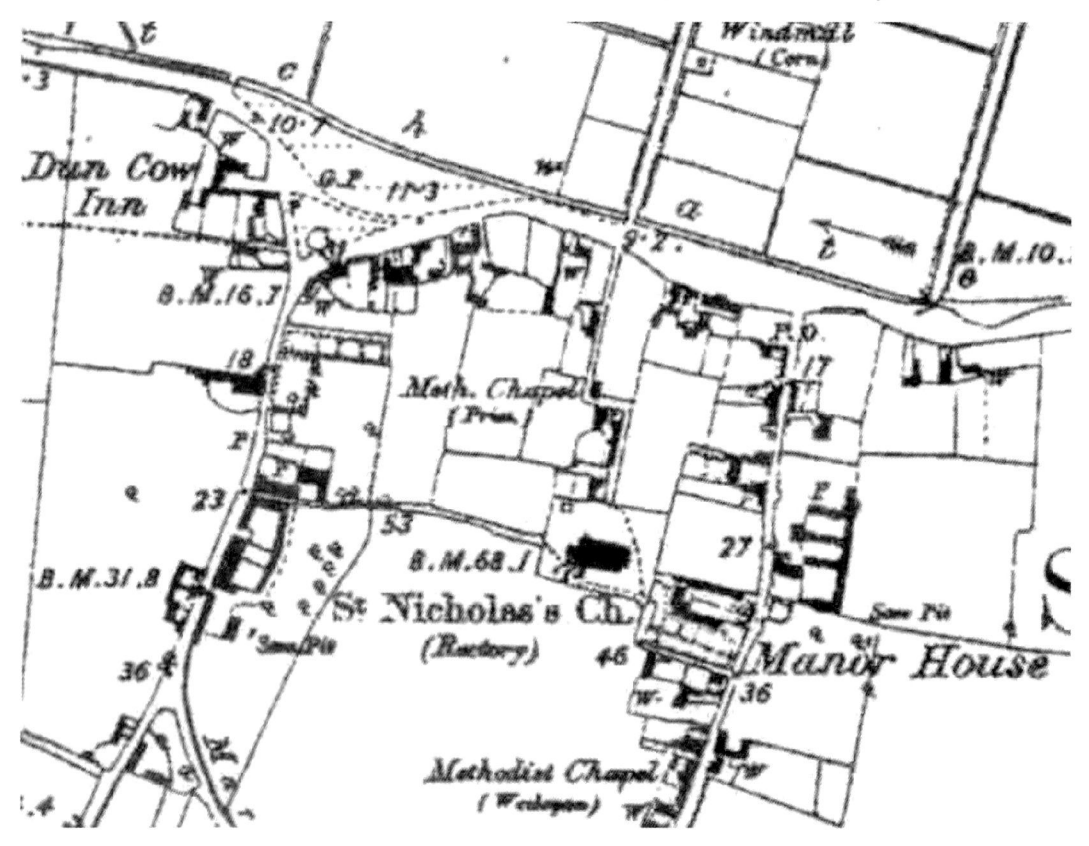

This 1950 map (below) shows the position of the 3rd and last Methodist chapel in the village—the one built on the coast road in 1891 (OS sheet TG 04SL).

The 1851 Religious Census

Primitive Methodism reached Norfolk in 1820 and quickly gained an enthusiastic following throughout the county. Very many villages had two, even three chapels offering differing styles of Methodist worship, and Salthouse was no exception.

In 1851 a census of Attendance and Accommodation at Worship—popularly known as the 'Religious Census'—was introduced. A further one was proposed during the planning of the population census for 1861, but its critics complained that it was clearly favourable to the Church of England and, in the face of the heated opposition of Dissenters, the project was dropped. Hence the exercise in 1851 was unique. The entry for Salthouse appears below. The chapel on the coast road, remembered by older people in the following pages, had not then been built.

From the book of the 1851 Religious Census, published by the Norfolk Record Society.

188 Salthouse HO/129/231.65
WESLEYAN CHAPEL. *Erected* 1842. *Separate & Entire* Separate. *Exclusive* Exclusive except for a Sunday School. *Sittings free* 31, *other* 44, *space* 10.
On 30 March M A E (M A E : Morning, Afternoon and Evening)
Est. no. of persons 54 52
Remarks The number of Prechers on the Plan for this Quarter is 53 – 15 of which are appointed to assist in conducting the services in the Salthouse Chapel namely John Tuttle, Robert Fisher, Jonathan Dybale, Richard Copling, Samuel Bastard, Wm Bastard, Thomas Dawson, Robert Long, Robert Brown, H. Heywood, Robert Pigott, Jim Earl, Henry Mallett, Thomas Drake.
Signed 31st March William Hardingham, Preacher. Salthouse near Cley
[*White 1845 – William Hardingham, shopkeeper*]

189 Salthouse HO/129/231.66
PRIMITIVE METHODIST CHAPEL. *Erected* 1836. *Separate & Entire* Yes. *Exclusive* Yes. *Sittings free* 20, *other* 46, *space* 30.
On 30 March M A E *Average* M A E
Est. no. of persons 29   27* 12 mnths 30   30#
Remarks *The aggregate number on Sunday March 30th of the two congregations was 56. The services are conducted on Sunday morning and afternoon alternately but invariably in the evenings.
#The average number of the two congregations for the last 12 months has been 60.
Signed 2nd April William Dew, Manager. Grocer. Salthouse

[Florence Radley refers to this Mr Dew, who used to give a bit of cheese to her father when he was a small hungry boy.]

Jimmy High's Chapel memories

Jimmy, extreme left above, with his mother Polly, sister Ethel (Mary Lemmon's mother), Grandmother, brother Tom, brother Jack and father Henry in 1892. The following account is taken from his autobiography, written in 1940.

In those times, when I was young, religion was taken up with enthusiasm and even the people who did not profess to any religious order would help to build the chapels. I have seen the publican doing what he thought was his bit in building the new chapel in the village and I also assisted.

I was entrusted with the task of carting the stone and other building material, but I used to be very nervous when the Missioner came to our house, and would always be late for tea, for they tried hard to convert. Once my Uncle, who was full of the revival spirit, tried to convert me when we were both working on a hayrick. He began by saying, 'Would you like to join our little band?' and he never got a chance to say more as I had guessed the rest, and had slid down the rick and was off like a March hare!

No less than a week later I was in Chapel and wishing somebody would speak to me. It was getting on my nerves, so greatly moved was I. Whenever I heard a spider tick I thought it meant my doom, and I could hear one every night over my bed. As no one came to me and the mission ended I became brave again.

As a boy I liked going to Chapel. Strangely enough there was always plenty of excitement, if nothing else. I have seen preachers so worked up by their oratory they had to take off their coats. They did not seem to spare themselves one bit. I have seen a whole congregation cry when one man prayed. I have seen men standing up, their arms waving, shouting at the top of their voices so that they could have been heard a mile away.

I once heard a local preacher denouncing pride. He was a very personal man. One of the members of the congregation was a young lady who had a very gay hat, all flowers and feathers, and a large hat into the bargain. The preacher made a thrust: 'You with the flowers and feathers on your head,' he cried, 'will be cast into the pit,' and words similar in effect. This so affected the young lady that she jumped up and went out. Her brother* happened to be present, and he was also a Trustee of the Chapel. 'Come, come, my boy,' he cried, 'Don't get excited.' Whatever the outcome it livened things up for the onlookers.

* It's possible this was Amelia Pigott, and her brother Leonard

The Camp Meetings in connection with the Chapel were quite a sensational event in the quiet life of the village. These would be held on a suitable meadow when the weather was fine. Crowds would come from surrounding villages, and when word got round that so and so from a certain parish was coming to the meeting we would tell ourselves that we were in for a good time.

In the evenings they would hold what they called a 'Love Feast'. Everyone who wished could take part, and I found it of great interest to watch the attitudes of the different converts as they unfolded their feelings in public of how they came to be saved.

One of the 'Feasts' I have in mind was conducted by the fishermen from a neighbouring town. Never before had I seen such an array of jerseys. One of these fishermen had a striped shirt underneath his jersey, and I am not certain whether it was through pride in his garment or whether it was through nerves, but when ever he was on his feet speaking, he would roll up his jersey and then unroll it again after displaying a great deal of striped shirt. Another of them began by saying 'I could have preached you a rare sermon when I was walking over the golf links on my way to the meeting, but the bottom seems to have dropped out of the bag now'. To get the full effect of this sentence, one would have to hear it spoken in the local dialect, for instance the word 'sermon' sounded more like 'Sarinond'. This man got in a great muddle in trying to tell his audience of his experiences and convictions, as his opening sentence implies.

There was such a good muster of these men that they could not all get into the pulpit so they had to speak where they could find room to stand up. One of these bore the nickname 'Butcher' and I must say he looked like one, although he was a fisherman. I must describe his speech. I might have mentioned that this particular 'feast' was held in the Chapel on account of the weather and this 'Butcher' had been seated just in front of me. As soon as he rose in his pew to speak he gave himself full room for action, swinging his arms about wildly and shouting at the top of his voice. With each sentence he moved still further forward eventually forcing his way into the aisle. He looked very fierce, but seemed quite happy to relate his convictions in this manner.

After performing like this for a minute or so he felt fit to offer an apology for his lack of education, and shouted out at the top of his voice 'What matter if the words do come out arse-uppards!' No sooner had this been said than he calmed down and slunk back to his pew very much embarrassed.

When at the height of their oratory, speakers' movements were frequently a menace to those seated near them and you had to do some ducking if you sat in front of one of them, as my Uncle can testify. He came from the North and was not used to this kind of behaviour in Chapel, so instead of leaning forward in his seat when the man behind him got to his feet to speak, he remained seated upright, and it was not long before he received such a clout from the gesticulating man.

He said afterwards that the blow was entirely unexpected.

For more of Jimmy High's autobiography, see pp 156-162

Salthouse Chapel Preachers, 1932

The chapel on the coast road in its hey-day. It is still there today, turned into a private dwelling called 'Boreas'.

1932:
Salthouse is well represented in the list of preachers for the Sheringham and Holt circuit:

Gerald Cubitt's uncle, William Cubitt;

Sidney Craske's father, William Craske;

Herbert Pigott the baker; and Richard High, who was ex-Salthouse postmaster, turned farmer and then living at Lawn Farm near Holt.

United Methodist Church,
SHERINGHAM & HOLT CIRCUIT.

Preachers' Plan of Appointments.
From April 1932 to July 1932.

MINISTERS:
Rev. James Bullock, Hon. C.F., The Manse, Augusta Street, - Sheringham.
Rev. W. H. Paddon, Holt.

PRICE TWOPENCE.

Cheverton & Son, Sheringham & Cromer.

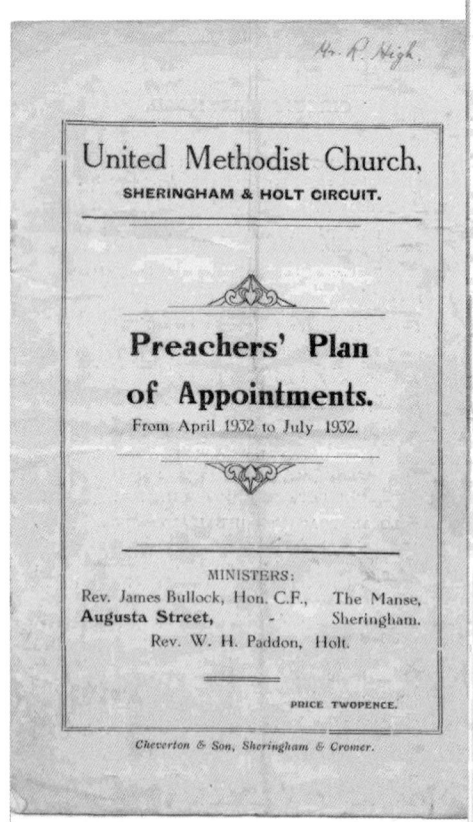

Names and Residences of Preachers.

Preach the Word.

1. J. BULLOCK, The Manse, Sheringham
2. W. H. PADDON, Holt
3. W. T. Barraclough, Sheringham
4. G. A. Lines, E. Runton
5. R. Walker, Cromer
6. J. Winn, Saxlingham
7. E. G. Pointon, Hunworth
8. W. J. Darby, Croydon
9. J. Gant, Bodham
10. H. B. Storey, Sheringham
11. W. Starling, Blakeney
12. H. Podmore, Felbrig
13. J. Rudderham, Cromer
14. R. Graveling, Thornage
15. T. High, Weybourne
16. R. J. High, Holt
17. W. Fish, Matlaske
18. W. Cubitt, Salthouse
19. W. Olley, Edgefield
20. W. Craske, Salthouse
21. J. Edwards, Sheringham
22. G. Wright, Edgefield
23. H. Pigott, Salthouse
24. D. Hazlewood, B'thorpe
25. A. Graveling, Swanton Novers
26. S. Gant, Bodham
27. R. Pegg, Sheringham
28. H. Burrell, Bodham
29. A. Boyce, Holt
30. P. A. Ditcham, Sheringham
31. C. E. Nunn, Sheringham
32. E. G. Holland,
33. F. R. Gracey, Sheringham
34. G. Daniels, Northrepps
35. E. Bullen, Beckham

The Preachers' Plan of Appointments is the property of Mr Raymond High.

Cyril Jolly looks back on the Chapel

The following article by Cyril Jolly is from the 'North Norfolk News' of 29th August 1980:

HEY-DAY OF A CHAPEL BY THE NORTH SEA

BESIDE the busy North Norfolk coast road, at Salthouse, where motorists stop to watch the ornamental ducks and geese in the creek, there stood a little Methodist chapel looking out over the far-famed marshes to the North Sea.

Few folk now recognise it because it has been converted into a dwelling. Yet the chapel, with four pointed side windows, tells of its former purpose.

Built of flint, brick and tile in 1891 by the United Methodists, it seated 150 and had a splendid hey-day. The Primitive Methodists had been in Salthouse since 1827, but the new chapel attracted large congregations and had a Sunday school of 70 scholars. In recent years numbers so declined that the chapel was closed, sold and turned into a house. But memories of its importance as a focal point of village life remain.

Salthouse, with its 300-acre heath, affords magnificent views of the coast, but has now lost both its Methodist chapels, the fine tower mill that stood on the seaward side of the coast road, and much of its marshland. The splendid parish church, however, still stands sentinel over the village. The hungry sea has not changed either, only crept ominously nearer the houses. Deceitfully benign in summer, it continues to gnaw irritably at the sea bank, and if goaded by an exceptional nor'easter, will break its bounds, sweep over the marshes and fling itself at the front line of the parish. Twice the chapel, right in the forefront, has had the wild waters surging through it.

Six years after the chapel was built a disastrous flood ravaged the coast. Surging water broke into the building, sweeping the forms and chairs to one end and ruining the harmonium and all books. When the water receded a major renovation was necessary. In 1953, the sea again breached the bank and created havoc in the exposed village. On that wild Saturday night, many people were marooned in their bedrooms; one person was drowned; seaweed was left hanging from telegraph wires and the chapel deeply flooded. The organ was ruined and the building closed for many weeks.

Reputation

When the chapel was built, a line of foundation stones, laid by well-known Methodist worthies, was placed on the north side, and a Sunday school teacher gave a shilling to each scholar to buy a brick for the building. One aged native can point to where her brick was placed. The site was given by Mrs. Sarah Johnson, of Manor Farm, and James High and his sister (later Mrs. Randall), started the Sunday school. There was no organ — the preacher read out the hymns, two lines at a time, and James High started the tune. Eventually, an organ was bought and a scholar walked the four miles to Holt to learn to play it.

The cause so flourished that there were 12 local preachers in the society and the chapel was filled for every service. A reputation for singing was gained, and a choir took Services of Song, usually read by "Willie" Long, the beloved fisherman-evangelist of Sheringham, to places far and near. At Salthouse, the sound of a hundred lusty voices singing some rousing hymns, carried far out over the marshes, and the oil-lamps, shining through the pointed windows, were a landmark for fishermen at sea.

Camp meetings were held on the Green and crowds from neighbouring parishes gathered to join in the "procession of witness" to the chapel.

Many local preachers had but little schooling, but sincerity and originality made up for it. "Willie" Long was a favourite with all ages. When he lost his sight his daughter accompanied him but the old man learned his lessons by heart and read as though he could see.

One preacher, a baker, illustrated his sermon on Noah by stepping from the pulpit and pretending it was the Ark. He opened the door and ushered in the imaginary animals saying, "Now, Mr. and Mrs. Lion, in you go." Then, "Mr. Tiger, it's your turn." Lastly, he said, "Now, Mr. Noah, in you go." He slammed the door behind the invisible Noah so emphatically it jammed and he had much difficulty opening it to resume his discourse. Another layman, speaking of Jonah being sent by God to go to Nineveh, observed: "But Jonah turned runty and wouldn't go." The simile of another speaker has stuck in local memories. He cried: "The Lord can save souls like He can blow the tiles off this roof."

Probably it was not forgotten for it was a winter's day when the howling wind and boom of the nearby breakers reminded the fishermen and relatives present of the power of the elements as well as testing the roof and walls of the bold little chapel that once stood by the sea.

Cyril Jolly

Willy Long, the Evangelist Fisherman from Sheringham.

SALTHOUSE LOOKING EAST

The Coast Road before it was tarred, with the last of the Methodist chapels just beyond the steamroller and the pony and cart.

Chapel memories from Florence Radley

The chapel was up here at first [Cross Street] where Mr Blackburn used to have that shop just opposite the new houses. Then they built that one down the road. I was a year old when they built that, in 1891. They collected enough money to pay for it. I still own a clothes brush made from the hairs of our pony's tail; things like this were made and sold and they built it free of debt. Sunday was a day of rest and for attending chapel. We never had cooked meals, and the only books to be read were the bible and the Christian Herald. No Sunday paper ever came into our house.

The chapel was the centre of our social life. My father and his sister Hannah started the Sunday School, and my father was superintendent there for twenty-one years. He had 72 children. Of course every family in those days had seven to nine children. Then there was the Anniversaries. Oh, we used to have to dress up. Mother used to send away and get remnants, and Ethel Dawson (she was a dress-maker) used to come up here and spend a week with us, and make us all new dresses for the Anniversary. We had new hats too. I remember having a black sailor hat, like a boater, with a red ribbon round it.

We used to have a special Service of Song at the Anniversary. Old Willy Long, do you remember him, the Evangelist fisherman from Sheringham, he always used to come, and he was a beautiful reader; he used to lead our Anniversary. He used to read a story and then we had all special hymns. Oh, they could sing! They had some beautiful voices in this village! The singing and beautiful readings would leave hardly a dry eye in the house.

The Methodist Sunday School circa 1909. Florence's brother Richard (Dick) High extreme right, and Mary his wife extreme left with Freda their two-year-old daughter, who later became Freda Morse.

Mary Lemmon's Chapel memories

It is with a sense of guilt and feeling of sadness that I write. My grandparents' generation worked, saved and gave to build this chapel, and my generation closed it. It was not only that they gave their time and money—a number of them were in danger of losing their jobs, homes and Christmas gift of coal and blankets if they continued to follow this different religion called Methodism, but in spite of the hardships it cost, the little chapel thrived.

It was different for my parents' generation, they were not forced to sacrifice in order to keep the chapel going, and no one was sent to try to stop their services. The chapel was strong. In my time, our Sunday worship was led by the minister from Sheringham or one of the Circuit Local Preachers. The chapel membership included at least six local preachers: Billy Cubitt, Billy Craske, Richard High, Tom High, Rodney High and Sidney Craske. These men travelled around the Cromer, Sheringham and Holt Circuit preaching at various churches, and were greatly appreciated.

Music played a great part in the services and we were fortunate to have so many organists and singers in the congregation. Sankey hymns were popular for the after-service sing-song, while Torrey-Alexander supplied the hymns they enjoyed for part-singing. Services of Song which included duets and solos were very popular and enjoyed by all. Herbert and Amelia Pigott were great favourites for their duets, as was Sidney Craske as a soloist, for my generation. Dick High's daughter Freda, and Gladys High, were organists at this time. Sunday School Anniversaries were wonderful for the children when, dressed in their best clothes, they recited and sang with all their heart to the enjoyment of members and friends and relations who filled the chapel. Freda (now 94) tells me that the first time she played a hymn to lead the singing of the chapel congregation it was 'news'! and she was heralded as the youngest girl to play for a congregation, with a photograph and a write-up in the local paper.

My memory of Sunday School is a happy one. I can still see the roll of wonderful pictures that Gladys showed to our class while she told us the Old Testament stories of Moses, Joseph and Daniel etc. in such a way that they have been special to me all my life. Freda and Gladys were organists for alternate services every Sunday, and Freda played for the Anniversary services which she arranged with her father and mother's help. When Dick High moved away, my mother Ethel Dawson became Superintendent, and things went on much as before. Sunday School treats were now trips further afield, to Hunstanton and even Great Yarmouth.

I took on the Sunday School when my mother retired, with the help of Norah Hayward, and other friends gave extra help at Anniversary time. Gladys and I shared the job of organist until, owing to family illness, Gladys was unable to do so. When she was free again she was invited to play for the parish church as they had no organist, and she felt that she should, so she played at the church on Sunday mornings and attended her chapel afternoons and evenings.

A Youth Club developed from the Sunday School, but the problem was where to meet. Mr and Mrs Tom Leach, who owned the Manor

House at this time, were kind enough to let us use their 'Barn Room' and with the help of others, such as Bill Curl and Eddy Hancock, the Club prospered.

But the chapel numbers gradually decreased by deaths and by people leaving the village, younger people marrying and moving away (myself included). Grace Craske took over as organist and her playing was greatly appreciated. She carried on until, with numbers so small, the chapel was closed in the seventies—a sad day for us all.

Mary Lemmon (née Dawson)

[*For Mary's childhood memories, see page 234*]

Mary Dawson as she was then, in the middle of her Methodist Sunday school in 1960.

Violet High and Janice Hayward present Mary with a farewell gift from the Sunday School.

Main landowners and Lords of the Manor

In the eleventh century there was no land without a lord and no lord without land. The responsibility of the lord of the manor, to the king and to his tenants, was a serious business. By the late twentieth century, manorial lordships became marketable commodities despite the fact that they brought with them little more than an archaic title. ('The Companion to the English Parish Church' p 268)

Kelly's Directory, though it does not cover every year, gives information as to the chief landowners and lords of the manor of Salthouse since 1836:

1836 The principal landowners in Salthouse are listed as John Francis Johnson living in the Manor House, Mrs A. Purdy in the Hall, and Mrs P.M. Girdlestone of Kelling, who is lady of the manor.

1845-1854 John Francis Johnson is dead and his widow Elizabeth is listed as one of the three chief landowners, with William Purdy and Mrs M. A. Girdlestone, who is now the lady of the manor and patroness of the church.

1864 Mrs Ann Girdlestone and William Purdy remain unchanged but William Johnson, Elizabeth's son (later to marry Sarah Ann Pigott), is now named as owner of the Manor House and farm. A year later, in **1865**, Elizabeth has died and her executors are listed as the third chief landowner.

1868 The living is in the gift of O. Randall Esq but the parish is 'principally the property of William Purdy and W. Johnson Esqrs'.

1869 O. Randall Esq is listed as lord of the manor and holds the gift of the living of the church, but is not listed as a chief landowner. The land is still 'principally the property' of Messrs William Purdy and William Johnson.

1872 There is no change.

1879 The trustees of the late O. Randall Esq are lord of the manor, and Messrs W. Purdy and W. Davy Esqrs, and Mrs Johnson, are the chief landowners. (William Johnson has died, and Sarah Ann his wife has become the owner of his land.)

1883 The parish belongs mainly to Mr Randall, lord of the manor and patron of the living, and to Mr William Purdy and Mrs Johnson.

1888 Onesiphorus Randall Esq is lord of the manor, and W. Davy Esq and Mrs Johnson are the chief landowners.

1890 The parish belongs mostly to Mr Randall and to the executors of Mr William Purdy and Mrs Johnson.

1892-1896 Onesiphorus Randall Esq lord of the manor; trustees of the late William Purdy Esq, W. Davy Esq and Mrs Johnson are the chief landowners.

1900 Still Onesiphorus, but Thomas Purdy is now mentioned as a chief landowner and Mrs Johnson is not.

1904 Ronald Herbert Savory Esq of Kelling Hall is lord of the manor, Thomas Purdy and the trustees of William Purdy are chief landowners.

1908 H.W.A. Deterding is lord of the manor and he and Mrs Primrose are chief landowners.

1922 H.W.A. Deterding is lord of the manor and the Norfolk County Council and F. Primrose Esq are the chief landowners.

1929 Ronald Deterding Esq is lord of the manor, and Norfolk County Council and F. Primrose Esq are chief landowners.

1957 Ronald James Deterding Esq is lord of the manor (the Jim Deterding of today).

Onesiphorus Randall

The following is part of an article by Peter Brooks which was published by the Norfolk Journal in their June 2002 edition. It describes the hitherto unknown London life of this most illustrious and colourful of all the Salthouse lords of the manor.

Any boy christened Onesiphorus deserves to succeed in life, for this unusual name means 'bringing profit'. In the case of Onesiphorus Randall, it did just that. He was born in Cley on 11th August 1798, the youngest of five children, and nothing is known of his early life or interests, although his father, John, is thought to have been a clock or watchmaker.

What took Onesiphorus to London is not known but he is recorded to have settled in Poplar in the East End in 1819. At the age of 22 he was lisencee of the Silver Lion public house in Pennyfields, moving on to the Globe Tavern in Blackwall, where he stayed until 1835. In addition to his activities with public houses, he started to dabble in speculative building projects; so much so, that by 1831 he was being described as 'the local building speculator', amassing a fortune from developing cheap houses to rent. One of his projects was the building of a terrace of four houses on the East India Dock Road, which he named Randall's Terrace. One of these (No 185) became his permanent home, and it was there that he died in 1873 at the age of 75.

His early interests led to the development in London, in 1848, of what was to become known as Randall's Estate, on a seven-acre site called The Grove, the eastern boundary of which was marked by the Black Ditch—a local euphemism for a common sewer.

Louise Grattan Collection

Randall's Folly, in the early 20th century.

By 1908 this development comprised 188 houses, 42 shops with accommodation, 49 lock-up shops and a large property called the Market Tavern. It was originally a temperance house, but by the 1880s it had become a Watney pub. 'Speculative' appears to have been a good description of this development, for in 1850 Onesiphorus was being accused by the local council's Surveyor of building property of unsound materials and with insufficient foundations—to the extent that the Council ordered at least one of them to be demolished and rebuilt.

At the centre of this estate was Randall's Market, built between 1851-2 as an ambitious project to establish a shopping attraction north of the East India Dock Road. Onesiphorus obviously thought that the presence of costermongers in the market would lower its tone, so he banned them from trading there. This decision proved to be a costly one, for these hardened traders took to standing their barrows and stalls in nearby Crisp Street, making it what one local newspaper described as: 'one of the cheapest middle-class markets in the whole of London'.

The Market—built of cheap materials—rapidly deteriorated with few reputable traders left, a position not improved when the area became the haunt of prostitutes. By 1913 the southern part of the market was in decay, with the result that the remaining shops were closed and the site cleared for redevelopment. Although the northern half lingered on until the outbreak of World War II, it suffered considerable bomb damage and was finally cleared in the late 1950s to make way for new developments.

The 1841 Census records Onesiphorus' age as 44, and his wife Ann as 50. But when she died three years later in 1844, her tombstone rather mysteriously recorded her as being 62 years old. At the time of the 1851 Census, Onesiphorus' age had increased to 61 and his home had changed to 'Clay' in Norfolk, with 21-year-old Elizabeth Gascoigne at the same address, listed as his housekeeper. Ten years later, in the 1861 Census, Onesiphorus had slipped back to being just 56 years old and was described as a 'Gentleman, Householder'. By this time he had acquired a new wife, Mary Ann (née Vousey), a minor whom he had married on 21st June 1860 at the recorded age of 62!

Mary Ann gave birth to their only child, a boy, whom they also inflicted with the name of Onesiphorus. Interestingly, at the time of the 1871 census when Onesiphorus' age was given as 70 and his wife Mary Ann's as 29, they were accompanied by Mary A. Spence—a 'general servant', whose birthplace was given as Salthouse, Norfolk.

Onesiphorus Senior, like so many people born in Norfolk who move away, evidently had felt the need to return, and in 1866 he is recorded as being present at a meeting of the Proprietors of Salthouse Broads and Marshes. He had bought a substantial quantity of land, and he was living at Woodlands House in Holt (now part of Gresham's School). Later he bought Kelling Old Hall (now ruined) which brought with it the title of lord of the manor.

He built his famous castle-like structure on land known as the Great Eye, adjoining Salthouse beach. Photographs show it to have been a square building, with large doors back and front so that Onesiphorus could drive his horses and carriage straight through, over a small bridge onto the flat grassland on the seaward side (known as 'Flat Eye'), turn around and then back again through the house. This strange structure became known locally as Randall's Folly, although villagers had alternative, saucier names for it because of the number of ladies he entertained there.

When Onesiphorus Senior died in 1873, his castle was bought by the Board of Trade for use as a Coastguard Station (No 304), and because the rocket and life-saving equipment were kept there, it became known as the Rocket House. There was a rocket pole on the beach and training sessions in the art of using the breeches buoy were held there much to the interest and entertainment of visitors and locals alike

During WWI, the building was used as a detention centre for soldiers on disciplinary charges, after which it was sold off as a private house. In 1937 local builder William Craske, and his son Sydney, were employed to build on a new wing to accommodate an extra bedroom, bathroom and entrance hall; a septic tank was also provided. Small repairs were also made to an existing well on the site.

Commander Frederick Champion de Crespigny
with his loader, Alec Morse.

and he was always here—the 'Companion in Arms' (above) refers to my father. I remember as a child going to Salthouse Hall. Mabel de Crespigny had a big picture of animals which she spread on the floor and we sat on them! The garden of the Hall was so immaculate, they always had wild strawberry beds, and we went and picked them.

They had an old roller in the garden and there was a steep hill going up. It sticks in my mind—we towed it up to the top of the hill—then we let it go, and it went down the hill with the handle going up and down, over and over. It didn't do the shrubbery at the bottom much good—Mabel de Crespigny was furious.

Bill and Fred were the sons of old Sir Claude Champion de Crespigny. My father always used to say that Sir Claude was one of the last bare-fisted prize fighters of those days of aristocratic sportsmen; no doubt he took on the local blacksmith and that sort of thing. It was when Sir Claude died that the de Crespignys left Salthouse Hall to go and manage the family estate in the midlands.

Jim Deterding, lord of the manor of Salthouse and Kelling.

The view from the top of the garden at the Hall, from where we let the roller go.

Mr Olley, 'Old Balaklava', 1832-1920

James Olley was already an old man when he came to live at Salthouse in the house that is now known as Marsh Cottage. His fame, as a soldier who fought in the Crimean War and actually took part in the Charge of the Light Brigade, was widely known and, due to the fact that he lived over the years in many different places in North Norfolk, there are probably many villages besides Salthouse who remember him as their own hero.

Steve Benson, when he was a housemaster at Gresham's School, wrote an article on James Olley for the special edition of 'The Grasshopper' of 1982, which was a parting tribute to Logie Bruce Lockhart on his retirement after twenty-seven years as headmaster. The following account is largely taken from that article.

INTO THE VALLEY OF DEATH RODE THE SIX HUNDRED

Cannon to right of them,
Cannon to left of them,
Cannon in front of them,
    Volleyed and thundered;
    Stormed at with shot and shell,
Boldly they rode and well,
Into the jaws of Death,
Into the mouth of Hell,
    Rode the six hundred.

Tennyson's poem made 'The Charge of the Light Brigade' in the Crimean War famous, and excited the public in the romanticism of the 'do or die' blind obedience of the British Soldier, but the very few who amazingly survived that famous charge were more or less forgotten.

Life in the British Army in the 1880s was hard enough, but unless he had a trade to take up when his time was served, an ex-soldier's outlook was often even harder. James Olley fell on hard times after his return to civilian life. He was reduced to begging in the streets of Knapton with a placard round his neck. But he was noticed and was identified as having played the part he did by the Squire, Mr H.M. Robinson of Knapton Hall, who was a Justice of the Peace. He took action to put things right in a stirring article deploring the fact that some one who had taken part in one of the most celebrated military events of the time, should be forced to beg. In the *Dereham and Fakenham Times* of 14 January 1888, he declared publicly that 'No one of the gallant six hundred should have to petition for the means to put himself in the way of earning a livelihood'. He called upon readers to donate to a fund to put James Olley 'into some little business'.

In the same article James Olley's own account of that charge showed that Tennyson's description of flashing sabres and the mouth-of-hell situation was no exaggeration:

'It was very queer going down the valley, a good deal worse than it was when I got to the guns . . . The first man I happened with at the guns was a Russian gunner who attacked me with a ramrod. I felled him at the muzzle of the gun he was defending with two strokes of my sword . . . Just as I killed the gunner, I saw several Russians dash at the Earl of Cardigan who was near the breech of a big gun; but his horse brought him safely over the limber towards us. I never saw him again in the battle . . .

'Whilst fighting at the guns, I received two lance wounds, one in the ribs and one in the neck from behind. The Russian lancer in the rear who stabbed me was killed by a comrade and I struck down the other. In this cavalry encounter, I was wounded with a sabre across the forehead by a Russian dragoon. He made "Cut 7" at me . . . I gave him point and stabbed him. The sword fell from his hand and the point penetrated my foot . . .

'When we were retiring we met some Russian lancers. We made a charge and they fled to the left incline and rode past. Just after passing the cavalry I got a ball from the Russian infantry on my left. It went through my left eye, passed through my nostrils and the roof of my mouth and came out against my right eye. I did not know at the time that my eye was out. It was not painful at the time; afterwards the suffering was dreadful. After being thus wounded, I still kept the saddle [he had already had one horse shot from under him but had managed to remount that of a fallen trooper] though blood was pouring from my mouth and nostrils, as well as running from my forehead . . . When I came out of battle the Paymaster did not recognise me. I was then blind . . .'

* * *

Even allowing for some romanticising on the part of raconteur and reporter, it was a gripping tale and certainly helped to increase the flow of cash into Mr Robinson's fund.

Mr Olley further recalled how he was nursed by Florence Nightingale at Scutari (he was certainly taken to hospital there) and then, on his return to England, was presented to the Queen at Brompton Barracks in March 1855 when she visited the wounded there in company with Prince Albert and the Duke of Cambridge, who had commanded a division in the Crimea and who commented, apparently, on Olley's 'miraculous escape'. Her Majesty seems to have been somewhat overcome by the occasion for she asked Olley whether he would like to go back again. He replied in suitably patriotic vein, and was pleased to receive when he got home 'a present of stockings, cuffs, scarves and mittens from the Queen'. Again, as he must have been one of the prize occupants of the Barracks, all this is quite possible, even likely, and with these five wounds and a lost eye, the scars of which he took to the grave, it does seem a little less than just that a new book, *Casualty Roll for the Crimea*, should refer to him as having been 'wounded slightly'!

And so, thirty three years after his discharge from the army, James Olley, by now a local celebrity, came to Holt. He trained horses for the local gentry, including Lord Hastings and Sir Alfred Jodrell of Bayfield Hall, and had his stables in Church Street where the public library is now situated and which had been the stables of Wansbeck House behind Hubbard's.

He was a regular at the Bull (now a baker's shop almost opposite the Cottage Boutique) and in the yard at the rear would prove his considerable strength by throwing two 56lb weights over his shoulders a distance of over 13 feet. This legendary exercise he could still perform at the age of seventy. He had an aggressive nature, and would return regularly from the annual horse-traders' fair on Aldborough Green with plenty of bruises to testify to his pugilistic encounters behind the tents. But this fiery side to his character was reserved for two-footed creatures only. He was, as his obituary testified, 'a great lover of animals who ruled his horses with kindness'.

Eventually Mr Olley was forced, through illness, to give up his business and he went to live in Blakeney in a cottage in the High Street which is still called 'Alma Cottage' after one of the battles of the Crimea. He also christened his son by this name, which was not appreciated. Although he too became a soldier for a while, Alma Olley was always known as Wallam.

Later, 'Old Balaklava' moved on to Salthouse. He lived in the house beside the Post Office, which bears the date of 1891, and he named this house 'Balaklava Cottage', after another battle. He was a Salthouse Churchwarden for a time, and Jane Hales remembers as a child being introduced to him in the early 1900s, on a visit with her father to Salthouse marshes.

Born in Salthouse Post Office, next door to Balaklava Cottage, Freda Morse and her brothers Ray and Roland High (all living in Holt today) can just remember the old man with a black eye-patch who lived the other side of the garden fence. Then later, after James Olley had left Salthouse, Freda's father, Richard High, having just sold the Post Office, bought Balaklava Cottage and moved his family into it while waiting to find a farm to rent. Being a peace-loving man, however, he couldn't bear to live in a house bearing the name of a battle and renamed it 'Beulah Cottage'.

SALTHOUSE VILLAGE GREEN c 1890
'Balaklava Cottage' centre (called 'Marsh Cottage' today) with the Post Office on the right.

Salthouse Heath: its ancient and natural history

BY STEVE HARRIS

Steve Harris

Thousands of years ago, an advancing ice sheet ground to a halt more or less where Salthouse village now stands. As climate warmed, the ice began to melt, disgorging millions of tons of sands, gravels and larger stones over the landscape to the south. Tens of metres' depth of this debris, rounded by the action of ice and water, accumulated at the front of the glacier. This outwash plain, sloping gently southwards, now forms the well-known feature of the Holt-Cromer Ridge. This feature's highest point, at Pretty Corner just inland of Sheringham, reaches 100m—the highest in Norfolk—and gives impressive views northwards over the sea where once there was nothing but ice.

As the ice retreated and, over centuries, the days warmed, vegetation re-clothed the barren high-arctic landscape; tundra was replaced by low woody scrub, and eventually trees appeared. This was a time when there would have been a complete range of animals browsing the vegetation, from rodents to large mammals such as deer, wild cattle and wild boar. Latest thinking suggests that temperate forest, before intervention by Man, far from being closed-canopy woodland, would have been broken up into a patchwork including large, open, grazed areas, particularly on thinner soils. It is now thought likely that heathlands, which develop on thin, acidic and unproductive soils, may have always existed in some form, perhaps resembling parts of the New Forest, and were modified by Man rather than created by him as had been thought. When early livestock farmers appeared on the scene, some 5,000 years ago, it is likely that they simply managed their animals on existing clearings, and that the combination of their fuel-gathering and browsing livestock merely made the existing patchwork heaths more extensive.

That Salthouse Heath was a place of great activity in the Bronze Age is demonstrated by the many burial mounds that are scattered over the site. There are nine large mounds, including 'Three Halfpenny' Hill, 'Three Farthing' Hill, and Gallow Hill (actually in Kelling parish) and many smaller ones, including a cluster of over thirty, which make Salthouse Heath the largest Bronze Age cemetery in Norfolk. In contrast, Kelling Heath has only one such mound. All are scheduled Ancient Monuments.

In the Middle Ages, grazing animals continued to keep heaths as open country. At this time wool was wealth, and sheep were therefore the economically worthwhile animal. Sheep do well on dry ground, and it is ironic that, in contrast to later history, it was Norfolk's poorest soils that contributed to the area's great medieval wealth and made it one of England's pre-eminent counties. This fact is demonstrated by the huge churches dominating small villages, of which Salthouse church is a prime example.

In the more recent past, Salthouse Heath was an integral part of the local economy, and would have been worked very hard by virtue of the needs of the villagers in the days of 'living off the locality'. Gorse provided hot-burning fuelwood. There are some people living in the village today who recall the ovens of the bakery being fired up with faggots (bundles) of gorse, and the bread or collective Sunday roasts being cooked in the residual heat from the walls of the oven. Farmers used gorse bushes as bases for haystacks and, in some parts, even as agricultural implements: a gorse bush dragged behind a horse, produces a fine seedbed. Turf or 'flag' cutting was known to have been carried out at Salthouse.*

See article on flag-cutting, page 144

Elsewhere such material was used as fuel and was certainly different from the peat dug from sphagnum moss mires that develop in wet hollows on heaths, but the details of this activity, as carried out on dry heaths, seem to have been lost. Heather ('ling') was harvested, as Salthouse records show, though it is not clear for what purpose. In other parts of Britain it has been used for thatching. Bracken was certainly used as bedding material and, last but not least, the heath was a good source of protein in the form of rabbits. From Norman times, rabbits had been 'farmed' on sandy areas, and the name 'warren' is associated with such deliberate management. Immediately to the south of Salthouse Heath, Faden's map of 1797 shows an area called Kelling Warren.

The relatively intense use of heathland is likely to have begun to wane in the nineteenth century, and declined to virtually nothing by the middle of the twentieth. As traditional activities declined, invasion by bushes and trees accelerated, and the open grazing land was gradually encroached by woodland. Where grazing for livestock was still required, it is likely that fire was used regularly in a controlled way to encourage plants palatable to cattle, sheep and horses. This appears to have been the case at Salthouse, where controlled burning and, more recently, uncontrolled and damaging summer fires, have kept the heath open in places.

Latterly, with the rise in interest in habitat conservation, it has been clear that heathlands are a landscape under threat. Over the last 200 years Norfolk's heathland area has dwindled by perhaps as much as 90%, notwithstanding the huge areas that had been ploughed up before 1800. The special wildlife of heaths, deprived of its habitat, has declined in proportion, so that many heathland plants and animals are now rare. What is more, until recently, the heaths that did survive were becoming unsuitable for heathland specialist species due to the encroachment of trees.

Salthouse has a good share of heath-specialist wildlife. Its plant life includes dodder, a parasite that lives off heather; the western gorse, the small gorse that flowers in August and September, and normally grows in western Britain; heath violets and of course the two heathers: *Erica cinerea*, the bell heather, and the true heather *Calluna vulgaris* that flowers a bit later with the western gorse. The sandy soils are good for burrowing insects and one of them, the Minotaur beetle, leaves a conspicuous hole about 10mm across, down which this British dung beetle rolls rabbit droppings in which to lay eggs.

Reptiles also love the dry soils that warm quickly in the sun. Common lizards, slow worms ('legless' lizards), and adders are all at home on the heath, if elusive to see. Easier to see (and hear) are the heath birds. Churring nightjars, nightingales singing in the blackthorn thickets and the chance to see 'roding' woodcock make the heath a popular evening stop for birdwatchers. The stonechat is now breeding again, after an absence of some years, adding to the Norfolk population that is barely a dozen pairs in a good year. Of great interest has been the return, after a 50-year-absence, of woodlarks. These fairly drab-looking birds have a beautiful song, which can now be heard once more over the heath from February onwards. This rare bird's population is expanding, largely in response to the conservation management that is now a high priority on most surviving heathland.

Now that Salthouse Heath is benefiting from conservation management, under the auspices of the Trustees and funded by English Nature's 'Tomorrow's Heathland Heritage' lottery grant, wildlife on the heath has a more secure future and residents and visitors alike can enjoy the open views over beautiful landscape, full of interest and cultural history.

Steve Harris, 2003

This summary of events, produced as propaganda for votes, gives a good idea of the difficulties faced by the Heath Trustees in the execution of their duties!

The History and Truth about Salthouse Heath and Parish Affairs.

1882. It was agreed "to prosecute all persons found trespassing on the Heaths."
1884. Complaints were made against Lodgers trespassing and exercising Common Rights, when it was agreed to take Counsel's opinion.
1884. Counsel's opinion being against the Lodgers—the Common Reeves were directed to report all cases of trespass.
1888. It was agreed "that no rabbiting should be allowed on the Heaths on Sundays."
1889. It was agreed "that no rabbits or game be taken off the Heaths between April 1st and September 1st."
1893. It was agreed "That Non-Common Righters should not be allowed to catch rabbits on the Heaths, and that the Heaths be closed from March 1st till the end of harvest on both farms, as regards taking game, rabbits, or vermin."
1896. An application to hire the Sporting Rights on the Heaths was refused by "your old and tried member."
1897. It was unanimously agreed "to close the Heaths," but afterwards, owing to a Common Righter declaring "he should continue to go upon the Heaths as formerly, whether closed or not," the resolution was not enforced.
It was also suggested that guns be not allowed on the Heath after sunset, or before sunrise.
1898. Question of letting Sporting Rights again considered, and again objected to.
1899. Question of closing Heaths considered and postponed.
1899. Ditto considered and postponed.
1903. Another offer to hire Sporting Rights on Heath considered, when "your old and tried member" objected to letting same.
1903. Several Common Righters claimed Sporting Rights in Bix's Lane.
1904. Agreed to close Heaths from April to August, but "your old and tried member" objected to same.
1905. A proposition was made to close the Heaths as before, and again opposed, by "your old and tried member."
1905. An official letter was received, stating that neither the Inclosure Act, or Award appeared to give any Sporting Rights as claimed in Bix's Lane.
1905. It was agreed to prosecute a person for trespassing on the Heath, this "your old and tried member" supported.
1907. It was agreed to close the Heath on Sundays against all persons, and a warning was given to Non-Common Righters, that if found trespassing on same, proceedings would be taken against them. This also received the approval of "your old and tried member."

1907.	It was agreed to prosecute two men for trespassing on the Heath, and again "your old and tried member" agreed to prosecute.
1907.	It was agreed to prosecute two more persons for trespassing on the Heath in pursuit of game &c., when "your old and tried member" supported prosecution.
1908. Jan.	It was unanimously agreed to let the Sporting Rights on the Heaths, which "your old and tried member" then agreed to do.
1908. March	The question of inviting tenders to let said Sporting Rights was considered, when "your old and tried member" changed his mind and objected to same being let.
1908. Oct.	Meeting of Common Righters considered an offer for the hire of Sporting Rights, when "your old and tried member" again changed his course of action, and seconded a motion to make the best possible arrangement with the Lord of the Manor for the hire of said rights.
1909. Jan.	Again the same gentleman agreed to warn Non-Common Righters, that if found on the Heaths in pursuit of game or rabbits, they would be dealt with as trespassers.
1909. April	"Your old and tried member" moved a resolution to close the Heath to the 1st September, to all persons, whether Common Righters or not, carrying guns or accompanied by dogs, or otherwise searching for or taking game, rabbits, or game eggs.
1909. July	It was agreed by all present, including "your old and tried member" to prosecute a "Widow's Son" for trespassing on the Heath lands in search of rabbits.
1909. Aug.	"Your old and tried member" seconded a motion to ask the Charity Commissioners to intervene, and try to bring about a friendly settlement of the disputed rights of Sporting on the Heaths.
1910. Feb.	On receipt of the Charity Commisioners' offer and suggestions for a settlement "your old and tried member" seconded a motion, thanking them for their offered assistance, and at the same time declined their services.
1910. March	At the Conference between the Charity Commissioners' Representative, who endeavoured to bring about a friendly settlement of these disputed Sporting Rights, "your old and trusted member" protested against same, and strongly advocated fighting the matter out in the Law Courts.

Comment is needless beyond this. For some thirty years the Heath Pot has been, and is on the boil, and this owing to the action of certain individuals.

Why has not "your old and tried member," who now seeks your votes, carried out his duties according to settled law and practice, as well as justice? Why has he all these years been working to benefit a few, at the same time by his and other's actions kept the people of Salthouse out of some £500 which they might have had? Men of Salthouse! Stand this sort of thing no longer. Exercise your rights on Monday next by voting for a man who has always acted straight, fair, and consistent in the management of your affairs.

March 31st, 1910.

These pages are reproduced from a poster kindly lent by Mary Lemmon.

Tracey's summary of the Heath Award

Tracey Large (née Wright), of Salthouse, compiled a terrific project on Salthouse for her History CSE at Sheringham High School in the 1970s. This page is taken from it. She had access to her grandfather's copy of the 50-page Heath Award document, and summarised it— expertly skimming over the incomprehensible bits. She has treated Zurishaddai's unusual name as more fittingly a title than a Christian name. [For more of Tracey see page 163]

The Inclosure Award of 1781 extinguished 'all rights of sheepwalk, common and shackage' in the two parishes of Salthouse and Kelling and referred to 130 acres of land known as Salthouse Warren and a further 300 acres of commons and heaths. The land was allotted and divided, between the lord of the manor the Zurishaddai Girdlestone and local residents, of property 'to value not exceeding £10 per year'. They were given the right to pasture one cow or heifer, or one mare and foal or three calves, and to cut, take, and carry away flags, furze and whins 'for their firing'.

There was a direction that the lord of the manor and others should 'within the first fortnight in January in every year' meet in the church porch to appoint two or more common Reeves to be responsible for seeing that the provisions of the Award were observed, including the keeping in good repair of all fences and the raising of 'a sufficient number of large doles of mounds of earth' to mark the boundaries of the allotments.

The heath as we see it today has been retained for the 'poor' of the parish, but with no property having a rateable value under £10, the old Common Rights have become somewhat archaic.* The present Trustees—'Seven competent persons'—have recently completed six years of discussion and consultation aimed to produce more money to help those in need in the parish. The major part of the heath is leased to the Ministry of Defence for training purposes and although there are some public Rights of Way, the Trustees emphasize that it is not public land although they do not stop the public enjoying its attractions. They point out, however, that they can still exercise some quite considerable powers, including 'the removal of any caravans, banning any vehicle going in more than 45 feet from any road and stopping thoughtless people digging up turf and causing malicious damage.'

*In 1781 only the poor, occupying or owning houses with a rateable value of £10 or less, had a right to profit from the Common land. They were known as 'Common Righters'. In 1905 this limit was amended from £10 to £20 (see opposite).

Left: An unidentified Salthouse smallholder on the Heath.

Ernest Porter High, Overseer of the Poor
and the Charity Commission's Amendment to the 1781 Heath Award

CHARITY COMMISSION.

The Board of Charity Commissioners for England and Wales, upon an application made to them on the 29th November 1905, in writing, under the seal of

The RURAL DISTRICT COUNCIL of Erpingham; being a Council interested in the above-mentioned Charities; and signed by

    The Reverend WILLIAM BRAMLEY SAYLE DALBY, Rector of Kelling with Salthouse;
    RONALD HERBERT SAVORY, then Lord of the Manors of Salthouse, Salthouse Witchinghams, Salthouse Netherhalls, Kelling, Kelling Ilketshall, and Bardolphs otherwise Bardwells;
    JAMES PLATTEN NURSE, of Kelling, Retired Miller; and
    JAMES DUFFIELD (since deceased);
    ERNEST PORTER HIGH, and
    JOHN DEW, both of Salthouse, Farmers;
    JOHN WILLIAM LAKE, of Norwich Road, Holt, Harness Maker; and
    SAMUEL CRITOPH CLARE, of No. 55, Wrottesley Road, Plumstead, Retired Postmaster;

being then the Trustees of the Charities:

And after due notice of the intention to make this Order published according to the direction of the Board by being affixed to or near a principal outer door of the Parish Churches of Kelling and Salthouse on the 12th June 1906, and by advertisement in the newspapers called "The People's Weekly Journal" and "The Cromer and North Walsham Post" on the 23rd June 1906 (being in each case more than one calendar month before the date hereof); and also sent through the post

(1.) On the 19th May 1908 to
    FREDERICK GEORGE HANNANT, of Kelling, Farmer;
    IVIE ROSS, of Kelling Hall, Farmer;
    HORACE FOULGER, of Salthouse, Farmer; and
    ROBERT GREEN, of Sheringham, Plasterer; and

(2.) On the 25th June 1908 to
    HENRI WILHELM AUGUST DETERDING, now Lord of the above-mentioned Manors;

being those of the present Trustees of the Charities who were not privy to the said application, at their respective last known places of abode in Great Britain or Ireland:

In 1902, The Parish Council appointed Mr Ernest High and Mr John Dew as Overseers of the Poor. In 1905 they were concerned with the attempt to amend the Heath Award's ruling that only the poor occupying houses of a rateable value of £10 or less should be receivers of Common Rights. But it was not until 1908 that the £10 house valuation limit was increased to £20, as may be seen left and below:

Ernest Porter High
As a young man, he walked to York to seek work.

And after due communication of the draft of the subjoined Scheme to the Parish Council of Salthouse and to the Chairman of the Parish Meeting of Kelling:

Do hereby Order as follows:—
The subjoined Scheme is approved and established.

SCHEME.
The above-mentioned Award shall have effect as if in place of the words—
"not occupying lands or tenements of more than the yearly value of ten pounds"
wheresoever they occur therein, the following words were substituted—
"not being owners or occupiers of lands or tenements of more "than the rateable value of 20*l*."

Sealed by Order of the Board this 30th day of June 1908.

These documents are reproduced by courtesy of Kathleen Gray, granddaughter of Ernest High.

THE HEATH

1882 Meeting to appoint Common Reeves

Below: A page from the Parish Minute Book of Vestry Meetings. James Moy and John Ives retired from being Common Reeves. Twenty-two people including two Heath Trustees—the Rev J.W. Flavell and local farmer Mr F. Page—were present to witness the appointment of Charles High (proposed by Samuel Hancock, seconded by Henry High) and John Hancock (proposed by William Spence, seconded by John Parke).

At an adjourned Meeting held at Church 31 Jany 1882 for the purpose of appointing Common Reeves &c

Present

The Revd J. W. Flavell (Trustee) Mr. F. Page (Trustee) J. D. Jarvis, H. High Senr, John Hancock, Wm Dew Jas. Brown, Thos. High, John Parke, Richd. Pigott, Chas High Jas. Hancock, Jas. High, Saml. Hancock, Wm Spence A. Banes, Chas. Bastard Hy. High Junr., W. Dew M Dack Jno. Pigott Senr. and Hy Lewis —

It was proposed by Mr. F. Page and seconded by J. D. Jarvis, that the Revd J. W. Flavell be Chairman of the Meeting Unanimous — The retiring Common Reeves Jas Moy & John Ives — It was proposed by S. Hancock and seconded by Hy High. that Chas. High be appointed one of the Common Reeves It was also proposed by W. Spence and seconded by Jno. Parke that Jno. Hancock be the other Common Reeve both propositions were carried Unanimously

Below: The minutes of the meeting continue, with specific directions restricting the areas where flags should be cut, and the time for the cutting to begin. Heath management was a communal affair.

> It was unanimously agreed that the Flags be cut the same places as last year viz the south of the Riding Road Green Pit & New Marl Pit. The time to commence Cutting 1st April next. The Stock kept to be two heads of any kind.
>
> It was proposed by H. High Senr and seconded by T. High and Unanimously agreed that Mr H. Page be allowed to cut what Ling he require at 1/6 per load. It was proposed by Mr H. Page and seconded by S. D. Jarvis that all meetings for the future be entered in the Parish Minute Book.
>
> It was proposed by Richd Pigott and seconded by S. D. Jarvis that all persons found tresspassing on the Heaths be prosecuted Carried Unanimously —

Gerald Cubitt Collection

The approach road to Salthouse down Bard Hill in the early 1900s, surrounded by grazing land. Where were 'the Riding Road' and the 'Green Pit', mentioned in the Minutes of the January 1882 meeting above? Doreen Sayer, daughter of Clifford High, says that it was *Harry High's Riding Road* and that Harry—her great-great-grandfather on her mother's side, was farm steward for the Purdys. He frequently rode between the two farms in the village, and the way he went was called after him.

Flag-cutting

In the eighteenth and early nineteenth centuries, turves were a standard source of fuel for the poor, yet it is very hard to find any information concerning them in this district. The extracts below are from Colin Wells' detailed research on this subject, taken from his article 'Post-Medieval Turf-Digging in Norfolk' which appeared in the Norfolk Archaeological Society's Journal Volume XLIII Part III, 2000.

In Norfolk, and also the rest of East Anglia, peat was known as *turf* and the combustible dried blocks derived from it as *turves*. These were associated with deeper, more humified and homogeneous sub-surface material, in contrast to looser and more fibrous superficial deposits which were usually referred to as *flag*. Fuel blocks were also made from this material and these were called *flags* or sometimes *hover*. The former items made for a superior fuel compared to the latter, which was poor in terms of calorific content.

Although the two types could often be exploited on the same site, specific references to flags are commoner from sites where peat deposits were very thin, such as heathland.

The implement to cut turves in East Anglia was a special elongated spade known as a becket, which was a rectangular flat spade made usually from wood and shod at the bottom with iron. It carried a short triangular iron flange placed at right-angles to the main blade which allowed two cuts to be made together with one downward stroke providing rectangular turves to be cut in succession from the peat face.

It is remarkable such a relatively recent industry has apparently disappeared completely from the collective folk-memory. Too much time has elapsed since the turf-cutting heyday, for there to have survived an oral tradition pertaining to the skills and methods used in extracting Norfolk turf.

Right: An excerpt from another meeting of Heath Trustees shows that the cutting of flags was a regulated affair, and the area from which they could be cut changed each year. The sixpences mentioned here are the yearly dues which each Common Righter had to pay. 'Two head of stock' could be grazed on the heath for this fee, but the cutting of 'Ling and Furze' (heather and gorse) had to be paid for separately. The money paid went to reimburse the Common Reeves for their work.

"Flags to be cut from forepart of Heath to Direction Post leading to Kelling – No Part of Heath to be burnt this Year – The sixpences of each Right to be paid in the month of June – Two head of Stock to be kept – Ling an Furze to be paid for as last Year – Proposed by Saml. Hancock and Seconded by N. High junr. that no Rabbits or Game be followed or taken off the Heath between April 1st and Sept 1st Carried by eleven against five – Resolved that the Trustees shall treat with the Eastern & Midland Rly. Company for payment for Heath Land taken by them; also try to get compensation for damage by fire to the Heath on Feb. 26th 1884 – Vote of thanks was given to the Chairman – C. E. Lowe (Chairman"

'The birthright of the poor' and 'a place of beauty'

The cutting below was found in the church chest. It has no date but a guess would be early 1900s. It is pointing the finger at the administration of the Award rather than at the Award itself, but it is not clear who were those participants in the 'spoliation of the birthright of the poor'.

To the Editor—

Sir,—I notice in your last Friday's issue a report to the effect that the Kelling people propose to ask for an enquiry into the administration of the Enclosure Act, 1781. It is surely high time that a Commission did sit, take evidence, and amend the present condition of things, both as regards Kelling and other Poor's land in adjacent parishes. Such an enquiry would probably shed a lurid light on the unspeakable selfishness of those who mis-read and misinterpret the intention and purport of the aforementioned Act and award. We read that the Act of 1781 awarded Kelling 122 acres 35 perches for fuel, and 28 acres to supply the poor with pasturage for one cow each. Also, that the poor of Salthouse received an award of 349 acres 3 roods and 6 perches for fuel and pasturage, and yet we hear complaints on all hands, that many of the real poor are getting no share or benefit from this common heritage. Perhaps a Commission will find out in the broad daylight of a public enquiry the names of men who greedily monopolise the rights of the people. And, it may be that we, too, will find that the knights and squires and their relations whom we hear so glibly quoted on local platforms at election times as prime offenders in the aforementioned matters, are shining angels in comparison with some of the other particpants in the spoliation of the birthright of the poor. I congratulate the good folk of Kelling on their pluck in tackling this question. More power to their elbow.—Yours, etc.,

JOHN WAINER.

Cley-next-Sea. Norfolk; March 30th.

Vivian

During the Second World War, when Vivian High was serving overseas, his mother sent him a cutting from the local paper. In it, Salthouse Heath is described as a place of beauty. To Vivian, surrounded by war, it brought vivid memories of home. (It isn't very clear which 'by-way' is being referred to, but there is no doubt that it is Salthouse Heath.)

BY-WAY TO THE HEATH

There are many by-ways leading from the village and one of the pleasantest is the way to the heath. It is a very old by-road, for one of the fields that border it bears the name of its thirteenth century owner, and for hundreds of years the heavy wheels of farm carts and wagons have jolted over its ruts in summer and churned through its mud in winter. It is a quiet way, this shady lane where the silence is broken only by the cooing of the wood pigeons, the low calls and joyous notes of the birds, the crescendo and diminuendo of the wind in the trees, the rippling and gurgling of the tiny brook which flows along part of its length. The lane leads through a belt of woodland to the highway, no busy road this for it is little used and, unlike most North Norfolk roads, has wide grass verges. We follow it past the lonely Peewit Cottages, rightly named for they stand at the corner of a field beloved of plovers and sea gulls, until in less than a mile we reach the lane that leads directly to the heath. If it is summer time, and the wind blows from the sea, the air is filled with the scent of gorse blossoms and the blossoms and the smell of pinewoods long before we reach the expanse of the heath. Its acres stretch far away merging in the distance with those of Kelling and Weybourne, where Beacon Hill and Muckleboro' stand clear against the blue line of Sheringham woods. The heath is always beautiful; in summer a golden sea of gorse and tossing waving broom, in autumn purple with heather and perhaps most beautiful in the early morn of a September day, when its bushes are covered with gossamers that have travelled perhaps some thirty or forty miles on some warm current of air, whose silken threads glitter in the sun with the colours of opal and transform the heath into a veritable fairyland.

Gossamer cobwebs on the bushes

The road leads to the top of the hill, and in front of us lies one of the finest views in North Norfolk. The descent is steep and directly before us and far below lies the village of Salthouse, its stone-built cottages stretched along one side of the coast road. There are few hedges in Salthouse, deep creeks intersect the marshes and separate them from the road, beyond them lies the pebble ridge of the beach.

There are some things in life, small things, everyday things, which leave an ineffaceable imprint on the mind—the lilt of a song, a picture, a beautiful face—and as long as memory lasts I shall remember an August evening on Salthouse Heath. L had brought her boys from her Fenland farm to Salthouse; she and I with P, a boy of seven, climbed the hill above the church to watch the sunset. It had been a beautiful cloudless August day but, towards evening, light clouds gathered in the west and against them the sun went down in all its splendour. We sat there watching the ever-changing light on land and sea, the stretching marshes with their reed beds and pools of water, now golden-brown, now roseate red, now purple and green as the sun sank lower and the blue of the distance turned to grey. It was very still on the heath that evening, we did not speak, for Beauty had laid her spell on us, and no sound broke the silence till somewhere a boy whistled a tune. 'How well that boy whistles!' exclaimed L. 'So clear and true.' 'It is not a boy, Mother,' said P. 'It's Pan calling. I knew we should find him here.' 'I think P has expressed it,' said L, her gesture embracing the fading loveliness of land and sea. I think he had.

E.H.

On the reverse side of the above newspaper cutting the war was being reported:

' . . . British, Canadian and Polish troops are pushing through the outskirts of Cabourg . . . To the south-west, another British column of armour and infantry has bridged the Orme and driven forward six miles to capture Sentilly . . . Between August 11th and 18th the British Second Army has taken 4048 prisoners which brings the total of prisoners since 'D' day to 20,792 . . . .'

PART THREE

PEOPLE

Memories of fishing, farming and family life

Salthouse, Norfolk.

Jim Sutton Collection

Salthouse in the early 1900s

by Florence M. Daw

An undated fragment of newspaper clipping, found blowing about on the floor of Wendy Elsden's garage, contains this graphic appreciation of the Salthouse of many years ago, and sets the scene for the living memories which follow. This is Wendy's transcription of it.

Salthouse, the very name smacks of the salt breeze and strong, rough built houses to resist the 'nor-easter' as it sweeps across the marshes from the North Sea.

Yes, the houses are built of smooth, round cobbles off the beach, with tiny windows to face the gales and a front door that opens to the south on to a plot of garden filled with flowers. There are small, crooked lanes, steep and stony with ever the flint walls on either side; a patch of lavender in the corner of a garden, and a brilliant red snap-dragon clinging to a high wall that looks as if the next gust of wind would sweep it from its slender hold.

There are farmyards that open to the road, with young pigs scampering over the manure as a brown spaniel pokes his nose beneath the gate. There are cows that walk leisurely along the highway from one rich feeding place to another. A grey goat takes four or five to pasture every morning and brings them back every evening. He walks in front with a dignified jaunty tread like a showman at the head of his circus.

There is a river that winds by the side of the road that skirts the village, where ducks dip and splash and float at ease or come to the green banks to clean and preen their feathers. Beyond the river lie the marshes, smooth and still, with ever their colour changing from hour to hour; every cloud that floats across the sky throws its shadow on to their smooth surface. With a high wind blowing the long shadows race and chase each other across the dark green, sage green, yellow and brown. In the distance, where clouds sweep low to kiss the earth, a heron rises from the reeds, slowly beating its great wings.

Beyond the ridge of shingle that borders the marshes rides the sea; the swell from the lonely north falls with a thud on the beach, where the rollers break as calmly, evenly, and unhurriedly as time itself.

When evening falls the tints from the western sky make deep pools of light on the glassy surface of the river, and dusk creeps over the marshes, levelling the colours to soft greys and greens. Behind the village a young moon looks down on a ripe cornfield. That is Salthouse in August. As my eyes sweep the lonely marshes and fall on the soft light in the river I send up a prayer of thankfulness there are still such places on God's earth.

Florence M. Daw

Florence Radley

Florence Radley was full of memories, and Eileen High (wife of her nephew Ray) made a recording of her when Florence was in her later years. The following is transcribed from that recording.

My grandson Peter has traced our family back to 1600—there was an Amy and Christopher High in Salthouse in 1600. I should think we are one of the oldest families and the Pigotts, they're old too. My mother was a Pigott, and my grandmother, and they lived at Kelling, the Pigotts did, at that time and my mother's grandfather was a shoe maker. Grandmother High was very poor. Grandfather died when he was fifty, he had cancer on the lip. He walked to Norwich Hospital and he was operated on, but in doing it they broke his jaw by mistake. That wouldn't happen now. They lived in that house where Rodney used to live. Oh, they were poor! My father never went to school. Well, he went one day, and Johnson went there and got him out of school to go and keep some hens in a field up on the heath. He was six, and he was terrified, and he came and sat on the stile at the top there, so he could see the houses.

My grandfather earned eight shillings a week and Uncle Harry earned four. Flour was four shillings a stone, and all my mother could make was bread. They used to give the bullocks molasses to treat them, and the boys used to come up and get some of that to eat with their bread. There was an old chap kept a shop up Cross Street, an old man called Dew, and when Father was going up the road, he used to say 'Come here, boy, and let's see what your mother bring you for your dinner,' and he'd put a bit of cheese in for him. And they'd get a turnip, and scoop that out and put blackberries in when the blackberries were ripe and they'd eat that with the bread. My father never did forget the first taste he had of goose! He worked for Johnsons in the Manor House and they had maids and one of them gave him the drum stick of a goose. He got in the stable and ate it and ooh!—he said he never tasted anything like it.

There was an old lady who lived next door in Sunnycroft, she was a widow and she paid £4 a year rent for her cottage. I think her husband had been lost at sea. Her only income was 2/6 a week allowed her from the Parish, and we used to give her some milk and butter. I remember taking in the bread and milk, and seeing her sitting up in bed in a white night-dress and bonnet. She wore a woollen cross-over, they didn't have cardigans in those days.*

[*see photo following page]

Florence Radley 1960

Florence 1905

Grandmother High (born Hannah Pigott) with her youngest daughter Lucy

All our family was Chapel. My father worked for Sir Alfred Jodrell at Bayfield, and my eldest brother Dick when he left school went to work there with him. Well, there was an election going on and Sir Alfred Jodrell asked Father what he voted, and he told him he was a Radical and he sacked him straight away. And he went round and told all the farmers not to employ that feller High if he had the cheek to tell him he was Radical!

My father was out of work two years. My mother took in sewing and washing. You know, for her principles she was ever so strong my mother was. Then Johnsons owned this farm where Don farms now, and Johnson, he was squiring the village. Mrs Johnson was my grandfather's sister,* she was a pretty woman and the Squire married her. He was only thirty-one when he died—he drank himself to death—and he left the farm to her, and she cut the farm up into smallholdings. She lent money to Uncle Harry, that's Harry Dawson's grandfather, and Uncle Ernest, that's Haddon's father, and another man, Robert Pigott, and she wouldn't lend my father money because he wouldn't borrow, he never would borrow. Father just had one field, he managed it on his own, he had eleven acres, but the others each had more, she cut it all up into smallholdings. Then my father he went to work for my Uncle Ernest, who never would work on the land, he used to be on these different boards, and Father used to work for him and then go and do his own field. Oh, he did work hard.

Later, the council bought the smallholdings, but before then, there were several different farmers who had them. I can remember my uncle and aunt—my father's sister, Aunt Susan. They went to East Rudham. He was steward there, and I can remember we used to go and stay, and I was there when the Dutchman came and taught them how to till the land for sugar beet when they first started to grow it. [*Was that before the First World War?*] Oh yes! I was only a little girl.

During the First World War, we made this little tea shop, you know. Of course there were no end of soldiers in the village then, more than there was in the Second War. It was a camp over the wall, where the houses are now [the council houses]* and my sister and I were at home you see, Margaret was teaching at Kelling and Doris was a little girl at home here with us. I used to do all the cooking, used to have a ten-stone bag of flour and I used to be cooking all night! Mother and Father used to get up about five o'clock in

My father, James High

Old Mrs Lynn who lived at Sunnycroft next door and the chair she always sat in.

*Mrs Johnson was actually aunt to both of Florence's parents (who were first cousins).
Florence's Grandmother High and Grandfather Pigott were brother and sister.   * The Cross Street Council Houses

the morning, getting ready for the soldiers coming in for an early morning cup of tea and then as soon as they were off duty they were in here again. We would get to bed about 3 o'clock in the morning, and get up again about half past nine or ten and start cooking again! I know mother bought great big trays of plums and I made forty plum tarts. We had an oven in this room—a Dutch oven, you know, an oven in the wall. I could cook six at a time and I'd made forty, and my sister then sold them all at dinner time.

We used to charge them a penny a piece, 6d for a tart. I used to make a great big milk-pan full of gingerbread mixture, and then cook them in tins and sell them a penny each, and a penny a cup of tea or cocoa—never had coffee, no—cocoa and tea.

One night I made this great big pan of gingerbread—of course they used to go to Sheringham, I forgot to tell you that bit—and I'd made all this gingerbread and it wouldn't rise! But the soldiers kept buying them and they said they taste all right. They kept eating them. My mother had a sitting-room upstairs and when she got tired she went up there to rest a bit, when she came down she said 'Do you know what you've done? You've put boracic powder in, instead of bicarbonate of soda!' My father nearly died, I don't think he slept all night! At any rate, when we looked out in the morning we saw the men all about, so we said, 'That's all right!' Do you know they never had any money till then. My sister and I, we worked so hard and saved a bit of money for Mother and Father.

Some of the soldiers on their way to church. On the left is the wall of the Manor House and the furthest house is Pear Tree Cottage, where Florence grew up and lived all her life.

They used to send drafts of men away. They marched to Holt station, but before they left they used to stop outside here and shout, 'Three cheers for the Wad Shop!'

After Father left off working, Uncle Ernest's boys got big, Havelock and Haddon, and they worked on the farm and there was Clifford the eldest and they didn't need my father. Somehow or other he managed to buy a pony, I don't know how they managed it, Mother and Father, and they went to Sheringham with the chickens and rabbits and eggs and that sort of thing. And I always remember Mother telling us when she was coming out of Sheringham, she counted what money she'd taken and it was twenty shillings. Those visits were twice a week, we used to go round buying eggs and garden produce to take to Sheringham. My mother had some big houses in Sheringham, good customers, and she'd get an order, and she'd say, 'You got to go to Sheringham with a chicken' and we'd get on the bike and we'd go back to Sheringham.

Mum was over 46 when she had my youngest sister. Fancy over twenty years having children, what a life. We were seven girls and two boys. My older sister went away when Grandmother went. My mother's three sisters had gone to Middlesborough, and when my grandfather died my grandmother and her eldest daughter went to join them, and Father and Mother came to live up here.

Grandmother and Grandfather [Gabriel and Elizabeth Pigott] lived in this house. They came here in 1850. Before that it was the village almshouse: there was one big room with a fire-place at either end, each with its own door, and there was an old couple at this end and an old couple at that end. Well then, when Grandfather and Grandmother got married, Mrs Johnson—or 'Aunt Johnson' they called her—had it rebuilt for Grandmother and Grandfather. When Father and Mother came here there was still just the two rooms. Well as we got bigger that was not enough bedrooms. I always remember we had two beds in this room, Dick and Edmund slept in the same bedroom as us! Between the house and Church Lane was just a shed, a lean-to, and they asked Aunt Johnson if she'd have the walls raised up and make two extra rooms. We've been here ever since. Nearly ninety years I've lived here. [*Now Pear Tree Cottage*]

Florence has credited her great aunt, 'Aunt Johnson', with the buying and converting of the original almshouse, but Sarah Ann Pigott didn't marry William Johnson until 1869. When the Church sold the almshouse in 1849 it may have been William's father, John Francis Johnson, who bought it and subsequently leased it to Florence's grandfather Gabriel Pigott and his wife. In Florence's time, when she and her brothers and sisters were all getting too big to sleep in one room, 'Aunt Johnson' was well established at the Manor, and had the means to do the alteration for her brother Gabriel's daughter and for her family.

Father was a quiet, gentle man, I never did know him to hit me except once. Mother was the one who kept order—we weren't allowed to talk at the table—if Mother looked at us, that was enough! But Father, he once hit me with his hat. We had cows, you see, and we had to drive them home once we came home from school. Well, I'd come home without doing the cows home, and I was told to go back. I said I wouldn't go, so he took his hat and layed into me and I soon went for the cows!

We always used to hang our stockings up at Christmas. We got a penny in the toe and an apple and an orange and a handkerchief and a hair ribbon. The stockings were hung up in the

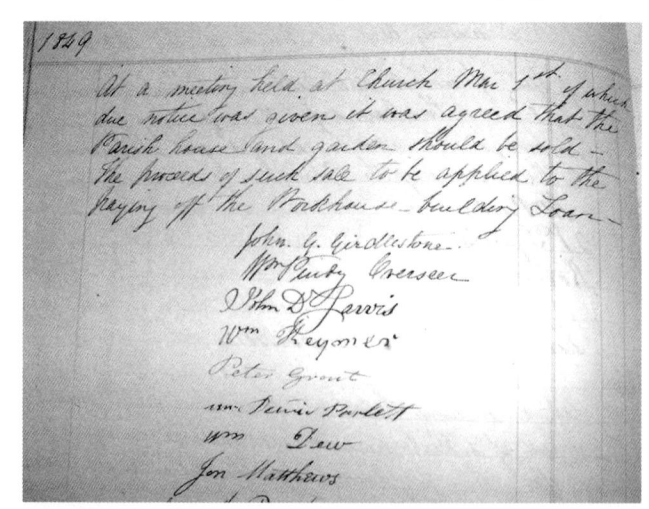

The above page, from one of the church books of Vestry Meetings, may refer to the selling of Pear Tree Cottage when it belonged to the church and was still an almshouse.

other room at Christmas, they put them there on purpose because we were awake so early we weren't allowed to come down till that was daylight. There used to be a penny on the side of Mother's and Father's bed, and whoever wished them a Merry Christmas first, had the penny! But we were never allowed to go and spend it unless Mother told us, and then we had to bring the sweets home and share them. We always had to do that. That was learning us not to be greedy, wasn't it?

I remember we got up a concert, we always had an instrument of some kind. I remember singing a solo, with a great big music book. What did I sing? 'Won't You Buy My Pretty Flowers.' I pretended I was Mrs Pigott, she used to open her mouth and sing! I remember once we were all in the big bedroom—we were playing at making fields. That's all we knew, you see, farming. We were making the fields out of buttons from Mother's button tin.

When Dick and Alice first started at school, my mother had to pay for them, tuppence a week. They went to school one day without the money and they sent them home again. I suppose Mother hadn't got the money to give them, I don't know, or she hadn't got any change or something. It was a long walk, wasn't it, in the rough hard weather. A long way to go, and you know, we only had one pair of boots.

When my sister started teaching, she was ashamed to walk up to the school. Sometimes you had chilblains and you couldn't get your boots on. They had iron plates on the heels and we used to have to clean them Saturday nights, Margaret and I, and I remember we were quarrelling one Saturday night who should blacken and who should shine. They used to be wet sometimes, and they wouldn't let us do it on a Sunday you know. My sister she got the blacking brush and she dubbed it down my face. I come howling in, and Father went for Margaret. She pushed Father, she thought he was going to hit her you see, and he fell back into the swill-pan. Oh, she was frightened! He pretended he was hurt. He used always to go to bed at nine, Father did, because he had to be up early in the morning. She crept up into the bedroom and kissed him, she thought he was asleep, but he was awake, poor old fellow! Mother was ever so ambitious for us all, I mean she put Dick to brick-laying here, and Alice went to Sarah's. Alice never had a lot of ambition of any kind. And Hannah, my sister who lived in Briston (Beck her name was), she was a dress-maker. Margaret was teaching, and I started to be a teacher, but I failed.

Richard Joseph High, Florence's eldest brother Dick.*

For Dick High's story, see his daughter Freda Morse, p 198-200

I went in for the pupil-teacher exam, and I failed. That was when Holt school was in New Street. I went to Holt school for the examination. [*Did you only try once?*] I didn't *try* to pass it. I could have passed it, but I was crazy to get into the shop. I loved shop-work. Of course I was seventeen when I left school. Then my brother next to me, Edmund, was a grocer. He was apprenticed to the International Stores. Of course Muriel was the baby, and she stayed at home. Margaret was clever: she could play the organ and she could make people sing. She had correspondence classes through the post, and that's how she got so she could be more than a pupil-teacher you see, but of course my mother couldn't afford to let her go to college. It's a shame really, isn't it, people had the brains but there was no chance for them. When my father got the sack, he was working at Bayfield and my mother took my brother Dick away too. They wouldn't let him stop. They apprenticed him to a bricklayer at Holt, to a Mr Woods, for half a crown a week. And he used to pay that to an old lady called Mrs Igmore for his lodging. She lived in Bluestone Row and Mother used to cook things for Dick and we used to say 'Oh Mother, give us a bit,' and she'd say 'You can't have that, that's for Dick!' We used to have to walk to Holt and take him his food and then he came home at weekends, then he'd walk back to work.

Then they managed to buy him a bicycle, and that had cushion tyres, you know, just a rubber. That was ever so hard, and very often he'd come home with the tyre round his neck, and that had come out of the rim! We used to have to come in here and light the fire—we had heaters in those days and irons. We used to heat them red hot, and hold them round this rim to melt the cement to put the tyre on.

When he had learned his trade, Dick worked at Sheringham and we used to go with the donkey cart to meet him on a Saturday.

Florence remembers her brother Edmund

(recorded and written by her cousin Mary Lemmon)

Once at brewing time, my younger brother Edmund nearly lost his life. We were holding hands and swinging back and forth, singing 'His Love Makes Us Ready To Die' (we weren't allowed to sing songs, only hymns) and his hand slipped from mine, and he fell into the bath full of nearly boiling beer where it had been put to cool. How he survived I shall never know, but he was pulled out and wrapped in a clean cotton sheet and his life was saved.

Edmund loved music and when he got older he longed for a gramophone. My father refused to let him buy one, saying that if he had one of those things he'd play songs. Edmund promised he'd use it only for hymns and band music, and in the end, being Edmund, he had his way, and he got one. Imagine his dismay when he'd paid for it and he found he was given a free record. It was 'Squeeze her, Squeeze her, Ebenezer'. The temptation to play it became too great. Care had to be taken that Father didn't hear it, and so my young sister was set to watch for his return from feeding the chickens housed up the street, while we all enjoyed this 'wicked' record!

Now the clouds of war were gathering. My elder brother Dick, was unfit, but Edmund was 'called up' and sent to France. We missed him very much, but life had to go on.

My mother had a habit of sitting quietly on her own after we'd all gone to bed. It was on one of these nights, a beautiful moonlit night, that she heard Edmund call her. She hurried to the door thinking he had been granted leave but no one was there. She knew then, what was to be confirmed later, that she would never see Edmund again. Like so many young men, Edmund had died in France.

An R.A.M.C. Chaplain found his bible and sent it to my parents. He had died on 7th May of his wounds. He who had been so full of fun and laughter, whose rich voice had given us so much pleasure, would never laugh and sing in this world again.

My husband was a soldier in the Hertford regiment. He survived the war, but was invalided back to England with trench feet, lungs damaged by gas, and the Mons Star. Here he was attached to the Military Police, until his discharge. We received no pension, although he was often ill due to 'the gas', and he had to work as a labourer to a building firm.

Our own two sons were called upon to fight in another war but thankfully returned safely, one from the Catering Corps and one from the R.A.S.C. My grandchildren and great-grandchildren are often with me and my life is full of interest.

So much has changed, the chapel my people fought so hard to build is closed through lack of support, even the name of my cottage has changed—but I can still sit here and remember.

Edmund George High who was killed in France 1917

[*For more of Florence's memories, see pages 124 and 282.*]

Jimmy High

James Henry High was born in Cross Street in 1881 and he worked on the land before he left school at the age of 11. He boarded out of the village in his apprentice blacksmith years, and later married a Sheringham girl and started a business there in Priory Road. He became an important man in Sheringham. His early life, however, belongs to Salthouse, and the following excerpts are taken from his autobiography, by kind permission of his granddaughter Gillian Read.

My father (Henry) was the eldest son of a family of sixteen, and his parents were of humble descent. As is only natural with such a family, they suffered a great deal of privation. Some characteristics of my father must now be related. He had no schooling during his boyhood, although in later life he taught himself to read. He was a local preacher of the Methodist chapel, often very much in demand. He had a nice suave manner, enabling him to mix with rich and poor alike. Mother (Mary) came from the same humble stock, she had to support her parents as her father was an invalid.

My parents kept ducks, and I have known dealers to wait all night if there was any hatching in progress. They would give a shilling for each duckling—a good price that—and their object was quick profit. These ducklings were fattened up by forced feeding and would be killed in six weeks, which is why they fetched such a good price.

It was my job on Saturdays, when there was no school to attend, to go on the farm where my father was employed. I had to follow the plough picking up worms for the ducks that did not get sold, as it was only those that came early in the season that attracted dealers.

[Several of the older residents in Salthouse today tell about the trade in just-hatched ducklings—with different explanations of what the dealers wanted them for!]

My father always had livestock of his own even when working for a master. He was what is known as a 'Common-Righter', which meant he had the right to graze a certain number of stock on the heath. This heath had an area of about one hundred acres, mainly furze, but quite a lot of grass.

LOST ON THE HEATH

My eldest brother would by this time be out at work, so it became my job during the winter months to take the old pony my father had to the heath and also to bring it back at night.

On one occasion I could not find the old pony at all, snow was on the ground and it

Jimmy and his first wife Laura.

Jimmy, the son of Henry High, was first cousin to Florence (on previous pages).

was also a bit foggy, so that it got dark sooner than usual. I was then very nervous in the dark and so, on returning from my search, I found another boy who had a pony and a cart. He had been using the cart to collect a load of firewood from the heath. I kept with him rather than face the journey home alone. This would be about five in the afternoon but he got in a muddle so the time passed away very quickly. Presently we started for home and came by a roundabout way, experiencing more trouble as the load of wood kept slipping. When I eventually arrived home I walked indoors quite unconcerned, only to find that everyone was greatly put out by my non-appearance. My father was out looking for me, and did not return until about half an hour later, this would be about 9 pm. He was absolutely overcome, and I think tears were general as we all thought that he was going to die. He had called out several of the men to go and look for me. They had been shouting my name and wondering what had happened to me, thinking doubtless that I had fallen and injured myself in some lonely spot where I might lay for hours untraced. No doubt it also occurred to them that I might have been captured by some gypsy band, who were frequently on the common.

FURZE FOR THE FIRE

On another occasion we were sitting at home shivering from the cold, owing to a lack of fuel and doubtless hungry as well. My father came in and saw us sitting there so glum. 'I'll have no more of this' he cried, and went out. He came back about two minutes later with the biggest load of furze I have ever seen one man carry. I ought to explain that the fireplace was of the old-fashioned, open-hearth type. Into the hearth went two of the faggots. He wasn't going to have his children cold, not he, but he had forgotten there was a beam of wood reaching right across the top of the fireplace. The flames shot up and outwards, or so it appeared to me. Presently they caught the beam and with that we ran out of the room, shrieking for help. Our home was on fire. My mother jawed my father for his panicky ways, and I think that even he was warm by this time.

MAN'S WORK AT AGE ELEVEN

When I look at boys of the present age and compare them with those of my childhood, I feel a sense of alarm. I was entrusted at the age of 11 with a team of horses and a wagon, driving them over bridges with no side-rails and laden so heavily that the wagon would sway with the load. I used to sit sideways on the shaft-horse, trotting across the fields or marshes, and the faster they went the better I was pleased. I should explain to those of my readers not versed in the ways of farming that there were no reins to the front horse. He was governed by touches of the whip, or by various calls. They all were trained to this language and only the bad ones amongst them would cause any trouble by refusing to acknowledge this language and, more often than not, temper was the cause of their troubles. I remember having a young colt amongst the team one day, and this colt was not used to the language. When I shouted for him to go forward he came round to where I was walking beside his shoulder. I was not expecting this, and consequently he trod on my foot. I can never remember how I got out of the way of the team when this happened.

It was a boy's job to cart water from the water pit to the stockyards. This was done with a water-tank on wheels pulled by one horse, a rotary pump being out of the question in those times. The water had to be drawn up by the old-style pump. I used to ride on the horse's back and guide him into the pit, and back the tank up to the deep part so it was not so far for me to lift the jet. A good horse would pull this load out of the pit but another would refuse, and that meant getting another horse to pull with him to shift the load. This meant, with the procedure I followed, that I either had to sit there till someone came to find out what had happened to the water-cart, or get wet in going for help. I have had the latter experience.

This is Robin Cooke, a bit older than Jimmy on the church occasion, but he is wearing much the same clothing as Jimmy.

CHASED OUT OF CHURCH

Writing of water-tanks reminds me of a queer experience I once had. I was told to take a tank of water to the church where some repairs were being done. I took my load to the church door, left my horse and went inside to find someone to tell me where the water should be left. Now at that time I would be wearing leather leggings, heavy boots, a large cap pulled over my eyes and with the stick in my hand would be tapping on the legs in an idle way, while the boots trampling around added to the noise I was creating, which was intensified in the atmosphere of the church. I could not see anyone in the church, so I went in further, but just then I heard a noise in the steeple. Yes! There was someone coming. I was still clumping around, and tapping my leggings with the stick as was my habit, when the sound of steps seemed to quicken considerably. It seemed as though someone was coming down the steps from the steeple in a mighty hurry. When the footsteps were heard at the bottom of the steps, I heard the door flung open and just then a very loud voice addressed itself presumably to me, asking 'Are you a Christian?' I turned and found that the voice was that of my master's brother, a very religious man, so I said softly 'No, Sir.' With that he ordered me to remove my cap but, before I could attempt to take it off, he had knocked it off, taken me by the scruff of the neck and pushed me outside, and threw my hat after me. When I related my adventure with my master's brother to the men on the farm they were highly amused, one even went so far as to say he mistook me for a foreigner.

MINDING THE SHEEP

My job during the summer would be minding sheep on the marshes. I have had as many as twenty score, and had to count them night and morning. Anyone who has had any dealings with sheep will appreciate the work I was called upon to do. If one ran away the others would follow, and if one went through a hole in the fence then all the others would follow suit. I got to understand them eventually, and after they had had a good feed of grass I would drive them into a corner of the marsh. When one of them laid down the others would soon follow its example. I had no hurdles to make a fold, but my idea worked. Perhaps they would lie for an hour, when I could get a bit of fun with one of the other youthful shepherds. I would sometimes have to go about half a mile away to join some other boy.

When the sheep were restive one of them would get up after only a short time, and all would soon follow its example, and I had to leave my games to rush back, but I got my own back on them. I would rush them over a bridge that had no parapet, some would fall over into the ditch and have to swim under the bridge. Great fun for a lonely boy.

I have spent some lonely hours on these marshes tending sheep. Up at four in the morning so that the sheep could get a rest during the summer heat—that was the farmer's idea, not mine. It was two miles from any other habitation and it seemed twenty times that distance at times, especially when it thundered and rained, and then I got frightened. I used to cry and run miles to get in someone's company but all the same I had some good days as well as bad. Some days other boys would come minding sheep and we'd all meet at the pond. One might have sheep to mind, another bullocks to look after, another cows. These would be great days when we met. If the weather was fine, and sometimes there would be several such days, we would all meet at this pond about ten in the morning. The bullocks might stray to the other side and, as a punishment, we used to rush them down a steep part of the pond into deep water and make them swim across. It was quite a good distance, and I have often wondered since that they were not all drowned.

We were quite expert at fishing for flat fish in the pond, and our sole tackle was our bare hands. This was our method. First of all we would wade in and startle the fish, which would dart off quickly at our approach, putting up a muddy track as they fled close to the bottom. They would then dart back and hide in their own smoke-screen, whereupon we would touch them with both hands, and so fling them out of the water. Another part of

Thunder over the marsh

the pond was shallow and had a cockle bed, and also clams could be found there. These delicacies used to attract many people seeking for them.

To show things were not always as pleasant as this I had better relate a winter's tale. I was sent into a field to mind some sheep on a bitterly cold day. Snow had fallen, and the sheep did not seem inclined to stir so I sat down to rest. Sometime later my father came to look for me, and I heard him say afterwards that it was a good job for me that he did or I should have died of cold. I felt myself sink into a kind of coma.

I worked for the same farmer as did my father, but when this farmer died the farm was split up into smallholdings which were taken up by my uncle who had about sixty acres, my father who farmed about thirty, and another who had a similar amount of land to that held by my father.

My father's land was not enough to afford me sole employment, as my eldest brother was helping him, so I was found a job with the other smallholders at the princely sum of six shillings a week. This was almost double what I had previously been paid so I was well content.

All the above kept cows, and I (being the youngest) was posted to the task of cow-keeper. They had agreed to run all the stock together to minimise expenses and this brought me back to my old haunts where I used to mind the sheep. The cows were not so difficult a job to mind as the sheep had been, and I soon learnt to milk them, for which I got two shillings extra from all three smallholders each week.

I was not nearly so lonely on the marshes during this time as I had previously been, as I was allowed a dog to help me with the cows and also to protect me against the bull. The boy who kept stock for another dealer also had a bull on the marsh, and we took great delight in letting them get together. Sometimes they would butt each other for hours, and when they fought as they invariably did and the fight brought them into the pond we were highly delighted.

In the summer we often used to take all our clothes off and run around naked all day. That will give my readers an idea of the desolate nature of the marshland. One day a boy who was sent to mind the bullocks declared he could ride one. We at once challenged him to do this. We helped him to capture the mount so that he could get on. He rode it all right. He was so pleased with his prowess that he rode it too long, and the animal got tired of such unusual treatment. It made a dash for the pond, walked in till it was nearly covered, and there the boy had to sit, as he could not swim, until the bullock decided that he had had enough. The animal truly got his own back as the boy had to sit there naked all the time.

I was not always confined to the marshes. In the winter I was given other jobs to do, such as driving a horse and cart laden with manure from the stockyard to the field. Part of my task on these occasions would be to supply the men spreading manure in the field with drink. I suppose it must have been thirsty work.

The custom of those days was to entrust the pouring out of the beer or stout to a young boy, who for this reason was called the 'skinker', who then had to hand round the drinks, and of course had his own share when the men had been served.

EXPERIMENT WITH DRINKING

One day I was entrusted with a two gallon jar of beer and stout to cart to the men in the field. To do this I had to go down a lane, a nice short one that was well-screened by high banks. A feeling came over me that it would be a nice sensation to get drunk, so I stopped the horse in this lane, well away from observation, pulled the cork out of the bottle, and filled the drinking-horn three times before going on to the men in the field, where I was as usual given another drink. This would total about three pints, not bad for a small boy, but as time went on I began to lose control of my feelings. I felt dazed the whole of the day after that, and never remember how I got home. I believe the foreman noticed my condition when I had to go and help him, he also liked to drink a great deal. My people were out when I did get home so I was fortunately recovered by the time they returned.

GUY FAWKES DAY

I am certain that there was not much in the village round that did not have my mark on it. I'll just give you an idea of the fun we had on Guy Fawkes day. I had heard someone say that to get a loud explosion a piece of tube about eighteen inches in length was required. This was to be stopped at one end, and the other end left open. A hole was to be drilled near the stopped end. That was the weapon. Now for the bang. Get some gunpowder, ram it into the tube then plug it. Now to create the noise. Light a fire and heat in this a rod of iron. This was the 'touch'. Get a certain distance away from the tube, and apply the heated rod to the tube above the drilled hole. The heat from the rod would ignite the gunpowder and cause an explosion. It was a simple sort of weapon and one that was well within my capabilities as an apprentice smith, so I made six of these pop-guns, and armed with them, we began our evening's sport. There were originally four of us in the team, but we soon had a crowd as our guns were a great success and were really making right loud explosions.

Someone suggested that he was thirsty, and we all found that we were in the same condition, so off to the local pub, where we stayed till turning-out time, 10 pm. On wending our way home we were joined by two others and we were all feeling merry and it was suggested that it would be fun to set fire to one of the shelters on the marshes. These shelters were used for the cattle for their comfort in rough or wet weather. No sooner was this idea suggested, than we were all for it. We set fire to one, then lay down to watch the blaze. 'There's another one over there!' said one of the party. Off we went and it soon joined its fellow for our amusement. This did not satisfy our mania for fires, so we went from one to another of the shelters and from there to the fringe of the beach where there was some gorse, this too followed in flames. Then to a hill to watch our handiwork. Then away to a barn containing straw. See how little ideas always lead to bigger things. This barn was the property of a farmer whose son was with us on this adventure, and we had great difficulty in restraining him from setting the barn and straw on fire.

I think that we had by this time worked some of the beer out of our system and we were afraid our chain of fires would lead to our discovery. This boy did succeed in setting fire to some few portions of straw, but we soon had that out. We got him away from there as soon as we possibly could. Just to finish up, we burned the bottom of a hayrick.

We lost a real good friend over that night's performance. One of the ladies in Salthouse had taken an interest in the young men of the village, providing us with cricket sets and so forth, but after the Guy Fawkes episode which I have just related, she gave us up altogether. The reason for this action was that one of her uncle's shelters had been burnt down that night. It was a bad day's work for us in that respect.

In mentioning guns, I might say that I have always been fond of using a gun, but never had enough to purchase one, and indeed if I had had the money I would not have been allowed to buy one. The outcome of this was that I made one. This weapon was made from one of the pop guns I have already mentioned, which I fastened on to a suitably shaped stick to form the stock. My ammunition was provided by collecting small round stones. My crude weapon was used principally against birds. I would stalk up to them, and apply a match to the touch hole when I had got my aim, and that was that. I was doing this one day when the idea occurred to me that the more gunpowder I put in, the more force I should be able to muster. I did this and fired the gun which went off with a terrific crack. I found that the barrel was bent almost double, and I had lost most of the flesh off my fingers, and that finished my experiments in armaments.

In mentioning gunpowder, I might have said that we used to eat this to make us strong, and I used this to advantage in my first advent into the boxing world. We bought some boxing gloves—we being the four already mentioned, but not by name, for obvious reasons—and we would practise the art behind a hill near the beach. When I first started, my nose used to bleed at the lightest touch, but after a time, and thanks to several liberal doses of gunpowder, I managed to overcome that handicap. I finally was able to stand up to some terrific hammerings, and also to give some. I liked this pastime immensely.

Other excerpts from Jimmy High's Autobiography appear on pages 118 and 283.

Tracey Wright describes Gabriel Pigott the marshman

Tracey Wright (now Tracey Large, and mother of 4 children) made a project on Salthouse, when she was at school, which filled two large ring-binders. She has very kindly allowed some of her research to appear in this book. On page 140 she sums up the complicated Heath Award of 1781, and here, on this page, her summary of Gabriel Pigott and the true story of his mother who sought refuge in the church porch, provides an introduction to this famous Salthouse marshman:

TRACEY

I had to do a project for my history C S E at Sheringham High School and I chose to do mine on Salthouse. I got top grades in History, and enjoyed doing the project so much. I then found out more when I was 17 to 18 years old. I lived in Norwich so I used to sit in the library going through all their archives. When my project was finished, I presented it to my dad.

THREE IMPORTANT EARLY SALTHOUSE CHARACTERS:

Gabriel Pigott *(the famous marshman)*, and his two sisters **Sarah Ann Pigott** *(who became the redoubtable Mrs Johnson of the Manor, see p 235)* and **Hannah Pigott** *(referred to as 'Granny High', the Matriarch of the High family, see p 149)* — all suffered eviction in their childhood and a temporary home in the church porch, as Tracey describes on this page. All three are foundation stones in the story of Salthouse.

The name Gabriel Pigott is to be found in any history or Project on Salthouse. He was born in 1821 and lived in the post office but moved into Heath Cottage round cross street and now he lies buried close to the south porch of St Nicholas church. His strength and mind power came from his mother for when evicted from her cottage, she took her family and campaigned in the church Porch, one of the last surely to seek such refuge in this part of the county, forced with such determination her landlord. Relented and she was Returned to her cottage.

Gabriels life centred around the wildlife of the area and when he became a marshman he gradually built up a Reputation as one of the best wildfowlers along this side of the coast. His gun was Responsible for supplying many Rare species wich included a black stork and montaglu harriers, white egles and avocets to the collections of individuals and organisations including the norwich museam, and to show how common avocets were gabriel used their eggs to make puddings.

Churchwarden Mrs R. Matthews (1925-30) in her 'commonplace book', which was discovered in the church chest, noted that the church must once have been a sanctuary church, because of the deep slot in the wall beside the north porch door where a beam could be kept and pulled out to barricade the door from inside.

Gabriel Pigott

H. N. Pashley, the naturalist and taxidermist living at Cley in Gabriel's time, gives us a first-hand description of this grand old man of Salthouse, who is the ancestor of so many Salthouse people today. Pashley's book, 'Notes on the Birds of Cley Norfolk', was first published in 1925, and was republished by Christopher Frost in 1992.

In his 'Recollections', at the beginning of the book, Pashley remembers the men who supplied him with specimens:

First and foremost among these men was Gabriel Pigott. He was (as a gentleman said of him when speaking to me about him) one of Nature's gentlemen. He was a fine portly man with a long beard; he would have made a good model for a Patriarch. He had a fine deep voice too, and his character was in keeping with the outer man. He and I have had many a shore tramp together and he has sent me many a specimen in summer plumage; all this was long before a close time was thought of.

I was also acquainted with several good old gunners later on. Two or three of them were Salthouse men, one of them named Moy, who when I knew him had given up shooting. I have often talked with him and he told me of having taken the eggs of the avocet ('Clinkers' he called them) when a boy, and of the alterations on the marshes which drove them away.

This photograph of Gabriel Pigott (c1885) was in the possession of his granddaughter Florence Radley, when 'Sea Pie' (C.D. Borrer) came to search for those who still remembered him.

The following excerpts are taken from an article by 'Sea Pie' which appeared in 'The Shooting Times and Country Magazine', 6 November 1959:

Last of the Dyke Reeves

Time was when men who lived in the fenlands of Lincolnshire and East Anglia, and looked after the dykes and ditches and marsh drains and sea-banks, were known as 'dyke-reeves'. Certain landowners and village elders in areas around the Wash had the onus planked firmly on their shoulders of seeing that their marshes were 'dyched scowred and clensed as often as neyde shall require by the lordes freeholders and copyholders', according to one 16th-century document.

I suppose old Gabriel Pigott of Salthouse-beside-the-sea on the North Norfolk coast may well have been a lineal descendant of some ancient dyke-reeve, for the above quaint description describes his work exactly, though he lived as recently as the latter part of the 19th century and his title was no more romantic than that of 'marsh-man'.

But the name of Gabriel Pigott is remembered today, not only as that of an amender of marsh drains and cattle paths but as the greatest wildfowler and specimen hunter that Salthouse ever produced—a man to rank with Ramm of Cley and the John Thomases of Breydon. Some of the rarest birds in many Norfolk collections fell to his gun, for in those far-off days the arrival of any feathered rarity was the signal for every local fowler to set out at once in its pursuit. He is remembered as the last of that semi-amphibious race of marsh-men who lived almost entirely by means of gun and net.

SHOOTING THE AVOCETS

In those days, when Gabriel was young, no sort or kind of protection for birds or animals existed, and in later years he told how returning punt-gunners emptied their great muzzle loaders by shooting the avocets to avoid the trouble of 'drawing the charges'.

When the craze for egg-collecting was at its height in the 1870s, Gabriel earned many an honest pound by finding the nests of the Montagu's harriers which bred on the wild uplands above Salthouse and Kelling.

But his heart was forever on his beloved marshes. His work as a marsh-man gave him wonderful opportunities for wildfowling, and many a rare specimen in the Norwich museum or the famous Connop collection bears witness to his prowess.

Perhaps his most spectacular trophy was a black stork, which frequented Salthouse marshes one April, and was reputed to bear a charmed life, so eagerly was it pursued and so frequently shot at without success by the local gunners. At length the great bird became utterly unapproachable, as it constantly fed in an open part of the flats. One foggy morning, however, Gabriel, who of course knew every yard of his ground when making his way across the marshes, was surprised to encounter what he first took to be a decayed post standing upright in the mud. When the supposed wooden object suddenly rose into the air, it was lucky for Gabriel that he had his gun all ready, for the stork almost instantly 'vanished in the thick', as Gabriel used to put it when telling the story, adding that 'I fired where I thought it ought to be.'

TWO WHITE-TAILED EAGLES

Gabriel Pigott is said to have accounted for two white-tailed eagles in the course of his many adventures ashore and afloat. These great birds were by no means uncommon in winter on the salt marshes and inland heaths of East Anglia, for in the middle of the last century sea eagles nested in many of the wilder districts of Scotland. Gabriel is credited with more than one bagged on the upland warrens, where these great creatures were attracted by the swarming rabbits.

My friend Mr Fred Pashley, still living at Cley, well remembers Gabriel Pigott as a living link with the days when much of what is now grazing marshland was a vast stretch of shingle and mud, partly covered by every flowing tide. The line of the beach was in places half-a-mile further to the north than at present [*Sea Pie was writing in the 50s*] and a tidal channel, the outline of which can yet be traced below the Dun Cow, ran up to Salthouse village. Indeed, so rapidly has the sea encroached upon the land during the past hundred years that I have myself talked with men who carted hay from fields now far beneath the sea.

In the year 1853 a protective grassy sea-wall was constructed for a distance of some two miles from Weybourne Sluice as far as the east bank adjoining Cley levels. No doubt Gabriel Pigott, as a true dyke-reeve, worked on this causeway which was to have so great an effect on his beloved Salthouse marshes. It was a big undertaking, but ten years after it was completed the sea, banked up by a northerly gale, breached the bank—which was never properly repaired.

None of it remains at the present time, the whole being completely buried by thousands of tons of shingle driven over its site on the brackish marshland. A mere fifty years or so ago, I often walked along the top of this dyke. Many delectable salt pools haunted by diving duck and grebes are now under the beach; and many a wintry day I have spent beneath the shelter of the old bank waiting for fowl to come in off the sea. On such occasions it was easy to picture the scene as it must have appeared in Gabriel Pigott's boyhood.

I recently made a pilgrimage to Salthouse in company with Mr Lindsay Fleming, a noted Sussex antiquary, in order to ascertain if memory of the old marsh-man still remained green in his native village. We first visited the splendid old church, which has weathered so many centuries of storm and sunshine, high above the marshland and the red roofs of Salthouse village, that ancient land mark visible to distant ships far out at sea beyond the Sheringham shoal. Here we discovered Gabriel's gravestone among the long grass beside the south door. Within a hundred yards of his last resting place is the little house wherein he lived and died.

We were fortunate enough to find two elderly ladies, granddaughters of Gabriel, still residing in the village and one of them living in that same cottage, Pear Tree Cottage, which was Gabriel's home for the last 39 years of his life. It remains exactly as in his lifetime. The date 1850—which is the year when he went there—is inscribed above the doorway, and a pear tree planted by Gabriel still flourishes over the front wall. The elder of his granddaughters (Alice) vividly remembers him and tells of how he would come home laden with fish and fowl, lean his muzzle-loading guns and his nets against the wall and place his powder-flask and wads in a dry corner of the shelf. I sometimes wish that something could have been added to his epitaph to the effect that here lies the last of the Norfolk dyke-reeves.

Sea Pie

Pashley records the last bird shot by Gabriel to have been: 'a fine adult male avocet' on 17 July 1887, two years before his death.

Jim Radley

Jim is the son of Florence Radley, whose memories were recorded by Ray High's wife, Eileen (see page 149). He is the grandson of James High and the great-grandson, on his mother's side, of the famous marshman Gabriel Pigott.

Jim, who was so enthusiastic about this book, and provided so many of the photographs and so much of the information, died on 6th December 2002, just 7 months before it was published.

1985— four generations
Jim Radley, his mother Florence (aged 95), Jim's eldest daughter Susan, and her two boys, Stuart and Paul.

It was over towards the East Bank where Grandfather Gabriel used to get his shooting. He was also a Dyke Reeve and he was in charge of the sluices, to open them when the marsh flooded. Mother always said that Gabriel dug an urn up off one of the hills on the heath and that should be in Norwich museum. I don't think Mother could remember much about my great-grandfather Gabriel, but my Aunt Alice who lived down the street from her, she was the older granddaughter and remembered him.

Of course they used muzzle-loading guns with loose shot and powder in those days, and I can remember Mother saying that Grandmother, if she wanted to clean the flues in the copper, would get a little bit of gunpowder and wrap it in a piece of paper, and stick it up the oven. She'd hold the door shut with the poker and that would go *whoom* and clean the flues out! My mother told me that her own mother, Grandmother High, used to do it.

Knowledge was very sparse you know, the only learning they had was from the Bible. My grandfather learnt to read and write from the Bible. They were so down-trodden. The Church and the State were all-powerful, and I think had it not been for the Methodist Chapel religion, there would have been a revolution—their fervour went into their preaching. That was waning a bit by my time, but Mother used to tell such tales about those prayer meetings!

As children we had no restrictions on us and that was lovely. We all walked to school—traffic was so slow then, it was the natural thing to do. In the past, when people were so poor, poaching was not seen as a crime amongst the village people but more a way of life for some people, and as boys we'd be looking for game on the way to school. If we spotted any partridges or pheasants over the hedge, one of us would go round and put them up while the rest set behind the hedge, then we'd jump up when the covey flew over, trying to frighten them into the telegraph wires hoping to get one, but we never did!

One particular morning I was late going to school and I was on my own. Just before you get to the school there's a road come down off the heath, Wood Lane we call it. There used to be a stack in the corner of the field there, and this particular morning there were some pheasants behind it. Of course we all carried catapults, and I crept in hoping perhaps I'd get a shot at one of them. Of course when I went round they'd all gone, but there was a heap of straw from the stack and I thought perhaps they were hiding in there. I was kicking into this straw *and suddenly an arm come out!* . . . I can tell you my feet didn't touch the ground from there to school . . . of course there was a tramp asleep in the straw and I'd woken him up poor chap.

To get home from school quickly, we'd have hoops! We had little money, so you made hoops of what was thrown about and Father would cut the spokes out of the rim of a bicycle wheel. You'd run a stick inside the wheel to guide it, and you'd get home in ten minutes from Kelling easily, or you'd lose the thing going down the hill!

It's so different today. We're too careful because the situation has developed whereby we've got to be, but years ago you never thought about locking a door, it would seem very foreign to have done so, and if you went anywhere to catch a bus, you'd bike in and leave your bike lying in the hedge and that'd be there when you came back. Salthouse was a lovely place to live you know, it was so free and easy. Nobody cared where you went; you roamed the fields and the marshes. In summer time we'd be running rabbits in the harvest field. It would be nothing to get twenty or thirty rabbits out of a field, and you can imagine how many more must have got away. The heath would be closed in summer: nobody was allowed on there with a dog from 1st April to 1st September.

In those days when things were so poor there were a lot of tramps about, and if a tramp called at a house he was always given something—you don't know, do you, you could be in the same position, couldn't you! Billy West who lived in Cross Street, I remember him telling a tale about Harry Fitt who came from Kelling. He walked to the North Country for work—where in the North Country I don't know—but he walked there; and he walked home again because there *was* no work (as there was nowhere you see). He tramped on the way home and begged for food where he could. He said this particular day he knocked on a door (of course it wasn't allowed to beg, that was against the law) and when the man opened the door Harry could see a policeman's helmet hanging on the wall in the passage. So he said—quickly thinking—'Does Jimmy Smith the well-sinker live here?' So the feller said 'Just wait a minute and I'll go and see if I can find him', and he went in and came back with a great big piece of bread and cheese and he said 'Is this him?' Harry said, 'That's jest the feller'. That would have been between the two wars I think. But that's amazing

Nearly seventy years ago! Myself and Gerald Cubitt. We were inseparable.

how people did travel to the North Country. I suppose it was to the docks or even the coal mines, hoping for work. There was industry up there.

People of nowadays don't realise how desperately hard up people were in those days. I was fortunate because there was only me at home. But where there was a big family, how they managed goodness knows. My brother Percy was nine years older than me; he was apprenticed to a grocer at Holt and he worked long hours. I was in bed by the time he came home so we didn't spend much time together.

THE HEATH

The language of the 1781 'Heath Award' is very hard to understand, but the part that always pleases me is where it says:

'left from this day forward for all time'

The legal document says *'for all time'*. So no one can ever take it away. The Charity Commissioners are all powerful in that respect, you know, because of that being a charitable organisation. I'm one of the Heath Trustees, and we had to make new rulings because the old Heath Award let the land so that any household with a £10 hire could use the heath for grazing and rabbits and whatever, and of course they said, well, £10 hire is ridiculous today. So we had to change it, and that took us I think five or six years to settle it. We were all pretty well of the same mind, Salthouse people, but it took a long time to get it right. The heath is all powerful. That's our heritage you see, and we fought for it through all sorts of troubles and trials, so everybody is in agreement that it is sacrosanct.

Our family had two Common Rights: we had one with the house, and one with the little pightle up the road, called Rosie's Pightle because there was an old house in there. As long as you had the hearthstone, you were all right, and the whole chimney-breast was there and everything. Once Grandfather died, and I grew up, I could go and use the heath and Father could go. *[see p 140 for Common Rights]*

MY FATHER

Not that he could take much advantage of his rights though. My father came home from the first war and he'd been frozen in the trenches. He had special surgical boots but he couldn't work on the land. When the means testing was on, you had to go round a half a dozen farms to get them to say that you'd been seeking work, so he had to go round but he couldn't work on the land because of his feet. It wasn't trench feet, that's a different thing; his feet had been frozen and his ankle bone was near his heel. He was gassed as well. The means test was a dreadful thing, it really was. You see, there was no work and you couldn't get Parish Relief, or whatever the poor law was at that time, unless you'd been round seeking work. Somebody had to sign to say you'd been to that particular place, and I know several farmers wouldn't sign his paper because they said he wouldn't work; but my poor old father *couldn't* work on the land, you see. Then, when the first huts were built at Weybourne Camp around 1935, he got a job decorating

My father, a young soldier, ready for World War One.

inside the buildings and at last he really was 'on his feet'. I think that was the best time we ever had. Money-wise, things were getting better and there were more jobs about.

THE WEYBOURNE CAMP

It was an artillery practice camp. They had big guns along there, 4.5mm guns, and an aeroplane going along trailing a drogue behind it. That was red with a white net tail on the end of it. It had a great pole in the front with a weight in the bottom to keep the thing upright, and they'd fire at this as the plane dragged it along. I can remember the first rocket firing down there. They had an artillery barrage of rockets. I remember coming down Cross Street when those rockets were firing for the first time, and the house where Mrs Elsden now lives, that had a tin roof, and all the nails were jumping out of the roof and running down it. The vibration was so much!

There were gunning places all over the area, and there was a dummy aerodrome on the heath as well. On the cross roads at the top of Bard Hill—you know, the first cross roads you come to—there was a light there that they called a 'lion light'. It was a big revolving light to simulate an aerodrome. Do you know where Bix's Lane is? Well down there, which was the Deterdings' Warren, that was all part of the dummy aerodrome. We had dummy tanks and lorries all made out of canvas stood about all over the place.

Father worked down at the camp on the Nissen huts. Then as the camp progressed and got bigger, there were more Nissen huts, and they had a barrack warden stores where they issued the blankets and linen and every-

My father, Percy Radley

thing, and he had the job of stores labourer, until he became barrack warden, and the poor old boy was there until died.

In the first part of the war there was a German plane crashed on the marsh up Purdy's Drift. There was a great tank trap made out of piping right across the marsh; that ran at angles right up to the beach as well. We boys used to walk along, holding on to the uprights and walking along the pipe, that way we could walk up to this plane. There was bits of it scattered everywhere and there was bullets laid about there in their hundreds. We used to take these damn things to pieces. When I think about it now it makes me shudder: they were explosive bullets and we used to unscrew them and take the firing-pin out, you see. If we had screwed them the wrong way...

We had all sorts of different types of soldiers in the village: infantry, artillery, armour and whatever. The last thing I remember here were

Pauline Lemon Collection

Above: An Airman called Paddy, and Geoffrey Woodhouse (son of Fred and Julia), sitting in front of the tank trap across the marsh described by Jim above.

the Essex Yeomanry and they were an artillery regiment with field guns and an armoured vehicle to tow them. They were on the heath, and I remember them building that pylon. They lodged with my Aunt Alice who lived round in the council houses then, and I can remember seeing the plans and thinking how interesting that was to see them build it. It had a hoist—a lift in it—the pylon did, with a cabin at the top, and they went up in the lift to do their spell of duty there. The Eighteenth Division was here until they went to Singapore, the Norfolks and Suffolks and Cambridgeshires they were here training; they were infantry. It was them who laid the mines along here on the beach.

The mines were stored at the bottom of Cross Street behind the council houses. Do you remember how cheeses used to come years ago, two to a crate, big round cheeses, well that's how these mines were. Well, along come Jerry Sunday morning and dropped those bloody bombs on the coast road and it played hell with the soldiers, they thought he was after those mines. I don't think so though—they were hit and run raids. Anyway, after that, they laid them. There were eighteen thousand mines laid on the beach, and there were two boys got killed laying those mines. They had to prime them themselves, you see, and they weren't taught—they weren't sappers or anything like that—they were just ordinary privates. One young soldier, Leason his name was, he's buried up in the churchyard. We reckon he screwed the detonator in too tight and that blew up and killed him. I believe the villagers told the soldiers not to set them on the beach but on the marsh, because they knew they would be blown up by the first high tide. In fact, the first high tide, there was eighty blew up. The waves beat on them. If a rabbit had run over them they would have exploded they were so sensitive. After the war they come up with bull-dozers and they bull-dozed the whole beach away and I'm convinced to this day that's what caused the trouble. They broke the hard panel of the clay bank that Purdy had put down.

I know when the soldiers first came here in 1939, duck shooting was just about to start and I was talking to someone in the street and I said, 'Don't forget that'll be duck shooting tomorrow morning, so don't think that's an invasion starting!' They said later, 'Thank goodness you told us because we'd no idea.' That just show you how a silly little thing could cause all sorts of problems.

I joined up towards the end of the war, in 1943, and I went to Carlisle. I tell my children about this now. They gave me a hessian sack which I had to fill with straw. We had double bunks and the wires in the bottom were four inches apart and you lay on that. When you think I came out of a feather bed, you can imagine what that was like. My first breakfast was a spoonful of beans and a small rasher of bacon. They put a basket of bread on the table and I suppose we were about eight of us to a table, and I thought: that'll go round and that'll come to me when the time comes, and I looked at it and there weren't a bloody crumb left! So I thought, 'Well, I'll be first in the queue tomorrow morning!'

From being sheltered, you mixed with all walks of life and that rubbed all the corners off I can tell you. That was an experience I think many of us would not have missed. I know some people had a hell of a time, like poor George Cooke in Japanese imprisonment. But by and large when you think about the comradeship you developed, you would give your last shilling to anyone you knew, that was how you were. You were so reliant on one another for your life you see.

Jim, 1943

Betty Holman's photos

Roy and John on Ginger

Betty remembers:
'Ginger was our pony for us to ride but she would pull a cart too. We used to go to Holt early mornings—Mother and Father and some of us by pony and cart. We would unyoke the pony at the back of the Station pub, leave it for the day in the stable there, and get on the train for Norwich. That was a real treat. I can't remember what we did in Norwich, but I remember getting on the train, it was fantastic.'

In the garden at Pit View. Bob, Doris, Nancy and puppies. Behind is the coast road and Spring Holes where the children had a boat.

Betty remembers her father: 'He was a brilliant shot with a gun. He used to go about in his pony and cart, and he would stand up in the cart and shoot pheasants. Later on in life, he was boilerman at Weybourne Camp, but in his early years he made his living from the heath and the marsh and his allotment. He was a warrener. Rabbits were the only meat most people had in those days.'

Roy remembers going rabbiting with his father. It was his job as a boy to catch the little rabbits. He would sell them to people for rabbit pies, at a shilling for four or five in a bunch.

Doris, Peggy and Nancy in their boat. What is usually now called the duck pond, was called Spring Holes because of the deep holes made by springs along the far side. They were deep enough to drown a horse.

Walter Holman, (better known as 'Rooter')

Above: Inside the Holmans' cottage Pit View after the debris from the flood of 1953 had been cleared away.

Roy and John Holman behind Pit View, the well is on the right.

Betty says: 'The water came up to just below the level of the mantelpiece in this picture, but the things on top of the shelf stayed there. After the water had gone down we didn't go into a caravan, we came back into the house. In the picture above, that's my mother standing with the partridge, then my eldest brother John is next (he's the one who lost his arm in the mangel shredder later in life), and my father is nearest to the camera.'

Before they lived at Pit View the Holman family had lived in the Corner Cottage beside the post office. Both these houses had the 'Common Right' which meant that the occupiers were free to shoot game on the common land (the heath), and graze a cow or horse there.* Common Righters often sold rabbits to other families in the village. (see p 251)

For information on the Common Right, see p140 and 169

173

Above: The Dun Cow from the east, after a flood has been over the road. The water is still on the marsh on the right.

Left to right: Alan Holman (son of Clem), Billy Cooke (son of Robin Cooke), and John Holman (son of Walter Holman).

From the left: Peggy (née Holman), her husband Sid Emery, Herbert 'Mickie' Graveling (killed in the Korean war), Terry Holman, Sammy Dix (rolling a cigarette) and 'Tiddles' Woodhouse from Kelling.

John Hancock, gamekeeper

The following story by 'Sea Pie' about John Hancock appeared in the local newspaper together with his story on Gabriel Piggot (see p164). The date must be between 1907 and 1910.

Near Gabriel's grave we find that of another 'worthy' of Old Salthouse, this time a *'fin de siècle'* gamekeeper called John Hancock. At the beginning of the twentieth century poaching was rife in this district of wild heaths and wooded uplands, and one night when the faithful John and his son were watching their young pheasants and ducks, a rough gang came up from Holt Lowes and began stoning the keeper. John at once sent the boy home, and stood his ground till the volleys of stones became a serious matter, whereupon he 'upped his gun'—as he subsequently described to the magistrates—and shot two of the miscreants, whereupon the rest of the gang ran away.

John Hancock poses for the newspaper.

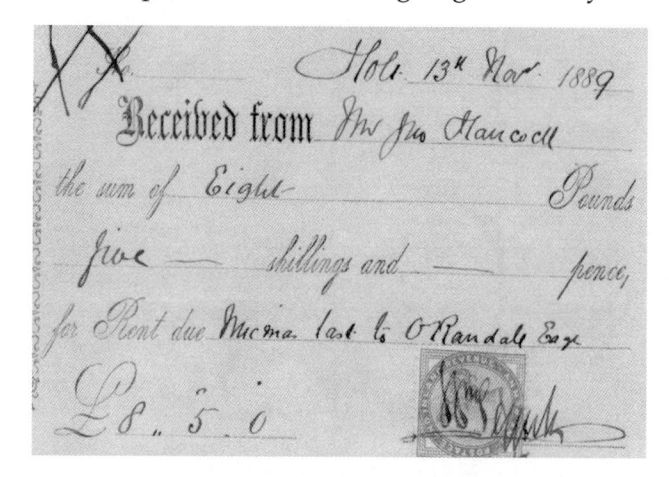

Above: A rent receipt paid to Onesiphorus Randall.

John's youngest son Arnold poses as a shot victim being revived with something out of a bottle.

Lorna and Tom Fox

Lorna and Tom Fox, just after their Diamond Wedding in March 2001. Lorna died in August the same year.

Lorna was the daughter of Leonard Hancock and granddaughter of gamekeeper John Hancock. Her great-grandfather was Samuel Hancock the baker. When Tom retired from farming they came to live in 'Lorcot' in Cross Street where generations of Hancock ancestors had lived. Lorna inherited her Aunt Amelia's organ, which John Hancock had sent for, from America. She also inherited Amelia's talent for music and played the church organ regularly in St. Nicholas' Church.
The following talk, together with the notes to her photographs, was recorded in May 2001.

Above: John Hancock gamekeeper born 1837, and Elizabeth (formerly Field) born 1843, with their children (*left to right*): Leonard (Lorna's father), Patty (eldest daughter) and Amelia, with Arnold sitting in front.

LORNA : This photo on the right is my father before the First World War. He was Coachman to Sir Edward Stearn in London. When they used to go to the country he was in charge of all the hunters, and when they were hunting, he would ride the spare horse for when Sir Edward's horse got tired.

TOM : He had the chance to be Coachman to King Edward VII. Now this is what he told me himself: he was groom at Sir Joseph Savory's, the Lord Mayor of London, and he decided he was going to leave.

LORNA : I don't remember all this.

TOM : Mrs Stearn was looking for a pack groom for her horses, and the King said to Sir Joseph

Leonard Field Hancock, groom to Sir Joseph Savory.

Savory, 'I understand your groom's leaving you and I would like him to come to me.' And the King sent word to Lorna's Dad and asked him to go for an interview, and Granddad went and they offered him the job and he turned it down.

Then the King asked him to go for a personal interview—he wanted to know why Leonard had turned the job down. He said 'If it's the money, you needn't worry about money; I'll give you anything you ask for almost.' But Lorna's Dad said 'No, I'm not going.' So the King said 'Well Hancock, I want you to forget I'm the King of England; I'm an ordinary man to you, and I want to know why you've turned this down.' 'Well, if you'd like to know' he said, 'any fool can drive your coaches!' 'How's that?' and Leonard said 'Because everything stops on the road for you; you don't have to control your horses because everything makes way for you.'

The King said 'What have you decided to do, Hancock?' and Leonard said 'I'm going pack groom to Lady Stearn.' 'Oh,' said the King, 'I shall not try to take you away from her'—for the simple reason, (but he didn't tell him this) that Lady Stearn was his special friend. It's true, that's what he told me.

LORNA : Dad never told me.

TOM : I shouldn't have known if he hadn't told me!

LORNA : He used to sit and talk to Tom.

TOM : I remember him saying, 'Any fool could drive the King's horses; everything stops for them on the road.' And he said to the King, 'A coachman that leaves you, has a job to get a job.'

LORNA : And they were paid in gold sovereigns, men on the land here were earning twelve shillings a week.

TOM : Lorna's Dad, he was a very nice lad in every shape and form, and anyone would give him nearly anything he asked for.

LORNA : He was marvellous with horses, he loved horses. That was his life.

TOM : And he could have been coachman to the King of England, but he turned it down, and I think *some*where Lorna's Mum had a letter where they were asking him to go. I can remember her saying about it; they kept it of course.

I know that's what he told me, else I shouldn't have known anything about it.

My father is standing at the head of the horses and they're all going to Ascot, Sir Edward and Lady Stearn and their guests. They are leaving Sunningdale near Windsor Great Park. I've still got the tail-coat he's wearing there.

Below right:
Here is my grandfather John Hancock with Amelia his youngest daughter.
Below, and far right:
Pages from his gamekeeper's notebook: The date of Amelia's first lesson in music shares a page with the date of Mrs Cubitt's heifer going on the marsh; and (below) the date he began work for Mr Savory.

My grandparents lived here, in Cross Street, and my great-grandparents before them. My aunt Patty and her husband (William Cubitt, the Methodist preacher) lived here when they retired from business in Cromer, and Amelia lived here too, after her husband died.

As I was the only one of the next generation, the house came to me. I used to let it as a holiday cottage as I didn't want to part with it, and Tom and I came and lived here twelve years ago.

My other aunt, Amelia, married Herbert Pigott, the baker. He did his apprentice at the Co-op and they gradually took the bake office over and lived there.

It was the Hancock's Bakery and my father (Leonard Hancock) was a bit hurt because when they came out of business they offered it to George Holmes instead of to him. They didn't think he would be any good for business and so it went out of the Hancock family.

My grandmother, Elizabeth Hancock, at 'Lorcot' in Cross Street.

Herbert Pigott the baker, Leonard Hancock his brother-in-law, and Amelia his wife with a little dog on her shoulder, outside the Hancock's Bake Office on the Coast Road. The outhouse behind them was washed away in the flood of 1953 but the bake office still stands, now known as 'The Old Bakery'.

Herbert Pigott must have delivered as far as Weybourne. Behind him here seems to be Weybourne Priory Church.

I think there may have been a bake office here at Lorcot, perhaps before the one on the Coast road, because when we came here that end room had an oven in the wall. We didn't take it out, we just bricked it up. I don't know if the Hancock's Bakery was in Cross Street, before Herbert and Amelia moved down there.

According to the 1844 property list, Lorna's house in Cross Street was a 'Dwelling house, Beer Shop and Baking Office' owned by James Hancock (her great-great-grandfather), and occupied by Samuel his son (John Hancock's father). In Kelly's Directory for 1864, Samuel's widow, Martha Hancock, is listed as the baker, but from 1868 it is her son Samuel until 1912, when Herbert Pigott is baker in the Hancock's bakery, and is married to young Samuel's niece Amelia Hancock.

The bake office on the coast road with ponies and bread carts, early 1900s.

Lorna tells about James Dix, Master Mariner

Lorna's great aunt married a mariner who had begun his sea-going life in 1848 as a cabin-boy registered at the port of Cley. Lorna has kept everything relating to him, and to his family. Here she explains:

This is James Dix the Master of the ship in that painting on the wall in our dining room [*see next page*]. He married my Great Aunt Mary, and they had six boys and most of them went to sea. Here is his 'ticket'. Notice the spelling of Cley!

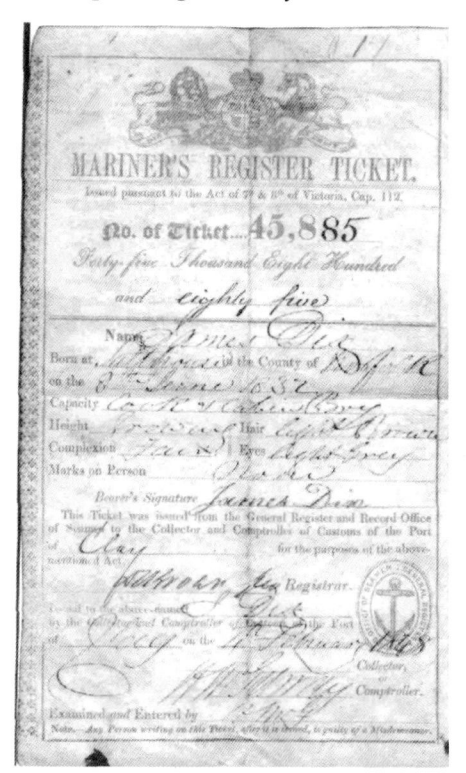

On 4th February 1848, James Dix registered at the port of 'Clay' as cook and cabin boy. According to his register ticket, he was of 'fair' complexion and still growing. He was sixteen years old.

James and Mary Dix were married in Salthouse Church, 7 April 1860.

My son-in-law wrote away to Lloyds of London to get information about the ship and about James Dix. And so we know that he became a Mate in the year 1863 and a Master in 1865, and in 1871 he was Captain of the *Jane Pardew*, a 120-foot barque built in Sunderland in 1857. Her port of registry was South Shields. I have here the marriage certificate of his daughter Martha, who was the youngest child of seven, to a William James Cooke, a dock labourer of South Shields.

Of Martha's six brothers at least three of them went to sea and two are recorded drowned. James himself was drowned at Potio in the Black Sea in 1885, when he was serving as Mate on the Steam Ship *Horner*. On the next two pages there is a sad glimpse of the short life of one of the sons, James, born in 1862.

The S.S. Jane Pardew

JAMES DIX'S SON, JAMES

A letter to his parents from James Dix, the son of the Master Mariner, dated 7th February 1879. He was 17 years old.

Friday Feb 7/79

Dear Parents Feb 7th

We are loaded and allready for sea we are going to sea to day I did not think we was going this week we are going to alexandria again I think we are going to load there write when you get this Letter we signed on thursday I have got the same wages 2/5 they are 3/5 here for AB My month commences today

I had 13/- to take it was no use sending that home they have taken care of it till I come back the talk is we are coming to shields to get new boilers in after this voyage so I will be all right It is blowing a gale of wind and we are not going till saturday all our crew have been in the ship before they are a nice lot of men so I hope we will have a comfortabler voyage this time give my kind

YOUNG JAMES' LETTER HOME

love to all I will bring martha & george a valentine home from alex:::: I was pleased to here from sam & John I hope John my have a fine & quick Passage and the same to us. addres to British counsel alex Egypt

I have nothing more to say at Present so I must say good bye :::: from your loving son. James Dix I got no advance

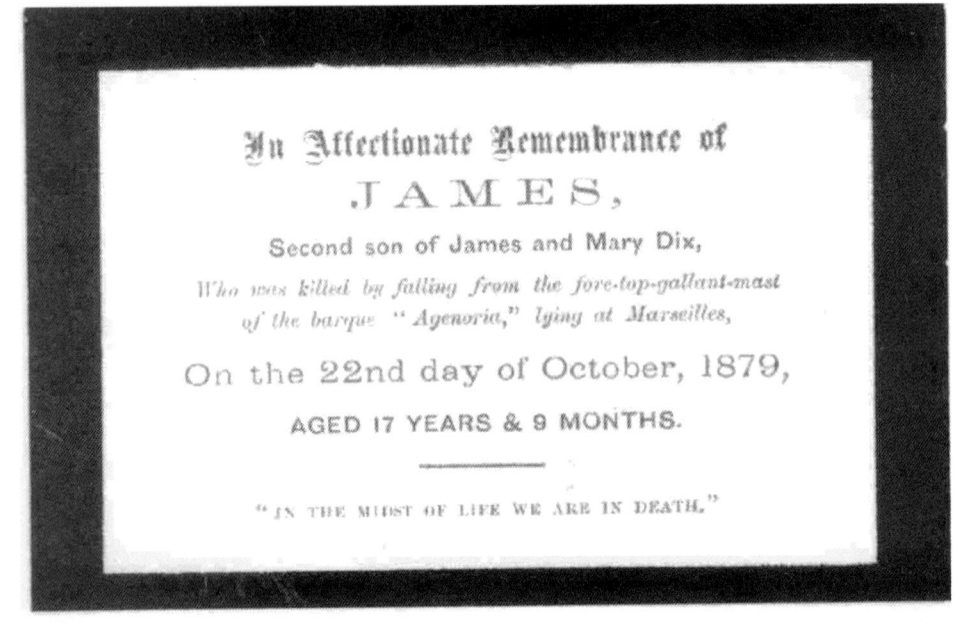

In Affectionate Remembrance of
JAMES,
Second son of James and Mary Dix,
Who was killed by falling from the fore-top-gallant-mast of the barque "Agenoria," lying at Marseilles,
On the 22nd day of October, 1879,
AGED 17 YEARS & 9 MONTHS.

"IN THE MIDST OF LIFE WE ARE IN DEATH."

The Remembrance card (left) shows that the date of his death at Marseilles was just seven months after he wrote the above letter, and drew the little picture.
His brother Sam, a year younger, lived to the age of thirty before being drowned off the coast of Ushant in the S.S. Heston.

Jasper Woodhouse

Left: Jasper minding piglets in Salthouse, 1921, and

Below: Jasper at Lenwade Concrete works, making bridges for motorways, 1951.

Jasper Woodhouse was born in 1917, and started working at the bake office when he was thirteen and still at school. Mr Holmes was the baker in those days.

Jim Manson said of Jasper, 'We all looked up to him when we were boys. He was only a bit older than us, but he was like a father figure.' Jasper, now in his eighties, has a clear memory of when he was a baker's apprentice.

I didn't work all the time, till I left school. Mr Holmes delivered round Cley and Wiveton in a van, and I used to bike home from school and take the bread up Cross Street every dinner time, but sometimes I used to work all night. I soon learnt how to do it: we used to have big troughs on the floor, and there was one in the middle where he used to make it all. He used to put 10 stone of flour, three big parts of water, four ounces of yeast and 1lb of salt. Sometimes we forgot to put the salt in, and that went hard. It used to lay all night. There would be flour bags all around the troughs on the floor and sometimes when we came back it had ris up and pushed the lid up and some of it laid on these bags. That used to be a job!

In the morning we'd cut it off with a trowel, put it on the table, and weigh it all off (when I was out on the round I used to get stopped by the inspector sometimes to see whether that was the proper weight of loaves), three-quarters of an hour in the oven: we'd fill all the bread tins up and put them all in the oven till it was full.

The faggots took about 10-15 minutes to burn, old smoke used to come out of the chimney! When the bricks all round the oven turned white, that's when the oven was hot enough, and then we had to clean the ashes out. We had a long pole with a chain and a sack on the end of it and we used to go down to the dyke—'the Crick' we call it—and put it in the water and wet it all, then bring it back and clean the ashes out with it. There was only about a dustpan of ashes left.

Joe Dack, he had a club foot since birth. He's the one who used to cut the faggots. When we used to go swimming, Joe Dack used to come with us, and his feet were full of furrah* points! You'd think he'd be poisoned. Furrah bushes, so sharp, and they were right in. He was only a little old feller but he got so used to it, he didn't notice it. He used to cut the furrahs [faggots] and 'Tarrow' Woodhouse, my Uncle Cliff, used to cart them, and they were put behind the bakery.

gorse

When we went swimming, there were about 20 or 30 of us used to meet at the bottom of Cross Street where there was a seat, and Sunday mornings we'd go up Beach Road. Years ago, there used to be planks along there so you could walk if it was flooded. We all learnt to swim in the sea when we were about 5 years old, nobody got into trouble you know. Joe Dack, he used to dive in like a porpoise-pig! He made us laugh.

When I was working for Mr Holmes, he kept the flour and corn in the Doll's House next door, and there was an old boy living in there then, Arnold Hancock.* 'Rat' we used to call him. He had a bit of land and he had this old horse he called 'Splash', blinking great feet he had! He had a field up Cley Lane, 'Scrib' that's called, right up at the end. He had one along Kelling way too. He used to go to work about 11 o'clock in the morning, and he'd get the horse in the plough—it was only a one-furrow plough, just one furrer at a time—and he'd go across the field and back again, and then he'd pack up and come home. That's all he used to do every day. He just didn't care!

Joe Dack and Arnold Hancock on a day trip to Yarmouth. They were great buddies.

Lorna Fox Collection

WAR TIME

I was in the army six years. Could have got off I think, I never did try. I followed my trade in the army. We were the first bakery after D-day in France to make bread for the troops. It was a Field Bakery. It was only two or three weeks after D-day, and they were glad to see us! They'd been living on biscuits. I shall never forget that, the day we landed over there. It was a lovely day, 5 o'clock in the morning I went on deck and had a look round. There was thousands of ships, from battleships down to crab boats. I'll never forget that sight. When we were going in, a message came on the intercom that we were approaching a mine, but anyway we missed it.

We had to wade through the water to get ashore, and we marched all that day to a place called Bayeux where they made that tapestry, that's where we slept you know, underneath the hedges. That's the first time we saw the French girls. They were looking out of the windows as we were walking up the street— French girls with all their hair shorn off because they'd been with the Germans. Then we camped down and started making the bread. That wasn't far from Caen. They took a bashing they did, there was a thousand-bomber raid on it. There was a battle ship laid off near where we were—it was the Prince of Wales— and they bombarded it one night, and the shells were whistling over the top of us.

We went to Belgium and Holland, and I finished up in Berlin, stationed near where Hesse was, Spandau. He was there all alone. That's a funny thing, when I was away in the army Salthouse was full of troops: Northumberland

*(son of John Hancock, the gamekeeper, photo p 175. For 'Scrib' see field map p 51)

Fusiliers, 5 Norfolks, Cambridgers, WAAFs too, and the Air Force. Soldiers in the Manor, and soldiers in the Hall. The de Crespignys, a Commander and a Colonel, both lived in the Hall and one of them was married. They were the only two to have a car. They were very nice people. Both of them got interned in Norway during the war. There used to be a bowling green in the walled garden that belonged to the Hall, but when the army took it over they messed it up really.

There were several people who came from Sheffield. There was the Britons, they brought a big old caravan and parked it where the mill was on the marsh. I saw it arrive on a lorry. They were friends of the Hawleys who came to the Hall and ran it as a Guest House. They were from Sheffield too and that's how they found out about Salthouse.

That's my grandfather there, the one on the left with the two horses, in front of the Hall. His nickname was 'Rummy'. He worked at the Hall when the Rosses were farming it. It was a lovely place then, it had that walled garden the other side of the road. There was a bowling green in there and all that garden.

Uncle Fred 'Hoss' Woodhouse.

Teamsmen Tom 'Rummy' Woodhouse and Jakey Matthews, in front of Ivy Hall c1906. (this old name for the Hall is now largely lost)

The man on the right is Jakey Matthews, he's the one that jumped over the churchyard wall to get married!

He was working in the field next to the church and he told his mate, 'I'm just going. I'll be about half an hour.' And he jumped over the wall, went in the church, got married and come back to work.

There was an old boy when I was young, called Martin Foulger. I don't know if he had any land down here, he might have. There are some Foulgers out Quidenham way, I don't know if he came from there. He was friendly with my grandfather, and he used to come down to the pub about once a year in an old van. He used to have meat and all sorts on the van, and he used to live in it while he was down here, in the pub yard. Of course they had some booze-ups. Martin Foulger his name was; he used to wear a big hat.

When I was 11, I went to London with my grandmother. It was Armistice week and my Uncle Fred, he was a Policeman, and he paid for us to go up for a week and stay with some people we knew. He was on duty in Westminster Abbey at the service there. He said 'I'll take you down Petticoat Lane Sunday morning, there's a market there, and they'll steal your watch as you go in one end of the lane, and sell it to you at the other end!' They knew him, because he's a Policeman up there.

So we went down there, and there was an old feller selling chickens and do you know who it was? That Martin Foulger who used to come down to the pub here. I'll *never* forget it! There was an old woman, she bought a chicken off him, and she was swearing at him because there was a great lump on the chicken's breast. I'll never forget it till the day I die, I never expected to see him down there selling chickens! Oh, she was swearing at him, this old girl! Martin Foulger, there wouldn't be no one now here remember him.

Twenty years before Jasper's visit to Petticoat Lane, Kelly's Directory for 1908 lists two Foulgers in Salthouse: Horace Foulger, farmer at Ivy Hall, and Martin, butcher and dealer.

On the left of the picture, a heap of faggots for the oven can be seen on the road outside the bake house, and directly behind the dark heap in the road can be seen Alfie Lynn's new cow house. The building extreme left is the old Parish Reading Room. Both of these buildings disappeared with the 1953 flood.

Myself on leave during the war, with Alfie Delamere.

Above: Tom 'Rummy' Woodhouse outside Victoria Cottage. Gramborough Hill and the old bake house can be seen behind him.

That's me on leave and the evacuee boy. My mother had him. He come from Dagenham, Alfie Delamere his name was. It's funny, my wife came from Sandy Way in Cheshire where I was stationed at one time, and Delamere Forest is joined there in Cheshire, and that's his name.

After the Rosses were gone, and Ivy Hall was sold, my grandfather had land of his own, a few acres and he kept 2 or 3 cows. He had a horse to work his few acres, most of us who lived here did. Victoria Cottage was washed out after the 1953 flood, and my grandfather died less than a week after it. The flood was Saturday, and he died on the Thursday. All of a sudden he caught cold that night when they took him out of the house and down to Weybourne camp. He was 84—the same age I am now.

Stephen Shipley writes about his grandfather
Charles Edward High

Stephen Shipley

Charles Edward High

When this book was already put together (and definitely too long) the editor received this lovely letter, and the following pages just had to be added.

I am writing to you as I would like to join the Salthouse History Group. I work for Royal Mail here at Beccles and noticed your newsletter which passed through our office as a missort which had accidently been routed through us and had been going to an address in Norfolk which happens sometimes through human error.

Now to my connection with the village. My Grandfather was Charles Edward High born 21st January 1889. His parents were father Edward and mother Anna Maria.

I have in my possesion my grandfathers Birth Certificate and Certificate of Baptism also photographs of a group of Farmworkers including Grandad at about the age of 13-14 years.

Also a photo of Grandads father and Brother and their father who I'm told was nicknamed Old Eggie.

From the left:
Steve's great-grandfather Edward High, Edward's brother Thomas, and their father Charles (known as 'Old Eggie').

Horace Foulger, farmer at Ivy Hall farm, stands with arms folded beside his workers. The right hand boy on the grass is Charles High.
Middle row from the right: Alph 'Hooshie' Dawson, Philip Dawson the shepherd, (father of Alph and grandfather of Primrose McGlinchey), Tom 'Rummy' Woodhouse(father of Alice Holman and grandfather of Jasper Woodhouse and Brian Holman).
Beside 'Rummy' Woodhouse: Charles Cubitt (Gerald Cubitt's father) and behind him Gerald's grandfather Robert Cubitt.

> My grandfather was a choirboy in the church at Salthouse, he met his future wife Bessie when she worked at the Hall cow. To save up enough money to get married and give them a future financialy together he joined the British Railways and travelled to Australia to help construct the railways there.

Margery and Doreen (Bessie and Charles's two daughters, now aged 87 and 80) say that when their mother was a maid at the Hall and she was hanging out the washing, their father (Charles High, the farm-worker boy in picture above) told her 'You should hang them up straight, Miss' whereupon she told him to mind his own business, and that's how they met!

Bessie Dickerson

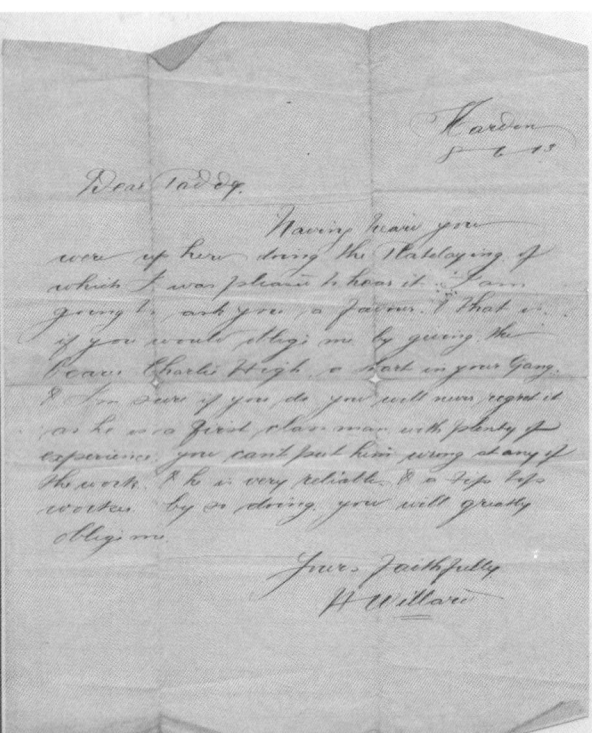

Left: An employer in Australia writes to a fellow employer. The letter gives a graphic description of Charles' character and skill as worker:

> Warden (?)
> 8 6 13
>
> Dear Paddy,
> Having heard you were up here doing the Platelaying of which I was pleased to hear it, I am going to ask you a favour, and that is if you would oblige me by giving the bearer Charles High a start in your Gang. I'm sure if you do you will never regret it, as he is a first class man with plenty of experience, you can't put him wrong at any of the work, he is very reliable and a tip top worker, by so doing you will greatly oblige me.
>
> Yours faithfully
> H. Willard

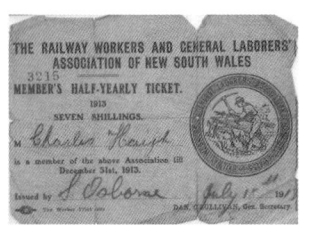

Charles and Bessie exchanged many postcards during the time he was on the railways in Australia and in 1915, having made enough money, he returned to England to wed Bessie and rear a family.

In 1926 they settled in Bungay where Charles was employed as signalman on the railway.

But he never forgot his native Salthouse where his ancestors had lived and worked for so many generations—as his letter (*opposite*) will testify.

Above: Charles High on the railways in Australia. The extraordinary machine that he's sitting on is a line-cutter.

CHARLES HIGH, SIGNALMAN, RETIRES

The occasion of the last train at Bungay Station, Charles High the signalman behind the others.

BUNGAY SIGNALMAN

MR. C. HIGH RECALLS THE BUSY DAYS

After 39 years' railway service in this country and a period in Australia, Mr. Charles High, of 66, Nethergate Street, Bungay, who had been in charge of the signal box at Bungay station since 1926, retired on January 23rd on reaching the age limit.

Mr. High returned to the station on Friday to receive a presentation subscribed for by his colleagues and their best wishes for his future. At a gathering in the goods office by Mr. M. Eyers, the stationmaster, asked Mr. High to accept an eight-day striking clock. He wished him health and happiness in his retirement.

In his reply, Mr. High recalled the days when crowds of passengers were to be seen on the station platform.

Mr. High joined the service of the Great Central Railway in 1907, being put in the Engineer's department. Emigrating to Australia in 1909, he worked on the construction of fresh railways in New South Wales for five years. Then he returned to England and resumed his duties on the Great Central. He was transferred to the operating department in 1915 and given charge of the signal box at Kirkby South Junction. After serving in various signal boxes in the Nottinghamshire and Derbyshire district he moved to Bungay.

Threat to Salthouse

Sir — I am especially interested in your articles about Salthouse village, as I was born there 76 yrs ago.

I admired your picture of the dear old church where I was choir boy for many years.

I am very much concerned about the ever encroaching sea. I can well remember when there were hundreds of acres of good marsh land reaching from Kelling to beyond Cley where many horses and hundreds of sheep and cattle grazed and grew fat, and when many householders in the village had a plot of marsh land where many stooks of sweet hay were cut and saved for winter.

If this had been Holland these acres would have been made secure years ago.

Millions of pounds have been wasted in useless missiles and weapons of destruction.

Can no money be found to save a bit of good old England? I sincerely hope that Bert Hazell M.P. will do everything possible to save the dear old village from a cruel sea.

C E High.

Nethergate St,
Bungay.
Dec. 1964.

In this letter to the newspaper, copied out by his daughter Doreen, Charles remembers the hay fields and pastures now covered by the sea.

He was held in high esteem by all who knew him and commanded the greatest respect as he had a most loving and caring personality. We visit Salthouse several times a year as I truly believe my ancestors are buried in the Bronze Age Barrows on the heath.

Yours Sincerely
Stephen. C. Shipley

'If Salthouse had been Holland, its marshes would have been made secure years ago.'

The Keymers of Salthouse

Dr Ian Keymer's family research on his 19th-century forebears fills an ill-documented gap in the Salthouse history. Here he relates how this research began, and his amazing family tree on the opposite page—though this is but a part of the complete Keymer pedigree—bears testimony to the far-reaching extent of his work.

Dr Ian Keymer

Keymer Cottage

This pedigree showing the Salthouse branch of the Keymer family shows how village people of that time were far more mobile than is generally supposed.

Only two Salthouse Keymers married somebody from the village, namely Charlotte who married Peter Williams a carpenter, after which they managed the Dun Cow, and Philip Keymer, a carpenter and millwright, who married Frances Cubitt. One Keymer related to the Salthouse branch married Thomas Dew of Salthouse.

The extraordinary thing is that all the other Keymers who lived or were baptised in the village married people from elsewhere, including places as far apart as London, South Shields, and Beverley in Yorkshire. The family tree shows links with 33 other families, and provides information about families from nearly 20 (mostly local) villages.

Probably 95% of the present indigenous population of this country is descended from the likes of my ancestors and their relations. Much research has been done on the aristocracy and 'gentry', while comparatively little is known about the social history of ordinary working people beyond the reach of living memory. The sort of research that I and many others have done illustrates how old records can be used to show how such people moved around, whom and where they married, how their fortunes could change and how they made a living.

Recently an old diary written in 1949 came to light, and this supplied information I had forgotten concerning my first encounters with those Salthouse people who inspired me to broaden my search. The first person I met was a Mrs Dew, who lived near the church, and I asked her if there were any Keymers living in Salthouse. She knew of none, but it happened that her husband's brother and sisters lived in a very old flint cottage on the coast road called Keymer Cottage, and she thought they might be able to tell me something of the Keymers who had lived there long ago, because they were some relation and took an interest in family history. Her husband George appeared and said that his father had talked a lot about the old gentleman who used to live in Keymer Cottage: he had played the violin and he was known as 'Fiddler' Keymer, but his real name was William Warnes Keymer. He had been an easy-going and trusting old man and was often teased by the village youths who would ask him to play the fiddle for them, while their friends were playing pranks in his garden and digging up his cabbages.

Later I was able to find out that this 'Fiddler' Keymer was my great-great-uncle. The Dews claimed to be related to him (*since confirmed: see family tree opposite*). They invited me to tea and showed me the Indenture made between William Warnes Keymer and George Dew, dated 1877, which recorded the sale of the Cottage property and land for £160. The eldest sister, who was stone deaf,* showed me a magnificent model of a sailing ship that had been left in the attic when the house was sold and which she said had been made by a Keymer. It was a masterpiece of craftsmanship; it had a lifeboat and even little wooden sailors climbing up rope ladders. The hull had been painted green, though its paintwork was faded and it was covered with dust and full of woodworm. On my next visit I asked if I could buy it, but this time I was told that Fiddler Keymer had given it

---

* *There were three Dew sisters: the eldest, Annie Wills, who was the widow of a Canadian soldier in W.W.I; a mousy, timid, stone-deaf one called Dorothy; and Sybil who no one ever saw, and was always shut up in a bedroom.*

PART OF THE KEYMER FAMILY TREE, SHOWING RELATED FAMILIES

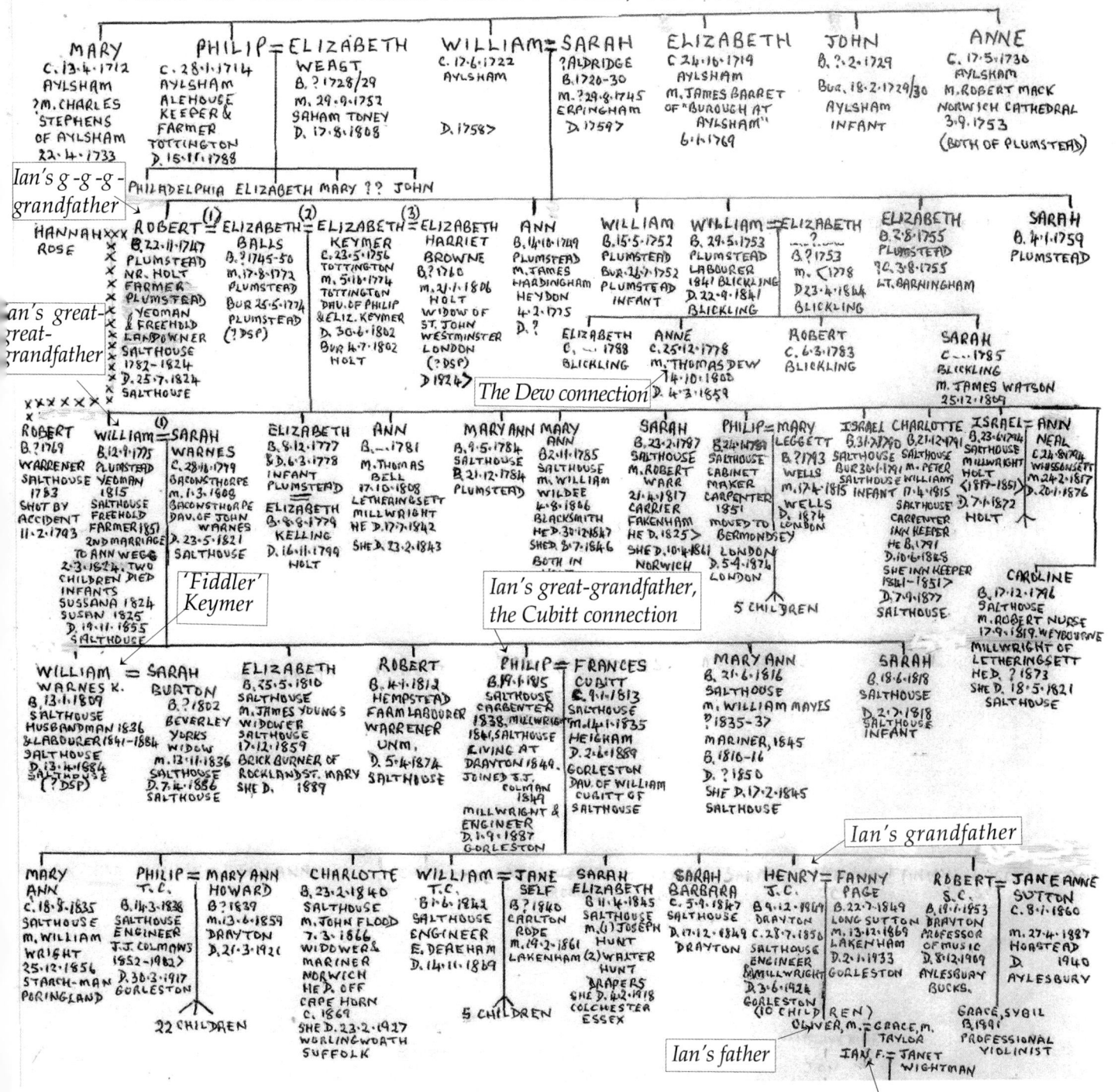

This tree in all its detail is reproduced here as an example of what may be achieved by dedicated amateur research.

to their father.

Next I went to see Mr Leach the churchwarden, living at the Manor House. My diary describes him as 'a very well-educated, tall, thin and rather hearty old gentleman', and his study as 'oak-panelled and littered with old copies of the Times'. I was invited to tea and heard 'the terrible news that, at the beginning of the war, the rector had wrapped up the old church records, dating from 1544, in a cloth and buried them in the churchyard, and when they were dug up at the end of the war they were in a terrible state'. I was told these precious records had been sent to an expert at the County Library in Norwich and were still there. Mr Leach then showed me a very interesting type-written manuscript: 'A History of Salthouse until 1840' written by Commander Stagg. I then departed and (according to my diary) I gave him 3/6d towards the church restoration fund and 'wished I could have given more'.

On the 5th January 1950 I went to the Norfolk County Library in Thorpe to enquire about the earlier church records, but the staff didn't even know they were meant to have them, and they suggested I went to Bolingbroke's in the Cathedral. My diary becomes a little patronising at this point—perhaps to make up for another disappointment—and records that 'I found two gents tucked away in a dark, dusty little room in the south transept. The gentleman who spoke to me wore a dingy blue pin-stripe suit which had never felt a clothes brush in its long career, I am sure. I told him I would like to see the old wills and church records of Salthouse, but he said he knew nothing about them'.

I visited the rector of Salthouse in Kelling Rectory and he told me that if it hadn't been for Commander de Crespigny, who had wanted to see them, the parish records would still be buried. He suggested that they might be being treated at the Castle Museum, but the curator of the Museum, like all the others, denied all knowledge of them and I really thought they were gone for good. When eventually the Norfolk Record Office was created, I was delighted and amazed to discover that the ancient Salthouse parish records were listed there and deposited in the archives.

By this time I was entirely committed to the research of my family history, and this commitment has remained with me until the present day. I can trace my family back to Henry Keymer, a copyhold landowner of Aylsham who lived there in the latter half of the sixteenth century. The Aylsham Keymers were mostly copyhold landowners, yeomen and tradesmen. The first Keymer to arrive in Salthouse was my great-great-great-grandfather Robert (1747-1824) who took up residence in 1782. The last Keymer to live in the village was Sarah, the wife of his grandson William Warnes Keymer ('Fiddler' Keymer), who died in Keymer Cottage in 1886.

It was in Commander Stagg's type-written *History of the Parish of Salthouse*, which Mr Leach showed me, that I found an intriguing burial: 'Robt. Son of Robt. Keymer and Hannah Rose shot by accident, 11 Feb 1793' [see page 46]. The Dews had heard of this incident and they confirmed that he was the eldest son of my grandfather Robert. Many years later, my research discovered a report of the accident in the Norwich Mercury of 16th February 1793:

> On Monday last, an inquisition was taken, at Salthouse, before Mr Munhall, Coroner, on the body of Rob. Keymer, warrener, who was accidentally killed by a gun unexpectedly going off, the contents of which lodged in his thigh and lower part of his body.

Robert was 24 when he was shot. His father, Robert Senior, was 22 and a bachelor when his son Robert was born, thus making him illegitimate. According to an uncle, Robert senior as a young man 'had taken a long ladder, placed it against an upper storey window and carried his fiancée down and eloped with her against her parents' wishes'. Since Robert appears to have had an illegitimate three-year-old son when he married Elizabeth Balls, her parents' disapproval would not have been surprising. However, according to the burial record confirmed in the Archdeacon's Transactions, the mother of Robert Keymer who was shot was Hannah Rose. Perhaps therefore it was Hannah Rose and not Elizabeth Balls (see family tree) with whom Robert senior eloped.

Unfortunately, after only two years, Robert senior's first wife Elizabeth died. Five months later he married his cousin Elizabeth Keymer at Tottington. When Robert and Elizabeth arrived in Salthouse from Plumstead (in 1782 according to the Church Rate Book for the Overseers of the Poor), he purchased a property with rateable value of £3 10s. 0d. A short time later he had no less than three properties, with a total rateable value of £24 10s. 0d. This was the fourth-highest value out of 65 people paying poor rates. The highest valuation was that of Mr Thomas Purdy, the churchwarden and big landowner; most were in the region of £5.

The reason Robert moved to Salthouse is unknown. Perhaps it was a better place to farm than Plumstead, not because the soil was better but because there was a plentiful supply of fish in the sea and wildfowl to shoot on the marshes.

During 1795-96 Robert was the fifth-highest rate payer out of 40, but during the period 1811-13 the valuation of his properties dropped from £24 10s. 0d to £15 15s. 0d. This tends to support the family story that Robert lost money due to gambling. He may have had to sell property to pay his debts. I wonder if his gambling venue was Holt Racecourse, which was situated at the site of the present Country Park. Holt races were popular in the latter half of the 18th century and up till 1810, when the course was enclosed because of the Enclosure Act.

Robert's death, on 31st July 1824, was announced in the *Norfolk Chronicle & Norwich Gazette*: 'Died Sunday last aged 76 Mr Keymer of Salthouse'. This was a news item, not an ordinary death notice, suggesting he was well known. It is interesting to note that he was entitled 'Mr'; in those class-conscious days, only three people in Salthouse were given the title of Mister. This denoted they were men of substance and therefore regarded as 'gentlemen'.

In his will, Robert divided his property between his daughters, and his three sons William, Philip and Israel. He bequeathed '5 shillings unto my wife Elizabeth should she come and make claim'.

William, the eldest son, married Sarah Warnes in Holt, and their first child William Warnes Keymer was born in Salthouse. William's presence at vestry meetings in the church, from 1839 to 1854, is proved by the regularity of his signature in the Assessment of Rates Books. *[He is number 34 on the 1854 valuation of property list on page 111.]*

The signature of William Warnes Keymer first appears in the church vestry records in 1845. He continued to follow in his father's footsteps till at least 1871, approving and signing documents for the relief of the poor, and in 1864 was appointed a Constable.

The appointment of Constables was the responsibility of the governing body of the parish, subject to the approval of Justices of the Peace. It was a position of responsibility with a wide range of duties—which included 'lock up' or imprisonment of offenders, inspection of ale houses, apprenticing of pauper children, removal from the parish of itinerant strangers, collection of rents, and assistance at shipwrecks. It was a centuries-old custom and originally a manorial appointment.

William Warnes' brother Philip (1815-87), whose name can be seen today among the graffiti on the choir-stalls, was first mentioned in the Rate Book in March 1837, and at the 1841 census he was living at Little's Folly, Salthouse. Philip and his family moved to Drayton near Norwich sometime between late 1847 and the summer of 1849. Although Philip's son Henry J.C. Keymer (my grandfather) was born in Drayton in December 1849, Philip and his wife Frances took him to Salthouse to be baptised in 1850. Philip became an engineer at Colman's and was left a legacy in J.J. Colman's will.

The family fortunes improved again when Henry—who, like his father, was also a millwright—became an engineer and moved to Gorleston-on-Sea where he developed a successful engineering business. Henry was the last to be baptised in the village and, in 1971, I was the last to be married there.

THE HIGH FAMILY

Richard (Dick) and Mary High with Freda aged 2, circa 1908. (Dick was the brother of Florence, see photo p 153)

Freda Morse (née High)

Freda aged 96

Freda is Salthouse born and bred. Her husband Alec, who came from Kelling, worked for a time for the de Crespignys at Salthouse Hall, where his mother was Cook. During the war, while she and Alec were living in Dawson's Cottage, Bard Hill, Freda took in evacuees. Later, Alec worked for Jim Deterding at Kelling Hall and they moved to Kelling to live.

This photo (above) of the post office is when my father first started in it. In his trade he was a bricklayer. He took those railings down and he built the front on, then he bought the shed next door and he made that into a hall. That had red and white bricks, like they used to years ago in a pattern. The stairs went straight up and we had a sitting room upstairs over the shop, and then he built the kitchen and another bedroom.

This later picture shows the porch which my father built.

198

But my father first started the post office in a little cottage in Cross Street. As you come from Kelling, on the right-hand side as you go up, first there is Mrs Talbot's shop (below and opposite), then the Jarvises, then the little house next to it almost opposite the Dacks (now

Mrs Talbot with her sister-in-law outside her house, where she kept shop.

Looking up Cross Street with the Talbots' shop on the right (see photo left) and, beyond it, the first post office, where I was born.

'the Seven Whistlers'). My Granny's house was behind the Dacks and a pightle at the back—we used to call them pightles, you'd call them meadows. Opposite Granny's house there used to be three or four houses and that's where the post office was started. I was born up there, and how my father managed to buy that house goodness only knows.

The old postman used to walk from Salthouse to Kelling with the letters. He was a funny little man. He had a uniform, and his hat had a peak each way! His name was Billy Lynn. He never had a bike. I remember having a bike in the First World War, one of the soldiers' wives taught me to ride it on the bottom road. There was no tar on the roads then. I can remember the big charabancs—you had to nearly crawl up the side to get in one of them, that was ever so steep. It had a great big hood that could come right over if it rained. It came from Cley along the coast road and we used to go to Sheringham on it, funny old things they were, great big things! But when we had a Sunday School outing we used to go in the farm wagon.

MY MOTHER

My mother was a Craske from Sheringham. Her family started selling pork pies at Salthouse, and she used to come on a bike selling them. My Uncle Craske had a tiny little shop next door to the chapel, you went up the side and they had part of the front room into a shop. Aunt Florrie, my father's sister,* came to housekeep for him when my mother died, and I was just a little girl of six. The only thing

*Florence Radley, see pages 149-155

I can remember about my mother is her having a policeman's helmet on! My uncle, her brother, was in the police force, so probably she just put it on for a laugh. Then I can remember everybody crying—I suppose it was the funeral day . . . The Pigotts, that's Herbert and Amelia in the bake office, they wanted to adopt me, but my father wouldn't let me go.

MY FATHER

Then, six months after my mother died, my father married Polly Dawson and he sold the post office to the Smiths and we went to live next door for a while.

Then my father took a smallholding from the council, and we went to live up Bard Hill in one of those Council Houses. I think Polly more or less agitated for him to go into farming. Then my father moved again, he gave up the smallholding, rented some land, and went to live at the Lawn on the way to Holt. He had cows and he used to take the milk to Holt every morning in a horse and tumbrel.

He went to the Lawn farm with £2,000, that was a lot of money in those days. He rented the house and I got married from there. This was in the 1930s when everything went slump, didn't it? My father lost his money—he went bankrupt. After that he went back to his old building trade. He lived at High Kelling and he used to bike to Sheringham. In the finish, he lived in Peacock Lane in Holt and he died there of consumption.

My first job, as soon as I left school, was working for the Smiths who now had the post office. Then Mr Stangroom, who had a big shop in Cley, asked me if I would go and work for him—Miss Smith was selling the post office to the Gents—so I used to bike to Cley every day and work in the big shop. We had grocery one side and drapery the other, and I worked in the grocery. Mr Stangroom's old aunt had a little shop also in Cley, and I went to be manager of that. We had china and grocery, lovely china we sold.

We used to have to weigh all the sugar in the blue bags, and cut all the lard and the butter. That was in great big slabs—nothing hygienic about it! We used to have to cut the ham, and that wasn't covered up or anything. I got so I could measure the sugar to a tee. I had a good business going there, whether they liked me or not I don't know, but a lot of the people that went to the big shop came to me in the little shop instead, so I stole their custom really!

GAS LIGHTS

We used to keep shop till 8 o'clock at night then, and that meant biking home in the dark in winter. You must have a light in the front and back of your bike. You used to have these old paraffin lamps and they used to smoke, but then the gas-lamps came in and that was much better. They had carbide at the bottom and water at the top, and that used to drip the water and make the gas. There was a gas-lamp in the shop; there were big rocks (carbide) in the bottom and a great big tank outside, that used to drip the water and that used to make the gas, and I had to look to see if that was going all right every day. I would crack this big old rock stuff, and put that in the bottom of my bike-lamp, and it made the gas. That gave you a lot better light, and it didn't smoke like the paraffin did.

When I got married, Mr Stangroom would have made me a nice flat above the little shop, so I could live there and go on managing it but, stupid-like, Oh no! I had to go and look after my husband.

I met Alec at a party—we used to have parties in those days, Christmas time, and all the friends went to each others' houses. We played games like postman's knock and musical chairs, and old-fashioned games like Old Mother McCoo:— 'Old Mother McCoo is dead, and how did she die? One finger up, and one blind eye!' You'd go right round, 'One finger up' and you'd sit with a finger up . . . And then finally it was, 'How did she die? One finger up, and one blind eye, and *all on the jig.*' That was a game. At one party my husband was there, and the man who was giving the party kept pretending that Alec was knocking for me (it was post man's knock you see) which he wasn't really, but the man knew he was sweet on me and so he kept me going out of the room with Alec!

That night Alec took me home, and then we started going together, but it was nearly five years before we got married because we couldn't get a house. Alec's mother had bought him a Raleigh motor bike for his 21st birthday, and we used to go out a lot on that to Cromer and different places, but when we got married we couldn't afford to run it, so we bought two bikes and we used to bike up to Holt pictures.

We lived in the bungalow opposite Beach Road. We furnished four rooms in that bungalow; we hadn't enough money to have the little

The bungalow opposite Beach Road where we first lived and had lodgers. (*Built by Friday Forsdick, see photo p 265*)

room furnished so we had that as a store-room. We bought a three-piece suite which was twelve pounds something. How my husband got enough money to furnish the bungalow, I don't know. I think his mother helped him. She was working as cook to the de Crespignys at the Hall, and my husband Alec was gardener there. When Alec asked for a raise in wages, the Commander said he couldn't afford it but there was that little cottage at the bottom of Bard Hill. When old Mr Dawson who lived there died, that became empty so the Commander said we could have it and we wouldn't have to pay 5 shillings a week, we could live there rent-free.

I didn't like moving really, because I liked my house. I used to let: 12/6 a week and 5/- for cooking! We lived in the little room; of course we hadn't got a bed, had we, because we let both the bedrooms. We had ever such lovely people come. They used to go out on the beach and they would come in for their evening meal, and I used to cook.

One gentleman visitor, all he wanted was blackberry and apple pudding, and he used to go and gather the blackberries for it himself!

We had an old sort of washhouse place and we made it into a kitchen. I don't know if you've seen these old cookers with a door like a copper underneath. You burnt coal or anything, and that heated the oven all round and I used to cook on that. Lovely, beautiful cooking-stove that was. And then, when we moved, we didn't take in lodgers any more. We had the soldiers stationed on us, and we had evacuees. One little boy, all he liked was the white of the egg, he didn't like the yolk.

They had lice. We *caught* lice! I caught them, Peter caught them, and Alec. They had impetigo, and Peter caught that. They come from East London. They weren't too bad, we didn't have them wet the bed like our friends did. The mother and father came over to visit the little boy and, Oh, she'd got him all in flannelette because she thought he'd be cold. They weren't too bad, but they didn't know how to eat, did they? They didn't like anything—only fish and chips.

Alec worked on the farm so he didn't have to go to war. Colonel de Crespigny and his wife, and the Colonel's brother, 'the Commander', lived at the Hall. I remember Mrs de Crespigny's brother, Commander Stagg, used to come to stay, and also a Miss Stagg came. The Colonel had an Alvis with a boot you could sit in. Once he took us for a ride and we went to visit an abbey and have a picnic. Going along the Stiffkey road, the Colonel said to my husband, would you like to go sixty miles an hour? And we went at sixty and it was marvellous in the dickey.

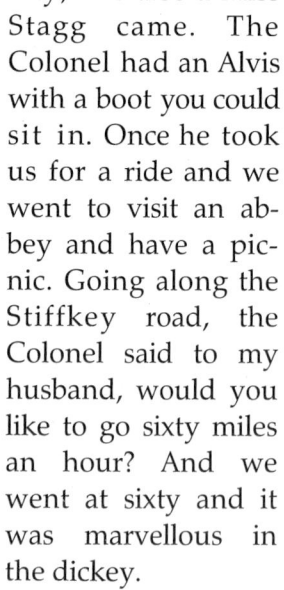

The de Crespignys were very good to us. We were very happy in our marriage.

Me and baby Peter

Alec and myself at Kelling

Ray High

Raymond High, stepbrother to Freda Morse, was born in 1915 in the post office. His mother was Polly Dawson, Jack Dawson's sister, and his father, Richard Joseph High, was oldest brother of Florence Radley. Before the war, when his father gave up his building trade, Ray kept the firm going and learnt the trade. When he got married and lived at Cley he worked with Newton & Co, until the Second World War.

Aged 87

Aged 8

I was born in 1915 in the post office and I left Salthouse in 1930. I was brought up a Methodist, married a Quaker, and I'm an agnostic. I think the War knocked it out of me—I couldn't accept religion and war—but when I get on that subject I get perhaps a bit heated at times!

My family was very mixed up with the Pigotts: my father's grandfather, he married a Pigott, and he was half a Pigott anyway. It was his sister who was Mrs Johnson of the Manor House. I don't know if she had been a maid at the Manor or what, we don't know, but she married him. I've heard he was an alcoholic and he died young and left her the estate. Then, of course, she split up the farm and rented it to her relations. That's how most of my family got their land. There was my grandfather James, and there was Henry, and Ernest he was a farmer, and his granddaughter Kathleen Gray still lives in the Manor farm house.

I don't remember this, of course—I'd be about five. The Deterdings owned the other farm up Purdy Street. The Kelling and Salthouse part had belonged to the Savorys of Weybourne and they sold the whole Kelling and Salthouse estate—except the Manor and its farm land of course—to Sir Henry Deterding. Then, after the First World War, there were a lot of men wanted land. My father and Mr Levi High* (he was chairman of the Parish Council) and Mr Stangroom at Cley (he was clerk of the Council), they got together with my father and they got a lawyer, and I don't know who else was in it but they managed to get the Hall estate turned into Council holdings. This would be in 1920 I think.

The Hall from the east, c1930—the farm-house which was sold separately when its farmland was split up for WW1 ex-servicemen.

Some of the estates that were split up in this way, split up the houses too, and the people who had the land went in them. The Rosses were in the Hall (they had been tenant farmers

* Levi High was brother of Ray's grandfather James

of the Deterdings) but it was a big old house to have really. They sold Salthouse Hall away because I think no one wanted it. Most people had about fifty acres apiece. There were fifteen of them, and I can remember the excitement you know, but mind you, they knew a bit what it was like because the other estate (the Manor Farm) had been split up among ordinary people. So it was a different village from most villages.

When these men all got these holdings many of them had a few cows. There's a shed up Purdy Street called the Cow House, which is now turned into a private property, isn't it? [*This is now a converted barn called 'the Cow Shed'.*] Well, there was 'standing' in there for twenty or thirty cows. There was Mr Charles Cubitt had some cows, my father had some cows, Mr Duffield had some, Mr Clifford High and another one, I forget who he was [*possibly George Dew*], but my father formed a milk Co-operative.

They had a dairy there, and they bought a cooler to cool the milk and they bought a float and they used to bring it to Holt. There was a milk train in those days, about half past eight, and they took turns to bring it up. My father would use a horse to bring the float up and when I was fourteen I left school and *I* used to do it. The float had ten gallon and seventeen gallon churns in it. You couldn't go up Bard Hill: it was just tarred then, but it was too steep. You either went round Market Lane as they call it, and round and up, or you took the old Sandy Lane at the side of Bard Hill, and came out at the top. There was a pit over there on the other side, a plain they used to call it 'Bard Hole's Plain'! Of course that's all grown up now. It was all open in those days, no trees. All heaths were man-made, they were treeless by over-stocking. Have you ever read *Mary Hardy's Diary*—that's Mrs Hardy of Letheringsett Hall? They came to Letheringsett in 1780, and she drove from Holt to Cromer and she said it was one of the most dismal rides she ever had. It was heath the whole way! That was before it was enclosed then; it was over-production—sheep really.

Bard Hill, when there was much more grass on the heath for cattle.

I always remember the milk cheque coming. The milk used to go to the United Dairies in London. Welford Premier Dairies, I still remember the name. What happened you see is they had a communal dairy. They milked their cows—it was all done by hand of course—then they measured their milk and wrote it all down in a book. They must have trusted each other! My father would collate all this and then, when the milk cheque came, he would split the money up and every month they'd have a meeting at the dairy and he'd pay them. Of course it was a big income for them really.

My father sold the post office a little while after he took the land, and he bought the house next door, 'Balaklava Cottage' they called it. There was an old boy there, I can remember him, who'd been in the battle of the Light Brigade, Mr Olley.* He had a black patch over one eye and I can *just* remember him looking over the gate. My father, being not exactly a pacifist, but somebody who didn't like the war, said 'I'm not having Balaklava Cottage!' He called it Beulah Cottage instead and we stayed there till I was about twelve.

Now there was a bit of a fiddle I think, there must have been: they built four council houses—you know the first lot up Purdy Street—well, my father shouldn't have had one! He sold Beulah house and he was looking for a farm. Several of the men who had these smallholdings got on and wanted bigger farms: Mr Tom Pigott, he went away; Mr Cubitt went away; Cliff High went away and my father went to the Lawn. Anyway, after he sold Beulah we went up the hill for three or four years till he bought the Lawn farm. But I've often thought back. Nobody told me this, but I think it was a bit of a fiddle. It must have been, but anyway!

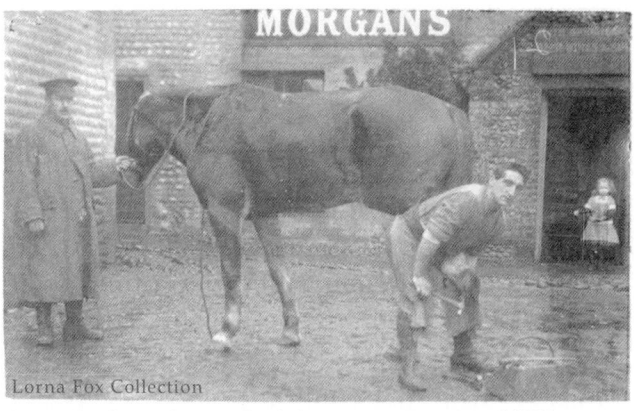

A cavalry horse being shod during the First World War at the Dun Cow.

and see Mr Olley page 133

Then, after we were at the Lawn, I still used to come down to Salthouse a lot because my father used to have his horses shod at the Dun Cow by Mr Graveling, and we used to come up Bix's Lane through the fields. My father bought an old cavalry horse out of the First World War. The date was stamped on him.

My father had a high-wheeled gig, and this horse could go! I used to ride him down to Salthouse to have him shod. I always remember one time my father gave me two half-crowns. I had to go to the post office and get some stamps; I suppose they were stamps he put on the men's cards. I was on this old horse and, as soon as we were on the grass, he went! and I was up and down and when I got there the money was gone. I never forgot it. I remember feeling so dreadful. It was a lot of money, farm labourers were getting thirty shillings a week then.

THE FIRST WORLD WAR

I don't know whether I remember, or whether I was told, but the soldiers used to drill on the Green. Of course you know the army flooded the marsh; they shut the sluices on the east bank. They used to call our marshes Salthouse Broads! When I first remember, it was one sheet of water. It was deliberate.

They built duck-boards all the way down the beach road. They had to have troops down on the beach, and the army built these boards along the side of the road to walk on above the water level. They stayed there for years after the war, up to the twenties and thirties. I used to run along there. It was an invasion area in that war as well as for the second, and the Rocket House was an observation post. In the Second World War, you weren't allowed on the beach at all. They put a big barrier up and dug a big ditch.

After the first war, they suddenly realised that the marsh was full of eels. I remember as a little boy sitting in the back of the boat and they got no end of eels. That had been covered for four years. There used to be lorries lying there waiting for the boats to come in, it didn't last long. Then, if you lived along the edge of the marsh, as so many did, you could keep ducks—but *only* Aylesburys. Some people had six or seven. Right from the white bungalow at the Kelling end of the village, they all had ducks. My mother had some when we were at the post office. Spring-time, they'd lay the eggs, and then they'd hatch them. The dealers would come down in the pony and traps, I remember there was one from Briston. They could come to Salthouse you see and get a whole cartload, whereas they'd have to go a long way to get as much in other villages. They'd take them inland where they'd be fattened up. Powder puffs? That's what they said, but—it *may* have happened, I don't know . . . They couldn't have made them into powder puffs, could they? My father bought some Indian Runner ducks. Walsey Hills was one of his fields, and he took them down there after the harvest, to pick up the corn. I can't remember how many he had, all I remember is the row about it! They got out and got in the marshes, and got among these Aylesbury ducks!

Aylesbury ducks beside 'Spring Holes' (the duck pond).

Indian Runner

So you see it was different from a lot of villages. They had a means of getting a living, and of course they had the heath with rabbits and the fishing in those days. After I left Salthouse, at the beginning of the war, I was courting a lady and she became Post Mistress at Cley post office, and I of course went to live there. Then I went into the army.

The first year I came back, after the war, some of the young men from Salthouse asked me to be a trustee of the Heath. Ronald Deterding was lord of the manor, and he had a seat on the Council. I was also on the Board of Governors for Kelling School—till they bought the computers and I said 'I don't know anything about computers, and "the time has come the Walrus said" for me to retire.'

The Stock and Cattle Association

This page summarising the Association is by Tracey Large—taken from her C S E History project on Salthouse (other parts of her project appear on pages 140 and 163)

Tracey

The grazing value of the marshes, and livestock generally, was very important to the village. So on 24th April 1858 the 'Salthouse Stock and Cattle Association' membership was opened to the inhabitants of the parish in order to meet the necessities of each other in cases of illness or death of any stock that shall be insured. Members of a visiting and valuing committee ascertained the state of health and condition of stock insured, and each member of the Association paid an entrance fee of 7/6d and 2d in the pound quarterly for all animals insured. Some of the animals which got insured were horses, cows, heifers, steers, foals and even donkeys and pigs.

In the case of illness, half of the veterinary expenses would be paid, subject to production of the vet's bill, and in the case of death, 'the full amount the said animal is insured at, will be paid within six weeks'. An animal was to be seen 'at least once a year' by the visiting committee.

One is left wondering what prompted rule 26: 'Any member entering the place of meeting in a state of intoxication so as to disturb or annoy during the hours of business, shall be fined 1/- for each offence.' The original document set out the rules, and was signed by three members of the association: Peter Williams, Gabriel Pigott and James Fitt. Testimony as to the need for such an association is born out in the fact that it continued in use for so many years, amendments being made to its rules in April 1912 and in April 1923.

Tracey Large (née Wright)

This lovely picture of cattle cooling off is part of Doreen Sayer (née High)'s collection, but the location is not certain. Is it the marl pit, or could it be the pond that used to be on the heath?

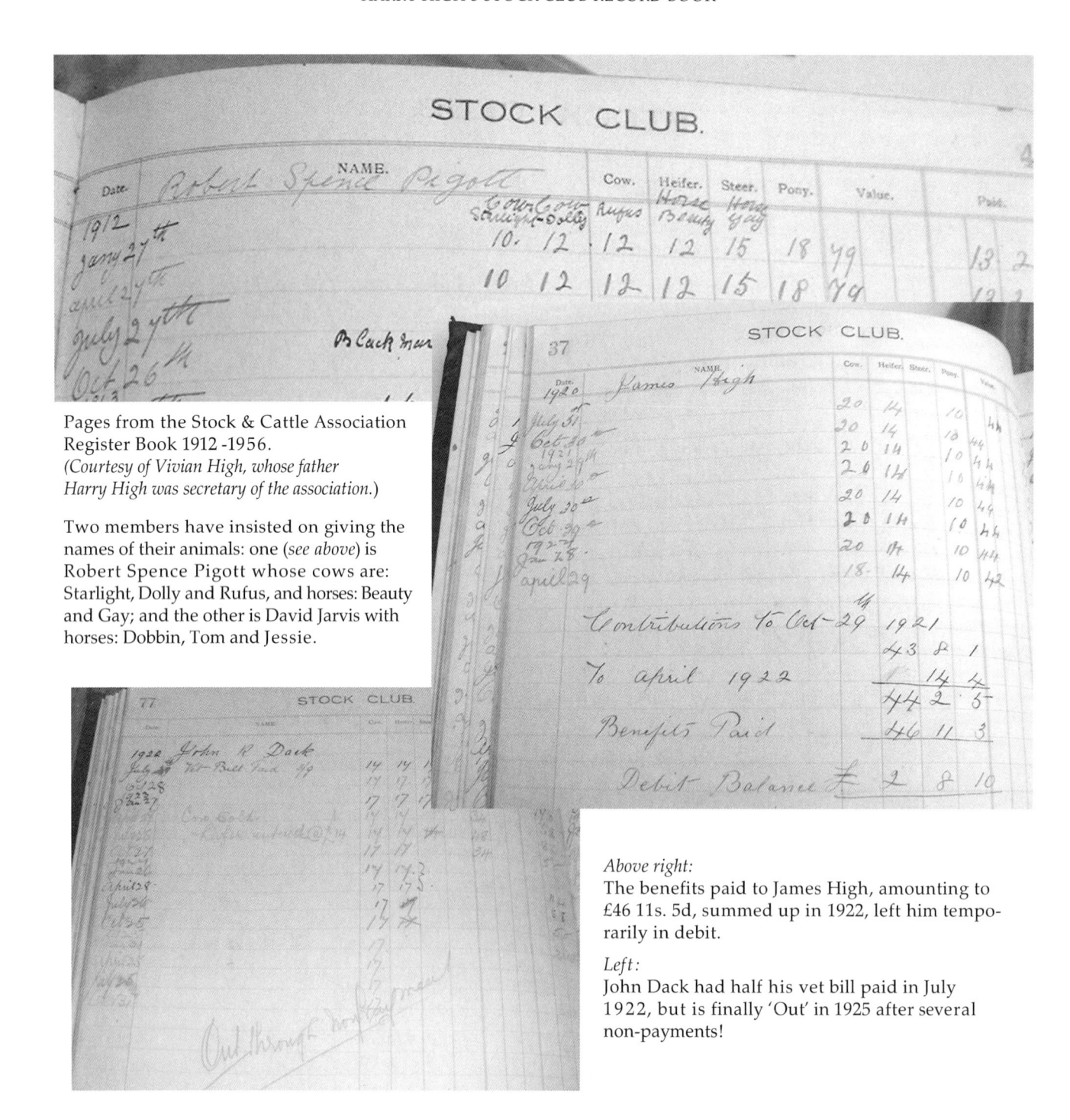

Pages from the Stock & Cattle Association Register Book 1912 -1956.
(Courtesy of Vivian High, whose father Harry High was secretary of the association.)

Two members have insisted on giving the names of their animals: one (*see above*) is Robert Spence Pigott whose cows are: Starlight, Dolly and Rufus, and horses: Beauty and Gay; and the other is David Jarvis with horses: Dobbin, Tom and Jessie.

Above right:
The benefits paid to James High, amounting to £46 11s. 5d, summed up in 1922, left him temporarily in debit.

Left:
John Dack had half his vet bill paid in July 1922, but is finally 'Out' in 1925 after several non-payments!

1912

Member	stock	value	fee paid
John Hancock	1 cow 1 heifer	£19	3s - 2d
Richard Pigott			6d
Henry High	4 cows	£66	11s - 0d
Robert Spence Pigott	3 cows 2 horses 1 pony	£79	13s - 2d
James High	2 cows 1 pony	£37	6s - 2d
William Dix			1s - 0d
Daniel Pigott			6d
James Hancock			6d
Levi High	1 heifer 1 donkey	£14	2s - 4d
Charles Pinson			6d
Robert Lynn	1 cow 1 pony	£26	4s - 4d
William Cubitt	1 cow 1 heifer	£19	3s - 2d
Ann Pigott	1 cow	£12	2s - 0d
David Jarvis	2 cows 3 horses	£64	£1-1s-4d
Mrs John Pigott			6d
Matthew Talbot			6d
Matthew Dack	1 foal 1 pony	£19	3s - 2d
Robert Woodhouse	2 cows 1 pony	£42	7s - 0d
Mrs Edith Graveling	1 pony	£18	3s - 0d
Herbert Pigott	2 ponies	£26	4s - 4d
Richard Joseph High	1 pony	£8	1s - 4d

MEMBERSHIP BETWEEN THE YEARS 1912 AND 1959

There were 21 members in the village in 1912, owning a total of twenty cows, fifteen horses and one donkey, according to the entries for that year in the Stock and Cattle Association register, which begins in 1912 after the Association has been going fifty-four years, and ends with its closure in 1959.

Each member fills a separate page with entries at each quarterly payment of their subscription. There must have been another book for the benefits paid, but at the summing-up (which comes ten years after the start of the book in April 1922, before beginning all over again), one has a chance to see who claimed benefits and who didn't. For example, see James High's summing-up on the page opposite

Not everyone in the village who kept stock was a member, but the majority—even if they had only one horse to register—certainly were, and many kept up their quarterly payment during the time they were without any stock at all. William Dix, for example, paid 1 shilling every half year until 31 Oct 1914 and then waited a year before paying a lump sum of 2/- and finally discontinuing. David Jarvis (by this time no longer a miller but a coal dealer) was in the habit of paying irregularly, which accounts for his £1 1s. 4d in the list on this page.

Membership could not be conveniently cancelled and recommenced when one bought new stock; rule 15 required that a member who had ceased to keep cattle must pay 6d a quarter if he wanted to retain his membership.

STOCK DEALING

In the 1920s and 1930s several Salthouse people start dealing in cattle. There are frequent entries of steers and bullocks kept for a year or a few months and then sold and more bought. Herbert Pigott the baker was one of these, and others were: William Cubitt, Herbert Dix, Harry High, Charles Cubitt, Arnold Hancock and Stephen Cooke (see *below and right*). They often have as much as 8 to 10 bullocks and steers at one time, before selling and buying in new stock.

Above: Stephen Cooke and wife Gertrude and dog, driving his ex-World War I mule.

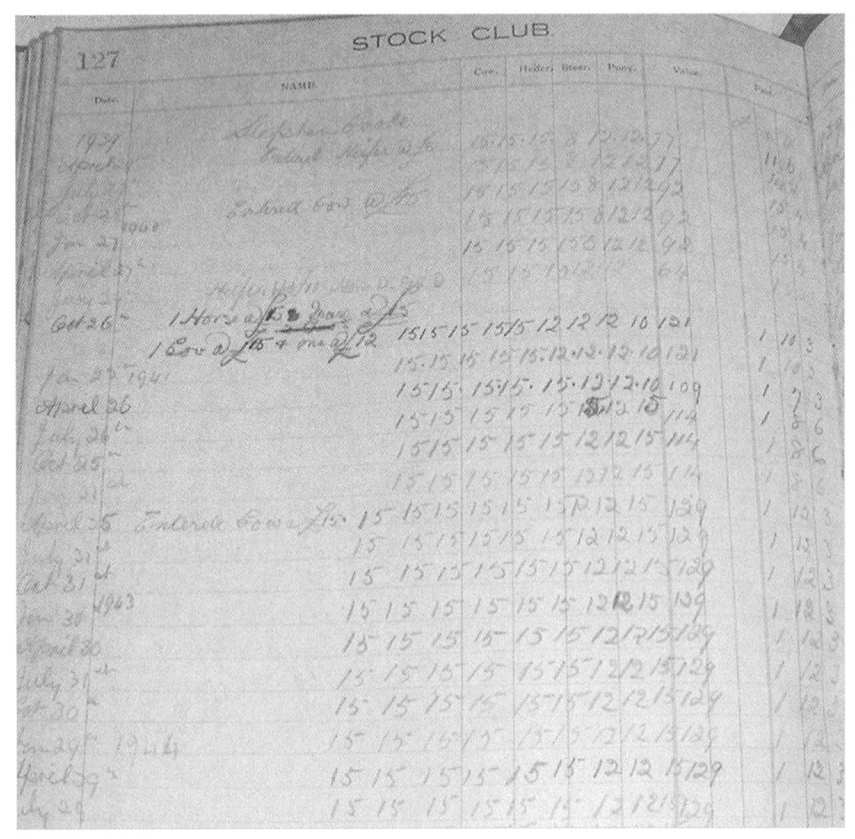

Jim Radley Collection

Salthouse is said to have been a village of donkeys and ducks, but from 1912 to 1959 only Levi High's donkey is mentioned. In fact after the First World War donkeys began to die out. Ex-cavalry mules, like that of Stephen Cooke above, were quite plentiful for a while after the war. But, apart from those who were dealing in fat cattle, the number of people owning one or two cows and a pony remained very much the same over the hundred years of the Salthouse Stock and Cattle Association's existence.

Left: One of Stephen Cooke's pages shows that he bought and sold bullocks on quite a large scale.

Vivian High

Vivian Harry High was born in Salthouse in 1922. His parents were Harry, who was secretary of the Cattle Association, and Bessie High, and his grandparents were Levi and Elizabeth High, and Tom (Rummy) and Mary Woodhouse. The following is taken from his autobiography.

Above: Vivian at the Salthouse 'Get-together' at the Manor, 4 October 2001.

Vivian 1933

Both my parents went into service after leaving school. My mother's first job was as a domestic servant for Mr and Mrs Ross at Salthouse Hall, and later she worked for many years for Colonel and Mrs Watson Kennedy at Wiveton Hall. She also worked in London as a cook.

My father, after he left school, worked as a farm labourer for Mr Deterding at Kelling Hall, and later he went to London where he worked in a hotel in the Tottenham Court Road as a lift operator. He joined the police in London, but the First World War put an end to this career and he joined the Royal Norfolks. He was discharged from the army with heart problems, and I still have his discharge badge which men who had been discharged used to wear to let people know they had been in the forces. He then returned to the farming life and worked for Mr Tom High at Swan Lodge and then for Jimmy Duffield at Salthouse until he got his own smallholding, but he was a special constable in the village for many years, and one of my memories is of how he had to keep the peace on polling day at the Parish Room. He was on duty all day, and I took him his elevenses, dinner and fourses. When I was old enough I did jobs on my parents' smallholding. I remember burning quicks,

Father with the horses, ready for a day's work. He bought his first horse 'Peggy' from Mr R. High ('Uncle Dick').

which were small heaps of foulgrass forked up after chain harrowing. Also I remember leading the horse while horse-hoeing. This was to keep the horse between the rows to make it easy for Father to operate the mechanical hoe. This is the time when cutting out took place: thinning sugar beet, mangolds and turnip plants to a certain distance apart.

My parents also had a small dairy herd. Other farmers in the village sold milk in bulk; it was put through a cooler and into churns and then taken to Holt railway station by horse-drawn milk float for transportation to a milk marketing depot. But we kept our milk and sold it locally.

I did the job of delivering milk around the

Grandmother Woodhouse and her ducklings. Behind her are the post office and village green.

village on my bike, carrying pint and quart milk cans, and Mother made lots of butter. To make it, the cream was separated from the milk by a separator operated by hand. The cream was then put in a churn, also hand-operated. Sometimes Mother turned the churn for hours, waiting for the butter to appear. She would then flavour it and pat it into half pounds or pounds which she would then sell. I still have the butter scales, but sadly the patters and decorating wheel are gone. The skimmed milk from the separator was sold cheaper or given to the calves. Fresh cream was sold to customers when requested. Grandmother Woodhouse kept ducks, and in the spring she reared ducklings. The eggs were hatched by broody hens called sitting hens. Orange-boxes were used for hatching, and these were ideal because they had three compartments. After hatching the ducklings were reared for a couple of weeks or so, and then sold to a Mr Norton from Briston who travelled here by horse and cart. I don't know what happened to the ducklings; some said they were used for powder puffs. Mother reared chickens by the same method as Gran, but sometimes the hens would lay away in clumps of nettles, where they were prone to rodents. Hedgehogs too could steal eggs. Mother kept the pullets, and cock birds

Grandmother Woodhouse's house is the left half of the white house, and Mr Norton's horse and cart are parked outside. Behind, and to the right, is the Dun Cow public house with the blacksmith's smithy on the right of the yard.

were reared for Holt Sale or Christmas dinners. To encourage hens to lay, sometimes a china egg was placed in the nest box.

Mr W. Graveling was the publican at the Dun Cow, and he was also the Blacksmith. His smithy can be seen on the right of the photo showing the Dun Cow. Apart from the usual horse-shoeing, I can remember him repairing hurdles for Mr Everett, a farmer from Cley. These hurdles, for penning in farm animals, were a portable metal frame with bars, and four iron wheels. They were brought to Salthouse for repair by a horse pulling several at a time, and they made a terrible noise on the tarred road. The tin building which was Geoffrey Graveling's carpentry shop, just beside the smithy, can also be seen in the photo.

Mr George Holmes was the local baker when I was a boy. My cousin Jasper worked at the bake house. I remember how he used to do the hard-working job of punching the dough ready for baking early the next morning. The oven was heated by 'furrer' (gorse) bushes cut by another village character, Joe Dack, and carted to the bake house by my Uncle Cliff with his horse and cart. Flour was delivered by a steam wagon belonging to Dewing and Kersley from the granary at Wells.

Some cottages had Common Rights which gave the occupants the right to shoot on the heath. One stretch of heath, from Holt Road to Lawn farm at Holt, was called Bix's Lane, and had private land on either side. This could cause friction with the landowners at nesting time as game-birds would nest close to, or in the lane, and at the start of the shooting season the game would stray into the lane and be shot by the locals who had the right to be there.

In the spring, bird nesting would start. We had an ornithologist, a Mr Garnett, living in Kelling, who formed groups of us to find nests so that he could ring the fledglings and log their journeys. One year my group found a cuckoo's egg in a hedge sparrow's nest, but sadly the egg was taken, so no fledgling emerged. Mr Garnett would reward us with a bar of chocolate each meeting and, at the end of the nesting season, a party was held in the tea-rooms on the beach, and prizes were given to the group with the best results.

Swallows, robins, thrushes, blackbirds and tomtits could be found nesting in outbuildings. I remember lapwings (peewits) on the marshes; they were my favourite bird and I did an essay on it at school which was approved of by Mr Garnett. There were skylarks and bitterns on the marsh and I remember nightingales on the heath and night jars, shrikes and turtle doves, all sadly now in decline.

Mother feeding the calves

We had nicknames for most birds:

Chaffinch	—	Spink
Greenfinch	—	Green linnet
Mistle Thrush	—	Pullfer
Song Thrush	—	Mavich
Blue Tit	—	Pickcheese
Goldfinch	—	Draw-water
Yellowhammer	—	Goolie
Ringed Plover	—	Stone-runner
Moorhen	—	Waterhen
Wren	—	Tomtit
Heron	—	Harnser
Dunnock	—	Hedger
Sparrow	—	Spadger

Along the coast road to Cley there were two wooden bungalows on the marsh. One was near Purdy's Drift and was occupied by Amy and Hezekiah ('Butcher') Holman, and the other was near Walser (Walcey) Hills and that's where my Aunt Alice* and Uncle Billy (Holman) lived at birds' nesting time, and I used to stay there sometimes with my cousin Brian. My uncle was keeper of the marshes for Mr Roy Pope. I recall how he would collect gulls' eggs in a pail, and I remember sometimes on a Sunday morning he would take my cousin and me to see a Mr Bishop who looked after Cley marshes; he had a keeper's hut near East Bank and would bring out a packet of sweets and hand them around.

My Uncle Billy and Aunt Alice ran the tea-rooms on the beach for Mr Pope, and we supplied them with milk daily in the late spring and summer. There was a flag pole a few yards to the right of the picture of the

* *Alice was sister of Bessie, Vivian's mother.*

The marsh flooded in 1938
On the left is Little Eye, with the wooden bungalow and garage on it clearly visible. To the right is the Rocket House on Great Eye. The tea-rooms can just be seen on the very left of Great Eye and on the extreme right of the photo is a converted old solid-tyred bus— a holiday home, belonging to the Briton family, with sleeping-quarters attached to it. It stood on the site of the old windmill in Mill Drift.

tea-rooms (below), and on a very busy day, when milk ran short, a second flag would be hoisted which could be seen from our house, and this was the signal for me to hurry over with extra supplies. In later years the tea-rooms were sold to a Mr and Mrs Brooks of Billericay, Essex, and used as a holiday residence.

Randall's 'Folly' was renamed when the Board of Trade took it over and used it to store rockets and other breeches-buoy equipment for

Uncle Billy, Aunt Alice and Brian in the tea-rooms.

sea rescue. I can remember the pole, to which the breeches-buoy line would be attached, lying near the Rocket House, and Father saying that the smallest man in the team climbed the pole to do this. In the 1930s the Rocket House was bought by a Mr Briton from Sheffield who used it as a summer residence. On the sea side of it there was a car park and also a pill-box with a winch on top for pulling boats up the beach, and there was a car park on the land side just below the Rocket House. In the Second World War the place was used as an army detention centre, and after the war it was bought by Mr and Mrs Jopling. It was badly damaged in the floods of 1953 and finally blown up in 1956. The garage, which also housed the

Randall's Folly renamed 'the Rocket House'.*

engine-driven water pump, can be seen on the right of the above photo.

Two kind old ladies who lived in the bungalow on Little Eye took a group of us to see Scott's Air Display at Aylmerton, by chauffeur-driven car, and I still have the Scott's Air Display badge which they bought for me. Another vivid memory I have of planes occurred in Salthouse itself when one Sunday dinner-time two aeroplanes flew low over the village and landed on a field close to the Hall. The pilots were visiting Commander, Colonel and Mrs de Crespigny who lived there. People gathered round the planes as this was a rare occasion! As I delivered milk daily to the Hall, I came in contact with the de Crespignys, and I found them very kind people. One of the things they did was to leave partly-smoked cigarettes for me to give to an old village character called Mooch who would break them up to smoke in his clay pipe.

Salthouse Bowls Club was at the Hall, and my uncle Bertie Woodhouse was team captain. I used to wipe the bowls on damp occasions. Mr Alec Morse was the gardener at the Hall,

* *The main section on the Rocket House begins p 280.*

and he also looked after the bowling green in the walled garden.

When I started school, we had to walk the two miles to Kelling, taking packed dinners, and in cold weather we toasted our sandwiches by the open coal fire. In later years we biked there, which enabled us to come home for lunch. I remember when the currant crop was fit, Mother and other women walked with us to Kelling so as to catch transport to West Beckham for currant-picking. We had a school football team and a dancing team. One year we competed in a dance competition in Saint Andrew's Hall in Norwich. We came second—which was good considering we were competing against much larger schools.

Jock was a half-bred Scottie. He went with me everywhere, when possible. One night we

Kelling school dancing team outside St Andrew's Hall Norwich

Back row: Myself, Ivy Holman, Mary Dawson, Betty Holland, Sylvia Duffield, Billy Osborne.
Second row: Gracie Hill, Kenny Brown, Don High, Clarence Newstead, Philip Dawson, Margaret Moy.
Third row: Billy Dew, Irene Woodhouse, Florence Woodhouse, Joan Lee, Eileen Thirtle, Sylvia Batch, Nancy Cooke, Ronnie Clark.
Front row: Jasper Dawson, Willie Woodhouse, Arthur Moy, John Hill.

Jock and myself on Salthouse beach.

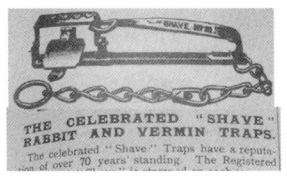

Above: A 'rabbit and vermin' trap of the time.

missed him; so early next day I went to search for him and found him in a gin trap. He had had the sense to stay still and not damage his leg too much. How pleased he was to see me!

Vermin caused lots of damage to the crops, and gin traps and snares were set to catch them. Rabbits would eat the young barley shoots and root-crop seedlings. Moles were also a problem. I have seen Father catch them by using a spade to dig them out at the moment they were making molehills. Stoats and weasels caused trouble with ground-nesting birds such as partridges and pheasants. To catch them, a trap was set in a wood tunnel, usually placed in a hedgerow between two fields.

Hay was cut and made into dome-shaped cocks. When being stacked, sometimes the cocks near the stack were pulled by a horse complete to the stack, by putting a chain round the bottom of the cock. The stack was left to mature ready for winter feed. Farmers had to be careful with hay as it could overheat. When it was ready for winter feed the hay was cut into blocks with a large-bladed stack knife and carted home. It was cut into chaff by a hand-operated chaff cutter and fed to the horses.

Both being smallholders, father and Uncle Cliff Woodhouse would help each other during harvest time. Barley was cut by a binder usually pulled by three horses. Before this was started, a strip the width of the binder was cut by scythe all round the edge of the cornfield. This was done to save the first round being trampled down. Shoofs (sheaves) were collected and made into shocks, six to eight leaning against each other for drying purposes. When the field was nearly cut and only a small strip was left, rabbits trapped in the remaining corn would run for safety, and people with sticks would do their best to catch them.

Bloom Stile in the foreground (before the housing estate was built), notice the footpath on the left and the stack on the right where we went ratting at night with sticks and torches.

A sail reaper cutting corn in Bloom Stile field, with rabbit chasers in action.

With the fields small and scattered, the binder would have to have its two auxiliary wheels fitted for the road. This was done by lowering the large driving wheel, so jacking up the binder. The shaft was then moved to be in line with the two wheels.

When the shocks had dried out, it was the time to build a stack. First the stack bottom (hedge-cuttings, straw etc.) had to be laid to protect the first layer of shoofs. These were collected by tumbler (tumbrel), and this was the time when, sitting on the horse, I would holler 'Holdyer!' to make sure that Father who was stacking the shoofs on the tumbler was aware it was about to move to the next shock.

Father (on top of the load), Brian Holman by the horse, and Uncle Cliff Woodhouse

When the stack was being built, warm dinners would be eaten in the field. Mother would bring well-wrapped meals in milk cans and basins to keep the dinner warm. How nice these meals were! Meat, potatoes, Norfolk dumplings and gravy. Drink was in a large bottle, mostly tea, and the horses had their well-earned meals from a nose bag.

SEA FISHING

I remember sea fishing—no rod, no reel, just a hank of line with hook and weight fitted to stronger string. This was swung round and round and then released. Lugworm bait was obtained from Ben Nockles or Jack Cooke.

Catching mackerel from the shore is not seen nowadays. Terns diving near the shore for whitebait used to be a sure sign that a shoal of mackerel was about. To catch them, a rowing boat was launched and a net was spread as the boat was rowed in a half circle. Then, with the boat beached, both ends of the net were pulled in.* The catch would then be sold or given to the helpers. The boat belonged to John 'Hopper' Holman and his family.

When an easterly wind blew for a few days, this would cause the beach to scour which would clear all the stones away to leave mud where coins, weights and other items could be found in the crevices. We would go beach-combing, finding amber and nice stones, lucky stones (with holes through them) and other bits of jetsam thrown into the sea from passing ships, as well as the round green glass balls used by fishermen to mark their crab pots. I remember one year after a bad storm thousands of oranges were washed ashore, having been swept off the deck-cargo of some merchant ship. In those days many ships could be seen at the same time, creating lots of smoke on the horizon. Porpoises used to be a common sight but are not seen nowadays off the beach.

Fishing for eels in the freshwater cricks was by hook or by bab. Hooks were used in shallow water where holes appeared in the mud. Babs were used in deeper water. These were bait threaded on wool made into three or four rings with a bamboo stick, line and a tell-tale cork. When biting, the eels' teeth would get caught in the wool, enabling them to be pulled out. This was done by a gentle pull on the bamboo stick.

On the beach there were large pools filled with tangle (weed). Using a stick to twist the tangle, small eels (elvers) could be caught when the weed was drawn out. Eels were also caught by using a glide which was a steel fork with five tines with barbs at the ends. Using a long pole to thrust into the mud, eels were caught between the barbs. [*see photo p 223*]

* *See photo p 266 of 'Friday' Forsdick with a mackerel catch.*

Eel Babbing 2001

Right: A visitor eel babbing in the creek at Salthouse in 2001. The occasion was an all-day Eel Babbing Contest arranged by Anne Wright, Winnie Walton and Charles Elsden. Joan Cooke and Anne Wright made the babs, threading the worms on wool in the traditional way—not everyone's idea of a pleasant task!

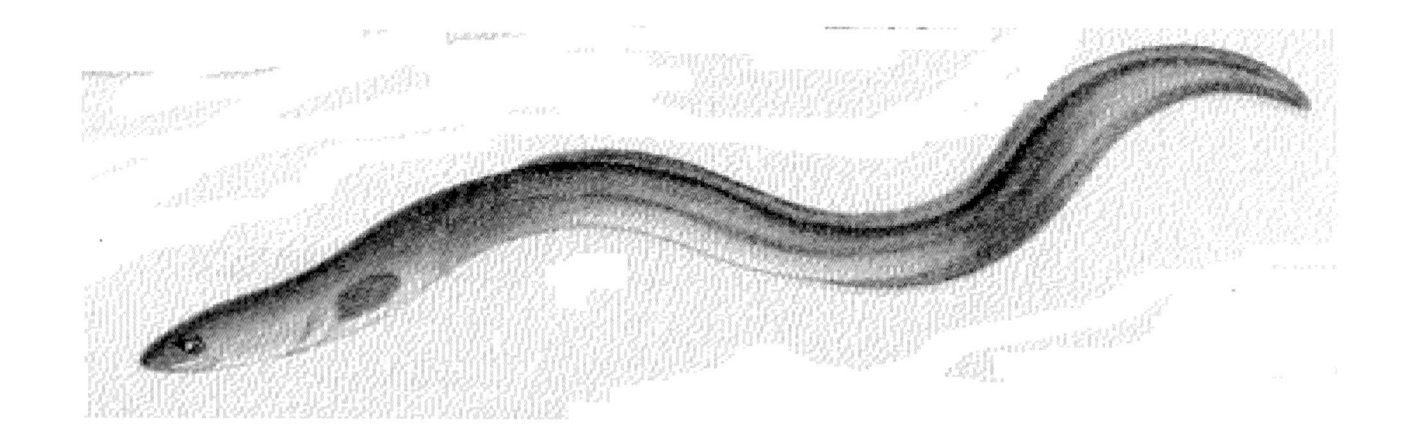

SALTHOUSE AND OTHER EELS.

The Salthouse Marsh has ceased to be a marsh in the proper sense. It is a square, shallow lake, divided from the sea by a bank of shingle and a broken, grass-covered dyke. It is crossed by the bed of the old river, and this river, now stagnant, is shut out from the Cley marshes by the East Bank sluice. The average depth of water on Salthouse Marsh is perhaps two feet.

A species of grass grows beneath the water, and hidden in the grass and mud are millions of eels, but eels of exceeding delicacy, which command the highest price on the London market.

A great deal has been discovered about eels and their amazing journeys across the ocean, and their departure from fresh water every decade; and those who have written learnedly about eels might with advantage study the Salthouse species, whose flavour may be due to their having been cut off effectively from the sea.

Once, when the sea mounted the banks, it is supposed that the Salthouse eels made a dash for liberty, and failed; for tons of them were captured in holes left by the tide.

The Salthouse eel lies inert under the mud in winter, and then he is most easily caught by means of a "glave" (sometimes pronounced "glide") or flat-pronged fork, which does not pierce him, but which grips him between its prongs. The "glave," as it is stabbed into the mud, is used to propel the flat-bottomed boats of Salthouse Marsh. And the use of a "glave" produces a swelling and hardness of the inner part of the thumb, by which a "glave" user can be instantly detected.

In the spring and summer the eel on Salthouse Marsh becomes agile and frisky, and will leap out of the water like a trout through very joy of life. Then to stab him is no easy task, and to land him in the boat when you have stabbed him is difficult.

From an undated newspaper clipping in the Tracey Large Collection

Summer Sea Angling in Norfolk

The following article describing the discovery of Salthouse—by a stranger from further afield than Holt—appeared in the local paper some time in the 1930s. It is from a cutting found in the Parliament Box.

Sea fishing on the Norfolk coast has hitherto been looked upon as a sport which can only be pursued in autumn or winter when the fringe of the vast shoals of whiting and cod passing down the North Sea strikes our coast, and during the summer the angler has naturally laid aside his tackle because he believes that there are no fish inshore for him to catch.

Recently a discovery has been made which bids fair to give the sea-angler good sport. In the course of his travels, Mr G. T. Atkinson, Chief Inspector of Fisheries of the Ministry of Agriculture and Fisheries stationed at Lowestoft, came into touch with Mr Nockolds of Salthouse and to his surprise learnt from him that he had taken good catches of fish in the summer from the beach at Salthouse.

Mr Atkinson passed on the news to me and asked me to look further into it, as he thought there were great possibilities in it, so the writer with some friends journeyed over to Salthouse last Thursday to investigate.

The wind was blowing half a gale and the sea was so rough that a pound lead would not hold bottom, but enquiries were made as to the results of the efforts of local people and a profitable and enjoyable afternoon followed. Salthouse is a weird-looking place: a little village at the foot of the hill-country looking out onto a broken sheet of water—the result of a flood a few years ago when the sea wall broke down—and, beyond this, the sand-hills and a narrow, quickly shelving beach down to the sea. This steep beach is the secret of the good fishing at Salthouse, for here the water is deep close inshore, and a moderate cast takes the angler's bait to the feeding grounds of the fish. The fish taken are usually of the flat varieties—dabs, plaice, with occasionally a good sole, varied by a mackerel or a bass now and again. On a suitable day, anything from twenty to forty fish may be taken, fishing the last two hours of the flood and the first hour of the ebb.

Anyone can partake of the fun. Last week a little lad with twenty yards of string caught several dabs, while a short time ago a policeman, in three hours' fishing, had 133 fish of various kinds. Here then is good sport for the sea angler. Let him choose a day when the tide suits the time of his fishing, and the wind is from some other direction than from the north, preferably from straight offshore. Get a supply of lugworms from Mr Nockolds, and enjoy good sport in the otherwise 'off season'.

That the possibilities of sport at Salthouse have not been discovered before, is due doubtless to its inaccessibility, there being no railway nearer than Holt or Weybourne; but it is a delightful motor car run from Norwich, and a return trip by the coast road to Cromer, as we did it, makes an enjoyable finish to the trip.   A.R.J.

The late Jim Radley was one of those 'little lads' mentioned above who fished off the beach with hand-lines, and he recalled exactly how he felt when outsiders came to Salthouse to fish and tended to disregard the natural laws of respect for fellow (local) fishermen: 'We used to work with several lines. We'd buy a ball of string and make four hand-lines about eighty yards long and three hooks on. We'd be fishing off Salthouse beach, and what used to infuriate us was when the Holt Sea Angling Club came along. We'd have our lines spaced four or five yards apart, and they'd come and plop in between us *and it used to infuriate us something shocking*! I mean—all they'd got to do was move further along the beach . . .'

George Cooke

George today, 2002.

George was born in Salthouse 84 years ago and still lives in the house where he was brought up, though he has travelled the world and was a prisoner of the Japanese in World War Two. He is one of a big fishing family who have made their living from the sea and the marsh for many generations.

Above: Crab boat LN268, in 'the Crick' outside George Cooke's house.

Left: George making a crab pot. Behind him is his eldest brother Jack (the original 'Cookie' of Cookie's Crab shop on the Green, and father of Suzanne McKnespiey, who now runs it with her husband Peter).

The water used to be on the road every year before the war. You used to go in the boat to fetch your coal from Cross Street, because the water couldn't get off the marshes. It used to have to go through the east bank to get off—half way up the east bank there's a sluice—and they wouldn't allow to let it go and flood Cley marshes and the bird sanctuary. That lay on there a week or more, a whole winter sometimes. You'd get in a boat and go as far as the east bank when I was a boy.

George with the business end of a glide which would have had a long pole. It was used for catching eels from a boat.

That would be just after the fourteen war. My father and I, we'd go eeling. It was full of eels these marshes—tons of eels we used to catch. I've heard my grandmother say that Hopper, my uncle, had the floor of the washroom next door thick with eels, and they used to come from Norwich and buy them. He used to put a board across the door and shoot all the eels in. Everybody had a boat in those days, and everybody in the village had a gun and it always hung over the door—or over the fireplace. The cartridges would sit on the mantelpiece too. As children we never touched the gun. We'd get a belting if we did. We knew better.

It was a village of ducks and donkeys! They used to have about five or six ducks and a drake, everybody, and you'd get them in at night (they come up when you feed them) and after they'd laid the eggs you'd turn them out in the morning. They hatched the young ducks off and you'd get a shilling each for them. They had to be yaller ducklings, no colour. If a coloured drake turned up, somebody killed it so they won't cross breed. They used to go for powder puffs—Perry Norton used to come all the way from Briston with a horse and cart, and sit and wait for the ducks to hatch. If somebody had some hatching, they'd sit up and go to the pub and wait—and go and get say another half-dozen. So good a trade that was.

Bob, he used to do taxidermy. He used to keep all them ducks on the marsh; he used to breed birds to sell to different parts and he used to do taxidermy as a hobby sort of thing. He used to go to college to learn it. Not many people did it. An old boy in Cley used to do that, old Borrer, he had all these birds round that he'd shot, and the dates.

They brought a new law in then, about 1950 time or earlier, before the flood. I think he shot a sandpiper, the last bird he shot. After that they took his guns away. I know I shot a smew drake along the bank there, I took it to him and 'It's no good to me,' he said, 'but I'll have it.' Beautiful coloured bird, similar to a shoveler. That's a nice colour.

Leslie Cooke was only fourteen when he shot a snow goose. They used to shoot everything. I can remember Beach Road lined with guns about every yard apart. Ducks used to drift along the sea as far as Yarmouth and then come back onto the mud flats along the marsh, and they'd shoot 'em like the Vietnam war.

I don't remember anything about flags for the fire, but I remember there was a 'Flag Heath' at Kelling. I used to turf-cut on the marshes. I done a lot, for bowling greens and that. They were thick—big thick rolls. That used to go to Norwich, Drayton, Leicester, Cromer—when they made a new road they banked the sides with turf. It would grow again in a year. I got a marsh up there, I got a lot off that. I stripped the lot off that and now it's all grown back again.

Twenty odd years ago it wasn't a bad trade. Now, they won't let you do it. What do you call it? 'Special scientific interest' or something.

They cut turves here for years. An old boy used to tell me how to do it, you know, how to get on with it. He reckon he used to cut a hundred and then go home. He said if he done too many they'd cut the price down. They would do, wouldn't they? That's what he always told me. 'Don't do too much', he said, 'You'll find you get your price drop.'

That picture [*opposite*] is about 1949. That's old Mrs Fielden in the distance standing there. She's an army officer's wife. They hired it off the Joplings. We're taking her husband or someone over, as we were going across onto the beach. She needn't have stayed there in the flood. The army come along after her, but she wouldn't go; she stayed there.

George at home

Mrs Fielden was marooned in the Rocket House during the flood of 1949. The cutting below, from the North Norfolk News of the time, gives a firsthand report on her story.

FRIDAY, MARCH 4, 1949

Relief Party Reaches Rocket House

Across the floods, standing in isolation on Salthouse beach, completely surrounded by water, was the old coastguard rocket house with its single occupant, Mrs. Fielden, the wife of Lieut.-Col S S Fielden, stationed at Weybourne.

Walking across two miles of shingle bank, out of which mines washed up by the heavy seas were showing, a party of troops and 2nd/Lieut. G. Harding, from Weybourne Camp, accompanied by a reporter, reached Mrs. Fielden on Wednesday. The troops brought bread, milk, three pails of water and candles.

Mrs. Fielden came out of the house to greet them. "It is lovely to see you," she said. She looked none the worse for her lonely ordeal. "It was too wonderful to frighten me," she said.

Mrs. Fielden said that when she awoke on Tuesday the sea was breaking over the shingle banks and swirling into the marshes towards Salthouse. At times the water washed very close to the house, which stands on a high mound of earth. In front of it a former military pill-box was washed away and the high shingle bank in front of it had disappeared. On either side of the house the shingle banks which normally keep the water from Salthouse marshes have been flattened.

GAINED HER WISH

"I always wanted to see a rough sea," said Mrs. Fielden, "and by Jove, I have seen one now. I spent most of Tuesday with my nose glued to the upstair sitting-room window, looking at the sea. It was a thrilling sight and the seas were terrifically rough. At times it was completely black and

Left: This picture, taken at the time, in 1949, did not appear in the press until the 1980s when Mrs Fielden's son Michael, who had taken it all those years ago, found it and sent it to the EDP. He is the one who is being rowed across the flooded marsh to bring food to his mother, and she can be seen in the photo watching from the 'Great Eye' (she is standing to the right of the Folly).

Michael 'had a vague recollection' that the men pulling towards the Folly 'belonged to the Cooke family' and he hoped that the photograph might stir memories among any of those pictured who were still alive.

He was right—they were all Cookes: three brothers (Bob, George and Charlie), and two cousins (Tom and Billy). Two brothers, Charlie and George, are still alive.

Left: Bob
Behind him: Billy
In the bows: Charlie
Middle-right: Tom
Near-right: George

> I could not tear myself away from the window. It was too wonderful."
> Mrs. Fielden showed herself outside the house during Tuesay in case the people at Salthouse were wondering if she was all right. "I would not wave in case they thought something was wrong and that I needed assistance. I felt so sorry for the people in Salthouse village who were flooded out. At least I was dry and in no real danger."
>
> NO WISH TO LEAVE
>
> Mrs. Fielden declined the rescue party's offer to escort her back to Weybourne Camp and said she intends to stay on as "the worst was over.'" At high tides Mrs. Fielden has been cut off again as the lowered shingle bank was partly covered by water and her contact with the land was cut off. It is possible, however, to reach her by boat from Salthouse. She has a good stock of tinned food. Mrs. Fielden will leave the Rocket House at the end of March, when she goes to join her husband who has been posted to Barnard Castle.

Leslie Cooke

Leslie is the son of Isaac Cooke. He is a cousin of George Cooke and is related to both the Hancock family and the Holman family. He has very strong feelings about change and the loss of the old way of managing the heath.

My father used to go wildfowling, and from the age of five I used to go with him. I can always remember my mother wrapping me up—about two jerseys and three scarves round my chest. That's no good going wildfowling on a sunny day like this; it had to be rough weather. When I was nine years old, my father gave me a four-ten and I used to shoot peewits. He wouldn't let me go alone; I had to be with him. And then he said 'I'm not going to buy you any more cartridges, you'll have to earn them with what you shoot.'

At that time there was a lot of green plover (peewits) used to come along during the shooting season every evening about chimney pot high and they set up Mill Drift, and I know I always had enough to buy more cartridges. I used to get threepence for them. It were no good for duck shooting, a four-ten, but they'd kill a green plover as high as a chimney pot.

There was a butcher used to come from Sheringham—Pigott his name was—with a big lorry. He used to go to London twice a week and he used to buy all the rabbits around here. His mother was Hannah Pigott, I think. They'd buy anything: pheasants, partridges—anything—ducks, rabbits, hares and peewits.

Mrs Morse used to live bottom of the lane, and she took a liking to me. She was a widow and she had a son, Ted his name was, and he was a gamekeeper. She called me in one day and said 'Ted is getting another gun, he's getting rid of the gun he's got, would you like it?' It was a sixteen bore, a hammer gun, and I think I given thirty shilling for it, and I could start shooting ducks with that.

George Cooke's father was my father's brother, Marshall Cooke. They called him 'Yorkie' because he walked to Yorkshire. My father was Isaac. He was a blacksmith, my father. He worked in the blacksmith's shop at Blakeney where the King's Arms pub is; there's a big yard and two blacksmiths worked there. He was in the army during the First World War, and he was a blacksmith then.

He told me when he left school he went to be an apprentice. They were strict you know—that was all done through the government. There used to be an inspector come round to take him to the man who wanted to employ him as an apprentice. He had to live-in with this blacksmith and his wife at Sheringham. They had to feed him and there was an inspector come down and see if he got the right food. They were strict. He got a shilling a week for himself and he got all his food, and they treated him like a son till his apprenticeship finished after five years. I know he said they had to do it properly because of the inspectors coming round. He used to come home once or twice a year for a week at a time.

Granny Rudd—born Mary Holman, she married a Hancock and then a Rudd.

My grandmother was related to Ruth Holman; she was a Holman, I think, before she married. She lived up the top, nearly the last house on the right going up Cross Street. Her name was Rudd. She was a widow living alone and she kept a pig—nearly everyone kept a pig. They used to breed the pig and have a litter every year. I know, because she told me. They'd have perhaps eight little pigs and that would pay her rent and rates for the whole year, and if anything went wrong and the sow didn't have any, they'd be in a muddle you know. That was their bank.

My father built his own house from the old chapel up Grout's Lane, and another of his brothers, Stephen, helped him. The marshes used to flood and the water lay on them all winter and he'd go across in a flat-bottomed boat and get a load of shingle, come as far as the coast road, shovel it out into a donkey cart and bring it up the hill to make his concrete.

He dug his own well too—him and his brother Stephen. He had an old mangle and he took one roller out and wound the rope round so he could turn the handle and get the buckets up. It was all chalk, absolutely hard chalk, after they got down about four or five foot, right down to the bottom. It was lovely clear water that chalk water when it settled. That was clear—crystal clear.

I was told that the water all run down into the sea, whether that be on the top of the ground or under the ground, that still run into the sea. When the tide come in, that back your fresh water up and of course it can't run through the salt water, can it? When the tide is up you can see it come half way up the beach. Well, the water that runs through the bottom of the beach can't run away when the tide is there, can it? As soon as the tide go out the fresh water go with it, and so there's always fresh water going into the sea. That don't run in the summer on top of the ground but there's a lot run under the ground. That water down the bottom of his well would perhaps rise up and down because, when the tide come in, that back it up and that can't get out. That do all round the coast like that.

When we were at school we heard rumours there was a tunnel run straight between the two churches from Salthouse to Kelling church. The old monks used to go from one place to another.

The man who cut the gorse to make faggots, Joe Dack, he never let the gorse get big like it is now. About as thick as your finger that went in the bake oven. All he did was make the faggots. He never tied them—he bent one of them round and twisted it and tucked it under. He never wore anything on his hands, and they were all full of gorse. Toughest man he was. He was up there on the heath all day and every day. He used to have his dinner up there, a round of bread no butter on it or anything, perhaps a piece of cheese. He made a great stack of faggots and Cliff Woodhouse would take three or four tumbrel loads a day and stack them on the green outside the bake house.

When the gorse bushes were only so high, there used to be a lot of little sand lizards on the heath and I used to like to watch them. They don't hardly move and then they dart like that, then if they see you they'll go in, and

Bard Hill before the road was tarred.

if you stand right still they'll come out again. Just like little newts, only slimmer. I've seen quite a lot of them, they'd be in a little bunch, then if you go on you'd come on another little bunch, three or four at a time.

There's a pit by Bard Hill, they call it Bard Hole. Between the road and that pit it was all grass and they used to call it Bard Hill Plain. There was no bushes and that—they used to keep cows on there. In those days nearly everybody had a cow to get milk.

They used to burn the gorse in the old days when Salthouse men looked after the heath. They burnt it in sections at a time. If they cut some roadways through now, like there used to be years ago—if they sent a bulldozer in from the road that runs across the Lowes and cut about eight fire-breaks 8 or 10 yards wide—they could burn one of those sections off easily. But now you've got to have firemen and police there and you've got to pay for them to be there, that's the thing.

There's about ten men now in the village of Salthouse, that's all, that are Salthouse people who were born here.

I remember Captain Borrer from Cley. He used to live on the corner between the George and what used to be Rust's shop. He was a shooting man. He used to shoot any birds, rare ones or anything, because he used to collect them.

He come along the bank once and he stopped me and he said 'Have you seen a smew about here? If you see one, let me know.' Next time I went along he said 'I got that duck but I can't get it—it's right in the middle of the water.' I sent my dog in and that fetched it out. That was in the middle of a hard winter. He thanked me for doing that and then he said 'If you'd like to come and see my birds, come down

Sunday morning and I'll be at home and I'll show you.' He had a great big room!—big as this house—and he had a swan sitting stuffed there. He had nearly everything there but he wouldn't have anything anyone else shot; he had to shoot it. That wouldn't be no good if it was the rarest bird on earth if someone shot it and said do you want it? He wouldn't have it. Borrer his name was. I remember when he died there was a bit in the paper about him and although he was a Norfolk man, I think he left his birds to some museum down south.

Billy Bishop of Cley knew Mr Borrer very well. He referred to him as the last of the Gentleman Gunners, and said that he wrote many nature articles for local papers and magazines under the name 'Sea Pie'. In one of these he left a fitting epitaph for the collectors who shot rare birds:

'Such were some of the Gentlemen Gunners and their Henchmen. They belonged to a race that has almost passed away, like may other denizens of the swamps and marshes. They may become extinct, like many butterflies and birds.'

Billy and Bernard Bishop, *Cley Marsh and its Birds,* 2nd edition, Hill House Press, Cley, 1996.

In the short article below, Borrer (writing in his old age) describes his first shooting at Salthouse before he came to live at the Old Manor House in Cley. He died in 1961 and left his collection to Cambridge University.

NORTH NORFOLK QUEST

A SMALL yellow-headed bird with a pair of tiny black feathered horns on its head first brought me to Salthouse on a cold December morning. I had walked along the beach from Sheringham looking for shore-larks, and bird watchers still come there on a similar quest in winter time in search of that hardy little rarity.

But I am speaking of fifty-five years ago. In those benighted days naturalists not only carried field glasses slung over their shoulders, but usually a double-barrelled hammer gun as well. I returned to London in triumph with a pair of shore-larks, which were duly stuffed by Rowland Ward, of Piccadilly, and the elegant little creatures can be seen to this day in the Museum of Natural History in Cambridge University. I subsequently enjoyed many a good day shooting and wildfowling in Salthouse marshes, and even bought a few acres of flooded salting below the Dun Cow Inn, which now forms part of the Norfolk Naturalists' bird-paradise.

Billy Bishop Collection

C.D. Borrer, about the age he was when he first came to Salthouse in search of shore-larks to shoot.

Arnold's Marsh given to the National Trust with shooting rights to C.D. Borrer

Thirty acres of Salthouse Broad have been bequeathed to the National Trust by Mr Edward Carleton Arnold, of 32a Furness Road Eastbourne. Mr Arnold, who died on October 20th at the age of 80, was headmaster of Eastbourne College from 1924 to 1929. In his will, Mr Arnold stated that the land was important from the ornithological aspect, and expressed a wish that his friend Mr C. D. Borrer of Cley be permitted to shoot over Salthouse Broad free of charge during his lifetime. *Eastern Daily Press, 18 Jan 1950.*

Suzanne and Peter of Cookie's Crab Shop

In 1956 Suzanne's father, Jack Cooke, bought the house where Emily Gray had lived and sold a few groceries before the 1953 flood (see page 289).

In the early days, Jack (known as 'Cookie' in his family) and Elsie first started selling crabs and bait outside the house. Crabs sold for a few shillings each, boiled and dressed, and lug worms for five shillings a hundred.

Since her parents died, the business they started has been developed by Suzanne and Peter McKnespiey, into the highly successful shop and restaurant it is today.

Elsie Cooke outside the Crab Shop

Jack Cooke

It must have been a freezing introduction to working life. Aged 15, Suzanne Cooke was put to work by her father, bait-digging on the marshes and creeks of the North Norfolk coast.

'We were absolutely freezing in the winter' says Suzanne. 'And you couldn't wear lots of clothes because that would have stopped you bending to pick up the worms when you had dug them up. The men I was with took pity on me and used to help me to fill up my bucket—it was hard work but even then it was wonderful to me being out in the open air on the coast with no one about for miles. It was beautiful.'

Once she had mastered bait-digging, life didn't get that much better. Her father asked her to help him when he went crabbing in his boat, Sunbeam. 'I was there to bale, and nothing else. While he would be pulling up the crab pots, I had to keep baling. She was a leaky old boat, and as fast as I baled her out the water came in.'

The business is very different nowadays from what it used to be. Cookie's Crab Shop has become famous for its seafood delicacies and people come from all over the country to eat here. Suzanne and Peter work round the clock.

But Suzanne's love affair with Salthouse and the mysterious creeks and gullies of this area of the coast has never diminished—even though the coastline and its inhabitants have changed. 'We employ other people to dig the bait and collect the samphire these days,' she says. 'But there is nothing like getting up early in the morning to pick samphire. Sometimes we get up as early as three in the morning and drive along the coast to where we think the best spots are—anywhere between here and the Wash. We know the place backwards but we are still finding new places to go. Last summer we found a glorious creek where the water was fresh and the samphire was thick.'

Suzanne and Peter McKnespiey outside the Crab Shop, December 2001

From the EDP, December 2001

Clifford High

Clifford, second son of Ernest and Mary High, was the only one of the three brothers to leave the country and adventure abroad. His daughter Doreen (right) and his niece Kathleen Gray (left)—daughter of his brother Haddon—tell what they remember of him and show some of their photographs. He was only twenty when he left. (For a photo of Cliff's father see p141)

Kathleen Gray

Doreen Sayer

Above: Mary High and her four daughters outside the Manor farm house, where the door was never locked.

Kath: Harry Dawson always said that Uncle Cliff could mix with the King and Queen or a gypsy. He was that type of man. Aunt Gladys said that Granny blamed herself for him going to Canada because she used to read to them a story about some pioneer family in Canada when they were children, and she did tell me the name of it but I can't remember.

Doreen: Gladys told me that after he went, his mother never locked the door again in case he suddenly came home. He left in 1913 and had a year out there before war broke out and he joined the Canadian army.

Ernest and Mary High's seven children. *From left to right:* Haddon, Gladys, Havelock, Gertrude, Kathleen, Miriam and Clifford.

Clifford High

Ernest High must have been a proud man when he read this article in the paper about the bravery of his son Clifford:

The Daily News & Leader

LONDON AND MANCHESTER. WEDNESDAY, APRIL 28, 1915

SALTHOUSE MAN WOUNDED AT ST. JULIEN.

Mr. E. P. High (District Councillor) has received information that his son Clifford, who returned to England with the 10th Battalion of the 1st Canadian Contingent, was severely wounded at the battle, in the course of which the Germans penetrated our lines to St. Julien. It appears a bullet struck Private High in the skull, inflicting a compound fracture. Mr. High has received letters from his son which, with characteristic modesty, refrain from mentioning the circumstances in which he got his wound, but describe his share in the battle. He says:—"I am getting on fine. Well, I will try to tell you something about it. We had just come out of the trenches, when the Germans started shelling us (this was Thursday afternoon). The game was too much for us to stand, and we had to leave. It was awful to see them coming over a hill to charge us after using their gas, and the shells were covering the ground all round. The French were almost mad. We had orders to stand to, and about 7 o'clock we started off to where they had broken through. All this time the Canadians were holding them back. An order came along that there was a wood full of Germans, and my Company (A) and C were to drive them out, and the other two companies to come up behind us. We started off, and the way the bullets came and went was thicker than a hailstorm. I was lucky enough to get right through. When we were within ten yards they ran as fast as they could, but our rifles can send a bullet as we can go just as quick. We got a lot of officers. The first I got was one, and he was on his knees. He carried on terribly, but he should have thought of that before. I had a good drink of cocoa off one. As for getting helmets, I picked up several, but did not carry them far. I had no idea of getting off so lucky. I expect I shall be all right in two or three weeks."

A few days later, writing from Bromley, Private High expresses the surprise his friends will have at finding him in England, and casually mentions that the doctors have removed a bullet from his skull. He goes on to wonder what has become of his chum, a Canadian named Merrifield, as there were only about a hundred left of the 10th and 16th Battalions when Private High got hit. By a coincidence Mr. High had just heard from Merrifield's mother that he is in hospital at Reading, with wounds in the arm and leg. A London friend of Private High, named Wallace, has journeyed to Bromley to see him, and writing to Mr. High, he explains the nature of the wound. The bullet entered the head at the right side, and carried small pieces of cap lining under the skull bone. The doctors had to remove a portion of the skull bone, and later on a second portion, before reaching the fragments of the cap. They pay a high tribute to the pluck of the patient, who stood it remarkably well. The surgeons were compelled to enlarge the area of the wound in order to clean it, as the black fragments of the cap were lodged on top of the cavity of the brain. It was a highly dangerous operation, and turned out most successful. Mr. E. P. High has just received a communication from the Canadian Red Cross Society, which states the patient has received a compound fracture of the skull, and that he underwent a serious operation for trepanning on April 31st, and is progressing exceedingly well. He is now at Oakley, Bromley Common.

Doreen tells the story that when her father was wounded he was first in the queue for an ambulance and, just as he was to be loaded on, a wounded officer turned up and took his place—officers were served first. The ambulance was then full and Cliff must wait for the next one to arrive. As the ambulance pulled away, he watched in horror as he saw it blown up by a direct hit from a bomb. He said 'I always felt sorry for that poor officer. They put him on first, and then—would you ever believe it—'

CLIFFORD HIGH

'You are thought one of the Heroes'

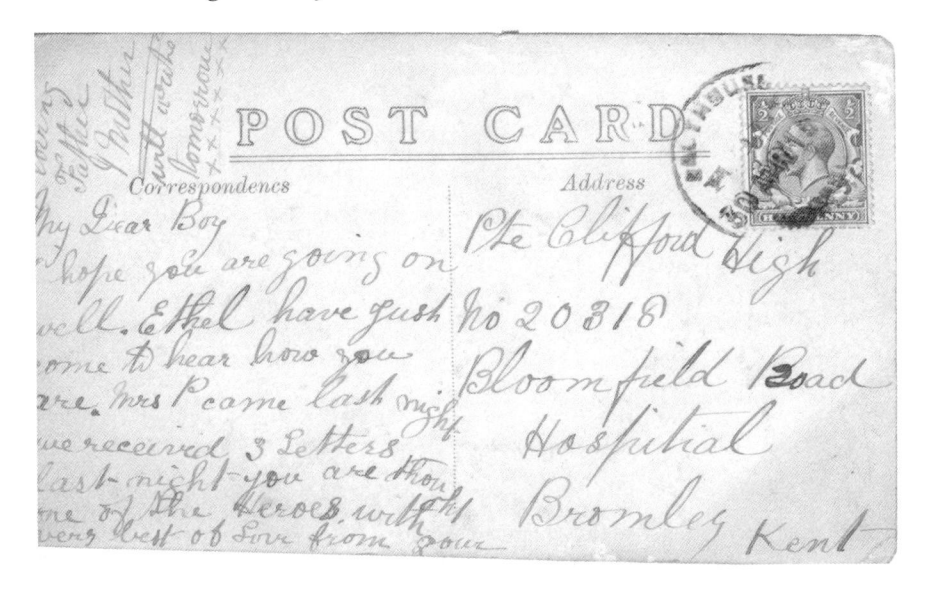

Left: A postcard sent to Cliff from his parents when he was brought home wounded and in hospital in Bromley, Kent—dated 30 August, 1915:

My Dear Boy,
I hope you are going on well. Ethel* have just come to hear how you are.
Mrs Peame last night. We received 3 letters last night. You are thought one of the Heroes. With very best of love from your loving Father and Mother will write tomorrow
x x x x x

(* *His cousin, Mary Lemmon's mother*)

He came home, got his demob and started farming in Salthouse—where Doreen was born—before moving to the Abbey Farm in Weybourne in 1931.

Left to right: Miriam, her husband Percy Ramm, Havelock, Doreen, Haddon, Bob Nurse (who was farm Steward), and Cliff High at the wheel of his jeep, in Cross Street on one of his Sunday visits to his family c1952.

Doreen today

The Manor House

MARY LEMMON (NÉE DAWSON) REMEMBERS HER CHILDHOOD IN THE MANOR HOUSE

Mary today

The first thing I heard about the Manor was a story of romance! Mr Johnson, I was told, a landowner, fell in love with and married a village girl from the Pigott family, and they lived in the Manor House. My grandfather, Henry High, either through birth or work, must have been connected to her,* as my mother referred to her as 'Aunt Johnson'. But Florrie, Mother's cousin [*Jim Radley's mother*] whose grandmother was a Pigott, for reasons known only to herself refused to call Mrs Johnson this, and was barred from the Manor House!

When the Johnsons died, my grandfather Henry and grandmother Mary (always called Polly), and Granny's mother, moved into the house. My mother, having completed her training as a dress-maker, returned to Salthouse to live with her parents. She and my father, a soldier in the First World War, married in 1915, and when he was invalided out of the army they took over the Manor House, using it as a Guest House. During the war, officers were billeted with them, and Captain Gunton's wife and daughter joined him there. They continued to return for holidays for many years.

* Mrs Johnson was aunt to Henry High and to his brother James, the father of Florrie.

Sarah Pigott ('Aunt Johnson') married the Squire

Sarah Ann Pigott became Mrs Johnson when she married the Squire's son William Johnson in 1869. At his death she found herself owner of the Manor House and farm, and we are told that she split up the farm among many tenant farmers but left the house to Ethel (her nephew Henry's daughter and Mary's mother). Mary (aged three) is seen below among her family on the occasion of her grandparents' Golden Wedding at the Manor House. Amazingly, it was not until this book was being written and facts sorted out, that Mary found out that her mother, as a girl, had become owner of the Manor.

The Golden Wedding at the Manor House

Standing: Tom High, Laura, Jack Dawson, Doris, Jimmy High, Mrs Dawson, Mr Dawson, Jack High.
Sitting: Letty (Tom's Wife), Ethel (Jack Dawson's wife), Henry High & Polly, Laura (Jimmy's wife), Sabra (Jack's wife).
Children, on the grass: Wallace, Harry (with me behind him), Harold, Douglas (with Elsie behind him) and Nancy.
[compare to photo p 118 of High family]

235

My brother Harry and the Guntons' daughter.

At this time the house consisted of a long low bedroom (servants' quarters perhaps?), six bedrooms, a kitchen, a pantry and two sculleries, hall, back stairs, dining room, drawing room, large hall and front stairs, study and a cellar. The yard contained a number of buildings, including wash-house and copper, stables (our Black Bess was stabled there), coach-house and workshops. Water was obtained from a pump in the yard and heated in the copper, or by the small tank part of the kitchen range. There were two earth closets, one at the front of the house and one at the back. Each contained two seats for adults, and one small seat for children—a family affair! Candles and oil lamps provided the lighting.

The garden was large and delightful. The lawns down which we rolled as children were kept in trim by my father with his scythe. He was responsible for the vegetables too, and these appeared in their season—potatoes, carrots, beans, peas, parsnips, onions. Mother was in charge of the flowers which always seemed to be in bloom. There were also gooseberries, raspberries, apples, figs, plums, damsons and pears. One corner of the garden was left wild.

My brother and I were born at the Manor House. The long low bedroom became our playroom and the garden our playground. We ate the fruit and got 'lost' in the wild parts of the garden. The glass summer-house was used as a tea-room when friends visited.

There were three things of which I was afraid. The painting on the cupboard door in the landing just outside my bedroom was one of them. This depicted the bears coming out of the wood to eat the children who had taunted the prophet Elisha. When put to bed, I stayed there! Then there was the haunted bedroom: a ghost was seen by visitors, but never by me—I not having been born at chime hours. She was a lady dressed in grey, weeping as she rocked herself in the chair by the window. Then there was the talk of a smugglers' tunnel from the beach to the Manor House, but we looked in vain to find this.

Visitors came back year after year. One family, the Bramfords, stayed all one summer. They brought their 'ayah' with them, but she was so cold and unhappy that they sent her home. They found a lovely girl from Wiveton, Mabel Parrot, to be their nurse, and they hired a girl from Cley called Lily to help with the house-work. The ayah used to take us to the beach for a swim. I and my cousin Nancy (Jack's daughter), who stayed with us during the summer holidays, went with the two Bramford children. Nancy hated the sea, and she and Mary Bramford found it very cold, but we all enjoyed the chocolates we were given when we got dry!

My father had two carts, a workaday one used by him sometimes to pick me up from school on a rainy day (I was very popular then), and one we called 'the car' used to take mother and we children shopping in Holt. We always got out and walked up Watering Hill, as it would have been too much for Black Bess to pull us all up there.

Gypsy the dog had her kennel in the back yard. In order to guard both yards she would lie on the top of the dividing wall. There were occasions when she got over-excited in her job of guarding, and fell off into the front yard and had to be rescued. One of her jobs was to go rabbiting with my father. He tried to keep down the rabbit population on Havelock's and Haddon's land. Later on, when he was old enough, Haddon's son Don went out with him.

Havelock and Haddon were Ernest High's sons. Havelock lived with his mother and sister Gladys at Manor Farm; Haddon and his family further down Cross Street. Gladys delivered our milk about nine o'clock each morning.

The time came when Manor House was to be sold. It was bought by Sir Michael Keen who had been Governor of Assam, and they modernised the house. Lady Keen was a lovely lady, and I remember happy hours with her as she taught us Indian games. We were very friendly with

The back yard area of the Manor House as it was in my childhood.

George and Gwen Martin, who worked for the Keens. The wash-house and chicken house were made into a cosy bungalow for them. The Keens' youngest daughter was married while they were there, and Mother made her trousseau of white silk, which I was never allowed to touch! Father and Sam Talbot fired over the heads of the happy couple, to drive off evil spirits, bursting a bag of confetti over them as they returned from the church through the gate in the garden wall.

Mr and Mrs T. Leach lived there next and were kind enough to allow the Youth Club to use the billiard room (the old coach house). So ended my links with the Manor House.

Mary Lemmon
(née Dawson)

Mother, me, Dad, and the Bramfords.

Harry and me

THE MANOR HOUSE IS OCCUPIED AGAIN BY A FAMILY OF DAWSONS

After the Leaches left, the Manor House was bought by Group Captain and Mrs Newman, who were very popular in the village. Then, in 1998, a Dawson family again became owners of the Manor, when Sarah and Rex Dawson (no relation to the previous Dawsons) moved in with their four children at the end of the school year. Both of them are doctors, Sarah a GP, and Rex a London gynaecologist. In recalling her first sight of the Manor, Sarah says 'We went up to the church and looked down on the house and garden. It was a lovely sunny day and the garden looked so perfect: it was a walled garden, near to the sea, it had a fruit cage, a greenhouse and a vegetable plot . . . it fulfilled all my criteria, and I knew we would live there, even before we entered the house!' Five years later, Sarah, like many other occupants of the Manor House before her, has taken on the role of Churchwarden. She is also on the village hall committee and is secretary for 'the Friends of Salthouse Church', a group of people battling to save this historic building from decay.

Gerald Cubitt

I was born in a cottage situated on the western side of Cross Street, one of the pair of cottages nearest the heath. This cottage and the one adjoining it stand in what is now known as Applewood Yard. This yard contains an old well which, when it was in use, was some 46 feet in depth. This well provided the drinking water for both of these cottages and also the two cottages below Applewood Yard.

The top part of Cross Street links up with Market Lane and then flows into Bloom Stile Lane. As a child I found this was the most interesting part of this street, as, tucked away on the heath side of this road junction, was an old horse pit known as the marl pit. Each spring the water in the pit contained a number of tadpoles and as children we always found them most interesting in the way in which they developed into small frogs over such a short period of time.

Gerald at work measuring an ancient brick.

Applewood Yard and its well today.

THE MARL PIT c1914

This small pit came about as a result of the need for marl which was dug here and used for the making-up of roads in the immediate area—Bloom Stile Lane, Cross Street and Market Lane.

When the much larger marl pits (located on the western side of the Dun Cow public house) came into use, the Cross Street pit was no longer needed and the bottom was sealed over by puddling a mixture of marl and water into it. It then provided a useful supply of water both for animals grazing on the heath and for allotment holders when planting out greens.

Above: Gerald as a boy, drilling corn with his father Charles Cubitt on the Crankham farm, circa 1932. Gramborough Hill can be seen in the background.

Above: The north end of Cross Street, where it meets the Coast Road, c1931.

Electricity didn't come to Salthouse until 1938. Sam and Ann Talbot's small grocery and provision store is on the right of the picture above. This picture was taken before the extension to the shop was built. The building with the sign on the east wall that faces Cross Street was used by the Talbots as a workshop and paraffin store. They also sold petrol and lubricating oil. On the east side of Cross Street, opposite the building which the Talbots used as a repair workshop, stands a traditional flint and brick-built gable-end. This type of gable-end is not uncommon in cottages which were built around that date on the east side of the village. This particular cottage, shown on the left of the picture, carries a built-in date of 1722. During the 1930s Joe and Matthew Dack were the residents there. Matthew was a retired poultry dealer, and Joe had been a cripple from birth but his will-power to work enabled him to cut furrow (gorse) faggots on the heath, which were then carted off by horse and cart.

The well behind Joe and Matthew Dack's house with one of the original well buckets they used.

The gorse faggots provided the fuel for George Holmes the village baker to heat his oven. The bake office was severely damaged in the great flood on 31 January 1953.

It is interesting to note that many of the approach roads to Salthouse, such as the top of Cross Street and part of Purdy Street as it runs down from Bard Hill, are all some 7 to 8 feet below the level of the fields on either side of them. It is true that before these roads were made up, water running down from the higher land would have helped to carve these roads out, but the depth of the road also indicates the great age of these approach roads which have carried the traffic of ages past, to and from the village of Salthouse.

The south end of Cross Street showing the typically sunken aspect of an old road.

Janette Dams (née Cooper)

Janette Dams tells her story which begins very normally—she was born in Salthouse the eldest of eight children. Then, at sixteen, she fell in love with a man who was at that time 'the enemy', and this must have presented problems. But Janette gives the impression of following her destiny in a specially joyful and untroubled manner.

I was born seventy years ago in what is now known as 'the Crab Shop'. I was the first of eight children: five girls and three boys. My grandmother owned the cottage, and my mother always 'come home' to have her babies.

I spent a lot of time with my grandparents and when I was about three years old, I went to live with them. However, my parents and brothers and sister lived in nearby Cross Street, so it seemed like I had two homes.

Grandma was a wonderful lady and like others of her generation had a hard and busy life. Monday was wash day, the copper in the wash house would be filled on Sunday (from the pump in the yard) and early Monday morning it would be lit. This would be the opportunity to get rid of any rubbish—and many a copper boiled on worn-out boots and shoes!

In would go the 'whites', bed-linen, tablecloths etc. for a good old boil. They were rinsed and then had a dip in 'blue-bag' water and would emerge dazzlingly white to blow on the line in the garden. A good housewife was judged by the whiteness of her washing. Later, after the washing was finished, there would be enough hot water over to scrub the step and to give another good scrub to the earth lavatory that was at the end of the garden. No chains to pull for us; Grandad dug a hole under the apple tree, and in went the contents of the bucket, and that apple tree had a marvellous crop every year!

Grandma was an excellent cook. I can still see her making a sponge cake, beating the eggs with two forks held together, and those sponges were 'as light as a feather'. She made jams and pickles, and in the summer the most wonderful ginger beer for us children. In August, she always pickled our local samphire (which I

Grandfather Jimmy 'Mot' Gray

Grandmother Emily Gray outside her cottage (now the crab shop).

have seen in Harrods labelled 'sea asparagus') and in the middle of winter we would have samphire and bread and butter for Sunday tea!

We had hens, ducks, and there was always a pig in the stye. When the piglets were born and then sold at a few weeks old, there was always one kept back to fatten up to be killed to provide the sausages, pork cheeses, pork joints, and leg of pork to be smoked and cured for hams. That was always a busy time, and Grandad would go 'rabbiting' so at least twice a week we would have a rabbit pie, or baked rabbit with a piece of that lovely pork.

We grew all our own vegetables in the garden or on the allotment, as well as raspberries, black and red currants, gooseberries and of course apples. The first of the early potatoes were grown in the garden; it was traditional to put them in on Good Friday (after the seed-tubers had spent a good few weeks in the darkness under the bed, to enable them to get good 'sprouts') and, if the weather was right, then we would have our first tasting on Whit Sunday.

To make a little 'pin money', Grandma in early spring would raise a quantity of baby ducks and chickens which would soon be sold on to a local buyer. Many mornings I would come down to breakfast to find a box, lined with an old blanket, full of newly-hatched ducks or chickens drying out in the warmth of the coal fire, or even sometimes a piglet who was a bit sickly. Grandma was also an expert at plucking and dressing all manner of fowl and so the local 'Gentry' would often bring their chickens etc. to her. At Christmas the house would be overflowing with chickens, ducks, geese, pheasants and the occasional turkey, all to be taken care of in the wash house. It was my job to deliver them when they were ready, and being as it was Christmas, many sixpences and three-penny pieces came my way!

We were a large scattered family. There was twenty years between me and my two youngest sisters, and my mother and I were actually pregnant together. She was always full of life, was my mum, but she had a long-term illness. She died of T. B. (that was a killer in those days) when she was only forty-five, leaving the eight of us (and the youngest was only four). The sister next to me was unmarried then, so she took over the house, which at that time was the end cottage next door to my grandparents. Then, after she married, the next sister down took it over,

Me the grammar school girl.

Centre, my mother.

and by the time she married, the younger girls were getting on to be early teenagers. But my father was a marvellous man. He trained as a baker; his mother was a Lusher, of the Lushers Bakery at Sheringham, and he went into the family business, but unfortunately he contracted flour dermatitis and he couldn't continue, so he had to finish.

Mum and Dad and the six of us, me bottom left.

I used to help Mrs Talbot in her shop, it was just a little general store she kept in her house at first, and I also used to help with Mr Holmes the baker on Saturday mornings. I used to get 2/6 a morning, and not only that, I got two bars of chocolate and it was rationed. It didn't matter that it was plain chocolate which I didn't like. It was an extra treat!

I used to go to the Manor, when the Leaches had it. Mrs Leach used to run a sort of girls' club one night a week, and one of the things she taught us was how to ring the hand-bells.

It was Christmas Eve 1946, and there was a whole group of us, because you need a lot of girls, and we were ringing the hand-bells and going round all the houses. We met up with a bunch of German prisoners of war and we thought we'd ring to them. When we played Silent Night, the tears ran down their cheeks. I was only fourteen at the time, and that sticks in my mind.

There must have been about 100 German prisoners of war arrived in this part of the world in August or September 1946. They came here to work on the beach and clear all the mines from Blakeney to Mundesley, and they took over the old army-camp which used to be where Catriona Court now stands, and before that Myngs Terrace. The RAF had it first, then the army. I think the POWs were in between the two. They were there for 15 months from August '46 to November '47, and the first winter they were there, the prisoners gave a party for all the younger children of Kelling School. They took them up to the camp here and every child had a

The 1946 view from Bard Hill, showing the nissen huts of the camp on the spot where, after the flood, Myngs Terrace was built and later still Catriona Court.

245

toy—I know my sister Jasmine had a doll's pram—and all the toys were made by the prisoners. They were very clever, they had wheels that went round and dolls' houses and I remember a big round board with chickens on it pecking. That Christmas, there was an appeal over the radio and in the press: 'If you have a Prisoner of War camp near you, invite a POW into your house for Christmas' and my mother—although we were six of us home at that time—she said, 'We'll invite somebody.' My father used to act as trainer to the local Salthouse football team and he knew the chap who ran the football team for the German prisoners of war, so he said 'We'll have Paul'. My sister and I, we happened to know this one who had been a prisoner of war in America and spoke English with American slang—you can imagine, can't you—so we said 'Can we have Helmut, Mother?' and then Mother said, 'I'll tell you what, we'll have a third. That chap who plays the goal-keeper in their football team, we'll invite him' . . . so that was how I met my husband.

Some of the toys the German prisoners made for the party they gave for the children of Salthouse.

The POWs at work on the beach in winter, Kurt squashed in the middle of them.

THE GERMAN PRISONERS OF WAR

The mines they have unearthed, laid out waiting to be exploded.

The mine-detector.

He came to the house for Christmas tea. I was going to be 15 in January, and I was 17 when we married. He was nine years older than me, but he looked very young, and he was very young in his outlook too. Eventually, after he finished here, he was moved away to another camp. He was still a prisoner of war for quite some time after that and I used to say to Mother, 'Could you write to the commander of his camp, and ask if Kurt could come down for Christmas?' Then he'd come down for a couple of days . . . and I wouldn't see him again for three or four months. But we kept in touch with letters, and eventually we got married. The war was over and I think the village people, individually, they liked the Germans who were here, but the war was very much in their minds still. Some people in the village had lost members of the family.

To think that one of the village girls actually wanted to marry a German—that didn't go down very well.

I remember people who I'd known all my life who looked the other way when I went past, and I remember one old lady who used to spit on the ground. But not everybody was like that, and we were very happily married for thirty-seven years.

Kurt and our two boys.
After the war, Kurt joined the Salthouse football team as goalie (see page 317).

247

Phyllis Jackson (née Brown)

Phyllis was born in 1916 in Church Cottage at the top of Grout's Lane. Her mother Evangeline was a daughter of Levi and Elizabeth High. Her grandfather Levi was one of those who helped to get the Hall farmland split up into smallholdings for the ex-servicemen coming home from the First World War.

My name was Brown before I was married. I am the fifth generation of Highs. I go to visit the village whenever I can, and I wish that I could live there.

Phyllis aged eighty-four, Bowls Trophy winner.

Four of my ancestors and countless uncles, aunts and cousins, and many more, lie in Salthouse Churchyard. In my childhood, I used to go across the graveyard and past the church to fetch water from George Dew's, and I remember when they were mending the church windows. As a little girl, I used to pick up bits of coloured glass because they were so pretty. As I remember it, there was a lovely window right at the front at the altar, and there was a lovely coloured window each side. I tried to find out about this when I first came back to Salthouse and saw all plain glass windows everywhere. The Rector was on a trip to the Holy Land at that time. I wrote to various people but I never was able to find out what happened to them. They were taken out during the war I think.

I was born in this house [Church Cottage]. We couldn't live in one of the rooms because the boards were bad. I remember that gate into the church yard; I knocked my teeth out on that blessed gate, I did! They used to set fire to the heath about every four years. They never did let it get overgrown,

Church Cottage where I was born is the building in the centre, Church House is on the right. This photo was taken before the connecting second-storey bit to the right of Church Cottage was built (you can just see a low roof and chimney to the right of it).

and the furrough bushes as we used to call them (you call them gorse now) their stumps were left. We couldn't afford much coal and we needed the extra fuel. They sent us out with a barrow and we had to go up and get the stumps out and bring them back to be burnt on the fire. So I was pushing this barrow, and I fell and knocked my teeth out on that gate.

Alice Graveling's name before she married was Alice Dix, and when we come home from school we used to hang on the back of her bread-cart, and if she didn't like it, she would hit us with her horse-whip.

Herbert Pigott the Baker, he used to sing duets in Chapel with his niece Alice; but Amelia his wife, she fancied herself as the best singer in the village! We used to enjoy going to chapel: in would come Amelia all dressed up in Sunday clothes. She'd swagger up the aisle, and she'd wear great big hats, and you'd hear Amelia's voice above everybody else's. Patty Cubitt, her sister, lived up above Mrs Radley on the right [now 'Lorcot'].

Every year, we used to have Anniversaries, and we all did a little bit—a piece of poetry or something. My mother Evangeline used to sing and once my young brother Ken had to say a piece; it was called 'Scotland Bill', and when he recited it, the last line came out wrong. It should have been:

'and through the crack,
the light came in . . .'

but poor Ken said:

'and through the light,
the crack came in . . .'

Everybody laughed and wiped their eyes—and he was so upset he's never been up on the stage since!

This is my favourite photo of my mother, about 1923. She looks really lovely.

MUD

When I was quite young me and my brother Russell, who was three years older than me, were sent to the beach to collect driftwood. On the way up the Mill Drift we were amusing ourselves by throwing stones at posts the other side of the crick as we walked along, and I got rather behind. My brother heard me call his name but when he looked back I was nowhere in sight. He ran back, and he just saw the corner part of my dress disappearing under the soft mud.

At that time, being the summer, the cricks as we called them were just soft slimy mud. Sometimes it would be just hard enough to walk on, but most times it was deep and soft. I threw a stone, overbalanced, and fell face down in the mud. Lucky for me I called Russell's name as I fell; he was some way ahead and that call saved my life. He ran back and by the time he got to where I fell there was just a bit of my blue dress visible. He got me out and tried to clean the mud from my eyes and mouth, and he said I shook myself like a dog! Gertie Dawson* ran out, but she wouldn't have been able to save me, she said—she'd never have got there in time. I would have been about seven and Russell ten. When we got back we were such a sight the neighbours were called to look at us—I can still remember it vividly. Mother put me in a hip bath in the back yard and they just poured water all over me. I was frozen because we didn't have hot water or anything!

Henry Dew (left) and my father, Charlie ('Quilter') Brown, at the Dun Cow.

The Dun Cow in the early 1900s.

MY FATHER

My father was half Irish and he was quite a character. He was never really accepted in the village. 'That foreigner', they called him, but they still looked up to him. He had a certain amount of education, and people used to bring any legal letters or documents to him to read and explain them. He was never too busy to help, and I remember him leaving his tea if someone called and needed him, but he was only a painter and decorator. It wasn't like today though, he mixed all his own paints and everything. Another thing he did, he put a ceiling up in the public bar at the Feathers in Holt, and it's still there.

Every weekend he used to go up to the Dun Cow. He was a good worker—but Saturday night was his night, and for years and years I thought he was carrying on with someone called Sally Walker. I'd ask my mother, 'Where's Father?' and 'Oh', she'd say, 'he's gone with old Sally Walker again.' He was the first female impersonator! He used to sing and dance at the Dun Cow, and 'Sally Walker' was his song—he had to dress up as a woman to sing it—he was Sally Walker.

My father was a tradesman and so he earned more money than other people in the village really, but wages were very poor in those days, and people working on a farm were better off with free milk and your house free, or it was a low rent. But my father had to pay for everything, he got no concessions, and in the end we were no better off than any one else. We were poor. I went out to work Saturday mornings when I was twelve,

* *Primrose McGlinchey's mother*

cleaning silver for George Dew.

My father was Church and my mother was Chapel, and so we went to Sunday school at the chapel in the mornings, and in the afternoons we went to Sunday school in the church. Afterwards, all we were allowed to do was go for walks. We were lucky enough to have a gramophone; it belonged to my elder sister and she was out of work at that time, but although my father wasn't a bit religious, he wouldn't let us play records on a Sunday unless they were hymns.

My father's career came to an end when a ladder he was using, when he was painting and decorating at the Grand Hotel in Sheringham, broke in half and he fell. He was off work for weeks. He never drank any more because he couldn't, it used to give him a bad head. That was really the end of his career.

MY MOTHER

She was a beautiful cook, my mother, she made us some wonderful dinners out of nearly nothing—but Saturdays was the best day. I had to go down to that house that adjoins the post office*—'Rooter' Holman lived there then, I don't know what his real name was. There was a little window overlooking the pathway as you go round to the post office and we used to knock on there and he'd come to the door and give you two rabbits for a shilling. He was allowed to shoot on the heath; he had the Common Right.

*See p 304 for the house that 'Rooter' lived in at that time and p 172 for a photo of Walter ('Rooter') Holman with rabbits

My father

Mother would skin the rabbits and stuff them with chopped up onions and things. She did it all herself, not with packets, and it was the most tasty meal you ever did have. We had it every Saturday. It cost a shilling and it fed the lot of us. To make the food last, you had a great big Norfolk dumpling, or a suet pudding, and you had that on a plate with a wonderful onion gravy she used to make. The gravy was lovely and you'd have that first, and then if you were lucky you got a piece of rabbit and your vegetables. The idea was that you'd fill yourself up and then you wouldn't want so much meat. On a Sunday you never had any meat; Father and Mother had the meat. But there was only one real luxury my mother used to have, as far as food was concerned. She used to have a quarter of a pound of butter every week from my Uncle Harry*, her brother, because Uncle and Auntie had a sort of a smallholding. We had 'Pheasant' margarine, in those days, I remember the pheasant on the packet. It's funny to think, if Mother had been alive today she would

My mother, Evangeline, when she was older.

* Harry High, father of Vivian High.

probably have chosen margarine. It's meant to be better for you than butter, isn't it?

Mother used to spend all day Friday cleaning the house, and Saturday was baking day. There was like a little kitchen off the kitchen, with a big oven in the wall, and once that fire was burning you had to do all your cooking because of the fuel. I can't think she had much of a life, but she seemed happy and I think she was. On Sunday she'd dress up and walk down to her mother's house, Granny High, at the bottom of Cross Street, and that was her outing. There used to be a houseful down there on a Sunday; all the family congregated there. I can just remember Granny High, a little old lady dressed in black always sitting in her armchair beside the fire, but she could make beautiful shortcakes.

She loved her garden, Mother did, when we went to Bard Hill. I don't know why we moved, but maybe Church Cottage was too small. There was one bedroom we couldn't use at all, at that time, because the boards were unsafe, so that only left two bedrooms. My mother and father had one, and seven of us all had to go in the other one, and I suppose we were cramped, so we got a council house.

CHILDBIRTH

I can't really remember being cramped, but I remember being in my mother and father's bedroom the night Kenneth was born. The other children were all in the other room. I'd been ill or something, I think I'd had shingles.

They used to have the doctor in those days. I remember being in the bedroom and I didn't know what was going on. I was six years old and I stood up and held onto the sides of the cot, and old Doctor Kay who was there said 'Get that child out of the room!' He's Scotch, and he said it in a Scottish way, and Father wrapped me up and took me downstairs and I can remember sitting on Father's lap, which is a thing we very seldom did—he never had time, he was always working. We sat there waiting until we heard the baby cry and then I think Father left me, but he came back and wrapped me up and he showed me Kenneth lying there on the bed, and he'd only just been born.

Of course Kenneth was my baby after that—I mean I did everything for him. He says I dragged him here and there, and I did, I never went anywhere without Kenneth, and I think we've still got that bond actually. I was the first one to see him, apart from Mother and Father. Aunt Agnes, who used to live in the house at the bottom of the pub, next to the Woodhouses, was midwife to the village. I think there must have been something wrong the night Kenneth was born, because the doctor and midwife were both there.

Granny Elizabeth High and Grandfather Levi High.

THE AIRSHIP AND THE MANOR HOUSE HOTEL

When I was biking home from my first job I actually saw the Airship, the R101, fly over the marsh. I was fourteen and a half at the time, and just started at the Manor House Hotel in Blakeney. I had to bike back along the coast road and there was this big Airship R101—must have been on trials or something—and I followed it from Cley to Salthouse. I could actually see people. And then I watched it go out to sea.

I lived in, at my job. When you work in a hotel you do what they call a split. You start early in the morning, and get two hours off—1 pm to 3 or 4 pm—and then you have to come back and start again. The time I had off I had to come home and see my mother. She wouldn't let me stay there while I was off. I had a bicycle and it was brand new; I suppose it was bought on the never-never. I don't know how it was done but I did have to pay for it each week out of my money, and the rest of it used to go to my mother. I got fifteen shillings which was quite a lot, and that helped to clothe Joan and Kenneth the two youngest.

My mother did tell me I could have the tips if there were any, but you never thought you ought to have your earnings yourself. It went to the family. You see, you just did need money in those days.

I was nearly sacked the first day at the Manor House Hotel because I was frightened of the telephone—they were horrified that I couldn't answer the phone; they didn't realise that we didn't have one and I'd never even seen one before! I wasn't the receptionist or anything like that, it was only if you were going through the hall and the phone rang, and you'd have to answer it because there wasn't a lot of us. I think there were only three or four of us working there. It was quite small; it wasn't the hotel it is today. It's called the Manor House Hotel because it was a Manor House, and all the annexe and that, was stables then. They've done them all up, haven't they? In fact, when I went back there the other day and had a meal there, I didn't recognise any of it—none of it at all! I couldn't even recognise the entrance hall. It was a long flagged hall—you could have driven a horse and cart in there easy—but I don't know where it's gone or how anything can change so much. The telephone used to be in a sort of alcove there, and it was coming down that big hall if the telephone rang—I was petrified.

I left the Manor Hotel when I was sixteen and went to London to work. I was married at twenty and we had two boys and one little girl—who died of meningitis and broke my heart.

We had three more boys, and when they all left home I trained as an occupational therapist and worked for many years with the mentally disabled. I have been living in Holt for four years now but I visit my beloved Salthouse as much as possible.

The ill-fated R101 at the Royal Air Pageant, Hendon, June 1930. It crashed in France 5 October 1930, with 48 lives lost.

Phyllis was not the only one who could remember seeing the R101 over Salthouse: Ken Brown and Vivian High remembered it too, and Vivian supplied this picture, kept safely since he was a boy.

Ken Brown's life in Salthouse

Phyllis Brown's youngest brother Ken writes of his childhood as a boy in Salthouse in the early 1920s.

Above: Ken today, and (*left*) in Salthouse football team c 1949. (*See p 317 for the team*)

I was born in 1922, November 12. What a problem I caused, because my grandfather died on November 8th and was buried on November 12th. My mother's bed was moved to the window so she could see her father's funeral. So, straight away, November 8th became very significant in my life—I will say more about this later on. I was born in 'The Nest' next to Salthouse Church, the cottage with no well, bathroom et cetera. Things must have been very hard for my parents. 'The Nest' became a significant part of my life once again later on, and I will explain later.

The earliest thing I can remember was when my sister Vera's boy-friend would visit her. I can see his motorbike chugging up the lane now. I was about three years old and wanted to sit on the seat—I found this was not good enough because I could not reach the handlebars. The old bike was a BSA with a long square tank, so they laid me out flat over the tank so I could just touch the handlebars, and this satisfied me.

I wanted to get down to the marshes when I was three or four years old. My mother said this was far too dangerous; I could go down as far as the road, but on no account was I to cross over (why, I could not understand—cars were a very rare sight in those days, only one or two being seen each week). So now I found myself at the bottom of Grout's Lane. I looked to the right and a car was just passing the beach road, which was quite a long way away, with lots of kids running alongside of it. This was the first car I had ever seen. I thought what do I do now, should I cross the road to the Mill Drift or wait? I was terrified of this car and thought I would be run over. I would have had plenty of time but decided to wait. The car came chugging up with the occupants exposed to the elements, dressed in big coats, and still with the children running along side. It passed me and, after I saw it reappear at the Dun Cow corner, I crossed over to the Mill Drift. The mill had long since gone but the brick rubble still laid around in heaps. There was an old railway carriage on the site with people living in it. They came out and said, 'Kenneth, does your mother know you are down here? I think you should go home.'

On another occasion I managed to get up and on to the beach at long last. As I went over the top of the beach it was littered with oranges. Cases were floating in the breakers. Instead of picking some up to prove my point, I ran back home as fast as I could and my sister Phyllis who was washing up said 'If this is not true, you'll get a big hiding from me,' but when we got there she realised I was telling the truth—and she hadn't brought anything to put them in. She said she would run home to get some baskets and bags and in the mean time I was to stop on the beach and gather as many oranges into a heap as I could. It appeared that a Spanish freighter had arrived in the North East with its load, to find that the port was on strike and they wouldn't let them off-load the oranges. The ship's crew was instructed by their bosses in Spain to go out to sea and dump their cargo overboard.

Another experience I would never forget was when I was about four. I heard a metal clanking going on from the farm buildings in Purdy Street. I decided to investigate, and found three or four men working on a well and fixing pipes down it. One man was looking down the well and lowering tools to his mate. I got nearer and nearer until I could almost look down the well myself, and I was told to get out of the way as it was very dangerous for me. I moved back, but when the man disappeared through to the road I thought now is my chance, I'm going to look down that well and see what is going on. So I crept to the edge and two men were down there, working on the pipes. Then, right out of the blue, I was grabbed from behind, tied up in a sack and lowered down the well on a rope. I passed the men and went down until my feet touched the water. All the men were laughing and I was hauled up and run home and explained to my mother that I had got my feet wet in the creek.

I had started school now and my sister Phyllis used to escort me. Another sister, Joan, had a huge mop of hair and this had to be brushed and finished before we could start our two-mile journey to Kelling School. Invariably we were late and we would run a post and walk a post [*from one telegraph post to the next*]. I was usually tired out when we got there and, in the winter, sodden wet. I can remember Mr Ridley was the headmaster and he was very brutal to everyone. Most of the children hated him and we were scared of him. I can remember him meeting my sister Phyllis—the time was five past nine—and striking her across the head as she was hanging up her clothes in the cloakroom, for being late. What a way to start the day.

Mr Ridley

About the age of nine years old, the farm buildings were quite a magnet for us boys. We had a bet which one of us would dare to climb on the large barn opposite Jimmy Duffield's house in Purdy Street and turn the weathercock around. The other boys agreed, as I was the smallest, I should do it. As the roof was very bad and there might be an accident, I was very scared indeed but did not show it. I climbed a wall and went up the middle of the main roof to the ridge and was scared out of my wits. All the boys were egging me on, shouting to me, 'Don't let it beat you,' and I was now sitting on the ridge of the biggest barn in Salthouse. I looked down and saw how far up I was. I had to go along the ridge to the gable-end where the weathercock was situated. I got there and tried to turn it, but it was rusted up and it was impossible to move it. Now I was facing the wrong way and had to get back, so I decided to go down the shortest way though this meant going over a bad section of roof. Suddenly a loud crack—and a hole opened up and tiles cascaded down the roof. Although I was very scared, I dared not show it to the other boys; I just froze. One of my friends alerted Mr Duffield and he told me not to move an inch. He got some other men to help with a large stack-ladder. They rescued me and I was a hero in all my friends' eyes.

At school I loved the modelling classes. We were each given a piece of plasticine the size of a tennis ball and were told to make what we liked. The plasticine was so hard we could not do anything with it. So the next week I made a small roller which I used to roll out the plasticine. The other kids near me kept asking me if they could borrow the roller. I said yes, but you must give me a piece of plasticine every time you borrow it. One girl borrowed my roller so much that at the end of the session she only had a small piece rolled flat, where I had enough to make a farmyard. When the teacher came round she said to the girl 'What's that?' The girl replied 'That's a mat, Miss.' My farmyard received first prize (two pennies).

There were about five of us boys all about the same age. One day we were at our wits' end to know what to do with ourselves. We only had a ha'penny between us and we wanted to buy gob-stoppers. I said 'Wait a minute. I've got a plan!—All of you keep looking down this drain. None of you must look up.' I had spotted the Colonel de Crespigny almost home from his walk. I had gambled on his generosity. When he got up to us he stopped and said 'What's the matter, boys?' I replied (as if I was crying), 'I have lost my penny down the drain.' He replied, 'Don't worry, you will never find it. Here is a shilling. Share it out among yourselves.'

I used to work some Saturday mornings for the de Crespigny's gardener. He gave me a large skip about the size of a dustbin, saying he would pay me a penny if I would fill it with weeds.

Kenny Brown the dare-devil

After two hours I was getting nowhere, as the weeds were very small in the flower beds, so I wandered over to a rough area of the grounds where the hogweed and docks were two to three feet high. I placed them in the bottom of the skip and soon filled it up. I done this for two to three weeks until the gardener realised what I was doing, and I was not asked to go anymore.

I remember being in the school playground when either the Hindenburg or the R101 Air Zeppelin came over, very low. It was a sight I will never forget. I could see people in the gondola quite clearly.

I found the following episode quite funny but I was quite scared at the time. At the school, our desks were in pairs: two boys and two girls. The girl sitting next to me had a skirt which had press-fasteners down the side. One or two of these fasteners had come undone. Unbeknown to her, I leaned over and undone the rest. We were reading one by one to the class and when the girl's turn came up to read, her skirt fell down. She was ridiculed, but no one knew it was my fault. Mr Coe, our new headmaster, always left the class for tea at his house during the afternoon. On this particular day, as soon as he left, I got up from my desk, climbed onto the guard-rail around the fire and put the clock on by fifteen minutes. When the headmaster returned, he glanced up at the clock and said 'Books away, class dismissed.' The next morning there was a witch-hunt. No one would split on me, but John Holman started bubbling with laughter and he received six strokes of the cane. We got our own back because we then cut the cane with a razor-blade in about six places. The next time he used it, it split into pieces.

On another occasion, during our lunch break at school, about a dozen of us boys went up Wood Lane near our school to a large straw stack. We had spread quite a lot of straw at the base and we used to dive twenty feet into it. Suddenly the gamekeeper appeared and said 'Come down and stand in a row.' When he got to me, he said 'What's your name and where do you come from?' I said, 'I'm Tommy Robinson and I'm from London.' He nearly blew his top and said, 'With an accent like yours, you are local and I can see you're one of Charlie Brown's children from Salthouse.'

Time was rolling on now and I was ten or eleven years old. The General Election was on, and the Tory candidate was Sir Thomas Cook. The village hall was packed. He started his speech, telling his audience in a very highbrow accent, 'Now, you must all adopt the crop rotation system and use fertilisers et cetera et cetera.' At this stage, the oldest lady in the village, Ruth Holman,* stood up and said in a very broad Norfolk accent, 'Why don't you shut your big gob, you can't even sow a tan-nup!' She nearly brought the place down. The meeting broke up and Sir Thomas moved on to Cley.

The war years were approaching fast. In 1938 I was working as a plumbing apprentice at Weybourne Camp. The army had laid on a meeting of 'bigwigs' from Germany et cetera to observe the launch of the 'Queen Bee', a pilotless aircraft. The idea was that it would be shot down by the 3.7 guns. Foolishly, myself and another apprentice had got inside one of the huge water-tanks which we were installing. When the guns opened up, our ear-drums almost burst, and we stayed in that tank for almost an hour with our hands over our ears. The guns fired like mad and could not hit the aircraft. Over fifty shots were fired, and then a loud cheer. The aircraft crashed into the sea. Afterwards we were talking to the soldiers who were operating the radio-controlled aircraft. One of them said his orders were to deliberately crash the plane if the gunners failed to hit it.

1939—the war had started and we were told to join the LDV (Local Defence Volunteers). Everyone aged 16 to 80 was asked to attend a meeting at the parish room about two days after the war had started. We were told to bring guns, pitchforks, hedge-slashers etc. etc.—anything which would harm a German. Our name had now been changed to the Home Guard. We were on parade outside the parish room; Mr Ronald Deterding was our Commanding Officer, and he was inspecting us. When he got to Robin Cooke* (quite a character was Robin), he looked down the barrel of Robin's twelve-bore gun and said, 'Robin, you have not cleaned your gun in years!' Robin replied 'Kill a bloody duck, kill a German!' When

* *For photos of Ruth, see pp 268 and 329*

* *For photo of Robin as a boy, see p 158*

Sunday, 1st February 1953. The scene of devastation: repeated, from the post office on the right, all the length of the Coast Road as far as Beach Road. Mrs Middleton's garage, where I had my workshop, has been demolished.

you look at 'Dad's Army' today, the things they got up to were very similar to what we did ourselves in the Home Guard. I remember once when we were on parade near the post office, our Sergeant in charge was Jack Dawson,* who had lost his foot in the 1914-18 War. He shouted 'Right turn, quick march!' and we progressed about 100 yards when he frantically called out 'Stop!' He couldn't keep up with us because his foot was missing. During this time, Salthouse was bombed several times, once in daylight and several times during the night.

I joined the Royal Air Force at eighteen, and when I was twenty-one I volunteered to go abroad. I was in a convoy when I was in the Mediterranean, when we were attacked by a Junkers 88 carrying torpedoes. Several ships in the convoy were sunk. Again, the date was *November 8th*.

After the war I got married, and once again 'The Nest' became my home when we moved back to Salthouse. It was still without running water or toilet facilities. Our first-born was Shirley, who arrived the same day as Princess Anne (15th August 1950). We received a very nice letter from the Queen. Our second daughter was Wendy—(wait for it)—born *November 8th*, 1955.

I started working for myself in 1949. Four years later, in 1953, we were heavily involved in the great floods. I lost my car, trailer and all my tools. My workshops were the two garage doors between the post office and the Crab Shop today. My landlady was Mrs Middleton who was drowned in the floods. In 1954 we moved to Holt to be more central for materials et cetera and to be among more people for the business. In the 1960s I was awarded the contract to install twenty-five basins at Sandringham House. I still have a copy of the account which was rendered by us direct to Buckingham Palace.

My story is a very brief outline of my life in Salthouse. On re-reading I realise I have missed so much out, I feel I could easily write a book. But that would really be another story.

* *For photo of Jack, see pp 331 and 332*

Dorothy Thomson

Dorothy Thomson, thirty years upholder of the church, is known and loved by everybody in the village. She has written a brief recollection of her earlier years:

I first came to Salthouse on Whit Monday 1960 and I loved it right away. We came for all the Easter and summer holidays until our children left school. We were soon able to buy 'The Greens' and we immediately started work on the garden. The vegetable garden had been home to a pony belonging to the then owners of the post office—no wonder it has done so well! The post office stores stocked only a limited variety of goods in those days and we had to go to Holt to shop, but with the arrival of the McInnes and Robertson family this all changed and a tea room filled the back half of the shop. Up until the Gulf War, we could even buy petrol there.

During my first August, Joan Haward introduced me to the church and from then it became a part of my life. I was enrolled on the list of helpers to decorate the church at Easter, Christmas and harvest. In my first years, older members, led by Mrs Neden of 'Springholes', were well organised and I was permitted at Easter to put violets and primroses in the gap in the lectern—and then I was given the windows of the north aisle to decorate. Later, I was also asked to distribute fruit, flowers and eggs to older parishioners, and I enjoyed these visits. Those I particularly remember are: Betsy Lynn, the two Hawley sisters, Jasper Woodhouse's mother Alice Holman, Fred Woodhouse's wife, and Alice Graveling and her sister (see photo below).

Mrs Graveling, in my earliest days, was the churchwarden and the oval brass flower-arranger in the church was given in her memory. She was succeeded by Mr Holland from 'The Cottage', Grout's Lane. He used to give classical recordings in the church on warmer Sunday evenings with his posh 'black box' gramophone.

Mrs Graveling, at one time the backbone of the church, told me that she was born in 'The Greens'. She was one of 7 children whose father died, and their widowed mother kept them on vegetables and eggs, the proceeds of the garden. Her own son was tragically killed in the Korean war.

After an interregnum, Michael Sellors was appointed rector and I became churchwarden and, when the Holland family left the village in 1980, I was the only one. This changed my life, because I then drove to Salthouse from London almost every weekend, until I moved in permanently, and I spent all my free time here. Sadly I have seen the congregations dwindle, but because of the concerts and exhibitions, and the inclusion in Simon Jenkins' book ('The 1,000 Best Churches'), visitors to our church have increased.

Dorothy at 'The Greens', counting money collected to sponsor a friend in the annual bicycle ride for the church.

Herbert Pigott the baker, his sister Charlotte Dix, and two of his nieces: Edie, and Alice (who later became Mrs Graveling and was born in 'the Greens').

Lorna Fox Collection

Freda Holman

Freda Holman is the granddaughter of Charles Duffield, who was one of the first to benefit when Henry Deterding, lord of the manor, gave up his land to the County Council—as did so many landowners in Norfolk—to be split up into smallholdings for the ex-servicemen coming back from the First World War. Freda's father was Jimmy Duffield (whose barn roof Kenny Brown nearly fell through), and she married John Holman.

Freda and her daughter Virginia Wright, the mother of Tracey Large (who did a prolonged study on Salthouse).

I used to work for Mr Haylock at the post office; I delivered the letters round the village during the war. The village people, they were all such friends, and that made it interesting for me. In the war-time they were all waiting for letters; I used to shout out, 'You've got one!' They'd give me a cup of tea and at Christmas they'd give me money. Money meant a lot then—two shillings or sixpence—and that was Christmas presents. And some of them would give me a drop of wine and a mince pie. Then I had to go back and report my time in. Mr Haylock looked stern, but he was a good boss.

I had no inkling about that telegram for Sylvia. Mr Haylock didn't say nothing to me, gave me no warning. My sister Sylvia (she's older than me), she lived up at the top of Cross Street, and I'd leave her to the last and have a cup of tea with her. This time I'd come up with the last few post to hers, and I didn't know I'd got this telegram. Oh, she ran down the road—she was crying. It was the telegram to say her husband Philip had been killed in the war.

The de Crespignys at the Hall, they used to take their dogs up on the heath, and we were children playing out on the road and we used to play hopscotch, and they were so fascinated they used to stand and watch us play hopscotch, the de Crespignys did! The Commander used to take me for a ride to Holt. Their car was a big excitement in those times, and he always bought me sweets. A Mr Halls used to keep a shop in Holt in those days, and the Commander used to come in there with me and say 'Pick what you like.'

I used to have a bee. You wound it up and that used to go 'brrrr' round on the window. They used to stand there and laugh at this bee... all these silly little things... But that was something big for us, you know. They used to take us to Holt to buy sweets and bring us back. That was a big thing, really.

It used to be beautiful down there at the Hall, especially the orchard, the opposite side of the road. We used to try and nip in that door and pinch an apple or something, but their gardener, Alec Morse,* he had a shed

* *For photo of Alec Morse, see p 202*

there and he could see us, and—Coo, we'd get wrong if he saw us! He'd rub us with whiskers, you know, rub our faces with his whiskers. He'd be rough, he hadn't shaved and our faces were tender, and that was our punishment! But oh, that was beautiful! All those figs and pear trees, all done against the wall. It was really gorgeous that garden was, and all little paths.

Freda, on the left, loved horses and could ride anything, Sylvia was rather more careful.

That's an old buoy from the beach, it's been here all these years; there's a sort of square handle on the other end. They wanted me to part with that, but I said no I wouldn't. That's been here ever since I came, I remember. Well, I mean—you couldn't get rid of that, could you? Somebody used to come round—one of the wreck dealers come round to John* when we were farming, and he would have given us *anything* to take that: he wanted it, he crazed after it.

Left: The enormous buoy in Freda's garden, once part of a boom that lay out to sea in the war years.

* *For photos of John and his family , see pp 172 - 174*

Brian Holman

Brian 'Brock' Holman is the son of Bertie 'Billy' Holman, the youngest son of Ruth. His mother was Alice, the daughter of Tom 'Rummy' Woodhouse. He is cousin to Vivian High and half-brother of Jasper Woodhouse. (Vivian's mother and Alice were sisters) Brian was able to shed some light on the history of the huge buoy, as soon as he saw the photo on the preceding page

Brian with the horse; Harry High on top of the load.

The cottages on the green as they were before the '53 flood.*

Old Clem, my uncle, when he lived in the end one of those three cottages [*above*] that were demolished after the flood, he knocked the hole in the top of that buoy with a hammer and chisel every night when he used to come home from work, and he was knocking with a hammer and chisel for two weeks. We'd hear the ringing of it every night—we were living in the Doll's House, right next door!

When he got it open, he had it round the back of the house for water. He had a tap in the bottom of it. [*And when Vivian and Bette High were living in the middle of the three cottages, Bette remembers Clem's wife Maggie letting them have a jug of soft water from it.*]

They took it up to that piece in Market Lane after the flood, but they left the top behind. When the Edens built their house there,* they found the top with all its shackles, and there it is on the wall today!

Old Hannah Pigott, she was a funny old woman, she was like a man. She had a greengrocer shop in Sheringham, but before that she lived in the cottage behind the pub, where we used to live and where we got flooded out. Her husband was a little man, Hilary Pigott. He was educated at Gresham's, Hilary was. He built a cart, a pony cart—built it in the front room, and he couldn't get it out, could he? Hannah says: 'You're a remarkable, educated man,' she say, 'and you've built a cart and can't get it out.' . . . But of course, he's pegged it together and he just took the pieces out and put them together.

He kidded her up one day that he was carrying on with someone up the street. She went and found him, carted him down to the sea front (in Sheringham), picked him up and held him over the wall. She said: 'Did yer or didn't yer?' And if he'd've said Yes, she would have dropped him. She would.

She smoked a clay pipe. She sold fish as well as greengrocery, and came to Salthouse with her cart. Then they got a lorry later on. They used to take a load of rabbits over to the market—Wisbech—somewhere away that was. Oh, she could skin a rabbit quick as a flash

---

* *See pages 345 and 347 for the three cottages after the flood . . .*

In the Dun Cow c1930.
From the left: Tom 'Rummy' Woodhouse (the grandfather of Brian Holman, Jasper Woodhouse and Vivian High), Harry Mace, Haddon High and Henry Dew.

while she was talking about something else.

My grandfather Tom Woodhouse, he told me about the mill up the top, when you go up Church Lane [Grout's Lane] that way past Mr Pringle's [now the Richards']. The house called Hilltop with the rounded edge is built that way so the wagons could get past. My grandfather, he worked for Mr Ross at the Hall and he used to take the corn up there.

They used to be out early mornings with the horses, and they'd sit on the corner of the field having a drink. Ross come up on his big horse and they were talking about big houses. My grandfather said 'I reckon I was born in a bigger house than you.' 'What do you mean boy,' he say. 'Where were you born then?' 'In the workhouse.' And Mr Ross turned his horse and went off and never spoke a word.

I don't know where my grandfather came from; maybe it was Beckham Workhouse, but we don't know. He never did go to school. I know he used to go courting my grandmother at Melton, and he used to walk to Melton! That was a long way to go courting, wasn't it? He told me when he was a young boy he walked from Norwich to Yarmouth on his own. He was a pretty hard old man.

My father had those beach huts on the beach. He bought them and let them out. People came out for a Sunday and used them. There was a double garage on Little Eye, at the bottom of the hill, and there was a road between Little Eye and Great Eye—just hard core.

Ivy Nightingale (née Holman)

Ivy is the daughter of Frank and Priscilla Holman.* Her husband Jack was a Londoner but he took a job in Norfolk so that they could live in Ivy's birthplace—Salthouse.

That's me when I was a little girl with my mother and my granny (Cooke), and two of my brothers: Stanley, who was killed in the war, and Harry.

During the war a friend from Leeds came to visit me. She came for a weekend and she stopped three years! We used to go to work together. We got those clothes at Norwich, the latest 'slacks'.

Here's the Rocket House taken from the beach. That's my son Michael in the boat and his friend Denis Burton. I've slept up there—lovely old house that was. I used to sleep there sometimes to keep Mrs Jopling company when she was there alone. Mr Jopling was a barrister. After the Rocket House got flooded out and Mrs Jopling had died, he still used to come to Salthouse on holiday and he'd stay in my house in Cross Street.

Above: My husband Jack.

Left: Clarice Westerman, the friend from Leeds, and myself, 1940.

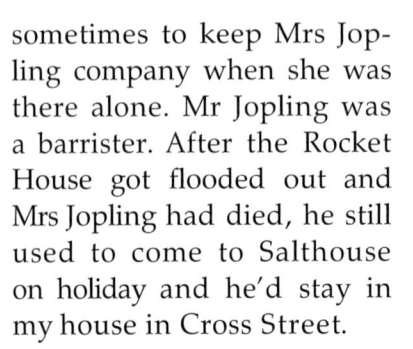

Above: In the British Colombia Hall (Village Hall) washing up after a sale and teas, with Richard (the son of Leslie Cooke and grandson of Isaac).

* *Priscilla was the sister of Stephen, Isaac, Marshall and Robin Cooke*

Friday Forsdick

Alexander Easter Forsdick, son of a gamekeeper, was himself gamekeeper to the lord of the manor, Mr Savory at Kelling Hall (as had been John Hancock of Salthouse, see page 175).

Born on Good Friday 1879, Alexander was known to everybody as 'Friday'. He enlisted in the army at the outbreak of WWI and served in Mesopatamia. After the war he made Salthouse his home, buying two derelict cottages at the east end of the village, opposite the road to the beach, and building himself a bungalow on the site. He lived there during the 1920s with his two sons Cyril and Alec. It was during this time that he made his living from the sea and from the heath (as a common righter) like his neighbours, the Cookes and the Holmans.

Friday's first marriage having failed, he eventually met and married Evelyn Fletcher of High Kelling (known as Flossie) in 1930. They then left Salthouse, having been offered a council holding, to take up farming in the North Walsham area where they both worked very hard to establish themselves. The white bungalow was let, and the first tenants were their friends, newly-weds Freda and Alec Morse.

[see page 201 for Freda's account of her time in the white bungalow]

Above: Friday and Flossie at the back of the white bungalow c1930, soon after their marriage.

Friday's pony Lizzie pulls his boat up the beach.

Above: Friday, in collar and tie and waders, with his boat on Salthouse beach, c1925.

MACKEREL CATCH

Above: Friday Forsdick (furthest right in the group around the net) hauling in his catch of mackerel on Salthouse beach c1923.

FRIDAY'S DAUGHER BETTY

Betty was born in 1933. Despite the slump in farming, Friday became very successful—moving on to increase the acreage of his farm in 1935 and in 1939. He retired from farming in 1946 and returned to live in the bungalow.

Betty has kept many newspaper cuttings and photos, and the picture on the right, from the EDP, shows Friday (second from the right) salvaging what he can of his beehives after the 1949

Above: The bungalow just after the 1949 flood, sea receding.

EASTERN DAILY PRESS, WEDNESDAY, MARCH 2, 1949

FLOODED COAST ROAD — Looking out across the flooded coastal road at Salthouse, over which yesterday's seas broke in waves. Occupants of some of the threatened houses are here seen collecting belongings that had been washed away.

266

Above: Beach picnic c1930, taken before Betty was born. Looking at this photo, Betty says 'No one would believe that when this was taken you could park cars on the beach.' *From the left*: Kenneth Allen of Blakeney, Betty's mother Flossie, Ernest and Edith Allen (Kenneth's parents and Betty's godparents-to-be), and other friends. Behind them: Fred Haylock's beach hut and Hopper Holman's old railway-carriage where Granny Ruth once served teas.

Above: Friday's pony Lizzie loaded with Salthouse children. His younger son Alec is standing second from the left c1925.

flood. Betty says 'I remember Father telling me that the Cookes used to run along the village shouting "The water's over! The water's over!" You see, it's always dark when this happens, or seems to be. The water never comes over when it's like a mill-pond—it's always a terrific gale. Every time a breaker came in, just as it does on the beach, the wave would break up and over the bungalow and the windows would be covered with flotsam and jetsam, and the chances are, something would be in it that would break your window and then the sea would be in. Very few houses in Salthouse had a front door in those days because of the sea. Father had extended the bungalow when he retired, and put a bathroom in; they then had a problem with water coming up the drains from the sea, and the wells were contaminated. That's when my mother said "Enough is enough; I'm going." And this decided my father to sell the bungalow and move to Stiffkey. Our Salthouse days were ended.'

Friday on Salthouse beach c1928.

Primrose McGlinchey

Primrose (née Dawson) is the granddaughter of the famous Ruth whose 1897 flood experiences were faithfully recorded by Jane Hales and are quoted on pages 329-30. Here Primrose describes her photos and recalls memories:

That's old Granny Ruth* (*photo, right*). I didn't like her, she was a hard lady. They had too many children, that was the trouble. That's Aunt Elsie on the left. And that's Aunt Ann (*top left*). She was nice, she went to Gresham's. She used to wear a mortar-board, that one did. That's Uncle Hopper and that's Alice and that's Mother.

Aunt Ann died 1940-something. Poor little Alice, she had all them kids and she was bent right over.

In this little photo, that's my brother that was killed in the war, and there's me pinching from his pockets.

Uncle Hopper used to go up to Holt which was an open market. They used to have a cattle market up there right near the pub, and when they used to take their chickens and stuff up there, they used to go in the pub, get blind drunk, get into the cart and the old pony would bring them home. When he was older, my Uncle Hopper, I've seen him fall out of the back of the cart many a time when I was a kid. The old pony used to go straight in the yard and stop, and out would fall Hopper. He's Ruth's son. She had him, and she had Uncle Rooter, and there was Brian Holman's father, Uncle Billy, and then there was another one who

Grandmother Ruth Holman with four daughters and Primmy's Uncle Hopper.

Me and my brother Philip in the garden behind my mother's house.

Pinching from Philip's jacket.

*Ruth Holman is pictured here with only some of her many children. Others were: Rooter (Walter), Billy (Bertie), Clem, Lottie and Butcher (Hezekiah). Gertie, seated on the right, was the mother of Primrose.

lived away (he used to be on the race courses).

Did you know anything about that old building along the Skirts? When you come out of Salthouse and you go that way to Kelling, and you go straight on where you could take the cattle onto the marshes, they call that the Skirts. If you walk along there you'll see those old stones. I used to hear Mother talk about that. She said that's the time when the ships used to come right up bringing the salt in. They used to bring it in there, and that is why that was called Salthouse.

Granny's brothers used to be on the old sailing ships—that's over two hundred years ago now, isn't it? My Dad,* he met my Mum on Sheringham promenade. My Dad's father was lovely, he had a great big white beard and he was a shepherd. In the autumn he used to take his flock right from Salthouse as far as Yarmouth, and back again in the spring when the sheep was due to have their young. He'd stop on the way, feeding, of course. He was a lay preacher, and Mother would say 'And how many more have we got laying out at Yarmouth?' (how many more cousins and relations?). The old man was gone all that while!

Granny Ruth had a sister who used to live in Sheringham, and she used to have a pony and cart and come all the way to Salthouse. Old Hannah Pigott. She wore a man's cap and britches, and she used to sell stuff off that pony cart; it was a right low cart. The old girl used to go in the Salt'us Dun Cow and get as drunk as a lord. Then that pony would come all the way to Sheringham with her.

When my Mum used to go to school, she was very good at sewing and knitting and she used to do all the things for the teacher's kids, so Mother didn't learn nothing at school, you see. But then when she left school she come to old Hannah's shop in Sheringham, and that's where they learned her to add up. And by Jingo nobody could add up quicker than what she could, although she never did learn when she went to school. She could add up, the old girl could!

I met Paddy when I went to the NAAFI at Weybourne Camp. Best job I ever got. He used to drive a staff car for the officers. He would meet me up the road, put my bike in the back of the staff car, and he'd take me home.

On the way down to Weybourne Camp, there used to be a big tree-thing across the road to stop lorries coming down, like a giant pole. This certain night, I was thinking to myself 'Hurry, Paddy's waiting for me up on the heath, to take me home in the staff car,' when a taxi come down and blinded me with his lights, and I smashed into that pole and went over the top, and there's all the troops coming in from the pub. I went over the top—the handlebars took the full force.

They took me back to the guard-room and they kept saying, 'Is she round, is she round?'—I could hear them—and then they said 'Where's McGlinchey? He can take her home.' But I *knew* where he was: he was waiting for me up on the heath! Oh dear, oh dear, I always was wild—but not like now; they do stupid things with drugs now . . .

---

* For a photo showing Primmy's dad, Alph Dawson, and her grandfather Philip, before Primmy was born, see p 191

Joyce Childs (née Dawson)

Joyce is the daughter of Freda Holman's sister Sylvia, and the niece of Primrose McGlinchey. Her father Philip Dawson was killed in the war when Joyce was only two. Today she runs a big guest house in Sheringham. Her talent for catering and entertaining first showed itself when she was a girl in Salthouse and worked for the Hawleys when the Hall was a guest house in the 1950s, after the de Crespignys had gone.

I never knew my father and I'd always said I wanted to go to Italy to see his grave. You know, he was someone I never recognised as a father until I saw his grave in Italy. I was two when he died. My auntie Margery, his sister, she had gone over to see his grave and she didn't think she'd be upset till she went there and then, when she saw all these young soldiers' graves, 22 and 23 years old, lines and lines of them and one of them with my father's name on . . . . It is very moving. When I saw it, you know, I couldn't believe it—and it was so lovely kept as well. His name is on the war memorial here at the church but to see the actual grave brought it home to me.

I used to live at the top of Cross Street. From my bedroom window I could see the radar going round all the time, and night-times that used to be all lit up and that was quite a point of the village—the village never had any lights. I was born in '42, so I don't remember a lot about the war. The RAF men used to come down to the main shop—that's the post office—for their lunch. Then in the mornings I used to go up with their sandwiches and drinks, for ten to half-past ten time, from Blackburn's shop.

They had a reunion a couple of years ago, and all the RAF came to the Feathers in Holt. They invited me to go up there and see them and we'd all got old, and we had a lovely chat up there! Sergeant Clark, who was one of the sergeants there at the time, put some photos of the radar station through my door. But I've moved since then, I'll have to have a search for them.

Blackburn's shop was only a little place. They used to call it 'Tiny Tot's tuck shop'. It was just the end part of a bungalow half-way down Cross Street. When I was at school I used to work there evenings and weekends and deliver all the bits and pieces all round the village, so I knew everybody in the village. I remember Mrs Cubitt,* she never used to come out. I never saw her out, apart from going to the well. Nowadays you'll call it hydrophobia or something.

I remember the Hawleys. He was an inventor, wasn't he, Old Hawley? He invented a thing called a 'Hawley Buoy'—you know, like a thing that you throw out to rescue anybody. Like a round ring, was a Hawley Buoy. And I don't know if he invented something else, like the gloss on a photograph. But they used to say: because he was so clever, that's why his children were like they were. He had one son who was clever and he had a steel factory in Sheffield.

They used to have a big old car, and they'd take in guests in the house. You know, at that

---

* *Patty Hancock (photo p 176) who married the Chapel preacher William Cubitt.*

time people loved bird watching and that kind of thing. Old Mr Hawley used to do the cooking and they had two daughters and two sons and I think the old lady had died, and they took in guests.

At the time I went to work there, about 1958, I was sixteen and I had just lost my mother, and that was one of my first jobs. Mary and Margaret, the two daughters, had gone away—I think they had been ill—and Kenny and Ernest, the two boys, did the rough work. I used to love domestic science at school, and I used to do all the puddings and I used to do the sweets for the evening and I used to serve and do the flowers on the table. There used to be callers to come for afternoon teas, and I used to do all these little sandwiches and I used to make the cakes. Old Hawley, he was a lovely old man. I can remember him cutting up the meat and putting it on the tables for the visitors.

The fisherman used to come round twice a week with a bell, and Mr Hawley used to buy crabs on a certain day. You know, I always remember doing this—he'd buy ten crabs and I used to make the 10 crabs go to 15, so everybody would have a crab! (We'd have extra shells.) They taught me a lot of things and I really enjoyed working there after working part-time at Blackburn's shop. That put me into the catering business, and from there I went to the Dormy Hotel.

The gates of Salthouse Hall Guest House.

The first 100 years of Kelling School

Jill Coleman produced a book, based on the discovery of the original Kelling School log book, for the School Centenary celebrations in 1977. The following article by Jill appeared in the EDP of Friday, 25 February 1977. It is reproduced here with her permission, and with the addition of some of her own illustrations from the book.

The inspector remarked that for a great part of the year the Infants' Department had been under-staffed, that the accommodation provided was inadequate and the ventilation unsuitable, adding that the children had not passed one happy half-hour.' So says the school log book of 1877. This year, the three-parish school of Kelling, Weybourne and Salthouse on the North Norfolk coast celebrates its centenary. The log book makes interesting reading. The school was built at a cost of £1,355, to accommodate 120 pupils, but as early as 5th October 1877 we read in the log book: 'No School kept owing to Inclement Weather. Only two came.' By far the biggest headache for the master of a village school a hundred years ago was attendance, upon which the next year's grant largely depended. The winter of 1877 seems to have been particularly grim.

From the end of September to the beginning of November, it is 'fearfully wet, and hardly any Salthouse and Wabourne children attend'. Fires had to be lit to dry the children before sending them home again. Then, on November 12th, 'Very heavy fall of Snow this morning. No school on account of Snow and not being able to light fires.' November 27th: 'Hard and disheartening as this week has been, it reached a climax this morning when only 11 were present—5 of those had come against their mother's wishes and without their dinner. The snow is 12 inches deep, and above a yard where it has drifted.'

Not only the weather kept children from school. A number were 'illegally employed', (some by members of the school board!). Others were at various times gleaning, raising mangolds, bird-scaring, leading horses in the hay-field, singling turnips, rearing pheasants, bush-beating, or they had other 'frivolous excuses'.

Salthouse club feast days crop up regularly in the log book as the cause of poor school attendance, as also do special occasions such as chapel treats, Holt fair day, Blakeney regatta, 'tea' at the Rectory, and Band of Hope meetings, while on 25th February 1895—'Owing to a stranded boat being launched this afternoon, many children intend going to the beach. I therefore marked the registers at 9.00 am and closed school at 11.15.'

In the school's opening year, on November 6th, we find: 'Most of the Wabourne children asked leave in the afternoon to follow a schoolfellow to the grave'—a not uncommon entry, we find, as we read on. An epidemic of diphtheria, which began in Salthouse in January 1893 and lasted two years, claimed many victims from the school.

9th January 1893: 'Salthouse children are absent on account of two deaths.'

The class show their slates.

30th January 1894: 'The sickness shows no sign of abatement. In some cases father, mother and all the children are ill in bed at once.'

5th November 1894: 'I regret to say that one of our scholars, Alice Beales, died from diphtheria at Weybourne yesterday.'

7th November : 'Another scholar from Weybourne, E. Beales, died today'.

On a cold Saturday in February 1977, standing among the first snowdrops in Weybourne churchyard, with flurries of snow swirling around the old Priory church and round the gravestone of Alice Ethel Beales, 6 years 10 months, and Ernest William Beales, 4 years 11 months, I shuddered at the sudden reality of it all. However, in spite of hardships—'one small fireplace, and classroom temperature at 43 degrees instead of 60 degrees as required by the Code', a dirt yard for playing, and no washing facilities other than the nearby beck—school did have its lighter moments for the pupils, if not for the master. Three boys were sent home after 'bathing in the dirty creeks' on a hot afternoon, and the master notes: 'No more bathing in School Hours'. Another evidence of high spirits is recorded by the entry:

'A coping from the Bell Turret fell down into the yard during the time a boy was ringing the Bell too violently', and another entry suggests a welcome relief from serious study: 'In place of the usual lessons, Mr John Abby gave a lesson on Temperance, with scientific illustrations'.

In October 1897 two boys played truant, and the entry reads: 'Whilst punishing one, his friend seized a slate and was just in time prevented from throwing it at the Master who with great difficulty succeeded in wresting the slate from him. The boy, who is a big heavy lad, began to kick out freely and made a large scar on the master's leg. I have expelled him from school.' During the next morning: 'The Rev W. B. Dalby called. As one of the members of the Board, and Rector of the parish, he spoke seriously to the assembled school and warned the children about a repetition of such unseemly behaviour.'

All this may contribute little to the great debate on education, but while the future of village schools appears to be in the melting pot, few dispute the fact that their contribution so far has been rich, colourful and valuable.

Daphne Hanlon

Daphne was the Head Mistress of Kelling School for thirty-two years from 1948 to 1979 when she reluctantly retired. At her presentation (pictured below) Ron Coleman, who had four children at the school, said how grateful everybody was to her for all she had done. He spoke of the enormous love she had for the children, the school, and all it stood for, and he said that she could always get the best out of a child. There was no way you could slack when Mrs Hanlon was around!

Daphne Hanlon in the midst of smiling children, at the School Christmas Party 1979.

Daphne remembers some of the problems during her earliest years at the School:

I had told the Norfolk Education Committee that I was ready to do some supplies, and they came up with the request would I take charge of this school, and I was horrified because I'd never taught children over eleven and I'd never been to a country school, I'd been teaching upper juniors in city schools, so it was a complete shock. When I arrived in 1948 the war just over, there was very, very little in the way of apparatus.

The war did starve us of everything—you wrote on both sides of the paper and round the edges. Nowadays they waste so much. The children were from four-plus to fourteen, and we were two teachers; life was difficult. There were two rooms, and the Infants up to seven year olds had one room and I took all the rest in the other room—but they were marvellous, they were wonderful children. It was a question of them showing *me* things rather than me showing them! The bigger ones told me how the boys went out and did the gardening and the girls stayed in and did needlework, and who went with them, but there was nothing there to do needlework with, and mostly they had to be on their own, because you couldn't be in two places at once.

Three teachers in 1950: Mary Dawson, Daphne Hanlon and Mrs Golding.

The parents were difficult at first. I think school was seen rather as the enemy: they thought you would be—well, unkind to them, I suppose! They didn't trust me. They thought as soon as I got their children, they didn't know what I was doing to them. There was a cane when I got there, and I'd never seen one before and it horrified me. I broke it in half and threw it on the fire in front of the class! We had open fires of course, which we had to make up with a scuttle of coal, and when it was very cold we all had to sit around it.

I had no experience of ordering; I'd never done anything of that kind before. You had to pay for what materials you wanted, on the limited budget that you had, and this went on as long as I was there. You had to manoeuvre your money around.

The toilets were earth-closets in 1948. They used to come round the village and collect it on certain nights. Then when water came to the village we had water closets—but they're still outside. There's nowhere inside you could put them.

There used to be a car that collected the

very smallest children from Weybourne and Salthouse. There were no restrictions then—the children were packed in like sardines, literally, and as they were setting off one day, one child fell out! Of course there was no fuss; you didn't make fusses about such things in those days. The child was Joyce Dawson.* I saw her not long ago and said 'Joyce, do you remember when you fell out of the car?' 'Oh yes,' she said, 'I was all right!'

It was very difficult teaching that large range, especially as some of them had not had a very good beginning and needed a lot of help with reading, and this went on for several years till the school got so full it was well over a hundred and we just couldn't pack them in any longer, although by 1950 we were three teachers.

The authorities realised we couldn't go on like that, so they decided to take the children of over eleven, and send them to another school. Meanwhile the older girls all went into Holt on a Tuesday for cookery—which they didn't like, and they never wanted to go! One boy, I won't say his name but he was a lovely boy, he had chickens and rabbits and he said to me 'On Friday I go to market.' I said 'Oh, do you?' He said 'I got to sell my rabbits.' He did very well; he made money and I accepted the fact. Nowadays you wouldn't be allowed to, would you? But he was doing actually more good there than he was at school. He was fourteen, not much good on the literary side but extremely good on the maths side.

I had a secretary for one day a week and there was nowhere to put her, so she sat on the edge of my table. There was no telephone of course, not for ages, it was a marvellous thing when we got the telephone, and we shouldn't have had one if it hadn't been for Mrs Watson-Cooke who was a councillor. She visited us and said 'Oh, you must have one, my dear!' She was a wonderful woman, she just went straight through like that. The phone had to be in the class room, obviously. Sometimes when it used to ring I'd pick it up and say very crossly 'Sorry, I can't talk to you now, I'm teaching.' The Education Office people thought they could ring up any time.

I was always terribly keen on drama, and every year each class did a play, and we did most elaborate things really. I remember one with a dragon in it. We never had one person not in the play. As I say, the parents didn't trust me with their children when I first came, but in no time at all they were being wonderful; I only had to say to them 'We'll have a fair, what will you do?' and they'd all come to sit in my room in my house and decide what stall they'd have. They all worked so well together, they were wonderful, and that money that was made on the fair was used to take the children away. The youth hostelling would be a week away, all over the country. It was my class, so it was ages 8-11, and my husband used to go as well to be with the boys in the youth hostels. We used Mr Sanders' first coach and he was superb. We went to the Lakes, and Derbyshire, and we went to Somerset. We worked on all aspects of where we were going, so they knew all about what they were going to see.

In the thirty years I was there, I taught the people's children who had been my first children!—I have very happy memories.

* Now Joyce Childs, see p 270—271

Kelling School children of 1977 report on life in days gone by

Daphne Hanlon, and the children of 1977, prepared a dramatic reconstruction of late nineteenth-century village-school life, as part of the school's centenary celebrations. One of the enterprises was to go out and talk to the old people in the three villages of Salthouse, Weybourne and Kelling—people who were old in 1977:

Dairy Maids

Most farmers also have 1 or 2 dairy maids. Sometimes the dairy maid had to milk the cows. Sometimes this was in a cold wet field. The cows have to be milked twice a day. When it was time to milk a cow the dairy maid would trot off with her little 3 legged stool and her bucket. Then she would sit down and start milking. They would milk by hand. Then she would carry the milk back with the help of a yoke. She would then take the milk in a big room which was called the dairy. When she got to the dairy she would tip the milk into a pan and then she would wait for the cream to come to the top. When it did she skimmed the milk. (Took the cream off for making butter.) What was left was called skimmed milk. Then cream was then put into a large churn. Then they would turn the handle of the churn and they would keep turning until they heard "flop-flop". That would mean there was a lump. It would get bigger and bigger. Then they would take the cream out and it would be called butter. The butter would be made into a nice shape with the butter pats. Then the farmers wife would take it to market to be sold.

Truants from school

Some children 100 years ago never went to school because they had no mothers or fathers, they where orphans. So there used to come round a man called an Attendance officer and sometimes a police man comes with him to find the children and take them to school. At Kelling a farmer used to have some children work on his farm to do some jobs. The Attendance officer would come round and tell the farmer that they should be at school and not at a farm. The children never went to school the next day because they were earning money because they were very poor. In my picture you can see a police man and a Attendance officer coming to take some children to school.

An attendance officer and a policeman capture their prey.

Alice Holman

Alice Holman (one of the seven children of Tom 'Rummy' Woodhouse, and mother of Jasper and Brian) was born in Salthouse in 1901 and lived all her life in the village. Carey Clark, who came to Salthouse in the 1980s, made a recording when Alice was 87 years old, and the following is taken from it. Alice's memories of her childhood go back to the beginning of the last century. She remembers nothing but happy times!

Alice in 1986, aged 84

Above: Kelling School and the road (in the foreground) that the Salthouse children walked to get there—as it was, in the early 1900s.

I spent a happy childhood. We used to walk to Kelling school and we used to have a lovely time going down and coming home. We really entirely enjoyed it, you know, when we were young, going to Kelling school.

Of course things were so much nicer in those days, we had the Chapel Anniversaries. We all took part with the reciting and we used to have a lovely party afterwards. That used to be up Cross Street, where the houses are now built. The head of the Chapel used to come and we had a lovely picnic. They used to throw sweets about and we used to love it all. It seems lovely in those days!

Every Saturday we used to go up and play on the heath. We made a sort of a house up there. We used to wear pinafores then, and we used to take them off and tie them round our waists instead—we thought it was wonderful to have a long skirt! We were quite busy really, we used to take some food with us. There'd be about a dozen of us and we had a lovely time. We seemed so happy in them days. There was no motor cars and that, you know. Of course nowadays you couldn't do that sort of thing, you couldn't go up there now.

Pinafores and hair ribbons at Kelling School in 1913. Alice would have been about this age, but no one is quite sure which she might be.

278

Walking the three miles to school in present times

In the 'old days' Salthouse children walked to Kelling school as a matter of course. But one September day in 1992, when present-day children did the same thing, it was a different matter. Anne Wright (third from the right, below) tells the story:

They wanted us to pay for our kids to go on the school bus, £32 a term! They said we could walk there, you see. We said we shouldn't have to pay when the road was too dangerous, but we had to demonstrate it before they backed down. We phoned the police up and said we were going to walk, and they said 'You can't walk that road without an escort.'

In the end two policemen were necessary to manage us and the tailback of cars! The Education authorities tried it on again a year or so later, but we reminded them about our walk and they backed down again.

The tailback of cars stretched nearly two miles between Kelling and Salthouse.

Shepherded by a policeman: Basil Cooke with Oliver, Julie Gibbons with Marybeth (walking) and Daniel in the push-chair, Anne Wright with George and Adam, Ivan Large carrying Zoë, and Mandy Holman leading the way with Kayleigh and Shaun.

Ten years later, Marybeth, Zoë and Kayleigh appear on the back cover of this book, George on the fly leaf (with Taffy).

The walkway to the Rocket Brigade House

These old postcards both show the raised plank walkway fixed to posts along the side of Beach Road.

It was erected during the First World War to enable the soldiers to march to the Rocket House when the marsh was flooded. (It is visible just behind the cows in the picture above, and in silhouette in the picture below.)

Jim Radley Collection

The extract below, describing it as 'the longest bridge in Norfolk', was written in 1921. In the distance, in the picture on the right, can be seen the mill on the marsh with its top blown off by the artillery in the First World War, when they used it for target practice.

Gerald Cubitt Collection

THE LONGEST BRIDGE IN NORFOLK

On a December day when the sun shone brilliantly in a cloudless sky, and a keen easterly wind swept the marshes and sand-hills, two of us walked almost round this coast broad, chiefly to examine the numerous wild fowl which here find a haven. We first crossed the longest bridge in Norfolk, which runs from the coast road to the Rocket Brigade House which stands gaunt and forlorn on the sand-hills. The bridge is of wood, two planks wide, without a handrail although on the easterly side is a row of posts, which give some kind of guidance on dark nights. The water was about 2 feet below the bridge and not very deep, and the structure curves first in a westerly and then in an easterly direction. A few obstructions rise above the surface of the water—the red brick parapets of two bridges, gorse-covered hurdles used as butts by wildfowlers, and the sere vegetation on one or two small islands.

The Rocket House (Randall's Folly)

In 1922, when the Rocket House was up for sale, the Eastern Daily Press published this letter from a reader in the know about the Rocket House. (To read about the man who built it, see Peter Brooks' article on Onesiphorus Randall on page 128.)

The familiar square-built stone house standing alone on the beach at Salthouse has been responsible for numerous questions as to origin, and so many enquiries have been made regarding its association with smugglers and such romantic enterprises, that one is sorry to destroy the illusion by the introduction of cold facts. The announcement of its forthcoming sale may make a brief note of its history interesting. It is only a commonplace history after all, for some seventy years ago the local landowner was one Onesiphorus Randall, who had prospered beyond his station in London and returned to his native county a landed proprietor. Mr Randall resided at that time at the Woodlands, Holt, now absorbed by Gresham's School, and being somewhat fond of visiting his estate at Salthouse and spending his leisure by the sea, he decided to build a substantial house which should at the same time answer as a small residence for himself and a shelter for shipwrecked sailors, for which beneficent purpose it has been sometimes used.

Another of the reasons, it is said, was that the owner fancied himself as lord of the manor and his entitlement to wreck, and the house on the beach was intended to store such stuff.

In a practical age, which did not give its builder the credit for his humane sympathies— the house being in a derelict condition, it became known as 'Randall's Folly', and ultimately passed into the hands of the Department of Mercantile Marine, Board of Trade, who utilised the ground floor for a rocket life-saving station. The Geddes axe having fallen, the department has decided the station is redundant and has removed the life-saving apparatus, and the house will be offered for sale. For a student of natural history, the place furnishes an excellent prospect as not only is the wildfowling good, but the marshes which are adjacent are the breeding grounds of a great variety of marine birds and, this season, nests and eggs have been exceptionally numerous.

The Rocket Apparatus

In 1975 the EDP paid tribute to the life-saving apparatus, with this account of a practice session:

Elderly people in Salthouse today remember the practices with the rocket apparatus, which was the ingenious invention of a Norfolk man, Captain Manby. The local brigade fired a rocket, with rope attached, eastward along the beach and over a mast set up to represent a ship in distress. A 'little ol' man' from Salthouse climbed the mast, secured the rope to it, and pulled up the breeches buoy and slid down in it to the apparatus, a spectacular performance watched with merriment by his neighbours on the beach.

Florence Remembers

Florence Radley's father, James High, was a member of the life-saving brigade. In her memoirs, recorded by Eileen High, Florence remembers one of the real-life rescues her father took part in from Salthouse beach:

I can remember the sea being so much further away. There was a mud bank which a man called Purdy put up. They gave him the marshes, Salthouse people did, so he could put protection up from the sea, you see.

He didn't build a wall, he just put the mud bank. Either side of the bank, where they dug the mud out, was a wide expanse of water this side and the beach side. Then there was grass the beach side, as well as that water. This was before the Rocket House was built. Randall, who built it, he lived at Holt. I musn't tell you this, but he was fond of women—that's what that house was built for! It had a big door either end and he used to drive up in his carriage and round into the house and right through the house with his coach and horses. The carriage used to stop in the house till he was ready to go. Then, you see, there was a bridge on the beach side of the Rocket House. He had that built and he would drive out of the house over the bridge and onto the beach, and I can remember jumping off the bridge.

Above: Evelyn Forsdick (wife of Friday Forsdick) leans against a part of the masonry of Randall's bridge, still remaining on Salthouse beach c1920.

Betty Rising Collection

Charles Edward High

Left: This meticulous and skilled drawing of Randall's Folly (known as 'The Rocket House' after the Board of Trade took it over) is the work of Charles High, whose story is told earlier in this book (see p190).

In the foreground of Charles' picture is the cannon that fired the rockets to send a line on board ships wrecked off the shore, to bring their crews to safety. Behind the rocket gun are the great doors inside which the life-saving apparatus was housed.

In the story below, Jimmy High describes a stormy night when he was a boy and found shipwrecked Sailors sheltering in the Rocket House:

Over the other side of the Rocket House there was one big expanse of grass where the village cows used to go. You see, first there was the marshes outside the village, then this wide expanse of water, then the bank, then another wide expanse of water, then grass, and then the beach. Oh, that's encroached no end. Half the marshes have gone. There's no bank now and all the water's gone—there's just marshes. When Randall died, the Board of Trade bought that house. They had a life-saving brigade in the village, and a rocket cart with all the apparatus on, and that was lodged in that house. There were so many men in the village in the brigade, and my father was one of them. They were wooden ships and they often used to come ashore and the men would have to go and rescue the people or try to. He wore a cork life-jacket, my father, and he used to have to go down into the sea and bring the people through the water. I remember, the last time he went, the captain's little girl was on the ship and he brought the little girl through the water and he said her hair floated on top of the water. They were alive—they rescued them.

Florence Radley

Rocket House in action

The rescue just described by Florence took place towards the end of the nineteenth century. The following account of another rescue of the same era is taken from the autobiography of Florence's cousin, Jimmy High.

Henry High and his sons, who lived in Cross Street, were called to a wreck in the night. Florence's father (Jimmy's Uncle James) was probably among the other rescuers on this occasion which is described so vividly by Jimmy High himself, who was only a boy at the time.

A gale sprung up in the early hours of the morning. There was a knock on our window and a voice crying out 'A ship has foundered'. We all dressed hastily and ran to the beach at great speed. A man told me to go across to the Rocket House and see if the crew of the apparatus wanted any assistance from us. As I ran into the room where the life-saving gear was housed, a dozen men met me. They all tried to speak at the same time, and were trying to tell me something in a foreign tongue. They were Norwegians. By the time I had got my breath the man who had sent me arrived, and at once asked the men if all had been saved. Another Babel broke out, but one came forward who could speak English, to tell us that the Captain, Mate and the ship's boy were still missing.

Off we ran towards the wreck, and I have never seen such a sight before or since. The men I had stumbled upon in the Rocket House had saved themselves by jumping from the bow of the ship, which was hard on the shingle beach. The three people they feared lost had been trapped by the cargo in the stern. This had broken away from the main part of the ship, and among the wreckage of this part we found the Captain, who had been so knocked about in the drifting wreckage, that he died. This was the first dead man I had seen. The boy could not be found anywhere, but the Mate lay trapped in the deck cargo, which was timber. He was clear except for one leg which was pinned down by the heavy wood, and every time a wave struck the ship it seemed to push the timber over him still further. It took hours of patient work by his rescuers to get him out, and it is a wonder that they were not all killed by the movement of the timber. Fortunately, some of the rigging got fast round it, after a time, and prevented it moving far.

The man was conscious for a long time, but lost consciousness before he could be rescued. However, they got him out and warmed him up near the fire and, when they had pumped some of the water out of him, he seemed little the worse for his ordeal.

Jimmy High

The Britons

'Millmarsh', the Britons' first holiday home in Salthouse, on the site of the mill in Mill Drift.

The Rocket House was bought by Mr and Mrs Briton from Sheffield, who had been obliged to vacate their odd holiday-hut which had been made of an old solid-tyred motor bus with a built-on sleeping quarters. This construction stood on the marsh opposite Grout's Lane, exactly where the old windmill had stood. The Rocket House must have seemed palatial!

Above: 1930s, Mrs Briton centre, and Amelia Pigott (née Hancock) (in the coloured frock) on the right of the group. She was a friend of the Britons and looked after the house for them in their absence.

The Joplings

LOUISE GRATTAN (NÉE JOPLING) REMEMBERS:

My parents bought the 'Rocket House', or Randall's Folly as it was then called, in 1937. They built on to it to provide a couple of bathrooms, another bedroom and a staircase, creating a practical if somewhat unusual and eccentric holiday house for the family. They renamed the house Great Eye Folly, as it stood on a low grassy hill or 'eye', the grounds of which sloped down to the beach some 200 yards away.

When the war came, the house was requisitioned by the war office and used as a kind of detention centre. The lads sent there had no heating, so they ripped out anything made of wood—doors, furniture, cupboards and so on—to make fires.

My parents repossessed in 1944, repaired the damage, and we lived there during all the school holidays except Christmas. The war was not quite over and one evening, from the sitting room window, we watched a dramatic air battle far away against the setting sun.

Our well was brackish so all drinking water was fetched, usually on foot, with a bucket from the village. The sea was cold, the beach pebbly and shelving, often with big waves, but we swam two or three times a day in the summer, and sometimes even at Easter, always starting with a dip before breakfast. It was always so windy that there was no garden in the ordinary sense. The rabbits trimmed the fine grass, and the gorse grew round their rabbit-holes. Our favourite game was deck-quoits, as the lawn was so like the deck of a ship. Indeed, from our upstairs sitting room you could see nothing but the sea. There was no electricity; my father spent hours cleaning and tending Aladdin lamps. The nearest telephone was at the post office, a mile away.

The people who lived in the village were wonderfully friendly and helpful in all sorts of ways. My mother wanted to have a VJ Day celebration, so she invited the whole village to tea. I remember the stream of people walking up the beach road to join us, playing games on the lawn and eating little square meat-paste sandwiches.

My mother, as Joan Elwes, had been a distinguished professional singer before the war;

1947 Three young Joplings. In the backgound can be seen part of the war-time defences across the marsh.

Beach road is flooded, but someone has been to the village with a bucket for drinking water!

she knew Elgar and Vaughan Williams well. When Dr Watson the organist came to stay at the Folly, he accompanied her in a concert in Salthouse church. That must have been about 1950.

We realised that Father Neptune claimed a little bit more of our land every year; the erosion was faster owing to the army gun-emplacements. But we were taken by surprise when, in January 1953, the combination of the spring tides and northerly gales produced a 'surge', causing floods and destruction all down the East Coast. Half the Folly was washed away that wild night. My parents found their bed on the beach, along with piles of plates from the kitchen cupboard. The piano was undamaged. But the remaining structure had to be destroyed soon after.

In the summer of 2000, Louis Grattan (née Jopling) read these 'Reflections' aloud in the church, before giving a concert of music by Bach, Handel and Loeillet to commemorate those pre-war times, in aid of the Friends of Salthouse Church. Louise played the violin; her husband Patrick Grattan, flute; Philip Coates, cello; and Michael Allard harpsichord.

Above: c1906. The Rocket House on Great Eye and the beach road, from the rising land behind the houses. Ruth Holman lived in one of these houses at the time of the Rage of 1897 and her grandchildren lived in the same houses at the time of the 1953 flood. (See photo p 359 of these houses taken from the marsh after the '53 flood) The little black squares on the beach are beach huts. The water this side of Great Eye is what remains of the Salthouse Main Channel. See aerial photograph p 63.

Sylvia Townsend Warner at the Folly

One wild winter, the Joplings let the Folly to Sylvia Townsend Warner, novelist and poet, a communist and a lesbian. She shared her time in Randall's Folly with her friend 'the extraordinary Valentine Ackland'—a six foot, boy-like, 'alcoholic Amazon'. The following extracts, chosen to show what their life in the Folly was like, are from 'The Diaries of Sylvia Townsend Warner', published by Virago Press, 1995. Unfortunately there is space here only for her sea and marsh descriptions—references to her letters written, books read or worked on and news from home, have had to be omitted.

1950

October 27. Still cold—and still tired we drove to G.E.F. [Great Eye Folly]. The fire was lit downstairs, there was tea ready for us, the table was covered with parcels and last thoughts from Mrs J. [Mrs Jopling]. Dreamily we read, unpacked, listened to the sea: it was the view from the upper room that suddenly woke us to a sense of place, and we knew we were here. We unpacked, put away, put out—it was almost dusk before we went out again, and picked up our first driftwood.

28. An intensely stormy day—we saw the sea darken and grow sullen, and an hour later it was rent with white horses. After waiting in for a baker called Jasper who did not come, we went off to the local stores, and bought staples like potatoes and toilet-paper, and then on to Holt, over a russet heath and through a violent hailstorm. Valentine bought nails at a shop resounding with anecdotes of cats, and everyone had Norfolk manners, and we much approve of Holt. In the evening, with the house practically settled, I sat writing, with the storm roaring outside, inside Niou [Siamese cat] sitting in his child's armchair, his little bell tinkling as he stirred.

November 1. *The newly caught skate*—still breathing—pink and ivory like a stormy sunrise, with pebbles still holding to its skin. The dusk, the sea coming out of the sky, no horizon, *the sky becoming sea*, rumpling, and breaking in very small cringing waves, and the boat being pushed ashore and up the shingle bank.

2. Shaw died early this morning—a comparable event to the death of Voltaire. I was very young when he was pointed out to me—that famous odious Mr Shaw—walking up Bond St in a pale homespun suit—that seemed to annoy my mother even more than the beard or the man.

In the morning of this fine calm day Niou was out playing among the fortifications—so stilly couched that we thought him a sea-white stone. I walked to the post, and heard about the flood of '47 and how a wave broke the shop-window and swept the wool off its shoulder-high shelf. The army, as usual, it appears. They dug into the sea wall and did not restore it. The flood in '43, at night, when no one dared show a light. But the charming young man who came from Holt about the Calor gas said there had been a flood in the thirties. He could remember a bridge where the fishermen now stand, and his father could remember cornfields under it—so much has the sea encroached. We saw a school of porpoises near the shore, and the fishermen went on by lamplight, after seven in the evening: but now the wind is rising and blows fiercely.

3. And this morning a gale, north, with the sea very high, and the Cley coastguard not supercilious when I rang up to ask the time of high tide. It was 11.30, and at 12 we drove to Sheringham and registered, and shopped, and on the way back the car boiled—so we went back to S. to have a new poultice fastened to the side of the radiator. Now, as the sea is still high, the car sits

on the front door mat. Spindrift like ghostly snow on the shingle, and flying everywhere around us.

6. In the afternoon we waited to buy a 2/6 poppy from a gentleman who rang—and this made our walk along the shore less glorious. I wrote ten thousand letters in the evening and the news is very bad. MacArthur detonating for war with China. He has been led up to the Korean border like a puppy after a gobbet on a string—and they have soundly enveloped and whacked him.

7. I awoke from a confused dream in which my mother was recently dead, but had not been senile—and she had sent a marlinspike iron object emmanchée in chocolate, and a remark—apparently in answer to something of mine—that bears were bad mothers.

14. My Love brought me breakfast while I was still in bed, and had cleaned and bowered my sitting-room. Still cold, windy, with brilliant colours on the marsh. Its dykes are now full of ruffled water—the curious look of the inland waterway flowing under the steep bank of seapebbles on our eastern beach. I darned a sheet—Niou killed two rats—and we drove in the afternoon round and about the Holt Heath. It would have been wholly happy if we had not met two gents and their keeper, the latter holding live pheasants upside-down: their wings fluttering and striving, and the gents awkwardly scrambling over a gate.

20. In the morning V.'s back was very bad—she had felt it give yesterday. And so I walked alone, by the sea's edge till I felt, like an animal—this is beyond any breathed air; and so it was, for climbing onto the shingle bank I found myself among the marram tufts, and seeing a superb piece of marsh: the pale sharp poppy-horns standing above green frizzed cushions, marsh

Great Eye Folly from the landward side.

michaelmas daisy in thick grey thistledown mackerel-sky clouds, and the marsh water like blue lead above cushions of green moss and edged with rust-dark vegetation. I got a quantity of wood too, looking east to Salthouse church under a dark purple cloud.

22. To Sheringham and Holt in the morning. It was cold wet and windy. In the afternoon I pawked by the marram tufts, and sat for a long while on my way back looking at the stern appearance of the smooth grey waves, and the tawny light in the north-west sky, and the band of dark slate blue of the eastern horizon between the grey of the sea and the blueish violet of cloud; and then as I went on with my bundle I saw My Love, tall and slender, coming across the plateau to meet me.

25. We have now most exquisite moonlight nights with foam as white as goatsmilk or Niou's bosom. The telephone restored.

December 15. Snow, hard frost, blizzards, icy roads, and the man cannot come from Walsingham. So we filled pails and buckets with snow, that sat in front of fires like large wet geese, refusing to thaw, and when at last they did were spotted with rabbits' dung. Meanwhile in a relenting interval the rainwater tank gave a trickle, and we got as far as Mrs Gray, who solved all our problems as usual, and has a father in law who is a rabbiteer. In the afternoon a terrific blizzard: the wind round to the north, and at gale force ever since, so in addition to hoarding water we may be flooded. But a most happy day, for all that.

16. A slight let-up—but the landscape still mostly snow, and the wind icy: it blows to us from Yorkshire & Lincolnshire, which are deep in snow.

Doris came in the morning, and so did the man from Walsingham—I found him with his lower half sunk in the well, like some Norfolk garden god with a scarlet face and a noble barrel. In the afternoon there was a blizzard. I worked on my pot-boiler, and read Donne, and in the evening my love read poetry aloud—Herbert, and Clare, and Fletcher, and the Afflictions of Richard, while I knitted on Niou's rug. The man from Walsingham, who talked politics—anti-Soviet, alas!—and glumly resigned to war, with the resignation turning to resolution, said 'You don't mind the old waves, then?' They have been vast and sombre, but with explosions of spray that run westward, as though kindling along the wave. My Love be-bellied, and badly so, with a violent headache.

1951

January 10. More pawking, more sawing, more chopping—for our wood supply runs low. A conversation with Mrs Gray—she still had no candles and no matches. They had been told there would be no [gas] cartridges for the next three months. On the same day, she had been told that price of knitting wool would go up from 1/8d an oz to 2/8d, and Mr Gray had learned at the garage that there would be very few small spare parts, as the factories were working—if at all—a 36 hour week because of the call-up of metal. She referred blastingly to the Festival of Britain (Oh! I forgot—they can expect very few tinned foods, no tin), and to the equality of sacrifice in which Europe equals USA. In that one sentence, Eisenhower seems to have achieved a lead in unpopularity over MacArthur—mirabile dictu.

February 2. A frittering day—and one of the coldest I have ever known. A south wind, again: a steady stealthy boring wind; and no sign of it, on this clean-shaved landscape, except on the sea. As the waves—very small ones—approached the shore, the wind turned them backward, aborted them: instead of breaking, they faded out on the sea, one following another, like bars on a mackerel; and the rim of sea and shore was as inexpressive as the shore of a lake. By the evening this wind has intensified, and blew in multitudinous gusts.

4. *Sunday.* And a tearing gale. We drove to Winterton, taking Niou hot-water-bottled with us, because it seemed that we might well be unable to get back. And at Walcott we had a puncture. It was opposite a kind house with a telephone, and a man who, when all garages proved to be sabbatical, came out in the storm and helped My Love. Then home, and it took both of us all our strength to turn back the garage door against the wind. Early this morning a boat hoved to, or whatever it is, just outside our beach, twisting and turning for all its two anchors.

11. Tonight, in my bath, I noticed that the wind was rising. This morning there was a violent n. e. gale, a Craske sea of looped breakers running sidelong to the shore, and indoors, the kitchen a swamp, the larder a waterfall, and fountains of windblown sink-water blowing up from the runaway. I noticed this aspect of it more, as I was feeling so ill, and let My Love do the outside jobs. But in flashes through the windows I saw how wildly lovely it was—and in the afternoon, the wind going down and the rain ceasing, I walked along the beach admiring the sea—sternly gay, destined and conscienceless.

21. A jet bomber has crossed the Atlantic in four hours. The BBC broke its news to say so.

Mrs Gray has given up being a grocer, because there are so few groceries, so much paper work, and the margin of profit has been cut again. So wags the world. And Norway, though it will increase its army, will have no foreign troops sent there unless it first asks for them.

24. It was a misty-moisty day, and in the afternoon a rare sexless fisher, with hair like Monica [Ring]'s, and long narrow scarlet hands and wrists, and a long heron's stride. A beautiful being, with a severe inattentive regard, it went away on a motor-bicycle, and we supposed it finally to be male. How such an incertitude would have surprised our grandparents.

March 8. A strong wind, and the sea roaring in with great plunging billows. So much so that with an eye on the pm tide, we took both animals in the car when we drove to East Dereham.

On our return the sea was almost up to the gap, with nearly three hours to run. I rang up the coast guards, who said Prevention was better than Cure. Not seeing how one can cure the state of being cut off from the mainland, we made a swift dusky get-away—and left for Winterton with the spindrift whirling after us and the wind dislodging the southern door post of the garage with one toss of the door.

Their stay in Great Eye Folly ended on the 20th March 1951. The following extract is from Sylvia's diary two years later:

1953

February 1. On the 6 pm news, the news of the flood on the east coast—all Holderness under salt water, Yarmouth & Lynn innundated, and the seaward end of Sea Palling flooded, with people drowned. Ruth, rung up, told how two local men who had left their boats at Gurleston, wanted to see about them, & hired Ronnie from Hemsby. He was told there was no road through, but remembered a side-lane. Halfway along it, he saw a boat coming towards him. The floods go all down as far as Kent—and on t'other side of the North Sea, worse floods and breakings of dykes in Holland.

2. An aerial photograph in the Daily Mail seems to be Salthouse, though it was called Sheringham. Either way, ruin and desolation, with a great elbow of sea thrust inland. Essex too; and the wretched bungalow towns and caravan towns destroyed, and hundreds drowned on Canvey Island.

5. A letter from Felix Young today tells of all the coast road houses in ruins or so badly damaged as to be uninhabitable. The poor old woman whom the sea killed in her kitchen—a tiger-kill, first it knocked her down, then when her old husband pulled her out of the water & set her on the kitchen table, another wave flowed in and carried her off in its mouth—was carried to the church, the only shelter: there she lay, while the wind raved in the high roof and shook the tall doors. The Patch, and the villa next to it are unhurt—so is *G. E. Folly*. But the village, the true village, lost. The sea came in, not by the Folly Gap, but sweeping from Cley, and swept through the Dun Cow, and the Post-Office. Done up, five pairs of trousers, my tan leather waistcoat, woollen vests and scarves, the shawl and the gloves Vera knit for me last year.

6. In the afternoon, the postman came up the drive with a letter from Felix Young. The seaward wall of G.E.F. has fallen, the house stands open to the sea. And alas for my Love!

Great Eye Folly 1953, its seaward wall fallen, but still standing.

Tale of a house that is no more

THE National Trust received a piece of Norfolk history when the Great Eye land was handed over by the Jopling family.

A large house once stood on the two-acre site and the Jopling family, which acquired it in 1937 spent their summer holidays there.

Mr John Jopling remembered his holidays there with great affection as he met National Trust officials on the site on Monday.

"My bedroom window faced inland and the view has not changed one bit.

"Quite often the house became an island. I would wake up in the morning following a storm and seawater had seeped through the shingle bank to create an inland 'sea'," he said.

Mr Jopling related one incident when the "inland sea" was so rough the house was cut off for three days before a boat could cross and evacuate the residents.

The great floods of 1953 heralded the end for The Rocket House when the north side of the house collapsed into the sea.

"My mother came here the following day to retrieve what she could. I can always remember her going to a drinks cupboard which stood in the part of the building which collapsed," said Mr Jopling.

"When she unlocked it the back of the cupboard had gone but all the bottles of drink and glasses remained neatly stacked," he said.

In June 1956 the remains of the house were demolished and the site is now covered by the present shingle bank sea defence.

Mr Merlin Waterson, left, the National Trust's regional director, and Mr John Jopling pictured on the land he has given to the trust.

At the time of the flood, workmen from the East Suffolk and Norfolk River Board were working on the beach to improve its sea defence capabilities and had left equipment there ready to continue their work the following day. Much of this disappeared in the flood and the lovely story was told that when the sea had receded, the lady of the house was walking along what was left of the shingle bank when she met one of the River Board workmen also apparently searching for something. There ensued the following conversation:

Lady: 'Good Morning. If you happen to find any silver cutlery, that will be mine.'

Workman: 'Yes, Ma'am. If you happen to find a bloody great bulldozer, that will be mine!'

Peter Brooks 2002

The Story behind the remnants of a Radar Pylon

Gerald Cubitt Collection

Many people visiting the heath today wonder about the remains to be seen there of a wartime radar pylon, and over the years a number of small wooden crosses have been placed on one of the four steel base-plates which still mark the site of the pylon. Gerald Cubitt tells how, on 15th January 1945, a Lancaster bomber returning after a night raid over Germany crashed into this 200-foot-high pylon and all of the seven crew members of the aircraft died.

On a visit to the heath in May 2001, Gerald said that he noticed a little note attached to one of the crosses which carried the following message:

> Remembering the crew of the Lancaster bomber squadron which crashed into this pylon in the night of 15th January 1945.
>
> The Boyce family.

Gerald felt he wanted to say a personal thanks to the Boyce family for their gesture of respect to the memory of those who lost their lives here.

On 5th March 2002, Adrian Lewis from Bristol was on Salthouse heath, remembering seeing Golden Orioles there thirty years before, when he came upon the pylon remains.

'I noticed that one of the pylon's feet had a bouquet of flowers attached to it and, walking over, found a note attached, addressed to the crew of LM720. It was a sign of remembrance from someone called Hilda and her family. Remembrance poppies and small wooden crosses were also tied there. It was getting towards sunset on that windswept hilltop and I found the memorial both fascinating and extremely moving, and it stays in my mind.'

On his return to Bristol, Adrian searched the internet for information about Salthouse heath—wanting to know the history of the site—and by this means he came in touch with the editor of this book.

THE BARD HILL RADAR PYLON

Gerald Cubitt Collection

THIS IS THE TANGLED REMAINS OF THE PYLON
ON SALTHOUSE HEATH AFTER THE CRASH

During the war all photography in this area was strictly forbidden.
This unique photograph was obtained by Gerald Cubitt
from Americans who had connections with it.

LOSS OF LANCASTER B3, LM720 AND CREW AT BARD HILL, SALTHOUSE

The following official account of how the Lancaster bomber came to be flying low over Salthouse heath on the night of its crash, was given to the Church by the RAF and discovered in the church safe along with an RAF book of missions and casualties.

We have heard several different stories as to how the crash came about—among them the theory that the plane had been hit by enemy anti-aircraft fire and was instructed to make a belly landing on the heath. Here is the official account, for good measure:

January 1945 was another busy day for the crew of Lancaster B3, LM720, based at Skellingthorpe, Lincs, with 61 Squadron. Take off was to be at 1630 hrs, for a raid on oil refineries at Leuna, near Mersberg. The crew had only just returned at 0245 hrs that very day, from a raid on Politz, near Stettin. The Captain and crew had reported a good concentration of bombing for this raid, with slight but heavy flak being encountered.

LM720 was now to be one of 573 Lancasters going to Leuna. The attacks on this target caused severe damage to the synthetic oil-plant, and indeed the German Minister Albert Speer, in his post-war interrogations, stated that 'This was one of a group of most damaging raids on the oil industry.' Ten aircraft were lost.

Due to bad weather whilst returning to Skellingthorpe, the aircraft of 61 Squadron were diverted to Carnaby but, for whatever reason, LM720 did not divert to this location and instead the aircraft was put on a heading to land at Langham, Norfolk.. Presumably descending for its approach to land, in very bad visibility due to drizzle and low cloud, the aircraft struck the RAF 200ft radar pylon at Bard Hill, Salthouse, at 0121 hrs on the 15th January. Six of the crew of seven were killed instantly. The seventh, F/Sgt Boakes, died from his injuries in hospital at 0625 hrs.

The pylon collapsed partially onto the Operations Nissen Hut in which the RADAR operators were working. Fortunately none were injured. The disintegrating Lancaster fell on the nearby heath, the tail section blocking the road at the entrance to the camp. The existence of the RAF RADAR Station and the pylon are still evident to those strolling on the heath. Poppies are sometimes placed at the pylon during Remembrance week.

Pilot:	F/O William G. Corewyn
Navigator:	F/Sgt Ronald C. Battersby
Flt/Engr:	Sgt Peter R. Earl
Air/Bomber:	F/Sgt Edward J. Boakes
W/op Air:	F/Sgt Sidney J. James
AG:	Sgt John Douglas
AG:	Sgt Richard Richardson

They were all in their twenties, the eldest was 24.

Sgts Earl and Douglas are interred in the parish cemetery at Wells, Norfolk; the remainder of the crew, in their respective home town cemeteries in England—with the exception of the Captain who came from Scotland.

In the Dark Days of the War

Russell Reeve (at that time of Cromer) researched and wrote this unusual account of a German pilot and his crew who turned up on Salthouse Heath in 1941. 50 years later, he contacted the German pilot and arranged a reunion.

Above right: The German pilot (left) and Russell, in 1991

In the dark days of the Second World War, Norfolk was no stranger to the sound of German aircraft engines.

Between 1940 and 1943, numerous raids on local targets took place. There were 44 separate raids on Norwich alone, with numerous other targets in the area receiving the same unwelcome visits with all the accompanying terror, death and damage.

But even when the Luftwaffe directed its attention elsewhere, there was no respite in Norfolk, night after night, as hostile aircraft overhead made their way from the airfields in North Germany and occupied Holland to targets in the west and north of the British Isles. The citizens of Norfolk who huddled in the smelly concrete town, garden or cellar shelters wondered whether they or some other unfortunates were the 'target for tonight'.

And so it was in the early hours of Sunday 4th May 1941, as the clearly identifiable engine noise of a Heinkel 111 was heard droning its ominous way over the North Norfolk skies.

The pilot, Lieutenant Alfred Plank von Bachselten, and his three other crew members were well satisfied with their night's work, having left the Liverpool docks ablaze as they made their way homewards towards the coast at Cromer.

Incredibly, despite strict blackout regulations, it is said that Cromer Lighthouse was kept burning as an essential navigational aid to North Sea shipping and was used as a reference point by aircraft.

What the German officers didn't know was that time was running out for them. From very poor results in the beginning, RAF night-fighting techniques using radar and improved training were at last beginning to pay off.

The powerful radar installations at West Beckham directed a Boulton and Paul Defiant of 151 Squadron, flown by Pilot Officer Bodien, and a Bristol Beaufighter, flown by Sergeant Hill, onto the track of the unsuspecting German crew members.

The burst of fire that raked the fuselage, almost certainly .303 calibre from the Defiant, crippled the aircraft and mortally wounded the airgunner, Bruno Kauhardt, with a bullet through the heart. Von Bachselten probably never saw his attackers, but dived to almost 10,000ft to evade them and at 01.04 hours made an almost perfect wheels up belly-flop across three fields, before coming to a halt near Breck Farm just north of Sharrington.

The three survivors removed their dead comrade from the plane before using documents and aviation fuel to set fire to and destroy the aircraft.

Retaining the heavy machine-gun and their individual pistols, the crew then divested themselves of German currency and other 'enemy items', intending to avoid internment by posing as Dutch airmen. They headed towards the Holt Road past the cottage of Mrs Allison, mother of two small children, whose husband was away in the army. As she watched the fire from the bedroom window, she heard them talking amongst themselves.

After a short while they abandoned the cumbersome machine-gun. What steps the authorities took at the time are not documented although it is thought that a Home Guard motor cyclist was shortly on the scene but left to seek assistance. Two local constables, PC Bunnett of Binham and PC Massingham who was on duty at Holt Police Station, arrived soon after and found the dead German in a ditch where his comrades had placed him, away from the now burnt-out plane.

Unseen by anyone, incredibly, the three fugitives made their way through the centre of Holt and, after sheltering for a while in a pill box in the centre of the town, headed towards Salthouse and the coast. By very early morning, somewhere in the area of Kelling Heath and Bard Hill, they opened fire on aircraft beacons at a small 'dummy' airfield and later made a small fire to warm themselves, no doubt causing considerable concern to the two RAF minders located in an adjacent caravan.

The RAF, doing what all good citizens do when things are not right, contacted PC Charles Henry Barnard, the local officer at Kelling Police House.

Setting out on his bicycle, the apparently unarmed officer found the three at Salthouse Heath on the coast. History does not tell us whether they still had pistols or whether their warlike intent had evaporated, but this incredibly brave man unhesitatingly approached them and at 6.10am they surrendered themselves to the lone representative of Great Britain's might.

What happened then, I venture to suggest, could only happen in 'dear old England'. Without any bluster or antagonism, Charles told the surprised Germans: 'You look all in. You had better come back and have some breakfast.' He then took them to Kelling Police House where his wife Vera, under the excited gaze of her two children, promptly proceeded to make tea and cook breakfast.

After much conversation and signing of the officer's notebook (still retained by the family), re-enforcements arrived in the shape of PS George Chapman, and the 'enemy' started on their journey to a prisoner of war camp, by way of Holt Police Station.

The whole event, no doubt due to wartime censorship and the typical low-key approach to policing at that time, passed off with only a few lines in the press to the effect that 'a Nazi plane had crashed and the crew had been arrested by police'. No mention of the incident appears in the officer's record retained in the force archives.

It is comforting to know that in the midst of all the hatred generated by the most horrific confrontation man had ever known, such acts of normality and humanity still happened.

The writer of this article, Russell Reeve, together with a friend of his, arranged in 1991 for Pilot Alfred Bachselten to come to Norfolk to meet the families of the late PC Barnard and PS Chapman, and visit the scene of his wartime adventures. The picture below was taken at that time.

Above: Alfred Plank von Bachselten, with his wife Dolly 50 years after the event, standing in the field where his Heinkel crashed. Even now, crops do not grow well on that spot (seen paler in the background).

The Windmill on the marsh

Left: The mill that once stood on the marsh at Mill Drift, seen from the coast road. It was the subject of many early picture postcards. Directly behind the mill, in the far distance, is Little Eye and, to the right of it, Great Eye with the Rocket House silhouetted against the sky.

The Mill Drift mill met its end in the First World War, not from enemy action but from our own. The artillery used it for target practice apparently seeing it as a dangerous landmark for enemy aircraft. Herbert Pigott, when he retired, used much of the brick from the ruined mill to build a house called 'Ducklands' in Grout's Lane (which can be seen on the right of the picture below).

Above: Looking east along the 'Crick', from the Dun Cow.

Right: David Jarvis with his wife and child outside their house at the bottom of Cross Street, c 1912. He was the one who was trapped in the mill during the Rage of 1897. The Jarvis family were millers for many generations, the earliest mention being 1835.

Above: The mill from the marsh—its remains can still be seen as a mound.

This watercolour belonging to Dr Ian Keymer, dated 1831, was the final piece in the jigsaw of Tony Palmer's research. This picture has been repeated on page 303 to compare it with a very similar painting recently found.

The Other Windmill: Harry Apling and Tony Palmer

Dr Tony Palmer and his wife Shirley, 2003.

Having camped on Bard Hill in the 1950s, and known Salthouse for many years as a holiday spot, Tony and Shirley Palmer bought the bungalow known as Windy Ridge at the top of Grout's Lane in 1971. Since that time, Tony has been absorbed in collecting evidence of a mill that once stood in his garden.

Establishing the history of the plot on which our bungalow was built has been an intriguing challenge. During our early years, we heard from a number of people who knew the place in the past, that at one time there had been a windmill in our garden. Mrs Radley (then aged 93) said that her mother had told her there used to be a smock mill on our plot (the 'Pightle'). This was confirmed by Mr K. Brown and his sister Mrs Phyllis Jackson who as children had lived in Church Cottage (later called 'the Nest', now St Nicholas Cottage). Mrs Jackson told us that, as a child, she remembered playing in the flint ruins of a windmill at the bottom of the garden (the west end) and, in a letter dated March 1981, her brother Mr K. L. Brown told how when he was given a vegetable garden on the plot (by the Harrison sisters who lived there in the 1950s), he remembered coming across terrific foundations which he could only conclude belonged to the mill. He said 'I exposed a few yards and then covered it up. It was not too deep, about 18" only', and he enclosed a plan which indicated a semicircle of foundations at the west end of our garden, next to the present vegetable patch.

No doubt the hauling of tumbrils loaded with sacks of corn up the hill to the mill would have presented a difficulty. An additional trace horse would have been used and the severe right-hand turn at the top of the narrow Grout's Lane would have been an impossibility if the corner of 'Hilltop' cottage had not been built in a rounded fashion (which may be seen today). Finally, I was told that Gerald Cubitt (whose family had lived in Salthouse for many years) said that one day the post mill at Mill Ridge 'ran away with itself' and disintegrated. He had heard that they had thrown coarse sand and gravel between the mill wheels in an attempt to slow it down— which had done it no good at all. Apparently it was destroyed in a gale when it broke free from the chains that normally shackled it. The late Harry Apling told me that a very strong wind could result in the mill turning and being blown over when the sails backed on to the wind—'tail winded'.

Above: The bungalow, taken from the exact spot in the vegetable garden where the mill must have stood.

Below: The diagram of site No 44, which Harry Apling included in his letter to me, with the approximate position of the mill about 60 yards west of the church, according to the 1" Ordnance Survey map of 1838 (which is the same year as the Edward Houghton survey map was made).

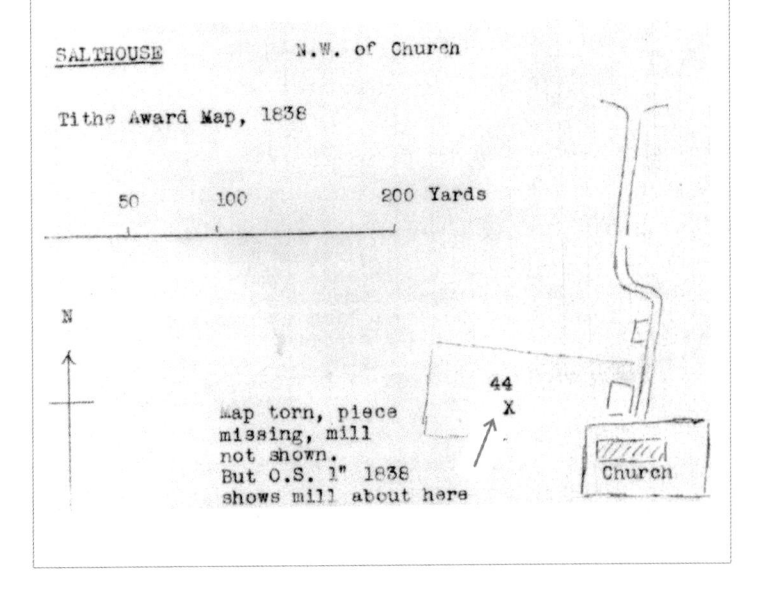

Historical evidence for the mill

This is derived from three sources:

1 **The Norfolk Record Office and Norwich City Library**

2 **Harry Apling's Research**
   (an authority on the History of Norfolk Mills and author of a book of that title)

3 **A watercolour painting owned by Dr Ian Keymer**
   depicting a windmill west of the church, probably by Thirtle of the Norwich School, dated 1831

1 The Norfolk Record Office:

At the Record Office I inspected a number of maps:

a) *Bryant's map of 1826*

This shows a smock mill north-west of Salthouse church, at the end of a track leading west, off Grout's Lane.

b) *Edward Houghton's Plan of Salthouse (no. 100) 1838*

Edward Houghton, a surveyor from Wells, was commissioned in 1838 to make this map to accompany the Tithe Award of 1839.* It is a large map measuring some 6 feet by 3. Each parcel of land is clearly numbered in ink and colour, except for the Mill Ridge plot which has been roughly pencilled-in as plot number 44. This anomaly may be due to damage (see Harry Apling's remarks below).

Plot 44 encompasses the area of the Mill Ridge property, which includes the two present-day houses (St Nicholas Cottage and Church Cottage). In the reference to the plan the total area is seen to be 3 rods 25 poles; the owner is named as Parlett Starling, and the occupier as George Larner Neave. The property is described as

> Dwelling house, Stable, Hayloft and Garden, Cottage, Wood Smock Mill containing Two Pairs of Stones, Flour Mill Jumper, Lower Room, Store Floor, and Stage Chamber.

Note, the windmill is not shown on the plan.

c) *Ordnance Survey Map 1886*

The Mill Ridge is not depicted, but there is a windmill shown on the marsh.

Norwich City Library:
(which I visited before the disastrous fire of 1994)

By consulting various years of *Kelly's Directory of Norfolk,* I discovered the following: In the year 1836 George Larner Neave was Corn Miller, but by 1845 John Jarvis was the only miller recorded, and he was almost certainly working the mill on the marsh.

Was the mill a post mill, smock mill or tower mill? Mrs Radley told us it was a post mill, but Harry Apling believed it was a smock mill (from the evidence of Bryant's map of 1826, and the Thirtle painting of 1831); yet all the 'for sale' notices describe it as a tower mill. The last description fits in with the finding of substantial brick foundations. It is possible that either a post or smock mill preceded the tower mill.

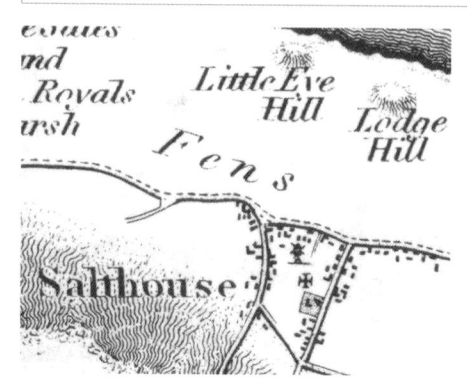

Left: A small section of Bryant's map showing a windmill north west of the church, but no windmill is marked on the marsh.

* For 3 sections of this map, see pp 50 and 51

2 Harry Apling's Research:

I first came across Mr Apling through a letter I addressed to the Friends of Norfolk Windmills. I was referred to him by the Secretary, Peter Woodrow. In his reply of 17 January 1984, Mr Apling enclosed photocopies of his findings concerning the mill near Salthouse church, and an extract from the 1839 Tithe Award which showed the rateable value of the property to have been £17 17s. 6d, and the tithe £1 1s. 10d.

In referring to the map which accompanied the 1839 Tithe Award, Mr Apling said 'Unfortunately this map at the Norfolk Record Office at Norwich is damaged and a piece is missing just where the windmill should be' (see page 299).

Sadly, Harry Apling died before finishing his second book and it was never published, but the results of his search for details of the history of this mill, culled from Norfolk Chronicle Property Sales advertisements, are reproduced here by kind permission of the Norfolk Windmills Trust:-

A smock mill shown on Bryant's Map of 1826 to the north-west of the church, was for sale by auction as 'newly erected' in March 1825:

Norfolk Chronicle, 19 March 1825

To Millers
To be Sold by Auction
By Wm Kendle   On Monday 28th instant
At the sign of the Dun Cow in Salthouse, Norfolk at 4 o'clock
(Unless sooner disposed of by Private Contract)
A Good new built Dwelling house, brick, stone and tiled, with a Shop or Flour house, yard, garden and pightle of Land to the same belonging, the pightle containing one acre (more or less), also a newly built Cottage adjoining the said dwelling house; and also a small TOWER WIND CORN MILL newly erected on the said pightle of land. Possession may be had at Lady day next.
The above Premises are all Freehold and situate in Salthouse aforesaid which is within two miles of Cley, a sea port town and four miles of Holt where a good Corn Market is held.
Apply (if by letter post paid) to Mr Ransom, Solicitor, Holt.

It was again for sale by auction in August 1826:

Norfolk Chronicle, 5 August 1826

To Millers
An Excellent WIND-MILL, Dwelling house etc. at Salthouse near Holt
To be Sold by Auction by Wm Spelman
At the Feathers Inn, Holt
On Friday August 11, 1826 at 3 o'clock
An exceedingly well built and substantial MESSUAGE with a Cottage and other Buildings, a Garden and piece of good Arable Land adjoining containing about one acre. Also a small TOWER WIND CORN MILL situate in Salthouse within two miles of the port of Cley and four miles of Holt, late in the occupation of Mr James Mackrell. The Mill stands exceedingly well for wind and the situation altogether is extremely desirable for a miller. If required one half of the Purchase Money may be had on Mortgage. Possession may be had at Michaelmas next.
To view the Mill and for further particulars apply to Mr Ransom, Solicitor, Holt or to Mr Cuddon, Conveyancer or the Auctioneer, both of Norwich.

By September 1834 its tenant miller, Leeds Richardson, had become insolvent and had made a Deed of Assignment:

Norfolk Chronicle, 20 September 1834

Notice to Debtors and Creditors of
Leeds Richardson of Salthouse, Miller

*Deed of Assignment for benefit of Creditors.
Mr Stokes, Solicitor, Fakenham. 18 September* 1834.

His stock in trade, furniture etc. were then sold by auction:

Norfolk Chronicle, 27 September 1834

*Sale by Wm Ansell on Tuesday 30 September 1834
All the STOCK in TRADE, Household Furniture etc. of Mr Leeds Richardson of Salthouse, Miller (Under a Deed of Assignment for the benefit of his Creditors) at 11 o'clock. Comprising about 8 coombs of wheat, seven and a half sacks of flour, quantity of meal and offal, sacks and sack barrows, bags, beams, scales and weights with all the mill fixtures belonging to the tenant such as jigger, jumper, straps, wedges, roller, brushes, sail cloths, lever, ladders, flour and meal bins and sundry other property in the mill. Also two flour carts and harness, capital harness mare, saddle and bridle, sow and 8 pigs, hay engine, iron crow, water cart, wheel-barrow, grindstone, about half a rood of potatoes, four pig troughs, small quantity of barley, small piece of hops, bushel and other measures etc.
The Household Furniture . . .*

The property was then to be let again:

Norfolk Chronicle, 11 October 1834

*To Millers
To be Let with Immediate Possession
A Small TOWER WINDMILL situate at Salthouse near the Market Town of Holt, driving two pair of French Stones, with comfortable Dwelling house, Garden and about one acre of Land.
Enquire of Mr Ransom, Solicitor, Holt; if by letter, free of postage.*

It was also offered to be sold or let in November. George Larner Neave, 1836, is given as occupier in the 1839 Tithe Award with Parlett Starling as owner. Evidently in the same ownership as the water paper mills at Upper Sheringham, the smock mill was again for sale or to be let in January 1840:

Norfolk Chronicle, 11 January 1840

*To be Sold or Let
All those PAPER MILLS at Sheringham . . .
Also a small TOWER CORN MILL situate at Salthouse in the said county, driving two pair of Stones with Going Geers complete.
Apply to Mr Ransom, Solicitor, Holt.*

3 Evidence from the Keymer watercolour:

Harry Apling told me that there was a picture of the mill, owned by Dr Ian F. Keymer who lived in Loughton, Essex. It so happened that I knew a Dr Ian Keymer, a fellow veterinary surgeon. I wrote to him in 1984 and this is his reply:

'I have a small watercolour painting attributed to Thirtle of the Norwich School of painters, dated 1831, that shows a windmill apparently a short distance away from the west end of the churchyard. My great-grandfather Philip Keymer (1815-1887) was a millwright in Salthouse in 1841 and I suspect this may have been where he worked . . . The Keymer family lived at Salthouse from 1782 to 1886 and one of their properties is still called 'Keymer Cottage'. It is situated on the Coast Road between the path to the church and the road junction.'

We finally arranged a meeting in 2001. He brought the watercolour and the final piece of the jigsaw was put in place.

A.C. Palmer, 2002

Right: The watercolour belonging to Dr Ian Keymer (seen below holding it). Dr Keymer writes, 'The painting is small and the windmill less than one inch high.'

Referring to Dr Keymer's picture, Harry Apling wrote, 'In this watercolour possibly by Thirtle, dated 1831, the mill appears to be an octagonal smock mill.'

Left: Another early watercolour painting of nearly the same view. This picture came into our hands by chance. Tim Groves of Sheringham produced it from his collection of Norfolk coast pictures. He photographed it himself from the original, but has no memory of when or where he was when he spotted it.

§

These two old paintings, together with Tony Palmer and Harry Apling's documentation, memorialise a windmill which might have been lost to memory forever.

The Royal Mail Postal Service to Salthouse

by GERALD CUBITT *from Kelly's Directory*

The first brief mention of Salthouse receiving mail appears in **1864**: 'Post from Holt', with no details. Four years later, in **1868**, we have a little more information: 'letters through Holt' which was the nearest money office. Post Town is Thetford.

1869 Letters received through Thetford via Holt. Cley-next-the-Sea is the nearest money order office.

1879 Letters received through Dereham via Holt, by foot messenger at about 10 am. A wall letter box was cleared at 3.05pm.

1892 In this year the first mention of a receiver of Salthouse letters appears: 'Post office Henry Lewis, receiver.' Letters were received through the Holt sorting office at about 9.30am and dispatched at 3.30pm.

1896 Henry Lewis sub-postmaster. There was no Sunday post.

1900 Miss Ruth Lewis was appointed village sub-postmistress. (The location of her shop was the cottage which later became Sam and Ann Talbot's shop in Cross Street.)

At the beginning of the twentieth century the number of letters was increasing. The mail was sorted at the Holt office and there were two deliveries in Salthouse by mail-cart: one at 8.20 in the morning, and one at 6.05 in the evening. There were two collections, the first at 7.20 am and the second at 5.05 pm. On Sunday there was no incoming nor outgoing mail.

In **1908** we find the village post office moved from Cross Street to the village green, where it

1908: The post office on the village green with Richard High standing in front of it. The house on the right, where Rooter Holman used to live, still had no windows on its northern side when Kathleen Thomas and her family were trapped there by the 1953 flood.

became established in a building which had previously served as the village coast-guard station, and Richard Joseph High was the new sub-postmaster. Letters were received and dispatched through the Holt sorting office as before, and again there was no postal service on a Sunday.

In **1923** a Miss Carrie Smith became sub-postmistress, and continued to run the post office and village store after her marriage to a Mr C. Pigott a few years later. During this time the postal service remained much as before except that the letter box was moved from where it had been in the wall in Cross Street to its new location in the wall of the new post office and village shop. The next change took place in **1929**, when George Gent became the new shop-owner and sub-postmaster, and it was during his time that the delivery by horse-drawn mail cart came to an end and a motor vehicle took over.

By **1937** George Gent had retired, and Mr and Mrs Frederick William Haylock took over the shop and post office. During the years they were there, the village experienced several sea floods. Fred Haylock told of experiencing no less than three, in the seventeen years they were there: 1 foot in 1938, 3 feet in 1947, and 'up to the ceiling' in 1953!

Gerald Cubitt

1936: Mr and Mrs Gent hand over the post office to the Haylock family. Fred Haylock took the picture.
From the left: Mr Gent, Kathleen and Madge Haylock, Ottoline Haylock and Mrs Gent (with her daughter behind her in the doorway).

The Haylocks

Kathleen and Madge Haylock were 12 and 15 when they first came to Salthouse to live in the post office in 1936. Their story of the 1953 flood makes exciting reading in the section on 'Flood' further on. Here Madge tells what it was like to come and live in Salthouse in 1936:

We didn't have any relations here. Everyone was related to everyone! Somebody told us when we first came here (of course we were only young girls) 'Be careful what you say, because you'll probably be talking about someone's relations!'

It was awful to come from a town where you were used to flush toilets and electricity—it was so strange to be dependent on lamps. They had a mantle in the centre, you'd only just got to knock it and it disintegrated. And we had those hanging in the shop. There was a real old brass one. We girls lit it and it was blowing black smoke, not being done properly, and I said we must put it out and start again and we had a little fight, my sister and I. We pushed each other and I pushed her through the window—the curtains were drawn, so it didn't hurt her, but the window was broken. My Dad nearly went mad: 'You've got to pay for it!'—but that was all the fault of the lamp!

There was a place on the heath, a pit where everybody took their rubbish until it got full. There was no dustbin collection of course . . . and the toilet . . . ! At Cley there was a 'honey cart' that collected the 'night soil', but here we had to dig holes in the garden. At first it was just buckets and later an Elsan, and finally my

Myself and Kathleen with one of the silk targets we used to collect from the marsh after the aircraft had been target-shooting over the sea.

Dad had his own septic tank. Janette's father, Mr Cooper, was a bricklayer and he built it.

Nancy and Ruth Cooke were our age and we were great friends, and we used to go there where they lived opposite Beach road. Charlie was the youngest and George was older than us. They had this long table and benches either side with all these children.* Their mum [Alice] was a little tiny lady with breathing difficulties. I used to wonder how she managed! I once went in a boat with George. I only went once because it was very deep and you could see the bottom although it was so deep, and I thought he might throw me over. They were all capable of throwing you out of the boat.
Kathleen: They didn't mean anything, really.
Madge: We used to go up there, nine o-clock at night, swimming. I remember they went out fishing and the weather changed and they couldn't get back in, and we were all sat on the beach crying because we thought they would never get back. There was Nancy, Ruth, June, Molly, Elsie and us, all sitting on the beach crying.

* *Alice (photo p 258) was one of Ruth Holman's daughters. Marshall and Alice Cooke had 9 children who were (in order of age): Jack ('Cookie'), Molly, Bob, George, Basil, Nancy, Ruth, Charlie and June. George's pages and a picture of 5 Cookes are 222-225.*

Of course they did get back, I suppose, but I just remember being afraid they were all drowned.

Mrs Talbot had a shop at the bottom of Cross Street and she desperately wanted the post office. It was a toss-up who got it. They vetted them both, and luckily my dad got it, because without the post office I don't think the shop would have been any good. Dad used to deliver groceries and it was usual for people to pay for them there and then, and he often had to sit there for hours waiting for his money; they'd talk, and then they'd nod off, and he would sit it out. He needed the money! John and Edna Massingham, who lived in Dad's cottage next to the post office, had a big table-shelter made of steel, to get under whenever the planes came over in droves after bombing inland. But Mum refused to have a shelter. She preferred to walk about all night even when the doodle bugs came over.

Salthouse beach with a solitary boat. The Holmans had the tea-place there—Ruth Holman. It was an old railway carriage, and my Dad had his beach hut beyond it.

Owen Hobbs and Tony Howard, the two soldiers billeted on us until the post office said it was all wrong as the PO was quite secret in those days!

Every Saturday we went delivering with a big baker's basket, things off the shelf like biscuits and chocolate and soap powders, and we'd go round to people's houses to see if they wanted anything One morning, when we were at the bottom of Grout's Lane a plane with a swastika on it came over so low, you could almost touch it—you could see the man in it. We crouched down with our basket of groceries. It flew over towards the sea. The beach was much flatter then than it is now, you could see the sea, and we saw it fly out and drop two bombs. There was a fishing boat out there, and a bomb went either side of it—lifted it out of the water! I couldn't believe I had seen it. People said they were trying to bomb the store of mines, which were housed opposite the Manor on spare ground, ready to be put down.

Gerald Cubitt saw the plane too

Gerald Cubitt was up on the heath with some other boys when the German plane came over (described by Madge and Kathleen on the previous page) and he saw it all from a higher vantage point. Later he found out what happened to the ship after it was attacked by the plane. He tells the story:

We were on the heath, just above the Butt Way—there was snow on the ground, I remember—and we actually saw it happen. The ship 'Boston Trader' was being bombed and machine-gunned, just off the beach between Gramborough Hill and the beach road. To avoid the bombs, the trawler was zig-zagging. The sea was quite rough, and an oil stove on board turned over, which set part of the ship on fire. The Sheringham lifeboat was launched and they came out and took the crew off—some of them were suffering from machine-gun wounds.

The unmanned ship drifted along the coast and came ashore on Blakeney Point. The rough sea put the fire on board out, and the ship was eventually repaired—the ladder is up against it, as you can see, and the men are working on it. Whether it was brought into the harbour or not I don't know, but the Boston Trader was too big to be brought up to Blakeney Quay.

Robin Cooke was duck shooting on the beach when the plane came over and he discharged two barrels of his shotgun into it. That must have given him some satisfaction! It was so low it was unbelievable. That doesn't surprise me at all that the girls could see the pilot sitting in it so clearly.

No fighter plane could really get at it, and it was too low for the guns at Weybourne camp to aim at, just above the waves.

It was a Dornier 215, a light bomber much larger than a Spitfire or a Hurricane.

The Boston Trader beached at Blakeney Point, after her narrow escape off Salthouse.

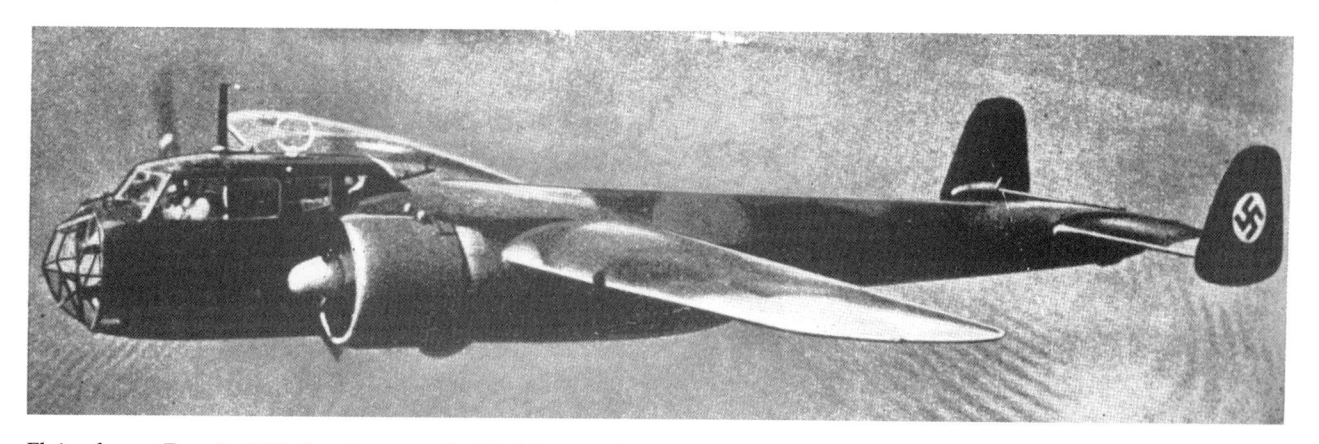

Flying low, a Dornier 215, the plane seen by Kathleen and Madge when delivering in Grout's Lane, and by Gerald up on the heath.

The view from Butt Way in Gerald's boyhood. Notice the little beach-huts to the left of Great Eye and the Rocket House.

Madge Barker (née Haylock) remembers the last year of rationing

Here is the inside of the shop in 1953, after the flood. The boy on the left is Tony Thomas, my sister Kathleen's eldest boy aged six. Standing in front of the counter is Julia Woodhouse ('Little' Fred Woodhouse's wife) with her little daughter Barbara, and standing next to her is Kathleen High (now Kathleen Gray). Behind the counter: myself and my mother, with my Dad at the meat-slicer. Behind the counter we used to have shelves of wood full of little drawers—I remember one held loose pepper—but the flood washed them all away. The biscuits from those tins on the left all had to be weighed out, as did the butter, lard, marge, sugar, cheese and even the dried fruit, which are all pre-packed today. The only thing we didn't have to weigh out was tea, which came in a dark wrapper tied with string.

Elizabeth Robertson and Catriona Galvin

Sadly, Elizabeth's sister 'Chip' died in 1996, and today Elizabeth runs the post office on her own with the help of her staff, Virginia and Sheila. In 1993 the two sisters held a party in the post office to celebrate their thirty years occupation. The picture and story are from the Eastern Daily Press 1993:

Party fun as shop sisters celebrate 30 years

A North Norfolk post office had more customers than usual this week, as the owners were entertaining in a big way.

Catriona "Chip" Galvin and her half-sister Elizabeth Robertson had more than 200 guests to the "open house" party at Salthouse post office and general stores, to celebrate 30 years of being in business.

The women, with their mother and brother, arrived in 1963 after farming in Wales and their native Scotland. "Mother and I took one look and decided it was for us," said Mrs Galvin.

Left to right: Barbara Brown, Elizabeth Robertson, Joan Cooke, the late Catriona 'Chip' Galvin, Sheila Jenkinson and Virginia Wright.

On Friday the staff spent the day dressed up in various costumes, including an angel, Father Christmas, Widow Twankey and a French maid.

"We were inundated with cards and flowers," said Mrs Galvin. "And the staff were the highlight. We also had a surprise when Walter Newstead, the father of one of the staff, came to play Scottish accordion music for us."

More than 200 people signed the card placed in the post office to commemorate the day. Mrs Galvin's brother, who moved out of the business some time ago, came to visit.

Mrs Galvin is vice-chairman of the parish council, a former youth club leader and treasurer for the local Royal British Legion Women's Section. Her half-sister has been a parish councillor, school governor and arthritis charity worker.

THE POST OFFICE STORES

Above:
Widow Twanky on duty behind the counter in the village shop.

Right:

Off to the pub! Widow Twanky, an angel and a French maid head for the Dun Cow.
   (Virginia Wright, Sheila Jenkinson and Joan Cooke)

The Dun Cow, 1950

Dr Ian Keymer, now nearing 80, was a young veterinary student in the early 1950s. His parents were living then at Overstrand and Ian, on his vacations from university in London, made many visits to Salthouse in search of evidence of his ancestors who once lived here (see page 194). Recently he discovered a diary he had kept at that time, which carefully recorded everything he did. Two entries (reproduced below) provide a picture of the Dun Cow as it was in those days, half a century ago, seen through the eyes of a visitor:

Thursday 5th January, 1950

I cycled to Salthouse. It was 12 noon by the time I arrived, so I went to the Dun Cow public house to eat my sandwiches with a glass of beer. It was a pleasant experience. I sat down on a wooden form (with a straight wooden back) at a wooden table in the deserted antiquated bar. I'm sure it must be almost the same now as it was when my great-great-great-grandfather Robert Keymer went in there for his pint, way back in the 18th century. The small window looks out across the desolate salt marshes enveloped in a fine dismal grey rain. The only sound I could hear was what seemed the almost deafening 'tick tock' of the Victorian clock hanging on the wall. The woman behind the bar was small and grey-haired, and silent most of the time. When she did speak, however, to the two old men who were sharing her kitchen, she left one in no doubt about it!

Thursday 20th April, 1950

I left home at 11 am to cycle to Salthouse. The sun was shining from a cloudless sky and it was a treat to be alive. At Weybourne, just past the Royal Artillery Camp at the top of the hill, I stopped to investigate the most marvellous chorus of bird song I've ever heard. After a picnic lunch I went to the Dun Cow for a glass of cider and watched an old inhabitant play 'Ring the Bull'—a very old game. From a hook screwed in a beam in the ceiling hung a metal ring about three inches in diameter on a length of cord. In line with the beam but on the wall, about six feet from the ground, was screwed another hook. To play the game, all that is necessary is to swing the ring on the string in such a way that it catches onto the hook—much easier said than done. Years ago it was a popular game and played '12 or 21 up'. Some experts could 'ring the bull' 11 times out of twelve, the old innkeeper said.

RINGING THE BULL

The game is one of the oldest in the country; legend has it that it was brought back by Crusaders from Jerusalem. The story seems to have come primarily from the most famous pub featuring the game: an old crusader's tavern called 'The Trip to Jerusalem', dating from 1189 and situated in the cliffs underneath Nottingham Castle.

Originally the hook was a bull's horn or a hook was embedded in the nose of a bull's head on the wall, the ring being dangled from a rope attached to the ceiling.

Jim Manson, landlord of the Dun Cow 1967-96

Jim Manson, born and brought up in Salthouse, was landlord of the Dun Cow for twenty-seven years before Kay and Tony Groom took it over in 1996

The Dun Cow, when Jim Manson was landlord.

I'm not the writing type of person. My brother Dick and I, we'd talk on a Saturday night over a couple of brandies. He'd been putting down notes for years and we was going to reminisce right from when we could remember. I was going to go over to his for a week and we was going to sit down with the old tape going and *mardle*, you know, and he was going to turn it into a book—just us two lads growing up.

My brother had cancer and died two years ago. I lost all the work that we did together. There's no one else I can really pick up memories with. When we were young we used to play on the village green—mind you, there were hardly any cars then. The grass used to be so short; I imagine it was the ducks and geese kept it like that. When we were eel-fishing we'd toss the eel with the bab on the bank and you'd find them easy. You'd never find them now, they'd be gone in the long grass.

My grandmother told me they used to sell the day-old ducklings for powder puffs. The horse and cart used to sit at the bottom of Grouts Lane where I lived, he just used to sit there and wait. Everybody used to have ducks and sell to this man. That was a nice little fortnightly bonus for everybody. They'd got to be a day old, so as they hatched out everybody took them down to him. And he'd give them 6d or whatever it was. That's what my grandmother told me. The man would be there about a fortnight. Everybody hatched out and away they all went for powder-puffs.

When the Joplings had the Rocket House, we used to have the village fêtes up there. I remember this big Rolls-Royce, or it might have been a Bentley car with an open back, and when they came through the village—of course we hardly ever saw a car—we'd be shouting 'The Joplings are here! The Joplings are here!' and there'd be these great big cases and trunks strapped on the back, when they used to come on holidays. They always treated us well. My Uncle Matt (Matthew Dack) was the man who used to look after the place, and when the walls

My Uncle Matt

got knocked down he used to build them up and look after what garden there was there. Mary Holman (Don's sister, Vic Holman's wife, who used to be the post lady for years), her and another lady Stella Wright, whose family come from Kelling, they had a little café up there. I think it was an old railway carriage, on Great Eye, and there used to be a bungalow there too.

I wasn't much of a pub chap before we moved into the Dun Cow. When I applied for the job of landlord I didn't think I'd have a chance, as a local chap. But the manager, he came round one night to see me, and he said 'Yes, you can have it', and we moved in at Christmas and we were there twenty-seven years.

That was mainly a locals' place at that time. There weren't so many tourists about then. We had some good old locals and they used to enjoy all the pub games like darts and dominoes. Donny High, Kath's brother, he was a regular. And I mean regular. Every day. There were lots of them, but Don was the chief.

Lunch time was the great time: they'd come in at twelve and stay till one, then the pub would empty. Sunday lunch time, they'd be queuing up at quarter to twelve. because if you didn't get there early you didn't get a game of darts. The first one in, put his name down. They all had their names down on the board but that all had to be over in an hour, because they all had to be home to lunch at one o'clock—that was lunch time.

Saturday night was the wives' night out and we always had music and a sing-song. My father-in-law, Morris, from Sheringham used to come and play the piano and we had some good nights. The songs we sang were the old wartime songs, all the ones that used to just roll off your tongue. There weren't no pop music and everybody would sing. It was all the old favourites that you never hear nowadays. A pub was a place to go and you knew you were going to have a good night out without getting drunk.

People never got drunk; they just enjoyed themselves. I had no trouble with that sort of thing, all the years I was there, and I enjoyed it as much as the customers.

1984, in the Dun Cow (*from the left*) Mervyn Stratton, Moira Cooke, Jim Sutton, Don High and Sandy Amis.

Landlords at the Dun Cow 1836-2003
(Earlier ones as mentioned over the years in Kelly's Directory)

MOST ARE LISTED AS 'DUN COW PUBLIC HOUSE' WITH THEIR OTHER TRADES MENTIONED

Peter Williams (1), Joiner and Victualler (mentioned 1836 and 1845, died 1848)

Charles Williams, Victualler (mentioned 1854)

Peter Williams (2), Joiner and Victualler and Carpenter (mentioned 1864, 1865, 1868, 1869, died 1870)

Sarah Ann Williams (Mrs), (mentioned 1872 and 1879)

James Brown, Victualler (mentioned 1883, 1888, 1890, 1892 and 1896)

Walter Graveling, Blacksmith (mentioned 1900, 1904 and 1908)

Edith Sarah Graveling (Mrs), (mentioned 1912, 1916, 1922, 1925, 1929, 1933 and 1937, died 1941)

(Walter Graveling, Blacksmith, then married Alice Dix. He died at the Dun Cow in 1955.)

Alice Graveling kept on the Public House for a short time, and was a member of the Ladies Bowling Club (*see photographs*).

Stanley and Kit Williamson (early 1960s)

John and Kath Ashton (late 1960s)

Donald James Manson and Brenda Manson / Judy Manson (December 1969 to December 1996)

Tony (Ginger) and Kay Groom (December 1996 up till today and onwards)

THE LADIES BOWLS TEAM AT THE DUN COW c1949

Above: (top left to right) Priscilla Holman, Primrose Dawson, Dolly Cooke, June Cooper, Alice Graveling, Alice Holman. The others have not yet been identified, except for Doris Leamon (*kneeling extreme right*).

Salthouse Bowls Club is now based at the bowling green outside the British Colombia Hall in Cross Street. Richard Cooke who has been the club's secretary/treasurer since 1977 says it is one of the last village organisations continuing to provide an amenity, now sadly becoming a rarity, for the benefit of local inhabitants of all ages.

Right: Ladies on the bowling green that was once at the Dun Cow. Behind the wall, a smoke house (now long-since gone), which belonged to the Hall farm, can be seen.

Ken Brown remembers football

Standing: 'Little' Fred Woodhouse, Isaac 'Dyke' Cooke, Peter Holman, Vic Holman, Fred 'Hoss' Woodhouse, Cockaday from Holt, Leslie Cooke, Colonel Shand, Ken Brown, unnamed from Cley, Charlie Hayward, Mr Hawley.
Kneeling: Rawlings from Bayfield, John Tyce from Holt, Ken Hawley, Tiddles Woodhouse from Kelling, Basil Holman.

We used to play football as boys on the green, and it was like a billiard table. We could never understand why they couldn't have taken the road along beside the crick and left the green in one piece. Instead of that, they took it straight through the middle. We used to play football there and we'd have one goal post one side of the road and the other over against Rummy Woodhouse's house. There'd be twenty a-side, and anybody who biked through, would stop and play football. When cars came, we didn't stop playing and they had to stop and wait! Later on we had a proper football team and here we are.

1949

Standing (from left to right): Wally Cooper, Ken Brown, Dan Harrison, Robin Cooke, Dougie Fuller, Kurt Dams (goalie), Vic Holman, Tom Cooke, John Holman. *Kneeling:* Don Woodhouse (from Kelling), Laurence Woodhouse (from Kelling), Basil Holman, Tiddles Woodhouse (from Kelling), Charlie Holland.

Alex Vines, Gresham's schoolboy, finds Roman relics on Gramborough Hill

A Roman bronze bird — thought to be a duck — which would have been used as a brooch.

Alex Vines was one of those who took part in an archaeological dig at Salthouse in Oct 1980. It was he who made the most valuable find of all, which was a bronze bird thought to be a duck, part of a Roman brooch. His report, part of which is reproduced below, was made while he was still a Gresham's schoolboy, and it was published in the Norfolk Research Committee's Bulletin in 1981.

Gramborough Hill, which belongs to the National Trust, lies on the coast road between Salthouse and Weybourne (OS 083444). As an archaeological site it is only of moderate importance, though it has produced some Mesolithic flints as well as a sherd from a Bronze Age food-vessel. But its chief significance lies in the Romano-British settlement which occupied the site from the early third century to the middle of the fourth. The site is a hill rising from the surrounding marsh to approximately the 30-metre contour; it is a natural look-out point, which on normal days gives clear views of the surrounding land as far as Warborough Hill, Stiffkey, Weybourne Hope and Muckleborough Hill. Today Gramborough Hill consists of rough grass pasture. Geologically there are gravels and sands with a thin layer of top soil. The Roman shore-line in the third century supposedly reached out into the sea another mile from today's coast line. It has been suggested that the hill was on the edge of an estuary, with a fort guarding the entrance.

Roman remains were first noticed in 1852-88 when Roman bricks and pottery sherds were found by workmen. This was duly reported and was interpreted as a pottery kiln.

The site was visited in 1937 by Rainbird Clark, who noted its gradual destruction on the NE side and picked up some Romano-British sherds from the cliff falls. The chief feature of the site is a small pit, about 100 cm in diameter and 90 cm deep, sunk in the natural gravel This was undoubtedly a storage or refuse pit, and was filled with earth much blacker, owing to the presence of carbonised material, than the surrounding humus. The earth contained an assortment of broken pottery, animal bones, oyster shells, iron nails and bronze coins. Burnt clay containing wattle impressions was present, which must have been the fabric of the building(s). Imbrex and tiles were uncovered, which would imply a substantial building. This theory is also supported by the two tegulae found on the NE side of the site. The other feature observed is a Roman ditch on the NE side, now destroyed through sea erosion . . . The soil contained a few pottery sherds from the late third century and a considerable amount of oyster shells.

Not enough has been found to show what type of settlement was situated on this bleak, windswept hillock. The pottery is entirely late-Roman, closely resembling that from other sites on the north coast, especially that from Warborough Hill. These sites suggest a defensive system connected with the signal stations which were essential for the safety of the Romano-British coastal settlements. All the pottery at Gramborough has been dated between 300 and 400 AD, which fits the hypothesis of a Roman defensive site. The system of signal stations was fully established in the third century.

Another idea is that the site was a trading post; this is suggested by the presence of amber pieces. But again this is unlikely since the coast may have been over a mile further out than today's shore line, although the river may have been navigable. There is one other possibility and this is shown through the name of the local village, SALTHOUSE. This is witness to known salt manufacture on the marshes in the late Middle Ages, and it is possible that it was already being produced in the Roman period, though we have no positive evidence to prove this theory. The most likely use for such a site as Gramborough is as a small look-out post, part of a chain around the Norfolk coast. This also explains the presence of a substantial building whose substructure and superstructure were built to stand up to the rough weather found on the coast and the possible danger of an armed assault.

The communications of the settlement are obscure. There may have been a road running on land now lost to the sea, or there may have been a road running on a causeway across the marshes to Gramborough Hill. This is more than likely, since the Romans preferred solid communications to ferries. This could then link up with the Romano-British site on the opposite side of the marshes (OS 089422). It would then join the suspected Roman road leading past Gallow Hill at Salthouse, and on past Lowes Farm to Holt. (*see location map below*)

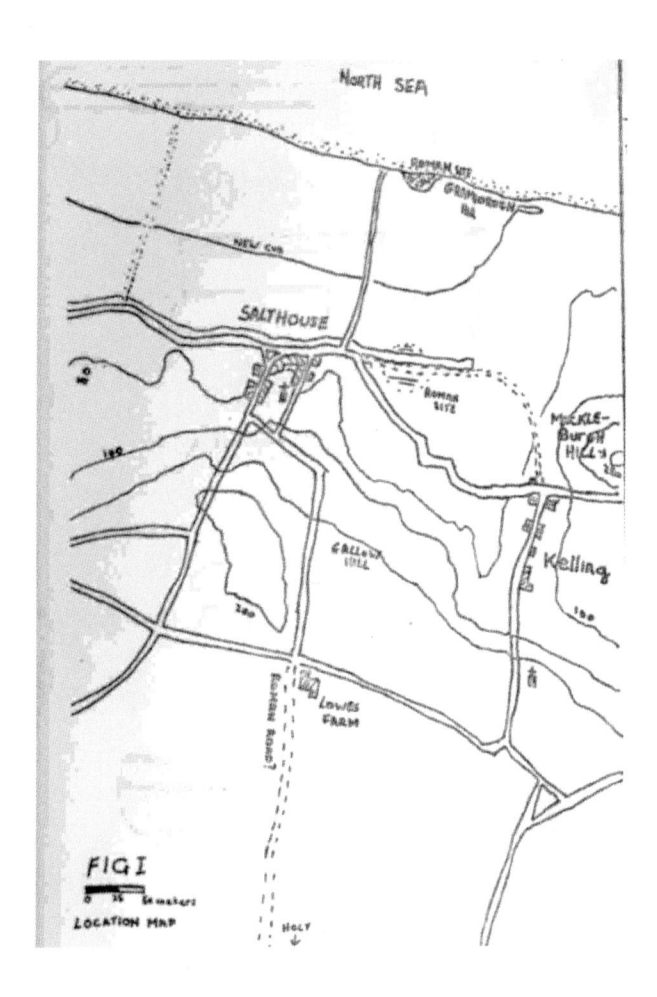

FIG I
LOCATION MAP

Local finds made by Paul High and his father Vivian

Paul High made a find on Salthouse beach a few years ago just under Gramborough Hill, after a scouring by the sea. As yet, the experts have been unable to define the origin of this little disc for certain. It is tiny and has no inscription on the reverse side—suggesting perhaps that it was an embellishment on the hilt of a sword or piece of armour. Andrew Rogerson, of Norfolk Landscape Archaeology at Gressenhall, thought it was probably Roman (though he only saw the photograph).

Above: Vivian High (with his autobiography under his arm) holds up the envelope with the coin or disc, the size of a one-pence coin, clearly visible in the photo as a black dot.

Above: The little object enlarged.

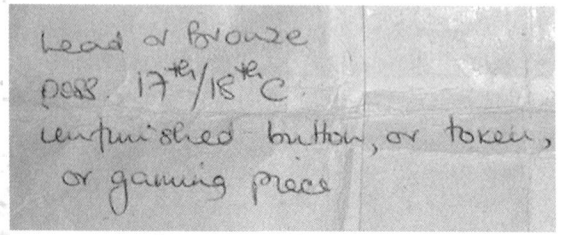

Above ↑: The Castle Museum's suggestion as to its origin.

← *Left:* Their comment! 'Never seen anything like this—<u>not</u> a coin.'

Above: Two silver pennies from the reign of Edward I (1279-1307).

Above right: A bronze rabbit, or is it a hare? And see the Castle Museum's report, *right* →

Above: The Castle Museum's report on the bronze hare.

Above: Vivian's son Paul, as he was when he found the dutch token on his way to school.

Above and below: Both sides of Paul High's 1788 token.

Above: 16th-century copper jetton (both sides).

Workmen were digging trenches for pipes at the bottom of Cross Street and Paul High spotted this coin among the earth dug out for the trench. It is thought to be a Dutch token, and possibly to have been dropped by one of the workers on the clay bank sea-defence completed in 1853. In the census for 1851 there are as many as forty men described as 'bankers and labourers' (all English) lodging with householders in the village. They were surely here to work on the clay bank. Is it possible that a Dutch overseer issued tokens to labourers to be redeemed later?

Carrie Large

I just found this piece of pot by chance. I was walking along and I wasn't particularly looking for anything. I thought it was a big stone, then I found it was shaped like the bottom of a bowl. We took it to Gressenhall and they said it was medieval.

Event Name & Type	Organisation	Event Dates
Casual find	Large, C.	2001

Description

October 2001 Found on shingle beach in mud exposed by sea, near low water line large basal sherd, slightly sagging, of large bowl in profusely shelly fabric, reduced, with sooting internally + externally. Not a 'local' product. Probably from Potter Hanworth Lincolnshire. 13th or 14th cent. Diam. of basal angle 340mm.

DATE 29/11/01.

Carrie with her medieval pottery find.

Right: It would have been either of these two shapes

Below: The piece of pot, showing the fine shells in its clay mixture.

We wrote this out in easy language to show it at school.

Its a large bowl, with a slightly sagging bottom.

It was made in the 13th or 14th century.

It was probably from Potter Hanworth Lincolnshire which is still there

The base diameter would be 34 cm if whole.

It was made grey colour when they fired the pottery. ~~down~~ closed down

MACALA LARGE AND MORE FINDS

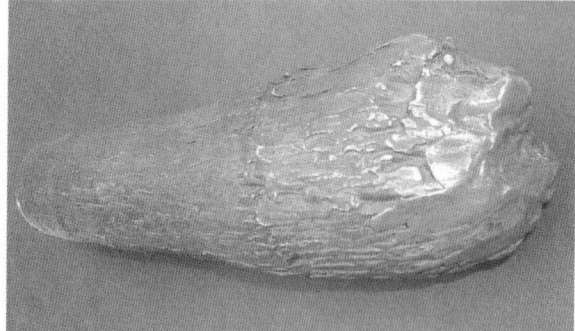

Above: The First World War bullet found on the beach.

Above: Macala (Carrie's sister) holds a bullet thought to have been fired at a target on the beach by cannon in the First World War. It is shiny brass and very heavy.

Below:
A fossil, a bullet, two coins and beads found recently.

Above: Macala didn't find this trophy—she won it at school for overall effort and achievement.

Myngs Terrace and Catriona Court

Eastern Daily Press 1953

Myngs Terrace was named after the famous Admiral, Sir Christopher Myngs, who owned land in Purdy Street in 1660 (known then as Westgate) and may have owned the very land it was built on.

Above: Myngs Terrace under construction. It was built to house the people who were made homeless after the 1953 flood and were living in borrowed caravans.

Right: The finished terrace. The houses, all with different-coloured front doors, were very smart, and most people were pleased to get into a proper house again. But for many the accommodation was too small and eventually people either moved back into their old homes (mended after the flood) or up the hill to the new council houses, and Myngs Terrace was filled with people from outside the village.

Wendy Elsden Collection

Myngs Terrace from Purdy Street 1996, forty three years later and soon to be demolished.

The demolition of Myngs Terrace

Wendy Elsden has lived in Salthouse since 1986, but has known it over forty years. She became the North Norfolk News Correspondent in 1989, reporting and photographing local events in the village, and never misses an occasion. These photographs depicting the end of Myngs Terrace and the beginning of Catriona Court are all hers—she got so friendly with the workmen they invited her into their hut for tea!

Wendy

Above: The demolition of Myngs Terrace began in 1997.

Above: Myngs Terrace reduced to rubble. *Below:* Catriona Court takes shape.

The Guinness Housing Trust, in partnership with the Council, began the construction of a superior fleet of ten houses and two bungalows.

Catriona Court

named after Catriona Galvin who gave so much time and energy to Salthouse concerns before she died in 1996.

Tenants of Catriona Court come and go but some, like Winnie Walton and her daughter Jade, have stayed. Winnie (below, with legs in air) is a magnificent fund-raiser and organiser—she started the Salthouse Seals Playgroup, and she makes enough money, with raffles and stalls on the green, to take all the children to the pantomime in Norwich each year, besides being a leading worker for church fêtes. She never misses a chance! Here she tells how she captured Belgian Leon and his bed of nails and brought him to Salthouse.

He was ever so nice—*a man of Peace*—that's what I liked. Me and Fiona saw him at Cley lying on his bed of nails to get money for the church there, and afterwards we saw him walking off pushing that trolley he had. I said to Fi, 'I wonder where he's going to sleep tonight?' So I went looking for him, didn't I? and I caught him in Weybourne at the Pheasant. He had passed us by! So I brought him all the way back here again, put his bed of nails in the car, and told him he must sleep with us and do a show on the green the next day.

It's true he didn't have much English, but he understood me.

Churchwarden Sarah Dawson and her daughter Amy see-saw on top of Leon.

Winnie testing the strength of travelling Belgian, Leon, who was collecting against re-armament and who lay on a bed of nails on the village green. Winnie fed him and her neighbour Fiona put him up for the night in Catriona Court.

He slept in Fiona's summer-house—it's like a big shed. Fi put him up, and I fed him and done his washing. He liked it so much he stayed three nights! The Tour de France was on, and he used to come in and watch it with us. He had this book full of cuttings and letters. He'd been everywhere, he'd met Prime Ministers and everyone, and he was going to London when he left Norfolk. He was a man of Peace, campaigning for World Peace.

Bloomstiles

The field called Bloom Stile was part of a farm owned by the late Haddon High who, before he died in 1969, gained planning permission to have 12 houses built on part of it, in a semi-circle. The farm was left to his sister Gladys High and his son Donald, and after Gladys died in 1971 the site was sold to cover death-duties. The first developer became bankrupt before starting work, but it was taken over by another firm and they proceeded to build the existing complex of 21 houses. One quarter of these today are holiday homes and only two are occupied by their original owners. Chris Evans, one of the first to buy a house there, tells his own story:

I first came to Salthouse in the early 1920s when my parents bought a house in Sheringham, where we spent every August. I remember Sheringham well when it was a small fishing village with great characters like 'Gofather' Peg, 'Chicken' Grice, the Emerys and many others, sitting on the benches along the East Promenade repairing fishing nets, and crab and lobster pots. I remember too how, within minutes of our arrival, someone from the local chapel (now converted into flats) would arrive to ask my father to play the organ at services so long as we were there. In these holidays I got to know the surrounding district very well.

My brother and I were on holiday in 1936 by ourselves and sharing the house with friends from Middlesex. They brought with them (in my then view) a simply ghastly schoolgirl in her early teens who annoyed me intensely with her practical jokes and other irritations. (Remember I was then a young man approaching maturity!) Later, when I came out of the Seaforth Highlanders, I came to my senses and the irritating (now beautiful) girl and I were married in 1946.

In 1975 we made an offer for a house in Cley which was refused. Disconsolately we made our way back to Tottenham, where we then lived, via Salthouse Heath. Pauline suggested that we should give our labrador a run on the Heath and, whilst there, she heard the noise of sawing. We looked down and observed a single house being built (now owned by the Olins), so we reversed direction and called on the Estate Agent and obtained particulars. The following week we returned, selected the position of the house to be built and its type, and clinched the deal immediately.

It is so good to be away from the frantic activities of suburban life, and to be enjoying the peace of the village. There is a big gap between those who have lived here all their lives, and us newcomers: we know we shall never be regarded as true 'Salthusians'. But we do feel part of the village—Salthouse is a small community and a very friendly one.

Chris Evans

THE FLOOD CAME AT NIGHT
Jane Hales

In the bitter wind-swept darkness, when the sea was breaking through, the immediate danger to life was all absorbing. But, on the morrow, as the cruel waters began to subside, folk saw the extent of the havoc. Some, who had been forced to flee elsewhere for safety, found their homes had been torn asunder. Other houses were gutted: torn flint walls were exposed, and yards choked with the debris of the marsh, under which lay cherished possessions. Apart from the loss of family or friends, there is nothing more heart-rending than the destruction of a home, but the owners rose above their grief. 'We are lucky to be alive' said someone [Clem Holman ?]. A huge buoy* had been lodged in his garden; his sitting room, once so neat and comfortable, was darkened for the window frame had been boarded up, but he had lighted a fire in an attempt to dry a few things. 'We had just finished our tea' said someone else,* 'when my daughter thought the tank must be leaking. Then the sea broke the door and in swam my dog.'

By Monday, after that terrible Saturday night [31st January 1953], the village street was no longer a water-way, and all was bustle. People were sweeping the filth from yards; in the fitful sunshine carpets and furniture had been put out to dry. 'Come and see for yourself' said the housewife. The windows were out, the door torn off its hinges, and the furniture thrown about within as though by some mischievous giant. 'Strangely enough, I didn't worry about the furniture when I was upstairs and the tide was down here. It was the little things—the trinkets and suchlike—that kept coming into my head. But I shan't know what I've lost till I miss them' she continued, thinking of all those useful odds and ends which must have gone. Could she go on living in the house? She looked at the desolation and wondered. At that moment the geese swam round the corner of the creek. They looked so spick and span, and they had been missing since the great tide. Then a pale sunbeam appeared over the drenched marsh. From time immemorial these Norfolk villages have lived under the threat of the Rage, and the comparative demerits of this one and that is the high topic of conversation. The aftermath of the flood is full of difficulties. Polluted wells cannot be used, and drinking water has to be fetched from the carts, which have been brought into the villages. Many have had their larders swept bare, others have no means of cooking and are dependent on the hot meals provided. Money and clothes have been lost, including indispensable water boots. There is no electric light, and no telephone to carry messages to anxious relations. Yet, in spite of it all, no one seems to complain.

*See page 261 for the huge buoy   * For Ethel Dawson, see p 331

Jane Hales' account of the Rage of 1897

On the preceding page, Jane Hales paints a picture of the grim horrors of the aftermath of flood. That excerpt, written soon after the great flood of 1953, and the one on this page—written much earlier when the historic Rage of 1897 was still in living memory—are taken from her book 'The East Wind', published in 1969 by Charles N. Veal & Co (now out of print). The many flood episodes relived on the pages which follow all bear out the truth of her words 'no one seems to complain'.

The spirit in which they are recounted fifty years later, almost light-heartedly, enhances the drama of the happenings, while the memory of fear and horror are left behind. The 'Ruth' in the story on this page is the great Salthouse character—Ruth Holman—when she was a young woman. One of her grandchildren, George Cooke, now lives in the house near Beach Road on the edge of the marsh where Ruth lived at the time of this account.

Ruth Holman in later life.*

Back into the mists of memory the people have lived under threat of the Rage. That of November 28th, 1897 is still remembered. All night long the north-westerly had swept over the waste of waters and the shuddering marsh, to the village on the skirts of the uplands. The people of Salthouse knew what it forebode, for 'the tide was in the eye of the wind' (the wind was with the tide). The Coastguards, however, strangers all, would not be forewarned, and well they rued it.

At 9 o'clock on the following morning, Ruth, a strong young woman with a houseful of children, was getting her breakfast. There were windows but no doors to the north side of the house, which overlooked the marshes. The doors opened to the south, into a yard, sheltered by the rising land. As she ate, and fed her husband and the noisy children, Ruth watched the foam flung skywards beyond the shingle bank. Then she saw something that she had never seen before, though, indeed, her mother had spoken of such a happening; waves were flowing on to the marsh through a gap near the Rocket House and were spreading rapidly.

The sea had overstepped its bounds, the steep grey wall of shingle. It was hardly more astonishing than if a piece of the sky had fallen! 'Here she come,' cried Ruth gleefully. She was high-hearted enough to defy the elements, as her fore-fathers had done. 'You don't need to laugh' grumbled her husband, knowing there was hard work ahead. In twenty minutes, the sea had burst through in many places. Soon the water over-swept the marsh and was in the village. Ruth 'set the children on the table and went to lay hold on a thing or two'. The hot cinders were carried hissing from the fireplace; the partitions between the rooms were broken down. With all she could gather, Ruth and her family walked over the fold of the meadows to the home of relations, in a higher part of the village. They stayed there 'come Valentine'.

Another woman on this grim morning saw 'the sea as high as houses, and all of a sudden that come slopping over'. Her husband, W... had gone to put chains on a barley stack in a field by the marsh. The stack was end-on to the marsh. Neither of his companions dare climb the ladder, the wind being so strong, so up went W... From the top he saw the flood coming. He had just time to descend, 'claw hold of the ladder, and get away with the tumbler and horses' when water surrounded the stack, floating it broadside to the marsh. By the time the men got back to the village, their help was needed. The water had risen so high that

For photo of Ruth with some of her children, see p 268

people were trapped in upper rooms, and had to be rescued with planks and ladders. Bread was swept from the oven in the bake office, a tumbril top was borne down the street. Floating timbers crashed against walls and through windows. W... had helped to break up these timbers months before, and pile them near the Rocket House. They were the remains of a three-masted barque which had run aground. Of all people, the heedless Coastguards suffered most, 'jewels and clocks swept from the mantel-shelf'. When relief funds were distributed—'parcels of beautiful black clothes and the like'—these Coastguards were entitled to a large share. However, in the end, the Salthouse people did not do so badly. Certainly they needed relief. Their houses had been damped for a generation; if they, too, had not lost jewels and clocks, it was only due to their native wit.

... When, after a few days, the water subsided, Salthouse looked a forlorn place, strewn with the muck of the marshes. Hundreds of head of poultry had been drowned. 'A deal of them was eaten before they went wrong', though some folk do not seem to have relished drowned fowl; no more they did the pig that perished, though the farmer would sell the pork at 2d. per lb. 'Seeing narthing hadn't come to that pig, and times weren't very grand, some of us baked a piece for our relations, that come away to see the place. They never knew narthing of it.'

So, at last, the great Rage spent itself. At length Ruth went back to her damp house as philosophically as her mother had done before her in another Rage. 'That Rage came the day after Pancake Day. There lay a piece of butter on the shelf that was over from frying o' the pancakes. When the sea went through the house, that swept the butter off the shelf, and they never see that no more.'

Of eighteenth-century flooding, only the written record remains: 'Being Sunday, about six o'clock in the evening, a great tide drowned all ye marshes, broke down ye greater part of ye marsh bankes. Morgan, who lived under the hill, had his wall broke down, and ye horse drowned in his stable. There were three or four feet of water in houses, two in ye Parsonage.'

* * *

MILLER TRAPPED IN MILL

Handed-down memory has preserved a relic of the night of the Rage of 1897 in the form of a doggerel verse. The miller, David Jarvis,* fled to the top of the mill to escape the rats off the marsh who were also escaping the waters. The villagers who huddled in the church on higher ground passed the night away by making up rhymes, one of which is still remembered:

> Upon a sack, to rest his back,
> He tried to keep from yawning.
> As the billows rang,
> We suppose he sang
> 'I won't be home till morning'.

The mill on the marsh with the church behind it on higher ground, as it all may have looked when the sea surged over the marsh and made an island of the mill!

For a photo of David Jarvis, see p 297

The Flood of 1953

Mary Lemmon (née Dawson) tells her Story:

Mary today.

This, in spite of the roaring gale, was to have been a 'fun' night. The Sergeant-Major's wife and I had been invited to a party/dance at Weybourne Camp. Leaving the sitting room, in order to get ready, I saw water seeping in under the door. I called to my father that the tank outside must have overflowed, but he and my mother knew better. 'The sea!' they shouted. Then began a frantic few minutes deciding what could be saved. We made a number of journeys up the stairs with various of our most precious items which were small enough to carry. Our thoughts were saddened by the fact that our dog—a working dog—was shut up in the shed at the bottom of the garden and there was no way we could save him.

Then a number of things all happened at once. I was amazed to see my mother struggling with the weight of a large green bowl containing an aspidistra! (my sister-in-law still has a cutting from this plant), the door burst open and in came the sea bringing the dog with it, and the grandfather clock was lifted up and landed on my father's head. We decided the time had come to escape and we made for the stairs. The sea followed us up to the penultimate step; we were safe so long as the walls remained firm.

My mother always had a small bottle of brandy on hand in the bedroom. We sat together on the bed, drying ourselves and the

In 1953 I was living with my parents in 'Harmary', the house extreme right above, now 'Combe Grove'.

dog, and taking sips of brandy. The gale roared and the downstairs furniture was lifted and began banging on the ceiling, but all held firm. We watched as in a dream, as a bath, a stove and all kinds of other objects floated past the kitchen window. There was nothing we could do but wait until the tide turned. At last it did, and we were rescued by my brother Harry from Weybourne and a friend, Don High. It was, of course, dark and we could only see that furniture had been smashed and much of it washed away. The following morning we returned to see the chaos left by the

My parents, Ethel and Jack Dawson, and our dog at 'Harmary' after the flood.

flood: sideboard, bookcase, suite, all smashed and vanished, and treasured books, ornaments and personal items, including most of our family photographs, all gone. In the midst of the rubble we found a perfectly whole wineglass and, just outside the window, Mother's yellow cooking bowl all in one piece!

My parents were loaned a caravan which they put in the pightle in Cross Street (where the village hall now stands) and from here the work of clearing up and repairing began. It was with some reluctance that, when the work was completed, my mother returned to 'Harmary'. I'm sure she would have preferred to stay in the caravan in Cross Street, after that ordeal.

My father, Jack Dawson, mends the flood gate at 'Harmary'.

The Lord Mayor of London's visit to the 1953 Salthouse flood victims. Myself and neighbour Sidney Craske tell him what we experienced.

Taking shelter

MORE than 60 people from Cley and Salthouse spent the night in the cinema of the army camp at Weybourne. Over their heads hung a net full of balloons which were to have been released during the sergeants' mess ball that evening.

This article, featuring Harry, Mary Lemmon's brother, is by David Blyth and is from the EDP Supplement of 27 January 1993, which commemorated the 40th Anniversary of the 1953 Flood. He is describing the events of forty years before and, according to Mary's comment below, he has got one or two things a bit wrong.

A chilling warning of what lies ahead

Warning: Harry Dawson.

North Norfolk district councillor Harry Dawson has campaigned for 40 years for improved sea defences around his home village of Weybourne and neighbouring Salthouse.

His main platform was as chairman of the district council coast protection sub-committee, of which the 76-year-old is still a member.

The present shingle bank is inadequate, he says, and the next time the sea breaks through it will sweep all the way up the Glaven Valley to Holt — and not recede.

He speaks with authority because he was on the scene of the tragedy 40 years ago, searching desperately for his parents, Jack and Ethel.

"They lived on the main road facing the marshes. Their house was six feet above the road, but even then the water was two foot from the downstairs ceiling."

The couple were found upstairs in a bedroom and refused to leave. A chair had been broken up to make a fire and the couple were drinking a bottle of rum. "They were both teetotal. It was the first time — and only time — they had ever had a drink."

He was born at Salthouse and is convinced another surge would erase it from the map. "We had a solid bank there then, now it is just shingle. I find it very frustrating. After the 1953 floods we could have had a solid bank built for £1¼ million; now it would cost seven times that amount."

A LAST WORD FROM MARY

My mother would 'turn in her grave' to have read that they'd drunk <u>rum</u>. Brandy was allowed to TT's for medicinal purposes, but rum <u>never</u>. And it was *sips*, not a bottle! Harry's enthusiasm carried him away, I fear. But I suppose it made the argument stronger to leave me out. I can't remember the chair being broken, but it's true they were reluctant to leave. I remember Harry carried Mother from the house and drove us to his house in Weybourne to a meal and a warm bed. We were very fortunate.

Kathleen Thomas (née Haylock), the '53 flood

An earlier flood (1938): → Madge and I were girls then. That's Alan Holman's boat. He took us for a trip across the flooded marsh to the beach, and here we are tethered to a telegraph pole while our dad took the photo. It was later a postcard sold in the post office.

In 1953, my husband and I were living in a cottage next door to the post office. There was one door, round the back of our house, and the stairs immediately in front of you with just one room either side and the same upstairs. We all had 'flu, and we stayed in the bedroom, and when the water went down we were taken to Weybourne Camp.

The flood knocked the door in and came to the top of the stairs, and when the water got to the switches, all the lights went out. We'd got some candles from Christmas, the sort you used to put on the Christmas trees, and the matches were in my pocket. But when I'd been down to rescue the cat while the water was only half-way (she was sitting on a chair across the downstairs room) I'd got soaked to the waist, and when I got back the matches were wet!

So I sat on them upstairs until they dried and we lit the little candles. Our two boys were aged four and six, and they went to sleep. My husband, he said 'If it gets any higher, you can have Tony and I'll take Christopher, and we'll try and float the mattresses out of the window.' You see, we hadn't got a loft to get into. There was no trap door in the ceiling where we could get up into the roof. It was frightening. I don't know how long the mattresses would have floated—I think they would have sunk. You hadn't got time for anything, and you think of all sorts of funny things. *[See photo of their house, p304]*

My husband went out as soon as the water went down, and went up to the council houses, and Mrs Gertie Dawson, that's Primrose's mother, made a great big bottle full of tea, and that's what warmed me up.

I'll never live again anywhere flat to the sea—I live on the top of a cliff now!

Kath today

Pages 306-7 tell how Madge and Kathleen Haylock came to the post office in 1936 as girls, with their parents.

AFTERMATH OF THE 1953 FLOOD

Left: The same view after the 1953 flood. The telephone box on its side, with the bakery behind. In the far distance, behind the telegraph pole, Great Eye and the battered Folly can still be seen.

Right: After the 1953 flood. Windowless houses on the village green after the water had subsided: the bakery extreme left, and the post office extreme right, with the petrol pump flat on the ground. All these houses completely lost their outhouses and 'wash houses'.

OTTOLINE AND FRED HAYLOCK RECEIVE £10 AWARD

Madge and Kath's father and mother, Fred and Ottoline Haylock, receiving their letter of congratulation. (*right* →)

TELEPHONE:
HEAdquarters 1234.

G.P.O. HEADQUARTERS,
ST. MARTIN'S LE GRAND,
LONDON, E.C.I.

7th April, 1953.

Dear Mr Haylock,

I have heard with great admiration of the way you rescued part of the Post Office stock, when the flood water was rushing through the Post Office, waist high, knocking down a wall, and destroying furniture and fittings, and how you reached an upstairs room just before the stairs were washed away.

Such devotion to duty is worthy of the highest praise, and I should like you to accept the enclosed warrant for £10 as a token of our sincere thanks for the action you took to safeguard Post Office stock.

Yours sincerely,
De La Warr

F. W. Haylock, Esq.

Madge (née Haylock) and husband Stan Barker

Kathleen and Madge came to Salthouse as girls in 1936. Their parents ran the post office. At the time of the 1953 flood they were both married. Kathleen was next door, but Madge and Stan were in the post office with Madge's parents. Together they tell the story of that night:

MADGE:

The old people who had experienced floods (there was a bad one sixty years before, in 1897) said Oh no, there wouldn't be a flood because the wind had been off the land for three days. But then, all of a sudden, wind tide and moon combined; it rushed down from Scotland apparently and it built up as it came, and then the wind changed and it just brought it on. We had only been married two years in 1953, and we were still living with my parents in the post office.

That particular night, my husband walked along with my Dad to empty the coin box in the telephone kiosk and, when they were just near it, my husband said 'Water!' and my Dad said 'Flood!'

STAN:

When we left the box, it was still stood up. We hadn't time to mess with the cash box, we left it and dashed back. My father-in-law, Fred Haylock, went indoors and I went into the garage to get the cars out. I'd chosen that time to take the starter out, to clean the brushes, but she started first turn with the handle. I couldn't open the doors for the wind, so I just revved up, let the clutch out, and battered the doors down. I went up over them! I got the two other cars out, the Thomases' as well, and left them up the hill.

Madge and Stan today

When I got in the post office again, I found my father-in-law Fred wandering about inside in the water. The ladies were upstairs. We had to get out. The front window broke with a bang and the water came along the top of the counter in a rush, and then we went through to the passage. It was coming at the rate of knots: the water had circled the house and was coming in fast at the back door bringing floating objects with it. There were all sorts come through, toilet buckets wizzing past! (That big fridge was on its back the next day, up on the bank behind, and my trailer with my plumbing stuff was up there too.) The only way out was the back window. Fred was a bit devastated; he had managed to get himself up into the window frame and I found him stuck there. He wouldn't go. He hovered in the middle there, unable to go out or get back, and all the time the electrics were flashing and going out, things were coming off the shelves, and I thought: Right! Best be out of this quick. I put my boot in the middle of his back, popped him out like a cork out of a bottle and followed him right quick and took him to higher ground (where the Galvins' bungalow 'Iona' now stands). I left him there and went back for the ladies.

MADGE:

We were upstairs, my Mum and I, and what

with the noise of the wind and everything, I didn't know where they were and I honestly thought they had drowned. What did the damage, was these poles floating around. They were putting poles and things on the beach, knocking them in, and they got half-way through the job— the sea got hold of them, they were long timbers. The stairs had gone and we had to save ourselves and the dog, and the only thing was to jump out of the back window. How I got my Mum out of that window I don't know. Stan was there and he's quite tall, so I was all right, but my Mum was a bit of a dead weight.

Above: Clem Holman* in the ruins of his wash house and outbuildings, with Cliff Woodhouse's house still standing behind.

STAN:

Well, Madge lowered her mother from the top window. *[Photo of the window on p 349]* She was a heavy little person—but anyway out she went. I could reach her legs and down she came, but she stumbled and fell and went under. I straddled her and hauled her out. Madge's poor father lost his boots and down he went. I had more trouble with him than with her mum!

* Clem Holman's house was the left-most of the three cottages (see p 345).

MADGE:

They'd dug all the garden then and it was very soft, and down she went—there was about three feet of water behind the house. My sister Kathleen and her husband were in the cottage next door, going towards Purdy Street, which my Dad bought for £100. They've got windows on the outside of that house now, but there were no windows then. They were upstairs. They both had 'flu, and the water was at the top of the stairs and they didn't know how much higher it was going to come. They saw something floating outside the back window and realised it was the big industrial shop fridge, which had been in a room built on to the back of the shop. The walls were thinner than the rest of the house and couldn't withstand the flood (see below). Afterwards, the stuff inside the fridge was quite edible. I don't think we ate it though! The Woodhouses nearby (in the house which is part of 'The Pightle', where Hermia Eden now lives) had got up in the roof, but had nowhere to get out

Above: After the flood, the fridge has been brought back inside though the room it was in, at the back of the post office, is swept away.

Above: From the marsh after the '53 flood. The buildings east of the post office: Cliff Woodhouse's house is on the left, then the three cottages together—Clem and Maggie Holman were in the first, Ruby and Tom Gray in the second, and Peter and Doris Holman in the third. The Crab Shop is on the right.

and, like us, they didn't know how much higher the water was going to come. They had to knock a hole in the end of the house.* Me and my husband couldn't help them because we had my Dad and Mum to look after. We got them up to my husband's shed, which was on higher ground, and we got my mother into a pair of my husband's overalls which were in the shed, and led them up through the hedge to Miss Cobbold's house. But her sister, who was in it while she was away, said 'I'm sorry, you can't come in because it's not my house,' which was understandable, but when we said we were desperate, she let us in. My poor parents were given a single bed for the two of them, and we sat in front of the fire all night. For the next few days we stayed there and had a mattress on the floor. Then we went up Cross Street and stayed in 'Sunny Croft' next to Jim Radley's Pear Tree Cottage.

Where Catriona Court now stands, there was an old army camp, and we lived for six months up there in a borrowed caravan.

* See page 342

From the Eastern Daily Press, 2 Feb 1953.

CARAVANS WANTED FOR HOMELESS

Appeal After Emergency Meeting of Villagers

Villagers of Salthouse held an emergency meeting last night, when Mrs. J. Watson-Cook, a county councillor, and officials of Erpingham R.D.C. were present. Emergency supplies of clothing, food, water and coal have been brought into the district, and early this morning Dr. J. H F Norbury, the Medical Officer of Health, appealed for the loan of caravans for homeless families.

The meeting was held at the Manor, the home of General T. A. Leech. Today volunteers will bring to the village a sectional summer house, offered by a person present, to be used as a temporary village shop. The village shop was badly damaged on Saturday night.

Clothing, hastily collected, was distributed to many of those at the meeting and Rural District Council officials promised to see to the provision of sanitation. They will also bring to the notice of tomorrow's meeting of the R.D.C. the urgent need for houses of some sort. Mr W J Bullock, the Clerk, warned people not to drink well water because it might be contaminated.

Villagers will use the parish church in which to store salvaged belongings. Earlier last evening a similar meeting was held at Cley.

Ration system: villagers and officials share out at Salthouse (P206).

Betty Smith (neé Wright) and Louise Deterding did a magnificent job dealing out supplies as they came in. Queuing up: Dick Manson (receiving sausages), Doris Holman, David Lynn, (lady unidentified) and Jim Manson.

Betty Wright

Early in the morning following the flood I arrived at Salthouse, as I was a member of the Red Cross. Everything was in turmoil, and we set about getting food and drink organised for the homeless, helping out where it was needed most.

Mrs Deterding (Senior) and I set up shop in a garage in Cross Street owned by Mr and Mrs Gordon Hancock [now the garage of Wendy Elsden's house]. There we gave out food. There was meat from the Holkham Estate—in the photo above, I am the one on the left dishing out the sausages!—and all sorts of other food came in.

The American Air Force gave quite a lot of food. There was tinned goods—I remember some very large tins of pineapple, which of course you couldn't get here in 1953—and they also provided a NAAFI wagon for hot drinks and sandwiches. We kept the garage store open for six weeks and we were there all day and every day till quite late.

The church was the venue for clothing, which came in great piles to be sorted and given out to people in need. I stored the furniture from the post office in my house at Lowes Farm, Kelling, for several months.

Jim Manson

I'll never forget 1953. I was in Devon Cottage—first house on the right going up Grout's Lane. That was our family house. The flood was a Saturday night and we always went to the pictures on a Saturday night; we travelled by bicycle to Sheringham. We were at the courting age then and we were after the Sheringham girls. My friend (my cousin actually) used to live next door in Lynn Place, and he would come round to collect me and off we'd go. This particular evening he left his bike in the alleyway by Devon Cottage while we were getting ready, and Uncle Alfie, the one who got killed by the tractor, came round and he said 'Have you seen Blind Billy?' He was a brother of Alfie and he lived with his sister Edie Dew but he used to spend the day with his mother, which was Alfie's mother, and then he'd go back home to Edie's to sleep the night. He went down just before the flood happened and they didn't know if he'd gone back. We asked Why? 'Well the water's on the road and it's half way up the lane.' So one of us rushed up to see if he was home and he was. And while one of us was doing that, the tide had come over and that was at least five foot up our house by that time, and our bicycles were gone.

Chaps were shooting on the marshes, Leslie Cooke and his friend Derek Howlett, and they thought they'd better come home. Leslie lived up Grout's Lane, he just got in the house and the water was right behind him. You could hardly walk against the wind and it was snowing as well.

That broke through just this side of the East Bank, and once that broke through there was this big wave and it came so quick. Within minutes it was all over. I know that just came through the door. My mother was ill, and Grandmother was in the front bedroom. We more or less had to carry them out the top end of the house, and we took them up to the church. That was very frightening. We went to the church first, but there were some people who lived in Church Cottage up the top, and they said 'That's too cold for you in there, come in our house'. It was Kenny Brown's sister Norah, and Charlie Hayward.

Devon Cottage in Grout's Lane

We stayed there a week. The house was in a mess—reeds and dead birds—it took us a long time to clean the house. I remember up Grout's Lane there was a kennel and a drowned dog still chained to it, a horrible sight, and down the road Alfie's cows all got drowned, and they laid on the bottom road for weeks and weeks till something came to take them away. There wasn't time to do anything.

It was a matter of minutes before seeing if Billy got home, that we went and knocked the wall down from next door so that Alfie could get his horses up our garden. They were trapped.

We watched the Parish Room fall down. That all happened when we were trying to pull Uncle Alfie up over the wall again from trying to save the cows. It looked as if it blew up, but that was just the electrics all flashing away, and then there was a terrific rumble and bang and it just disappeared. We were so busy that night. By the next morning it had all gone.

1953 FLOOD

Cliff Woodhouse, he escaped by making a hole upstairs in the gable—how he made it I don't know—you don't usually keep those sort of tools upstairs, but he escaped that way. So did Brian Holman and Mary, living in the Cley Corner cottage, the one cottage with two gables behind the pub. He made a hole in the end of the house to get out. They fell in the water when they jumped out, although the ground rises a bit. The water actually came in the bedroom in that house—a bit frightening when the bed starts floating.

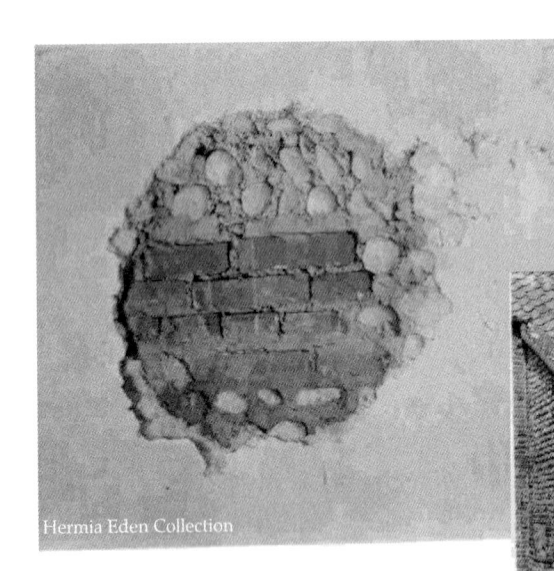

Above:
The hole which Cliff Woodhouse made to escape through, seen from the inside. It was just above the floor-level of the upstairs room, and only just above flood-level. Here it has been filled up by Peter Eden, who bought the house and rebuilt.

Inset:
The hole in the side of the house, made by the sea.

Above:
Back view of the Woodhouses' house, showing the position of the escape hole.

It was my brother Dick who actually found Mrs Middleton's body in the hedge the next morning. Everybody had been looking for her. What happened was they had bought a new carpet. I think it could have been laid only that day and she wasn't going to have that carpet destroyed so she went down to get it. She was messing about with this piece of carpet and the door broke open and the water took her straight out. She was entangled in that hedge where Tony Galvin's bungalow is now. They didn't know where she was, they couldn't find her early in the morning. My brother was in the forces, and he was home on leave.

Jim Manson

This cutting from the Eastern Daily Press, 2 February 1953, tells a slightly different story. We cannot really know what caused poor Mrs Middleton to be downstairs when the door burst in, but we can be thankful that she was the only one to lose her life to the 1953 flood in Salthouse.

In 30 Minutes Much of Salthouse Was Ravaged
Woman Killed and at Least Thirty Houses Destroyed

MUCH of the village of Salthouse was devastated in half an hour on Saturday night. A woman, aged 73, was swept through the window of her kitchen and was later found dead in the back garden. At least 30 houses were destroyed and another 20 so severely damaged as to be uninhabitable.

The dead woman was Mrs. M. Middleton, who had been put on a table in the kitchen by her husband after a fall. The back door was swept in by the sea, and both Mr. and Mrs. Middleton were carried out. Mr. Middleton was rescued and later found the body of his wife beside a tree in the garden.

At another house, Mr. Cliff Woodhouse made a hole through the wall of an upstairs room to which he and his wife had gone, and crawled through it to safety. From a third house, Mr. Leslie Cook, waded neck-deep in swirling, icy water in the dark to pass a rope to a man on the top floor of another house.

Leslie Cooke (whose own story is on pages 226-229) remembers that his friend Derek Howlett had a new three-piece suite, only two weeks old. They were familiar with floods and they expected no more than a foot of water in Derek's house behind the bakery (now 'The Greens'), and so they lifted the heavy couch onto the table. Derek ran upstairs to get his dog and was immediately trapped. Leslie raced home to get an anchor rope, 50 yards long. When he got back the water was so deep that men standing on higher ground above did not want to venture into it, but Kenny Brown appeared and though they managed to get the rope to Derek it was far too dangerous for him to use it. The words in the newspaper clipping above do not exaggerate: in deep swirling water and in the darkness Leslie and Ken struggled to help Derek, leaning out of a tiny window above. Next morning they discovered that the couch, which had been so difficult to get in through the door, had been swept out onto the bank behind.

1955 - the Edens buy the Woodhouses' cottage

Above:
The pressed grass that was rammed up the chimney by the waves.

Left:
The interior showing the kitchen and chimney of the Woodhouses' house.

Above: The Edens and friends build up the wall in front of the Woodhouses' cottage—which later becomes part of the house they are to build on the land occupied by the terraced cottages that were destroyed by the flood. (see opposite→)
From left to right: Gen Hawkins (on the stool) with her brother Oliver, Hermia Eden standing, Jonathan and Sebastian Eden on the top, and Simon Barley on the right.

Above: This is the scene just after the 1953 flood. On the right is the cottage and shop belonging to Jimmy and Emily Gray (where Janette Cooper was brought up, and which is today Cookie's Crab Shop). On the left of the picture are the three cottages, which were so badly ravaged by the sea that they had to be demolished for the Edens to build their house. At the time of the flood the first cottage on the left was occupied by Clem and Maggie Holman, the middle one by Ruby and Tommy Gray, and the last was the home of Peter and Doris Holman, who had only been married two years and lost all their wedding presents and photos. (See photos p 346-7)

Right: This is 1955, and the ruined cottages are still standing. The Eden family take time off from building up the wall—Hermia (*left*), her mother (Mrs Olivia Sowerby), Hermia's son Seb, and two friends Simon Barley and Oliver Hawkins.

Doris and Peter Holman

When they were first married, Doris and Peter Holman lived in the end cottage (previous page and opposite). Doris, one of the daughters of Sarah and Walter Holman, never had to change her name—she married Peter Holman in 1951. After the flood they were housed for a while in a caravan and also stayed with Peter's sister, Ivy Nightingale, in Cross Street, until they moved into Myngs Terrace.

W e had only been married two years at the time of the flood, and we lost all our wedding presents. Peter and I had gone to the cinema in Sheringham in the afternoon, and we didn't know anything about it till we got back. We were on the bus and it stopped at Kelling and couldn't go any further because of the water. We got a lift over the heath and came down Bard Hill. The dog was swimming about in the back garden; he was rescued but we couldn't save a thing from the house.

First we had a caravan and then we were with Ivy for a while. When Myngs Terrace was built we lived there till we got the farm. Mr Jimmy Duffield was in the farm house and when he retired he moved to Pembroke Cottage and we moved in. The farm belonged to the council. It was split up into smallholdings. People were coming out of the army in the First World War, and it was done to let them have land. They've gradually sold all the smallholdings now and none of them belong to Salthouse people at all, only the houses. After a while they let us buy our house. Peter bought ours. I used to do all sorts of work on the farm,

From the left: Nancy Foreman, Ivy Nightingale, Vic Holman, Peter and Doris Holman, Roy Holman, Peggy Emery, and Betty Holman. *

I went sugar beeting with the men and hoeing, and then with the cows. Peter used to milk the cows and I would take them out onto the marshes. I'd get them up in the afternoon, ready for when they came home, to milk. The smallholders all had their own individual dairies; there were three up the road [Purdy Street]. We had the top one, opposite our house, and we had our own dairy there. Those farm buildings are all standing empty now. My brother John Holman, Freda's husband, had the bottom one, and my brother Bob had the middle one.

You couldn't walk up the road for cows' dirt when we used to get the cows in. We had about 36 and the others had as many: we used to bring them all from the marsh up the road. Of course as you know, as soon as you start moving them they all make a mess. You couldn't hardly walk up the road in those days—I don't know what the people today would think of it!

* *Every person in this photograph is a Holman. Nancy, Roy, Peggy and Betty are sisters and brother of Doris. (see photos of them all as children p 172) Peter, Vic and Ivy are their first cousins.*

THE AFTERMATH OF THE 1953 FLOOD

Three views of those three cottages next door to the Crab Shop. *Top:* From the Holmans' album soon after the flood had done its damage. *Left:* A path cleared through the rubble. *Right:* The Lord Mayor of London visited Salthouse a few months after the flood (the grass had had time to grow), and he is seen here, with local dignitaries, inspecting the end cottage where Peter and Doris Homan spent their early married life. These cottages have now completely gone. Peter and Hermia Eden built their house on the site.

From the left: An unidentified lady, Sir Thomas Cook and Lady Cook (with unidentified man behind them), Fred Haylock, Mrs Nigel Parkinson, The Lord Mayor talking to the Reverend Felix Young (two unidentified men behind them), Nigel Parkinson, County Councillor Mrs Watson-Cook, and Tom Leach (who lived in the Manor House).

Jim Sutton's photos

Jim's folder of Salthouse photos, showing flood aftermath and attempts to strengthen the shingle bank, date from 1955. They are well-known at the Dun Cow but not everybody knows their history. Here Jim explains:

Some years ago I happened to wander into the post office, and it was just when the family who used to live in the Hall—the Hawleys—had just either died or moved out. Their cousins I think it was, from Sheffield, had come along and they were sorting the house out. They had come across an envelope dated 1955, with a number of large photographs in it. These Sheffield cousins were in the shop showing these things to Chip Galvin, and I persuaded them to let me take the pictures away for about an hour and put them through my photocopier, which I did, and brought them back. Later I believe Chip did get some copies made of the original A4-size prints but they were only snapshot size.

These photos are supposed to be around the time of the '53 flood, but there's a sort of quirk to this, which I'll come to in a minute.

These people are the Haylocks *(see top right)*. That's Fred Haylock, that is his wife Ottoline, that's his daughter Kathleen (Kathleen Thomas now) and the kiddy is her son Tony.

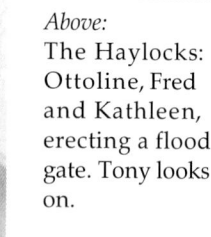

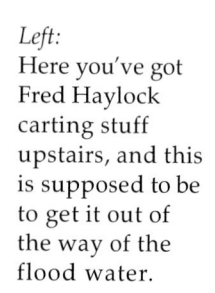

Above:
The Haylocks: Ottoline, Fred and Kathleen, erecting a flood gate. Tony looks on.

Left:
Here you've got Fred Haylock carting stuff upstairs, and this is supposed to be to get it out of the way of the flood water.

This is his daughter Madge *(near right)*, who married H.S. Barker the plumber in Blakeney. She's supposed to be sorting out the goodies, (stuff they've saved). You'll understand in a minute when we get to the relevant pictures.

There's Madge again *(far right)* hanging her feet out of the window and that's her father, not her husband, standing below. She's told me this story* about when the flood came. They couldn't get down the stairs and had to jump out of the window in pitch darkness. So this bloke who took the picture, he must have come along and got them to re-enact this. There's no water and it's broad daylight, so we assumed all the photographs were staged. This reporter bloke must have come down here, stayed in the Hall (it was a guest house at the time), took his photographs, and sent the Hawleys copies which they just put away. There they are *(left)* round a table at the Hall. Walter Graveling who had the pub and the blacksmith's shop, old Mr Hawley, Nigel Parkinson, Mary Hawley (standing behind) and Fred Haylock. It's a simulation, but they are the right people and in the right place.

Above: Walter Graveling, Mr Hawley, Nigel Parkinson and Fred Haylock. Mary Hawley stands behind.

* Madge and Stan tell the story on p 337-8

Now something very interesting, the same people out on the marsh, and that thing is a flood warning device, designed and created by Nigel Parkinson. He was Commander Parkinson, and somewhat like the mad professor-inventor type. He bought the bakery just before the flood. Afterwards he built an upper storey

Left and Above: Nigel Parkinson's flood warning device. Mr Hawley of the Hall Guest House, Walter Graveling the blacksmith and Fred Haylock of the post office look on.

to live in, with arches for the next flood to pass underneath!

The idea of the flood warning device was that when the water came up to it, it was set to have a siren that warned everybody. In actual fact if the water came up, it would probably have been washed away and never seen again—but that was the theory. Nigel Parkinson was sighted on TV, some years after he'd left Salthouse, officiating in Westminster Abbey on some state occasion.

Mr Hawley poses in the dark

Above: Here they are at the ruined Rocket House when all the floor was hanging out of it. The army blew it up. It was dangerous, but it stood there like that for two years.

Above: Mr Hawley and the buried brushwood.

Left: Mr Hawley, Billy Bishop and Sydney Craske inspecting brushwood on the beach.

Before the 1953 flood they drove a lot of railway lines into the shingle and they wired all these bushes and stuff onto them. The theory being that they'd build up and form a bank. Originally there was a natural clay core to the bank which meant that the water had to come to a certain level before it could even trickle through. They broke all that up with bulldozers and made it all porous, trying to make it better. They put all this stuff and they also wired logs to it. When the '53 surge came, the logs broke loose and knocked the houses down.

After the Rage of 1953

Above: An unusual view from Gramborough Hill in 1953, Rocket House in the distance on Great Eye.

By B. A. C. HAWARD

My father, Birkin Haward, took this picture from Gramborough in the summer of 1953. The Rocket House still stands and two bulldozers can be seen to the left on Little Eye. The flood deposited this inviting stretch of sand which can be seen in the picture with me, and my two brothers Bill and John, playing football on it.

At the time these pictures were taken, we were camping in what was left of Edenfield at the back of Baker's Yard, which had been badly damaged. My father had bought these two cottages in 1947 with his demob money. Both Fred Woodhouse, who lived in one cottage, and Mrs Wall, who lived in the other, had left after the flood. The house is still in our family and much loved.

Edenfield, the summer of 1953, after the flood.

The Shingle Ridge

Ever since the flood of 1953, feelings have been expressed on the inadequacy of the shingle ridge and the need for a stronger defence against the North Sea. The views of two Salthouse men—Jack Cooke (the original Cookie of Cookie's Crab Shop) and Harry Dawson—are reported in the local paper of 1958, expressing the beliefs of many:

[and see Harry on p 333]

'Salthouse's sea defences are about as effective as a sieve,' said fisherman Mr Jack Cooke yesterday. Mr Cooke (65) of the Green, who has been a fisherman at Salthouse all his life, said the Anglian Water Authority's measures for the upkeep of the twelve-foot-high shingle ridge were totally inadequate. 'Every year for the last five years they have sent in bulldozers. They build up the ridge but the sea and wind pull it all back again. It's about as effective as a sieve; all they are doing is pushing the bottom of the beach up onto the ridge. It is unstable, and the beach is being eaten away. What they want is a mud bank on the landward side of the ridge. As it is, if we get a good strong wind and a high tide, there won't be any ridge left.'

The Chairman of the North Norfolk District Council Coast Protection Committee, Mr Harry Dawson, endorsed Mr Cooke's fears. 'There is no doubt that things are critical,' he said. 'Because all the shingle has been taken from the beach, the sea has a straight run at the ridge and hits it with all its energy. The distance between the high tide mark and the ridge is decreasing all the time.'

He said that, at the last valuation, a proper bank would cost £3 million, but without it the marshes, which are unique in the world, would be lost.

Left: This picture, taken during the storm of 1996 (forty-three years after the opinions reported above), shows the shingle ridge reduced to a narrow line of pebbles. What appears to be a line of fencing posts is actually the remains of an elaborate structure of railway lines with logs wired to them, put there after the flood of 1953 in the hope that it would help the shingle to build up. The sea has simply removed both logs and shingle.

Above: Two years later, in 1998, the ridge has been rebuilt, and again diminished by a gale.

THE SHINGLE BANK

These great lumps are part of the ancient glacial loam of Great Eye.

Jim Manson

I remember them putting those metal things in, I believe they were railway lines. They drove them in and between each one they had what they call pit props, which are small pine trees, and they shoved them in between there. They went all the way along like that. In the end I used most of them for my fire because they all got smashed and washed out. They didn't do any good whatsoever. That was a good thought but it didn't work. The first tide, the sea was behind it and smashed it up.

Eventually the pylons got bent right over. Every now and then they reappear as the shingle gets worn away, and disappear when it's built up again. They used big old hammer things to get those in, and you could hear it all over the village.

Jim Manson knocks off gardening for a moment to remember those metal things.

FLOOD DEFENCES

Above: Two years after the 1953 flood, the Rocket House still standing, a group of Riverboard officials inspect the tops of the buried railway lines in the middle of the shingle ridge. Sidney Craske (second from the right) is the only person identified.

Left and Right: The rails were not all bent over: these pictures were taken thirty-eight years after the picture above. They show the railway lines temporarily uncovered after the storm of 1993, before the bulldozers built the shingle up again. Remnants of the timber props that were wired to them are clearly seen, and Steve Harris, who took these two photographs, said he recognised the wood as alder.

Jim Manson sees the last bit of Great Eye disappear

Above: During the 1996 flood, the three 'eyes' are clearly seen: Little Eye on the left, the remains of Great Eye in the middle, Gramborough Hill far right on the skyline. Great Eye was once twice the size of Little Eye; now it is only seen as a lump of sandstone when the shingle which covers it is washed away by a storm. The inset (*above*) shows this same fragment when it was bared in 1993, soon to be covered with shingle again by the bulldozers.

JIM CONTINUES:

After the 1993 and the 1996 floods, there was this big bit of Great Eye bared. A red sand lump. Me and my daughter went out to see what the damage was, early in the morning after the 1996 flood. We were walking past Steve and Liz Harris' place on that high bit of footpath. We stood there and we could see an extraordinary sight—water was gushing out of that bit, just like water coming out of a hose-pipe! It was rabbit holes, and we watched the water squirting out. And then, before our very eyes, the whole thing opened up and you could see it washing away. The marshes were flooded and the road was flooded, that was most probably the morning tide I should think. The whole thing disappeared in front of us. The hill was made of sand, a hard brown sandstone riddled with rabbit holes, and it did crumble. It was distributed all over the marshes.

Above: The evening of the same day: Little Eye is on the left; the shingle bank is quite level and there is no longer anything to be seen of Great Eye.

The Independent talks to Ivan Large, 1998

Ivan Large, Chairman of Salthouse Parish Council, Chairman of the Village Hall Committee and also a heath trustee, was interviewed by the Independent newspaper in 1998. The following excerpt is taken from an article which appeared on the front page of the Independent Sunday Review, of 31 August 1998. It compared the difference between the coastal defence needs for two different Norfolk villages, Brancaster and Salthouse, and the corresponding attitudes of the locals. It is written by Chris Arnot and entitled 'That Sinking Feeling':

Ivan today

Ivan Large takes a drag on his fag and peers from under the peak of his denim cap at the grey North Sea which is disgorging white foaming breakers onto the beach below us. 'This is all we've got between us and the North Pole' he says with a wry grin, digging his heel into the shingle ridge on which we are standing.

The ridge is about four miles long and fifteen foot high. It is the only major deviation from the horizontal in the thousand yards of marshland that separates the sea from the village of Salthouse in North Norfolk. Every winter since the terrible floods of 1953, bulldozers have arrived to shore up the shingle.

Above: Sixteen years earlier (than 1998), a group of flood-concerned parishioners on the shingle bank talk to MP Ralph Howell c1972.
From the left: John Lane (River Board official), Dick Manson, Tony and Catriona 'Chip' Galvin of the post office stores, Ralph Howell (MP for North Norfolk), Sidney Craske, Richard Cooke, Ivan Large and Eric Gray.

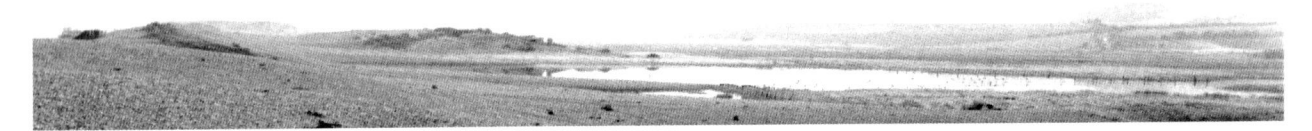

Forty five years on, the locals shake their heads and wonder how long it can last. The sea, they say, sucks back more and more of the beach before renewing its assault on this eroding coastal defence. Twice it has broken through in recent years—in 1993, and in 1996 (when the A149 through Salthouse was cut off for more than six weeks). 'If the sea were allowed to get in regularly, it could go six miles inland, come round the back of us and cut us off like an island,' says Ivan Large who has lived along this vulnerable coastline for more than sixty years. Like many another fisherman in these parts, he simply refuses to believe that higher tides are caused by global warming. 'It's just that we are in the lap of the gods with the weather,' he says. 'Every now and then we get big tides coupled with fierce north-westerly winds.'

On the face of it, the Environment Agency's proposal to spend more than £3 million on a secondary defence at Salthouse—a bank built of clay from the marshes and standing more than 12 foot high—would seem to go against the committee's recommendations. But the 1994 European Habitats Directive commits the British government to protect important wildlife sites. North Norfolk is well blest with them, and the bird-sanctuary at Cley-next-the-Sea (and next to Salthouse) is the jewel in the crown. 'If they look after the birds they'll have to look after the people as well,' says Ivan with another wry grin. 'If we get the bank, it'll be Cley bird sanctuary that gets us the money. There's little doubt about that.'

There's little doubt, either, that Salthouse is seen as one of the test cases for the implications of the Habitat Directive in a coastal environment. Brancaster, 20 miles along the coast, is another. But the Environment Agency's proposals for Brancaster are very different: 'managed retreat' from the sea, as opposed to 'managed realignment'. As a result, almost the entire local community [at Brancaster] is aligned against them.

In Salthouse the community is more split, even between families. But as much of the indigenous population seems to be related, perhaps that is not too surprising. We climbed into Mr Large's battered estate car and set off to see his brother-in-law George Cooke, who is in favour of the clay bank, and George's niece (and Ivan's cousin) Suzanne, who has raised a petition against it. 'Mostly signed by holiday-makers and twitchers' says Ivan, as we drive back through the marsh. The clay bank is scheduled to cut across it, roughly 400 yards inland from the shingle ridge. As we pass the spot where work should start next summer, a flock of the afore-said 'twitchers' are standing by the side of the road, with their binoculars and cameras poking through the reeds at whatever bird life lurks within. 'There'll be hundreds of them this afternoon,' Large goes on. 'There's some kind of rare tit in there.'

Surely, I suggest, the birdwatchers are good for the local economy. 'Not really,' he says. 'They're mainly day-trippers. Some people come here and buy holiday homes. That's why the prices are going way out of the reach of the working man. Just after the '53 floods, you could have bought half of Salthouse for £1,000.'

His brother-in-law George Cooke, now 78 and retired from fishing, had to leave his seafront home in a hurry in 1953. 'We moved the furniture upstairs but that got flooded as well' he recalls, as a hen and several chicks scurry into the hallway and begin pecking at a dog bowl. 'We've been lucky since then. The downstairs carpet got soaked a couple of years ago, but that didn't bother me much.'

All the same, George Cooke has had good reason to respect the power of the sea. 'This is such a small island,' he says, 'and you can't let the sea take too much of it. If you get a really rough'un, I don't know what'll stop the bugger. But this bank should take the sting out of it.'

His niece Suzanne, who runs Cookie's Crab Shop just down the road, will have none of it. 'How would you like to have a 12-foot high wall not far from your front window?' she asks, brandishing a sheaf of signatures at me. She doesn't believe the global warming theory, either, but adds: 'If it does get worse, I can't see a wall stopping a really severe flood.'

Above: After the '53 flood: George Cooke's house (on the left), with a path cleared through the rubble.

The Independent Monday Review, 31 August 1998

Meanwhile, until the bank finally gets built, the bulldozers continue to try to put the shingle back after each storm.

But, as this book goes to press, Ivan brought the news that plans for the long-discussed clay wall have been abandoned.

At Little Eye by E. A. E. (Ted Ellis)
From the Eastern Daily Press, 20th September 1971

Today we made a brief excursion to the Little Eye at Salthouse, one of three small mounds of red compacted glacial loam and pebbles standing like islands in the marsh just behind the great shingle ridge of the beach line. At various times in the past these hills have been battered by storm waves and they may well have formed a continuous mass in the past.

Even now, though protected from sea flooding, they are being eroded gradually by frost and rainwash year by year and as we saw today other destructive forces are at work. Wherever the loamy 'pan' of the hilltops was exposed, it was being riddled with holes by little burrowing bees of the species known as the 'Girdled Colletes'.

There were hundreds of these insects buzzing about the small crags, and many of them were arriving with loads of bright yellow pollen which they were storing for their broods underground. Like sand martins in the faces of the cliffs and sand pits, they were honeycombing and undermining the vertical brows of the hills.

The nearby marshes contained many of the elements of a relict salt marsh flora including dwarf sea asters and prostrate forms of glasswort and annual seablite, while the ditches held tall sea club-rushes and rice-grass, both in full flower.

The landward face of the shingle bank was bushy with yellow horned poppies, still blooming here and there, and there were still a few white blossoms on the rosettes of the sea campion, but the tall ragged sea docks were brown and carried vast spikes of seed.

The blue and gold sea asters were the chief attraction for numerous 'Silver Y' moths, bees and small tortoiseshell butterflies, ranging freely over the marshscape on this sunny autumn day.

Salthouse Beach

Sounds easy, looks simple, only consisting
of stones, water and air — three horizontal
bands of pale element, and just the gentle
wash of the North Sea in the English morning.

But at ease the mind is uneasy. Speculations
come inching with the tide across the sands.
Regrets dance on the wavetops. Absent friends
gleam and are gone. All sorts of silly questions
litter the sky, pollute the pebbled shore.

Slowly, insidiously, the dumb waves chant
articulate syllables. We simply can't
stand perfect nonsense; can't easily endure
— as the gull can before his single eye —
the shingle and the water and the sky.

Sebastian Eden

Acknowledgements

Janie Anderson and family, for permission to quote from Jane Hales' *East Wind*
Billy and Bernard Bishop, for permission to quote from *Cley Marsh and its Birds*
Jill Coleman, for excerpts from her book on the Kelling School logbook
Marilyn Eden, for the poem by Sebastian Eden
Carrie Clark, for permission to use her recording of Alice Holman
The Grasshopper, for Steve Benson's article on James Olley
Hulton Getty Picture Library, for photographs
Paul Long, for permission to copy and reproduce his ancient channel map
Peter Franzen, for photographs and articles from Eastern Counties Newspapers (articles by 'Sea Pie', Cyril Jolly and Ted Ellis)
Marion Lloyd for reproduction of the fold-out map
Susan Maddock, Principal Archivist at the Norfolk Record Office, for permission to reproduce the Salthouse Tithe map DN/TA 100
Norfolk Blueprint (police magazine) for Russell Reeve's article on German pilots
The Norfolk Churches Trust, for excerpt from *Sculptured Monuments in Norfolk Churches* by Noel Spencer
The Norfolk Journal, for Peter Brooks' article on O. Randall
Norfolk Museums and Archaeology Service, for permission to print a copyright aerial photograph by Derek A. Edwards
The Norfolk and Norwich Archaeological Society, for *Some Notes on the Ruin in Salthouse Churchyard* by C.L.S. Linnell
The Norfolk Record Society, for excerpts from *The 1851 Religious Census*
Norfolk Research Committee's Bulletin 1981, for excerpts from Alex Vines' article
Norfolk Windmills Trust, for permission to quote from the work of the late Harry Apling
Hugh and Tony Pashley, for permission to quote from *Notes on the Birds of Cley* by H. N. Pashley
The Random House Group Ltd, for permission to reprint extracts from *The Diaries of Sylvia Townsend Warner*, published by Chatto & Windus
Gillian Read, granddaughter of Jimmy High, for permission to use his manuscript
Gwen Szabó, for permission to reproduce and adapt the manuscript of her uncle, Frank Noel Stagg
Christian H. Warrant of the Independent Newspaper, for extracts from *That Sinking Feeling* by Chris Arnot
Dr Colin Wells, for extracts from his article *Post Medieval Turf-Digging in Norfolk*
Photographs in articles are from that person's private collection, unless otherwise credited

Sponsors who gave gifts of money

Kevin Aikens and Mrs Glenn Rolph
Madge and Stan Barker
the Rev Peter Barnes-Clay
Janet and Graham Benskin
Ralph Berney
Mo Blomfield
Geoffrey Burnaby
Rachel and Alan Chaple
Joan Cinnamon
Frank and Annette Clarke
Richard Cooke
Henry Cordeaux
Sarah and Rex Dawson
Angela and Keith Dugdale
Hermia Eden
Jay and Barbara Eden
Rosie Edgington
Chris and Pauline Evans
Bill Fiddian

Barbara Gibson
Louise Grattan (née Jopling)
Steve and Liz Harris
John Hart
Birkin and Jo Haward
Phyllis Jackson
Jim and Roma James
Janet Johnston
Ian and Janet Keymer
Dr and Mrs Leeming
Mary Lemmon
Jonathan and Marion Lloyd
Ray Loveday
Elizabeth Martin
Geoffrey Minns
Michael and Muriel Olin
Meyrick and Zoë Owen
Tony and Shirley Palmer

Mary Pringle
Derek and Maureen Schofield
Tony Theaker
Kathleen Thomas
Dorothy Thomson
Judith and Barry Thrower
Mr and Mrs Trevor Parkes
Merlin Turville-Petre
Dr and Mrs Urquhart
Paul and Amanda Vesty
Miranda Villiers
John and Sarah Walker
Winnie Walton
Robert and Rose Marie Warren
Graham and Tamara Watts
Chris and Ann Wilks
Gill and April Wilson
Karen Wortley and Olivier Johnson
Richard and Virgina Wright

MAP INDEX

Inside front cover: Salthouse village (Ordnance Survey map, 1904)

50   Edward Houghton's 1838 Plan of Salthouse, 3 sections
56   John Hunt's 1649 Salthouse Channel map (a copy)
62   "   "   "   "   (simplified version)
63   Aerial photo of marshes showing probable position of ancient channel shown on John Hunt's map
64   Area of saltmarsh reclaimed or lost to the sea
67   Salthouse Inclosure Award map 1853
71   "   "   "   "   (enlarged section)
81   Plan showing church, and position of ruined chapel in churchyard
116 Methodist chapels of Salthouse
131 'Weathervane map' of Salthouse and Kelling estate
300 Section of Bryants Map 1826, showing windmill
319 Sketch-map showing position of Roman Camp and road

Fold-out map (at the back): Where everybody lived in the village

INDEX

Text entries are like this: **99**, photograph references like this: *99*, references to maps like this: (map 99). Principal references are underlined like this: <u>**99**</u>, <u>*99*</u>. Husbands and wives appear on the same line. Both married and maiden names are given for women, like this: Florence (nee High) [married Percy Radley, cf]. See married name for page references. Most buildings mentioned appear on the folding map at the back.

Aerial photographs of Salthouse, <u>*63*</u>, *258*
Allotments on marsh, **71-3** (maps 67, 71); on heath **140**
Applewood Yard (top of Cross Street), **239**, **260**, **270**
apprentices, **154**, **161**, **169**, **185**, <u>**226**</u>
Army and RAF camps, **150-1**, **169-71**, **186**, **215**, **224**, **245-7**, **257-8**, **269-70**, **280**, **285**, **292-7**, *245*
   (and see war, radar station, Weybourne Camp)

Back Lane (see Purdy Street)
Baconsthorpe, **19-21**, **24-5**, **27**, **33**, **36**, **41**, *19*
bake office or bakehouse, **49**, **110**, **136**, **179-80**, **185-6**, **213**, **227**, **242**, **330**, *179*, *180*, *188-9*, *334*, *335*
Bard Hill, **110**, **170**, **204**, **228**, **296**, *143*, *204*, *228*
   (map inside front cover)
Barker, Madge (nee Haylock) and Stan, **306-7**, **310**, **337-9**, **349**, *2*, *305-6*, *310*, *334*, *337*, *349*
the beach, **48**, **101**, **205-6**, **219**, **249**, **255**, **263**, **285**, **361**, *63*, *130*, *265-7*, *282*, *290*, *307*, *351*, *353*, *359*, *361*
Beach Road, **90**, **186**, **280**, **285**, **286** (maps 50, 71)
bird-life, **68-70**, **137**, **165**, **213-4**, **228-9**
Bishop, Billy, **214**, **229**, *351*
Bix's Lane, **138**, **170**, **205**, <u>**213**</u>
Blackburn's shop (Tiny Tot's Tuck Shop), **124**, **270**
blacksmith, **110-11**, **205**, **213**, *205*, *212*,
Blakeney, **54-5**, **58**, **60-1**, **65-7**, **135**, **226**, **253**

Blakeney Point, **62**, **65-6**, **70**, **308** (map 64)
Blomefield's Report, **20**, **37**, **46-7**
Bloom Stile (a field), **53**, **217**, *218* (map 50, 51)
Bloomstile Lane (map front cover), **239**
Bloomstiles (housing estate), **327**, *327*
boats, **218-20**, **222-4**, **227**, **230**, **272**, **306-7**, *130*, *172*, *222*, *225*, *230*, *265-6*, *307* (and see fishing, and ships)
Borrer, C.D., **223**, **228-9**, *229* (and see 'Sea Pie')
British Columbia Hall (the Village Hall), **76**, **113**, **264**, **316**
the Britons, **187**, **214-5**, **284**, *284*
Brown, Charlie 'Quilter' and Evangeline (nee High), **248-52**, **254**, *249-51*
   Ken and Muriel, **249**, **252-8**, **260**, **298-9**, **317**, *2*, *216*, *254*, *256*, *317*
   Phyllis [married name Jackson, cf]
Butt Way, *309* (map 50)

Catriona Court, **326**, **339**, *325-6*
Chapels, Methodist, **49**, **112**, <u>**114-126**</u>, **156**, **167**, **227**, **249**, **251**, **272**, **278**, *114*, *120*, *123*, *126* (map 116)
Chapel Cottage, **227**
Childs, Joyce (nee Dawson), **270-1**, **276**, *270*
Church (St Nicholas'), **12**, <u>**16**</u>, **19-20**, <u>**25-7**</u>, **33**, **46-48**, <u>**75-90**</u>, **94-100**, **112-4**, **127**, **136**, **158**, **163**, **238**, **259**, **286**, **330**, **339**, **340**, **341** (plan 81) (map inside front cover)

363

INDEX

Church (cont.), outside views, *25, 59, 75, 77, 217, 298, 303*
    inside views, *47, 75, 79, 83-86, 87, 113, 114*
    Blomefield's report, **20, 37, 46-7**
    chapel in churchyard, in ruins, **18, 26, 46, 77, 81-2,** *44*
    church bells, **47, 77, 87,** *87*
    churchyard, **16, 39, 43, 44, 46, 48, 53, 76, 81-2, 88-90, 91-2, 96, 110, 248,** *31, 44, 76, 88-9*
    glebe, **16, 35, 46, 52-3, 76, 110-1,** *76*
    stained glass, **20, 33, 46-7, 77, 113-4, 248,** *113-4*
Church Cottage (the Nest), **248, 254, 258, 341,** *248*
Church House, *248*
Church Lane (the lane that runs up from Cross Street), **110-11,** *88, 151* — (but see also Grout's Lane)
    [not to be confused with Long Church Lane!]
clay bank (see Purdy's bank)
Cley, **9, 55, 60, 61, 65, 68, 70, 129, 181**
Cley Channel, **54, 65, 70, 74**
Cley Corner Cottage ('behind the pub'), **262, 342**
Cley East Bank, **54-8, 67, 166-7, 205, 214, 220, 222** (map 67)
Cley Lane (map 50) (NB: Cley Road is the coast road)
Cley marshes, **65, 70, 214, 358**
coast road, **49, 57, 63-4, 111, 120, 123, 147, 174, 188,** *278-9, 331* (map 50)
coastguards, **129, 215, 282-3, 287, 290, 305, 330**
coastline (changing position of), **166, 318,** *63* (map 64)
Common Right, **140, 144, 156, 169, 173, 213, 251, 265**
Cooke, **225, 264, 265, 267, 306,** *225, 315, 316*
    Basil, **306,** *279*
    Billy, *174,* **225**
    Bob, **223, 306,** *225*
    Charlie, **306,** *225*
    George, **171, 222-4, 306, 329, 358-9,** *222-5*
    Isaac 'Dyke' and Winnie (nee Hancock), **226-7,** *317*
    Jack 'Cookie' and Elsie, **218, 222, 230, 306, 353,** *222, 230*
    Joan, **219,** *311-2*
    June [married Ivan Large, cf]
    Leslie, **223, 226-9, 341, 343,** *226, 317*
    Marshall 'Yorkie' & Alice (nee Holman), **226, 268, 306,** *268, 316*
    Priscilla [married Frank Holman, cf]
    Richard, **35, 316,** *264, 357*
    Robin, **257, 308,** *158, 317*
    Stephen and Gertie (nee High), **210, 227,** *210, 231*
    Suzanne [married Peter McKnespiey, cf]
    Tom, **225,** *317*
Cooper, **243-5, 306,** *244-5, 317*
    Janette [married Kurt Dams, cf]
Corner Cottage (beside the post office), **251, 307, 334,** *304*
    [not to be confused with Cley Corner Cottage]
Crab Shop, **230, 243,** *230, 243, 339, 345*
Craske, **120, 126, 199**

Sidney, **112, 125, 129,** *332, 351, 355, 357*
William (preacher, father of Sidney), **125, 129**
de Crespigny, Champion, Lady Mabel, **5, 10, 132, 215, and**
    Commander Frederick, **131-2, 187, 196, 198, 260,** *132*
    Colonel Bill, **132, 187, 202, 215, 256**
'Crick' (Catchwater Drain), **185,** *123, 148, 188, 219, 222, 280* (map inside front cover)
Cross Street, **49, 62-4, 110, 124, 149, 179, 186, 199, 241, 252, 264, 278,** *114, 199, 233, 241, 242* (map 50)
Cubitt, **46, 49, 110-11, 178, 194-5**
    Charles, **204-5, 210,** *191, 240*
    Gerald and Bridget, **239-42, 292-3, 299, 304-5, 308-9,** *2, 168, 239-40, 308*
    William and Patty (nee Hancock), **120, 125, 179, 209-10, 249, 270,** *176*

Dack, Joe, **185-6, 199, 213, 227, 241,** *186*
    Matthew, **209, 241, 314,** *314*
Dams, Janette (nee Cooper) and Kurt, **243-7, 306, 345,** *2, 243-7, 317*
Dawney, Thomas and Edward (rectors), **25, 35-8, 40**
Dawson, Alph 'Hooshie' and Gertie (nee Holman), **250, 268-9, 334,** *191, 268*
    Harry, **150, 231, 331, 333,** *235-6, 238, 333*
    Jack and Ethel (nee High), **124-5, 234, 238, 258, 328, 331-3,** *118, 235, 238, 331-2*
    Joyce [married name Childs, cf]
    Mary [married name Lemmon, cf]
    old Philip, the shepherd, **269,** *191*
    Philip and Sylvia (nee Duffield), **268, 270,** *216, 261, 268*
    Primrose [married Paddy McGlinchey, cf]
Dawson, Sarah and Rex, **238,** *326*
Deterding, **127, 131, 203-4, 206, 211, 257, 260, 340**
    Jim, **127, 131-2, 198,** *131-2*
Devon Cottage, **341,** *341*
Dew, **43-4, 46, 49, 110-11, 141, 149, 194-5**
    George and Edie (nee Lynn), **204, 248, 251, 341**
    Henry, Annie, Sybil, Dorothy, **194,** *250, 263*
Dix, **38, 45, 49, 110-11, 181-4, 209-10**
    Alice [married Walter Graveling, cf]
    Charlotte and Edie, *259*
    James and Mary, **181-4,** *181*
    Sammy, *174*
Dogger Layer Point, **55,** *56,* **65,** *63* (maps 56, 63)
Doll's House, **186, 262**
ducks, **121, 156, 201, 206, 210, 212, 223, 314,** *206, 212*
duck pond (see Spring Holes)
duckboards along Beach Road, (see walkway)
Duffield, Freda [married John Holman, cf]
    Jimmy, **141, 204, 211, 255-6, 260, 346**

Sylvia [married Philip Dawson, cf]
Dun Cow, **49, 55, 69, 89, 113, 166, 205, 213, 229, 250, 313-16, 348,** *36, 205, 212, 250, 263, 314-6* (maps 50, 116)

East Bank (see Cley East Bank)
Eden, Hermia and family, **262, 342, 344-5, 347,** *344-5*
  Sebastian (poem), **361,** *344-5*
Elsden, Wendy and Charles, **148, 170, 219, 325,** *325*
embankments, <u>**55-6**</u>, **58,** <u>**61-2**</u>, **65, 67, 73, 166** (maps 64, 67)
  (and see Purdy's Bank, Hasedunck's bank, Cley East Bank, and shingle ridge)
enclosures, **67-73, 140, 145** (maps 51, 67, 71)
erosion, land lost to the sea, **65, 166,** <u>**282-3**</u>, **286-7**

farming, **150,** <u>**156-61**</u>, **186, 191, 200,** <u>**203-5**</u>, <u>**207-13**</u>, <u>**217-8**</u>, **235, 248, 346**
  grazing and stock, **136, 144-5, 149, 152,** <u>**158-161**</u>, **166, 169, 200,** <u>**207-10**</u>, **228**
fishing, **60,** <u>**218-24**</u>, **230, 265-6,** *222, 265-6* (and see boats)
Flat Eye, **54, 66,** <u>**129**</u>, *130* (maps 57, 62, 67, 71, inside cover)
flooding, **64, 68-70, 73-4, 121, 167, 205, 224-5, 227, 266-7, 286,** <u>**328-59**</u>, *74,* <u>*214*</u>, *225, 258, 266, 334*
  flood damage, *290, 335, 338-9, 342, 344-5, 347, 351-2*
  1953 flood, **121-2, 173, 179, 189, 242, 290-1, 304, 324, 328,** <u>**331-52**</u>
food and cooking, **149– 51, 171, 185-6, 200, 202, 212, 218, 226, 230, 236, 243-4, 251-2, 271, 277**
Forsdick, Friday and Evelyn, **265-7,** *265-7, 282*
Foulger, Horace and Martin, **187-8,** *191*
Fox, Lorna (nee Hancock) and Tom, **176-182,** *176*
furroughs, 'furrahs', furze, (see gorse)

Galvin, Chip and Tony, **311, 326, 348,** *311, 357*
Gibbons, Julie (nee Large), *279*
  Marybeth, *90, 279, and back cover*
Girdlestone, **30-1, 40,** <u>**41**</u>, **45-6,** <u>**52-3**</u>, **111, 127, 140**
Glaven river, <u>**60-1**</u>, **65, 68, 333** (map 64)
gorse faggots ('furroughs'), **157, 185, 188, 227, 241-2, 249**
  gorse, burning on the heath, **228, 248-9**
Gramborough Hill (Greenburrow) **12, 17, 53, 54-5, 57, 62, 64, 66, 318-9, 352,** *63, 189, 240, 356* (maps 50, 57, 62-3)
Graveling, Herbert ('Mickie'), **89,** *89, 174*
  Walter and Alice (nee Dix), **89, 112, 205, 249, 316, 349,** *259, 316, 349-50*
Gray, Kathleen (nee High) & Eric, **203, 231,** *231, 310, 357*
  Jimmy 'Mot' and Emily, **230, 243-4, 288-9, 345,** *243*
  Ruby and Tommy, **339, 345**
Great Eye (Lodge Hill on some maps), **54-5, 57, 64, 66,** <u>**129**</u>, **263, 291, 315, 354,** *63, 214, 297, 309, 354* (maps 50, 57, 63, 71)
'the Greens', **259,** *259*

Grout's Lane (still called Church Lane occasionally), **49, 110, 297, 314, 341,** *341* (map 50)
gunpowder, **161-2, 167**

The Hall (old name: Ivy Hall Farm), **10, 35, 43, 49, 52, 127, 131-2, 187, 203-4, 211, 215-6, 248, 260-1,** *36, 132, 203* (map 116)
Hall farm buildings, **255-6**
Hall Guesthouse (name used for the Hall when it was a guesthouse), **187, 215-6, 270-1,** *271*
Hancock, **49, 110-11, 126, 142, 176, 180, 209**
  Amelia [married Herbert Pigott, cf]
  Arnold, 'Rat', **175, 186, 210,** *175-6, 186*
  Gordon, **112, 340**
  John and Elizabeth, **175-6, 178-9, 209,** *175-6, 178-9*
  Leonard, **118, 176-9,** *176, 178-9*
  Lorna [married Tom Fox, cf]
  Patty [married William Cubitt, cf]
Hanlon, Daphne, **274-6,** *274-5*
Harmary (now Combe Grove), **331-2,** *331-2*
Hasedunck's embankment ('ould Banke' on John Hunt's map), **55, 61, 65** (map 56)
Hawley (of the Manor), **187, 270-1, 349,** *317, 349-51*
Haylock, Fred and Ottoline, **260, 305-7, 336-9, 348,** *305, 310, 336, 348-51*
  Kathleen [married Sidney Thomas, cf]
  Madge [married Stan Barker, cf]
Hayward, Charlie & Norah and Janice, **125-6, 341,** *126, 317*
the Heath, **12, 52-3,** <u>**136-46**</u>, **156-7, 168-70, 204, 213, 227-8, 248-9, 251, 292-4, 296,** *89, 140, 143, 204, 228, 292-3* (map inside front cover, plan showing the higher land that forms the heath 319) — (NB the heath was once called Salthouse Common, see map 50)
Heydon, as lords of the manor, <u>**16-27**</u>, **33, 36-7, 40**
  Sir Henry (builder of the church), **18-19,** <u>**25-6**</u>, **46**
High, <u>**45**</u>, **49, 110-11, 125-6, 142-3, 149,** *2, 118, 190, 235*
  Charles Edward and Bessie, **190-3,** *190-3*
  Clifford, **151, 204-5, 231-3,** *231, 233*
  Dick (see Richard—one of two Richard Highs)
  Don, **150, 237, 315, 327, 331,** *112, 216, 315*
  Doreen [married Mr Sayer, cf]
  Edmund, **152, 154-5,** *155*
  Ernest and Mary, **141, 150-1, 203, 231-3, 237,** *141, 231*
  Ethel [married Jack Dawson, cf]
  Evangeline [married Charlie Quilter Brown, cf]
  Florence [married Percy Radley, cf]
  Freda [married Alec Morse, cf]
  Gertrude [married Stephen Cooke, cf]
  Gladys, **112, 125, 231, 237, 327,** *231*
  Haddon and Daisy (nee Hancock), **112, 150-1, 231, 237, 327,** *112, 231, 233, 263*

INDEX

Harry and Bessie (nee Woodhouse), **208, 210-12, 217, 251,** *211, 213, 218, 262*
Havelock, **151, 237,** *231, 233*
Henry and Polly (nee Jeary), **149-50, 156, 160, 203, 209, 234-5, 283,** *118, 235* (sometimes called Harry)
James and Mary (nee Pigott), **122, 124, <u>149-55</u>, 167, 203, 208-9, 282-3,** *150*
Jimmy and Laura, **118-9, <u>156-162</u>, 283-4,** *118, 156, 235*
Kathleen (Haddon's daughter) [married Eric Gray, cf]
Kathleen (Haddon's sister), **231,** *231*
Levi and Elizabeth, **203, 209-211, 248, 252,** *252*
Mary [married Vic Holman, cf]
Miriam [married Percy Ramm, cf]
Ray and Eileen, **135, 149, 203-6,** *203*
Richard (Dick) & Mary (Craske) & Polly (Dawson) **110, 120, 124-5, 135, 150, <u>152-5</u>, <u>198-200</u>, <u>203-6</u>, 209, 305,** *124, 153, 198, 304*
Richard and Hannah ('Granny High') (nee Pigott), **149, 163, 167,** *149* (grandparents of other Richard)
Vivian and Bette, and son Paul, **145, 208, 211-19, 253, 262, 320-1,** *2, 145, 211, 216-7, 320, 321*
Hilltop (a house), **263,** *299*
Holland, **112, 259,** *317*
Holman, **174, 265,** *317*
    Alan, **334,** *174*
    Alice (nee Woodhouse), married Bertie, see below
    Alice [married Marshall Cooke, cf]
    Ann [married Billy West, cf]
    Bertie ('Billy') and Alice (nee Woodhouse), **214, 259, 262-3, 268, 278,** *215, 278*
    Betty, **172-3, 346,** *172, 346*
    Brian ('Brock') and Mary, **214, 262-3, 268, 278, 342,** *215, 218, 262*
    Clem and Maggie, **262, 328, 338-9, 345,** *338*
    Doris [married Peter Holman, cf]
    Frank and Priscilla (nee Cooke), **264,** *316*
    Freda (nee Duffield) married John, see below
    Gertie [married Alphie Dawson, cf]
    'Hopper' (John), **219, 223, 267-8,** *268*
    Ivy [married Jack Nightingale, cf]
    John & Freda (nee Duffield), **257, 260-1, 346,** *172-4, 260-1, 317*
    Kayleigh, *279 and back cover*
    Mandy (nee Large), and son Shaun, *279*
    Peter and Doris (nee Holman), **289, 345-6,** *172, 317, 340, 346*
    'Rooter' (Walter) and Sarah, **172-3, 268, 346,** *172-3*
    Ruth (nee Pigott) and John, **130, 227, 257, 262, <u>267-9</u>, 286, 307, <u>329-30</u>,** *268, 329*
    Vic and Mary (nee High), **315,** *317, 346*
    Virginia [married Richard Wright, cf]

Holmes, George, **179, 185-6, 213, 242, 245**
Holt, **37, 112-4, 120, 129, 135, 151, 154, 172, 197, 211, 221, 237, 268, 270, 276**

'inclosures', (see enclosures)
Ivy Hall Farm (early name for Hall, cf), *187, 191*

Jackson, Phyllis (nee Brown), **248-53, 255, 298,** *2, 248*
Jarvis, David, **199, 208, 209, 297, 330,** *297*
Johnson, John Francis, **42-3, <u>48-53</u>, 127, 149, 152**
    Sarah (nee Pigott) (known as 'Aunt Johnson') and William, **110, 122, 127, <u>150</u>, <u>152</u>, 163, 203, <u>234-5</u>,** *235*
Jopling, **215, 224, 264, <u>285-6</u>, 287, 291, 314,** *285, 291*

Kelling, **9, 12-7, 19, 21, 31-2, 37-8, 40-1, 43, 48, 53-5, 57, 62, 74, 115, 131, 136, 140-1, 145,** *278* (map in front cover)
Kelling Church, **16, 26, 32, 34-8, 40-1, 43, 47, 115**
Kelling Hall, **127, 131-2, 141, 265**
Kelling Old Hall, **15, 32, 41, 52, 129,** *15, 16*
Kelling Rectory, **35, 41, 112**
Kelling Road (old name for Cross Street, cf), **49, 53, 110-1**
Kelling School, *278* (see School)
Ketton-Cremer, R.W., **5, <u>10</u>, 29, 35, 42, 113**
Keymer, **46, 49, 111, 194-7**
    Ian, **194-7, 298, 302-3, 313,** *194, 303*

Large, Anne [married name Wright, cf]
    Carrie and Macala, **322-3,** *322-3*
    Ivan and June (nee Cooke), **306, 357-9,** *279, 357*
    Julie [married name Gibbons, cf]
    Mandy [married name Holman, cf]
    Tracey (nee Wright), **140, 163, 207,** *140, 163, 207*
Leach (at the Manor), **114, 125, 196, 238, 245, 339,** *347*
Lemmon, Mary (nee Dawson), **125-6, 234-8, 275, 331-3,** *126, 216, 234-5, 238, 275, 331-2*
Letheringsett church, **37, 41**
Little Eye, **54-5, 62, 64, 263, 360,** *63, 214, 297, 356, 360* (maps 56, 62, 63, 67, 71, 300, and inside front cover)
Lodge Hill (another name for Great Eye, cf), **53, 57** (map 50)
Long Church Lane, **35** (map 50)
Long, Willie, **122-4,** *123*
'Lorcot' (a house), **176, 179, 180, 249,** *179*
lords of the manor, **127-32**
Lynn, **49, 199, 209, 259,** *340*
    Alfie, **188,** *341*
    Betsy, **149,** *150*
    Blind Billy (Skidger), **341**
    Edie [married George Dew, cf]
Lynn Place, **341**

INDEX

Mace, Harry, *263*
Main Channel (see Salthouse Main Channel) (map 56-7)
Manor farmhouse, **35, 43, 49,** *36, 231*
Manor farm Cottage, **76**
Manor House, **35, 42, 44, 49, 53, 76, 110, 113-4, 125, 127, 149, 196, 203-4, 234-8,** *2, 42, 234-5, 237-8*
Manson, Dick, **314, 343,** *340, 357*
  Jim, **185, 314-6, 341-3, 354, 356,** *314, 340, 354*
Market Lane, **204, 239** (map inside front cover)
marl pit, **239-40,** *240*
Marsh Cottage (once Balaklava Cottage, once Beulah Cottage), **135, 205,** *135*
the Marshes, **54-8, 60-74, 158-61, 164-6, 205, 214, 222-4, 283, 287-90,** *27, 54, 63, 66, 74, 159, 280-1, 352, 356-8* (maps 50-1, 56-7, 63-4, and inside front cover)
Massingham, John and Edna, **307**
Matthews, Jakey, **187,** *187, 191*
McGlinchey, Primrose (nee Dawson) and Paddy, **268-69, 334,** *268, 316*
McKnespiey, Suzanne (nee Cooke) and Peter, **222, 230, 358-9,** *230*
Methodist Chapels (see Chapels)
Middleton, **258, 343**
Mill Drift, **249, 254, 297,** *27*
Morse, Freda (nee High) and Alec, **125, 131, 135, 198-202, 215, 260,** *124, 132, 198, 202*
Muckleborough Hill, **146, 318** (map 319)
Myngs, Sir Christopher, **34,** 38
Myngs Terrace, **245, 324-5,** *324-5*

New Cut middle drain, **68, 74** (maps 67, 71, 319)
Newman (at the Manor), **113, 238**
Nightingale, Ivy (nee Holman) and Jack, **264, 346,** *2, 216, 264, 346*
Nockolds, Ben, **218, 221**
Norton, Perry (from Briston), **212, 223**

Olley, James, **133-5, 205,** *135*
the Ould Banke (Van Hasedunche's Bank), **61,** (map 56)

parish boundary (Salthouse and Cley), **58, 63** (map 56, 62)
Parish (Reading) Room, **211, 341,** *188*
Parish Registers, **91-3**
Parish Town House (see Pear Tree Cottage)
Parkinson, Nigel, **350,** *347, 349-51*
Parliament Box, **5,** and some of the documents found in side it: **91-100, 101-3, 104-9, 110-111, 163, 294**
Parr, **27-31, 34-5, 37-8, 40-2, 44-5**
Parsonage (see Rectory)
Pashley, H.N., **68, 164, 166**
Pear Tree Cottage (formerly Parish Town House or alms house), **152, 166, 339,** *151*
Pembroke Cottage, **346**

Pigott, **49, 110-11, 149, 150, 205, 208-9, 226**
  Amelia (nee Hancock) and Herbert, **118, 120, 125, 176, 178-80, 200, 209-10, 249, 284, 297,** *176, 178-80, 259, 284*
  Gabriel, **110, 152, 163-6, 207,** *164*
  Hannah [matriarch of Highs, sister of Gabriel and Sarah, married Richard High, cf]
  Hannah, local character with a cart (sister of Ruth), married to Hilary, **226, 262, 269**
  Mary [married James High, cf, her first cousin]
  Ruth, known as 'Granny Ruth' [married John Holman, cf, matriarch of the Holmans]
  Sarah, 'Aunt Johnson' [sister of Gabriel and Hannah, see Johnson]
Pit View, **172-3,** *172-3*
Poor Relief, **72-3, 104-9, 141, 149, 169, 197**
Pope, Roy, **74, 214**
Post Office and Village Stores on green, **135, 163, 198-200, 259, 270, 285, 304-7, 310-12, 336-9, 348-9,** *135, 198, 258, 304-5, 310-2, 335, 348-9*
  (NB old post office was in Cross Street, map 116), **199**
Purdy, as landowners, **41-3, 45, 48-53, 110-11, 127**
Purdy's embankment (first clay bank), **67, 166, 171, 282, 321, 351,** *130* (map 67)
Purdy Street ('Back Lane'), **49, 62-3, 110, 205, 255** (map 50)

rabbits and rabbiting, **137-9, 168-9, 172-3, 217, 237, 244, 251, 262, 276,** *172, 218*
radar station, **170, 270, 292-4, 296,** *292, 293*
Radley, Florence (nee High) and Percy, **124, 149-155, 164, 167, 169-70, 199, 234, 282-3, 298,** *149, 167, 169-70*
  Jim and Elsie (nee Long), **167-71, 221, 339,** *2, 167-8, 171, 221*
RAF, see radar station (also war, and army & RAF camps)
Ramm, Miriam (nee High) and Percy, **231,** *233*
Randall, Onesiphorus, **127, 128-30, 175, 281-2**
Randall's Folly, **129,** *128* (and see Rocket House)
reclamation of marshland, **55-6, 65, 67, 70, 73-4, 282** (map 64)
Rectory, **16, 35, 37, 46, 76, 330,** *76* (or parsonage)
Robertson, Elizabeth, **259, 311,** *311*
Rocket House (also known as Randall's Folly and Great Eye Folly), **54, 129, 215, 224-5, 264, 280-291, 314,** *128, 130, 214-5, 225, 280-1, 283-6, 288, 290, 351-2, 355* (map inside front cover)
Rogerson, Andrew (of Gressenhall), **82-3, 320**
Roman finds & camp & road, **12, 318-9** (map 319 and inside front cover)
Ross (of the Hall), **187, 189, 203, 211, 263**
Rudd, Granny, **227,** *227*

Salthouse Broad, **53, 57, 65, 68-9, 129, 205, 229, 280,** *280*
Salthouse Common, (on 1649 map, 56-7, part of the marsh is called Salthouse Common) **61, 64, 68** — but→

367

INDEX

(on 1838 map, 50-51, the Heath is called Salthouse Common), 157
Salthouse Harbour or port, 12, 34, 54, 60-65
Salthouse Main Channel, 12, 54-8, 60-6, 220, *63* (map 56-7, 62)
Savory (of Kelling Hall), **127**, 141, 176-8, 203, 265
Sayer, Doreen (nee High), 143, 231-3, *231, 233*
School (Kelling School), 113, 149, 153, 156, 167-8, 216, 255-7, 272-9, *216, 274-5, 278-9*
sea defences, 282, 291, 333, 338, **351-9**, *351-9*
'Sea Pie' (C.D.Borrer) on Salthouse Jewel 80, on Gabriel Pigott 164-6, on John Hancock 175 (and see Borrer)
'the Seven Whistlers' (the Dacks' house), 199, 241, *241*
Sheringham, 12, 14, 32, 60, 115, 119-20, 122, 124-5, 136, 151, 156, 199
shingle ridge (or bank), **65-7**, 291, 333, 351-9, *36, 351-9* (map 67)
ships, 48, 54-58, 60-62, 65, 84-6, 181-4, 269, 282-4, 308, *84-86, 182, 308* (and see boats, and fishing)
shooting (see wildfowling, and rabbiting)
the Skirts (area of the marsh), 269 (map 50)
smallholdings (see farming)
Spanish Pits (a field), 12, 21, 53 (map 51)
Spring Holes (duck pond), 172, *172, 206*
Stagg, Frank Noel, 5, **8-9**, 10, 12, 29, 32, 35, 45, 47, 91, 196, 202, *8*
Stanforth (Standforth), 27-9, 35, 38-9, 41-3, 45-6
Sunday School, 115, 121-2, 124-6, 199, 251
Sunny Croft (a house), 149, 339
Sutton, Jim, 348-51, *315, 348*

Talbots' shop (and Talbot, Sam and Ann), **199**, 238, 241, 245, 304, 307, *199, 241*
tearooms on Great Eye (practically on the beach!), 213-5, *214-5* (run by Billy and Alice Holman)
tearooms in old railway carriage on beach (run by Ruth Holman, then used by Hopper), 267, *130, 267, 307*
Thomas, Kathleen (nee Haylock) and Sidney, 304, 306-7, 310, 334, 337, 348, *2, 305-6, 334, 348*
Thomson, Dorothy, 259, *259*
the three cottages (destroyed in the '53 flood), 262, **339**, 345, 347, *262, 339, 345, 347*
Three Farthing and Three Halfpenny and Gallows Hills (tumuli on heath), 12, 136 (map inside front cover)
Tuck, 27-31, 35, 38-9, 41, 45
Tucks Close (a field), 27, 41, 52 (map 50-51)

Van Hasedunck's Bank (see Hasedunck)
Victoria Cottage (Woodhouses' house), 189, 212, *212*
Village Hall (see British Columbia Hall)
Village Shop (see Post Office and Village Stores)

wages, 149, 154, 156, 160, <u>205</u>, 245, 253
walkway (duckboards) along Beach Road, 90, 186, 205, 280, *280*
Walsey Hills (Walcey or Wall Shawe Hills), 52, 54, 56, 58, 66 (map 56 and inside front cover)
Walton, Winnie, 219, 326, *326*
War, 129, 150-1, 169-71, 186-7, 205-7, 231-3, 257-8, 260, 270, 280, 285, 292-7
   Airship R101, 253, 256, *253*
   evacuees, 189, 202
   German prisoners of war, 245-7, *246-7*
   mines, 171, 245, 307, *247*
   war planes, 170, Dornier 307-9, *309*, Heinkel 295-6, Lancaster 292-4, *294*
   (and see army camps, radar station, walkway)
war memorial, 77, 88-9, 270, *88-9*
Warner, Sylvia Townsend, 287-90, *287*
Watson-Cook, Mrs, 276, 339, *347*
wells, 227, 239, 241, 255, 267, 270, 285, 289, *239, 241*
West, Billy and Ann (nee Holman), 168, 268, *268*
Weybourne, 12-4, 16, 21, 54-5, 65, 80, 221, 272, *180*
Weybourne Camp, **169-170**, 172, 189, 224, 269, 308, 334
the white bungalow, 201, 206, 265, *201, 202, 265-6*
wildfowling and shooting and guns, 69, 138-9, 162-7, 171-2, 175, 213, 223, 226, 228-9, 251, *172, 175*
Windmills,
   mill on the marsh (Mill Drift), 121, 187, 284, <u>297</u>, 330, *27, 280, 297, 330* (map 116 and inside front cover)
   mill on Mill Ridge, 263, <u>298-303</u>, *298, 303*, (map 300)
   Gramborough mill, 17, 55
   other windmills, 13, 15-6, 49
'Windy Ridge' (bungalow on Mill Ridge), 298-9
Wiveton, 37, 55, 60
Woodhouse, 45-6, 49, 209
   Alice [married Billy Holman, cf]
   Bessie [married Harry High, cf]
   Cliff 'Tarrow' and Ethel, 185, 213, 217, 227, 338-9, 342-3, *218*
   Fred 'Hoss' Woodhouse, 187-8, *187, 317*
   Little Fred and Julia (nee Rudd), 259, 352, *310, 317*
   Jasper, <u>185-9</u>, 213, 262, 278, 287, *2, 185, 189*
   Tom 'Rummy' and Mary, 187, 189, 211-2, 262-3, 278, *187, 189, 191, 212, 263*
wrecks, 39, 46, 48, 101, 282-4
Wright, Anne, 219, *279*
   George, *1, 279*
   Tracey [married name Large, cf]
   Virginia (nee Holman) and Richard, *260, 311-2*
   Zoë, 90, 279 *and back cover*

Young, Rev Felix, 112, 114, 290, *347*